MONEY AND THE MAKING
OF THE AMERICAN REVOLUTION

Frontispiece: Benjamin West's portrayal of Adam and Eve's expulsion from paradise includes an image of an eagle fighting a heron that was prominent on continental dollars, a possible allusion to the Revolutionary cause. West's monumental painting was intended for the private chapel of George III in Windsor Castle. The king rejected the painting, which now resides in the U.S. National Gallery of Art in Washington, DC.

Money and
the Making of
the American Revolution

Andrew David Edwards

PRINCETON UNIVERSITY PRESS

PRINCETON & OXFORD

Published by Princeton University Press
41 William Street, Princeton, New Jersey 08540
99 Banbury Road, Oxford OX2 6JX

press.princeton.edu

GPSR Authorized Representative: Easy Access System Europe - Mustamäe tee 50, 10621 Tallinn, Estonia, gpsr.requests@easproject.com

All Rights Reserved

ISBN 978-0-691-20026-2
ISBN (e-book) 978-0-691-28012-7

Library of Congress Control Number: 2025944247

British Library Cataloging-in-Publication Data is available

Editorial: Priya Nelson and Emma Wagh
Production Editorial: Jenny Wolkowicki
Jacket design: Chris Ferrante
Production: Erin Suydam
Publicity: William Pagdatoon
Copyeditor: Daniel Simon

Jacket image: Originally published in "Continental Money." *Harper's New Monthly Magazine*, Volume 26, Issue 154, fol. 438, 1863

This book has been composed in Miller

10 9 8 7 6 5 4 3 2 1

In memory of my fathers,

Martin (the historian) and Don (the poet)

FIG. 0.1. Three Dollars, United States, 1776, Obverse.

CONTENTS

The Burning Question

FIG. 1. Fifty Shillings, Pennsylvania, 1775, Reverse.

I. Money to Burn

This is the story of how money tore an empire apart, and how a revolution, ironically, brought it back together. It has two fundamental premises. First, to understand the American Revolution, we need to understand American money. This is less implausible than it may at first appear. The American Revolution was a revolt against taxation without representation, and taxes, as we will see, are fundamentally about money. Second, to understand a thing, it is important to lean into the parts of it that feel strangest. As Robert Darnton wrote in his classic study of early modern France, "When we cannot get a proverb, or a joke, or a ritual, or a poem we know we are on to something. By picking at the document where it is most opaque, we may be able to unravel an alien system of meaning. The thread might even lead into a strange and wonderful world view." Early America does not feel weird at times, but it was. So was its money. And perhaps the strangest thing about colonial America's money was the burning, so it is there that we must begin.[1]

Every year for the better part of a century, officials in Britain's North American colonies collected taxes in local paper currencies. In a world where overland transport was difficult and dangerous, each colony was effectively a watershed connected to Britain by the Atlantic Ocean. Taxes held them together. Most taxpayers were farmers who sold part of their annual harvest to a merchant or factor. Others were tradesmen, craftsmen, sailors, millers, coopers, or blacksmiths in the small towns that hugged the coast or lined rivers and streams that flowed towards seaport capitals. Each usually traded time, sweat, or property for tiny slips of paper that colonial treasurers and other officials had painstakingly signed by hand and printed with strange devices to prevent forgery. These treasurers in turn counted each note, checking its serial number against a list, sometimes punching a hole to prevent it from being reissued. Then, once each note had been counted, the treasurer would bundle them up and burn them in the presence of witnesses, including sometimes the governor himself. Rhode Islanders were typical in 1778 when they appointed a committee of three men—Paul Allen, Jabez Bowen, and John Updike—to gather the paper money paid in taxes over the previous three years—73,193 pounds, 15 shillings, and 5 pence—to see that it was "carefully counted and burnt."[2]

In the decades leading up to the Revolution, the colonies printed 53 million pounds-worth of paper money in a variety of shapes, denominations, and values. By the mid-eighteenth century, bills of credit, as they were called, were the dominant medium of exchange in colonial America. They were also, in virtually every colony before and during the Revolution, the primary means of financing war. They were central to what colonial America was, how it was organized, how it fought, and how it did business. And yet the colonies burned them. In some, the burning was an event, advertised in public newspapers and marked in legislative records.[3]

So why did Revolutionary Americans burn their money? And what can we learn from the fact that they did? The first question is relatively easy to answer. Colonial Americans burned their money because each bill represented a tax debt that had been repaid. Their money was called a 'bill of credit' precisely because each bill was a credit against a tax debt owed by colonial taxpayers. Each bill was matched by an equal and opposite tax. When the taxes were collected and the bills were received, colonial treasurers burned them because the debt had been repaid. The logic may be counterintuitive. We tend to think of governments as borrowing money from citizens and issuing IOUs, government debt, in return. Bills of credit were the opposite: UO-Me's, if you like. Each bill represented a debt owed by a colonial taxpayer. The debt had real power. If a colonist failed to pay their taxes, their land and property were forfeit. I remember reading through a rural court archive at the Maine Historical Society, where sheriffs in the 1760s were recorded collecting debts on tiny rocky islands, sailing away with whatever they could fit in their skiff. Payment included "six pair of gloves," chairs, and "a small calf," because the family in question did not have any money. With bills of credit, the government owed nothing. The citizens owed everything. The modern relationship was reversed.[4]

A second burning question is harder to answer. What can we learn from the fact that colonial Americans burned their money? Any adequate answer is broad. The burning reflected a different approach to money in general. Money for colonial Americans was a temporary means to social ends, a way of tackling projects bigger than any individual. Most of the money printed, signed, spent, taxed, and burned in the eighteenth century went to support colonial armies, but war was not their only collective project. Colonial governments also created money to protect farming families from short-term cash demands with state-issued mortgages, and to build lighthouses, prisons, and fortifications, often printing brilliant illustrations of their work on the notes themselves. In short, colonial money was not primarily a form of wealth. It was a way of making things happen.[5]

Money was a central economic institution in colonial America, just as it is now. It was "the Blood of the Body-Politick," as one Boston writer put it in 1739, diffused throughout the social fabric. The way it was organized had profound implications for the way power worked in the colonial world. Before a formal constitution was written, money was, in effect, constitutional. Everything money touched was shaped by the way colonial legislatures created it and colonists used it, and money touched everything. Thus the second "burning question" bleeds into every adjacent aspect of colonial life, where money shaped gender and class relations, helped organize violence and facilitate the theft of Native American land, and motivated politics, where money was a major source of controversy throughout the period. And this is all quite apart from what we tend to think of as money's natural realm, the world of commerce. Money was and

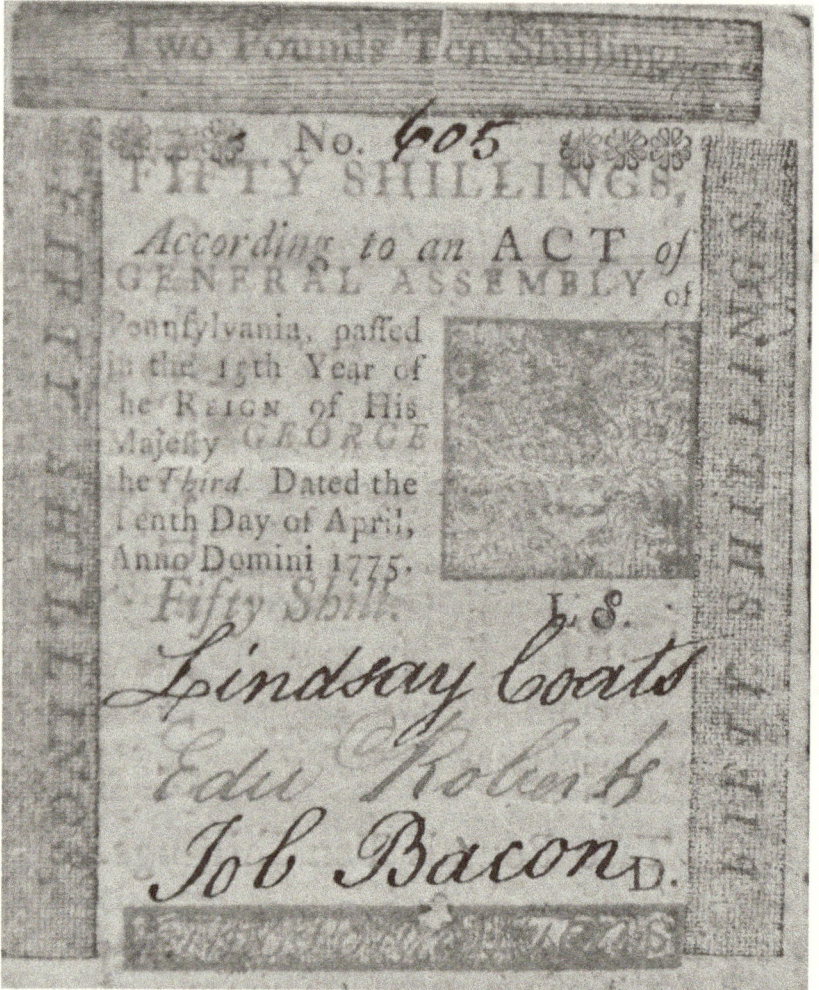

FIG. 2. Fifty Shillings, Pennsylvania, 1775, Obverse.

is diverse, difficult to tie down or control. The way it was made shaped the people who made it, and vice versa. This makes money extraordinarily interesting to study, especially in a time of revolution, when the nature of government itself was up for grabs.[6]

What burning meant in practice was that American colonial money did not behave like money as we typically think of it. The financial architecture of the modern world—from payments to pensions and central banks—relies on a form of money that at least in theory lasts forever. Its value may rise or fall, it may be expensive to borrow or cheap, we may owe it or earn it, spend it or save it, but it endures regardless and serves as a meaningful store of value. The ideal of permanence gives modern money what Mary Douglas identified as its ritualistic quality. Like religious rituals, money's permanence creates a meaningful link between the present, past, and future. Because money, like ritual, is rooted in belief, it is meant to last as long as that belief itself endures.[7]

Colonial Americans, however, had severed that link altogether. Burning severed it. Burning meant that colonial money, as a store of value, was temporary. Temporary money could not be saved or invested. It could not be hoarded or (except within strict temporal and geographical limits) lent or borrowed. This did not mean, of course, that the colonists had abandoned any vision of an economic future or that they had abolished credit. Quite the opposite. But when money was temporary, credit took on a different meaning. Credit was about the exchange of value, not the exchange of money. In fact, as we will have occasion to explore in more detail, colonial America did virtually all its business on credit, with almost no money changing hands. Money that was not a store of value was not a meaningful goal. Temporary money was not something people spent their lives trying to acquire. Again, this is counterintuitive; we are accustomed to thinking of money and wealth as one and the same, but when money is temporary, that connection is severed as well. Ironically, anglophone colonial America was, on average, among the wealthiest societies in the early modern world. The colonists simply located wealth elsewhere: in land, in their households, in credit relationships, in human beings, and, with their bills of credit, in the very continuity of colonial government.[8]

In turn, the temporal distinction between our money and colonial money suggests a deeper understanding of the differences between eighteenth-century society and our own. In the last century, for example, American historians spent several decades debating what some saw as the disinterest of colonial farmers in making money before the American Revolution. Colonial farmers, the economic historian Naomi Lamoreaux observed, "typically did not charge one another interest on debts," they "engaged in a variety of cooperative activities," and they "put family and community before profit" because "their goal was to achieve a competence," a comfortable if often hard-won living, "rather than to accumulate capital." But then, at a point roughly coinciding with the American Revolution, this community-oriented dynamic changed. For the first time, farmers began to calculate profits, build up substantial holdings of cash and securities, and invest their earnings. In other words, they began to behave like capitalists. But why? Was it to do with the Revolution itself?

With freedom, political independence, and its connection to economic culture, as some have suggested? Or is the answer simpler? Had they perhaps established the connection between the present and the future that continues in American money today? After the war, Americans stopped burning their money. New institutions produced new behavior, a monied revolution. This is not the full answer, of course, but it may be the beginning of a new one.[9]

II. Money and the Making
of the American Revolution

Perhaps the greatest mystery that the second burning question promises to resolve is the American Revolution itself. The central problem of Revolutionary history arises from the one fact that every schoolchild knows about the American Revolution: that it was an uprising against "taxation without representation." The problem is explaining why. Perhaps the most influential work on the history of the American Revolution in the twentieth century was Helen and Edmund Morgan's *The Stamp Act Crisis*, originally published in 1953. It was influential because it presented a puzzle that some of the most prominent historians in the United States spent the next half century trying to solve. There was an apparent incongruity between the causes and consequences of the Stamp Act of 1765, the first time in the long eighteenth century that colonial resistance to imperial authority turned into outright rebellion. The Stamp Act was a traditional turning point in American colonial history, at which the colonies, long secure in their allegiance to Great Britain, turned their thoughts for the first time to independence. The cause, the Morgans wrote, was almost unimaginably small. The taxes levied by Parliament were light and reasonable. The colonists were well able to pay them. And yet the consequences of those same taxes were epochal. For the first time, representatives from virtually all of Britain's North American colonies met in a "congress" in New York City to write a joint appeal to Parliament, asserting their exclusive right to tax themselves. This was the American origin of the famous phrase "no taxation without representation," the issue that, more than any other, galvanized American resistance to Parliament's demands and ultimately led to war. What is also striking in the Morgans' account is the way in which the American response to the Stamp Act combined high and low politics. Political leaders wrote pamphlets, delivered polemics, and sent official protests to London, while mobs thronged colonial towns demanding the resignation of stamp distributors and action from colonial officials: women marched alongside men, rich with poor, high with low. It was a wild, unifying moment that needed further explanation.[10]

The definitive answer to the question of why the Stamp Act triggered such fervor came in Bernard Bailyn's *The Ideological Origins of the American Revolution* in 1967. Bailyn argued that the violence of the colonial reaction to parliamentary taxation could only be explained by a shared ideology, which Bailyn defined as an "integrated group of attitudes and ideas" that gave meaning to political events. It was this, "above all else that in the end propelled [the American colonists] into Revolution," he argued. Bailyn's formulation resolved the dilemma posed by the Morgans fourteen years earlier. The difficulties posed by the Stamp Act were only minor in economic terms, Bailyn argued. If we fully inhabit the mindset of the eighteenth-century colonists, the reason for their violent reaction to parliamentary taxation becomes clear. Steeped in radical discourse, the colonists read Parliament's action as an abuse of legitimate power and a violation of their rights as Englishmen. It demanded a united response.[11]

Bailyn's interpretation was enormously influential, and he and his students used it to rewrite early American history. The interpretive challenges were enormous, but so were the rewards, which were as political as they were historical. This was American history for Cold War warriors, an antidote to the Marxist progressive histories of the 1920s and 1930s, a counterpoint to the rediscovery of critical theory by radical historians in the 1970s, and a powerful rejoinder to all historians who gave primacy to economic causation. Indeed, Bailyn and the Morgans' interpretation served as a towering demonstration that material oppression was not the only, or even the most interesting, motivation for revolution. The ideological interpretation required "investing the ethereal stuff of the mind with convincing social power," the intellectual historian Daniel Rodgers observed in 1992. Whatever its faults, and Rodgers believed there were many, it elevated the history of ideas in the process. An alternative school, including scholars such as Gary Nash, T. H. Breen, Woody Holton, and Marjoleine Kars, continued to insist on the materiality of the Revolutionary moment, but as Bailyn's student Jack Rakove commented, with taxation ruled out they struggled to find an alternative "nexus" linking all the colonies to the Revolutionary cause. The Revolution, Rodgers wrote, thus became "a particularly forceful example of what an ideology could do." By the end of the century, ideology also presented a formidable barrier to alternative interpretations.[12]

Rather than storm the ramparts, historians, beginning in the 1990s, increasingly turned away from the Revolution in new work. Some regretted it. Jack Greene, one of the Revolution's leading scholars for almost a half century, in 2010 lamented that the Bailyn interpretation had all but "closed off serious discussion," noting that in the previous twenty years only three scholars (by his count) had seriously grappled with the origins of the Revolution. The Princeton historian John Murrin decried the "self-immolation" of the field. In any case, most acknowledged that interpretive debates had grown stale, leaving little for new graduate students to pick over. Rodgers and many others still questioned the "simplification and exaggeration" that Bailyn and some of his successors resorted to, noting the "unraveling sense of what kind of entity republicanism"—the name Bailyn's students had arrived at for the Revolution's founding ideology— "actually was." Historians of Early America, meanwhile, began to explore ways of redefining the field that deemphasized the Revolutionary moment, finding new vitality in the history of Indigenous peoples and non-English-speaking empires across the North American continent. But neither Rodgers, nor even the most aggressive opponents of Bailyn and the Morgans' position, ever suggested that the Morgans' analysis of the stamp taxes, a foundational premise for so much brilliant prose and analysis, was flawed to begin with.[13]

But it was. There were hints everywhere. Any scholar facing the documentary record of the Revolution was forced to confront the colonists' own clearly stated positions that taxes were a real, material concern. The archival record of the Stamp Act crisis contradicted the Morgans' basic point—that the taxes would have been easy to pay—at every turn. Leading Boston merchant John Hancock called the stamp taxes a "Cruel hardship." Future president John Adams called the Stamp Act a "burdensome Tax, because, the Duties are so numerous and so high," declaring that it would be "totally impossible for the People to subsist under it." Twenty-seven delegates representing nine colonies, who assembled in New York City in October 1765 to formulate a unified petition to the king and Parliament, declared that the taxes were "extremely burthensome and grievous" because they would be "absolutely impracticable," meaning, impossible, to pay. Virtually every petition, pamphlet, and private letter addressing the Stamp Act makes similar claims—directly contrasting with the view that the taxes, themselves, were light. Indeed, the only people who made the Morgans' argument in 1765 were employed by the British ministry, attempting to justify by right what had turned out to be impossible in practice.[14]

If the taxes were heavy, though, the difficulty was understanding how. The few economic historians who took up the matter confirmed the Morgans' account. In 1965 Robert Thomas estimated that the combined effect of imperial regulations amounted to a loss of less than 1 percent of per capita income. The Stamp Act alone was even less onerous. In 1980 Edwin Perkins calculated that charges to the average taxpayer would amount to 5 pence sterling per year, or "less than 0.2 percent of per capita income"— hardly something worth rebelling over. A consensus emerged that colonists believed their taxes were "high" simply because Parliament had levied them. This was an essentially illogical position, but perhaps Americans took it, the story went, because of deeply held principles that had nothing to do with the amount they actually had to pay. That, essentially, was the Morgans' position. And to many Cold War–era American historians, the colonists' irrational preoccupation with the power to tax ennobled their cause. It distinguished the American crisis from those shaking the postcolonial world, arising from "social discontent, or economic disturbances, or of rising misery," as Bailyn put it. America's immaculate resistance could be the root of the American exception, a story that twentieth-century Americans wanted to believe. Contradictions in the record could be dismissed as rhetoric. The very notion of "hardship" could be seen as ideological. There was no need to look too closely.[15]

But what if the taxes were hard to pay because Britain's North American colonists burned their money instead of using gold and silver? Indeed, once one begins asking the question, the story of the Revolution begins to shift. The evidence becomes overwhelming that Americans opposed seemingly light taxes, not because they were paranoid, but because the taxes were charged in silver bullion, a money few colonists used on a regular basis and most never had. Thomas Paine had outlined the logic of resistance in June 1780. "There are two distinct things which make the payment of taxes difficult; the one is the large and real value of the sum to be paid, and the other is the scarcity of the thing in which the payment is to be made." Britain's North American colonists had found themselves in the latter situation in 1765. The Stamp Act Congress declared that "from the peculiar Circumstances of these Colonies, [the Stamp Act] will be extremely Burthensome & Grievous; and from the Scarcity of Specie, Payment of them absolutely impracticable." One Boston minister declared that the colonists would "have been stupid, had not a spirit been excited in us to apply, in all reasonable ways, for the removal of so insupportable a burden." Adam Gordon, an MP for Aberdeenshire who was traveling in Virginia in 1765, wrote that he was "at a loss to find how they," some of the wealthiest colonists in the New World,

Virginia's slave-driving tobacco planters, "will find Specie, to pay the Duties last imposed on them by the Parliament." Gordon was no American sympathizer. He would go on to be an avid supporter of the war against America, and even he saw the problem with the Stamp Act.[16] Not even a parliamentary decree could turn burning money into silver coin.

But looking at the Stamp Act with money and the "burning questions" in mind reveals something bigger than the problem of silver. It opens up a new way of understanding the Revolution itself. In a sense, it makes the American Revolution far more understandable than it might otherwise be. An answer to the burning questions might explain the relationship between revolution and taxation. The Americans revolted because taxes were levied in a currency they did not possess. But understanding why the Revolution happened does not explain its unique character. If anything, the money problem has the effect of making the idealism of the Revolutionary generation—their devotion to the ideal that "all men are created equal," to freedom of speech and religion, to democratic representation, and to a shared notion of liberty—all the more difficult to explain. It raises the question of how a set of fundamentally material concerns, such as money and taxation, could be translated into a profound and extraordinarily influential language of rights and freedoms without losing any of its force or specificity. I offer some suggestions here—particularly in the chapters following the work of John Dickinson, who was instrumental in developing what we might, following Greene, call the constitutional register of Revolutionary discourse—but this is the beginning of an answer, not the whole story.

Money and the Making of the American Revolution is a new narrative of the American Revolution with money at its center but not, I hope, its heart. Americans have long understood their Revolution as the birth of their democratic spirit, the expansive impulse to ensure that those created equal might have equal rights. That story is true. However, the political equality in democracy was also matched, from the beginning, by the material and social inequality implied by money as a form of individually held, propertied power. That, too, is part of America's Revolutionary legacy. One cannot understand American history without understanding the tension between them both. The literature on American democracy is justly voluminous. Money's is far less so. Thus, this book aims to retell the history of the Revolution through the lens of monetary contestation and transformation, in part, to restore a balance.

The choice of a narrative form for this book is deliberate, but it required making tradeoffs. Money is complex. Past money is arguably more so because it is so different from modern expectations. Explaining the Revolution in terms of money thus might require a richer analytical register than historical narratives typically allow. This is the choice that most, though not all, recent monetary historians have made, often with impressive results. However, this creates its own difficulties. Specialized analytical language has the advantage of precision, but precision can multiply rather than reduce confusions when the institutions in question are malleable. Analytical language also has the unfortunate tendency of reproducing the assumptions that produced it, flattening difference in a way that makes it difficult to explain historical change. Just as important, it tends to be all but unintelligible to the general reader—a massive disadvantage when the subject is of as much general interest, and importance, as the causes of the American Revolution.[17]

I tried something different. In writing *Money and the Making of the American Revolution*, I decided, wherever possible, to let the analysis emerge from the story itself, as told by the historical actors. Similarly, where possible, *Money and the Making of the American Revolution* tells its story through the lives of individuals rather than through statistics or broad social surveys. The reason for this is to emphasize that the history of Revolutionary money was, curiously enough, repeatedly transformed by individuals, albeit individuals empowered by the contingent and highly gendered dynamics of eighteenth-century political economy. The circumstances were not of their making, but the money was. The result may be neither fish nor fowl, neither analytical enough for specialists nor dramatic enough for a general audience. I leave that to the reader. As I wrote, however, I was continually surprised by the connections that emerged between people, institutions, and continents as I continued to follow the money. I hope that some of my delight in these discoveries comes through in the text. The goal is to explain the monetary roots of the American Revolution as accurately as historical language allows, and in terms that the actors themselves would have recognized. The results are sometimes complicated—money was as hard to understand then as it is now—but they are as faithful as I can make them to the confused times that produced them.

The most important reason for telling *Money and the Making of the American Revolution* as a narrative is the causal nature of the story being told. Narrative histories are implicitly arguments about the causes of historical change and the nature of that change. The causes in this case are largely, but not exclusively, monetary. Intellectual, imperial, and global registers naturally enter the analysis through the lives of Revolutionary actors trying to meet the challenges of their circumstances as best they could. Narrative history, as Lawrence Stone has observed, is attractive in part because it militates against the kind of monocausal argument one might expect from a book on, say, the monetary origins of the American Revolution. By forcing us to connect cause and effect, narrative forces us to look beyond our particular specialty, if only to maintain plausibility. It allows for surprise. Economic historians tend to treat money as a technical subject for static analysis. But no form of analysis that does not emphasize change can account for money in the time of the American Revolution.[18]

This story would not be possible to tell were it not for advances in the history of money over the past two decades.[19] Money is difficult to understand in part because, for most of us, it is the institution whose symbols and rituals most clearly touch the organization of the material world. The forces it marshals seem to be something like the weather, beyond individual control. And this is true up to a point. No individual can reshape money, but people as a whole certainly can. The aim of the best recent work on money has been, in part, to denaturalize it, to see it as what Karl Marx called a "human relation," too often "expressed as a relation between objects." Building on our historical awareness of the fact that money is not natural but a powerful form of political organization is one of the main aims of this book.[20]

Rethinking the relationship between money and the American Revolution also helps reframe the relationship between the Revolution and the history of capitalism. Historians often still talk about the American transition to capitalism as if the United States were somehow disconnected from the wider world. Capitalism, in this view, is internal to the state, a local order, characterized by local practices and local hierarchies, the result of purely local choices.[21] This internalist assumption has continued to hold, somewhat surprisingly, in the face of historians' renewed interest in global history, which at its best emphasizes the way that local processes intersect with broader trends and systems that ignore political frontiers.[22]

What I want to suggest, and what the story told here shows, is that capitalism is less an internal social order than one that is internalized, with money as a key vector of transformation. Capitalism cannot be understood within the confines of a single national history; it was international at birth, characterized by the explosive growth of European imperialism in addition to the transformations taking place in the Dutch or English countryside. While the precise connection between these two developments is still a matter of controversy, there should be no doubt that it exists. If that's true, then what we think of as national transitions to capitalism—like the American market revolution—are best understood as local iterations of developments within what was essentially an international regime, a system based on an intelligible—if malleable and contested—set of guiding rules and assumptions.[23]

This leaves open the relationship between capitalism and the state. Recent historians of capitalism have emphasized the way it is embodied in institutions. Nancy Fraser has called capitalism an "instituted social order." Douglass North, from a slightly different perspective, describes it as a set of "humanly devised constraints that shape human interaction." And this, as *Money and the Making of the American Revolution* shows, is essentially correct, but what changes in this new account is the role of capitalist institutions. If capitalism is an organism, then the state is a cell. Institutions are, in effect, cell walls, a semipermeable membrane that governs interaction with the whole. The result may seem paradoxical; capitalism is shaped by forces beyond the control of any one nation, even as nations taken together embody the system. Individual states, like the early American republic, faced a choice: either fight the regime by attempting to establish an alternative system that could reshape the whole, as the Americans tried to do in 1775, or embody capitalism so as to be empowered within it. The United States ultimately chose the latter path.[24]

But it did not do so on its own. It did so as a result of the Revolution. Money, as conflict over it shows, is not a natural extension of economic life. It is a means of exercising control, and, in an imperial context, extending the social power of national institutions—like money—onto a global terrain. In terms of money and finance, Britain won the Revolutionary War. As we will see in the next nine chapters, America's loss should come as no surprise. Britain did not simply lose its colonies in North America between 1775 and 1783; it reconstituted itself as an even more powerful imperial state. Indeed, the loss of the United States ushered in the Second British Empire that dominated the nineteenth century. Again, the story of money helps to explain why. In the eighteenth century, money divided Britain's North Atlantic Empire. Britain's failures in North America including the Revolutionary War resulted directly from its attempt to integrate its Atlantic colonies into what was, essentially, a monetary empire—what we might usefully term a "commonwealth." Despite the loss of political control in North America, the Revolutionary War healed this earlier division. Likewise, Britain's success in transforming money in the United States was arguably its first hard-won step in recreating a formal and informal— that is, financially led—empire that would, within a century, span the globe. With hindsight, it was the rules, assumptions, practices, and institutions of capitalism that would endure, not the empire. But its success and capitalism's global march were entangled in ways that the outcome of the American Revolution hardly slowed.[25]

There are at least two insights that follow from this analysis, one hopeful, the other less so. The first is that the American Revolution was a profoundly antisystemic and, in fact if not in intention, anticapitalist revolt. It was an attempt to carve out a space within the emerging British order for a different kind of political economy. If that attempt failed, as it did, the legacy of that resistance lives on in American democracy, a system designed to respond, however imperfectly, to people rather than merely the demands of wealth. Less than a century after the Revolution, Abraham Lincoln observed that many Americans held the "*liberty* of one man to be absolutely nothing, when in conflict with another man's right of *property*." His party, he wrote, were "for both the *man* and the *dollar*; but in cases of conflict, the man *before* the dollar." The fact that Lincoln helped turn democracy's power against slavery suggests that other kinds of resistance to the dollar are still possible. It is still a part of America's Revolutionary heritage, however dormant.[26]

Second, the idea that capitalism is bigger than America suggests there might be something inevitable about capitalist development. As we will see in the conclusion, the history of money suggests that this was not entirely true. American leaders could have chosen a different path, although they would likely have been punished for doing so. More importantly, the notion of capitalism as a world system, of which the American variety is at best a constituent part, can clarify the role of democracy in relation to the broader system. Democracy is the primary means by which Americans since 1776 have sought to counterbalance and contain, to reduce, the inequalities produced by capitalism and monied wealth itself. Democracy thus stands in imperfect opposition to capitalism; imperfect because, unlike capitalism, it is limited to the state; in opposition because democracy, the ideal embodied in the Declaration of Independence's insistence that "all men are created equal," is still a powerful contradiction to existing imbalances of political and economic power. Democracy supposes an equal division of power, inherent in each individual. Money, as an unequally held form of private wealth, is, in effect, its opposite. Money and democracy emerged from the American Revolution as opposing poles of social power in the United States. The places where they coincide constitute the mainstream of American life, the person and the dollar. But the unexpected moments when democracy has triumphed over the dollar—the Civil War, the New Deal, the Civil Rights movement—reveal the liberatory potential of the American Revolution at its strongest.[27]

III. Plan for the Book

This book is divided into three parts, each with three chapters. Part 1, "The Atlantic Divergence," sets up the burning question itself. It begins by showing how the American colonists created their temporary money in Massachusetts in 1690. This is (to specialists, if no one else) a familiar story, but *Money and the Making of the American Revolution*'s version differs from existing accounts in several crucial ways. First, it traces the ideas for temporary money back to John Blackwell, Oliver Cromwell's wartime treasurer. Blackwell's presence at the moment of creation is well known, but the centrality of his ideas is less well understood. As chapter 1 shows, they were crucial precisely because they were so radical: Blackwell, unlike virtually all his Atlantic colleagues, believed that money was essentially different from how it had been instituted in Britain, and he intended America to be the showcase for his ideas, as it turned out to be. Chapter 2 shows us the simultaneous transformations in eighteenth-century Britain and America through the life of Francis Fauquier, whose governorship in Virginia would have extraordinary monetary and imperial consequences. Chapter 3 shows how a conflict over money in Virginia prompted a British official to write perhaps the most important policy memo of his generation. This memo, once approved by the Privy Council, became the monetary basis of British policy for two decades. It was disastrous because of its strangely precise hostility to Blackwell's ideas about the nature of money.

Part 2, "The Conflict Begins," takes us through the Revolutionary crisis itself, showing in chapter 4 how a philosophical dispute over money, when written into a new law to tax the colonies, became the basis for American resistance to British taxation. After Parliament rejected America's burning money, the money they actually used, they were forced to tax them some other way. They settled on silver bullion, which the colonies did not have and increasingly could not get. The result, after a period of disbelief and consternation, was the first American Congress in New York in October 1765, and the first stirrings of a united resistance that would coalesce in 1776. Chapter 5 tells the story of one of the most influential thinkers of the crisis, John Dickinson, and the difficulties he had in creating a political or constitutional language for what was essentially a dispute over money. Money, like any property, he realized, was less important than the power to produce it, the political organization that made property itself possible. He began to articulate a new vision of what American political power should look like in a reconceived British Empire, one in which the Stamp Act would never have been possible, even as British politicians were trying to create just such a precedent. The reason these imperial politicians were so eager to assert new powers over the Americas becomes clear in chapter 6, when the scene shifts to India and the other half of Britain's imperial reform project. The conquest of India was part of a plan in which America played a key role as a consumer of East Indian goods. Indeed, the reform of American money was largely justified as part of a project to make the Atlantic colonists more reliable customers for British merchants like those of the East India Company. It shows how, in India too, silver was the key, and how a drought in 1769 led directly to renewed calls for taxation of America via the East India Company's new monopoly on tea. Finally, it shows how the throwing of tea into Boston Harbor provoked such an outsized, draconian response because it was not just tea that Americans were rejecting but their role as buyers in the new British Empire.

Part 3, "The Double Revolution," takes us into the Revolution itself and explains why Americans stopped burning their money. It begins, in chapter 7, with what was arguably temporary money's finest hour: the massive mobilization of burning money for war against Britain. It shows how the mass reintroduction of bills of credit spread south from New England and eventually took hold in the Continental Congress, whose decision to issue its own money—the Continental dollar—was perhaps its first step toward becoming a national government. Chapter 8 follows how the bold initial decision to finance the war with temporary money reached a dead end when states facing invasion found it all but impossible to collect the money in taxes and burn it at a reasonable rate. It also examines what Barbara Clark Smith called the "Patriot Economy," the bold, popular attempt to save the money that was still the only thing supporting the war. It shows how this attempt failed in the face of a new war-driven desire for a money that would serve as a durable asset, a store of value. Chapter 9 shows how a money was recreated on two fronts, in Philadelphia through a series of banking accidents and experiments, and in Paris through blunders in America's negotiations for independence. In 1782 Britain wanted to make sure that any peace would allow it to dictate the monetary terms under which postwar debt would be paid. The acquiescence of American negotiators had the effect of locking the monetary innovations of the last years of the war into national policy. This was the price, in effect, of British recognition. The combination of self-serving reform and diplomatic maneuvering brought the days of burning money to an end.

The conclusion returns again to the problem of capitalism in the America at the end of the eighteenth century, suggesting that what many historians have tended to see as a strength—America's nascent imperialism—was the result of a profound weakness. American leaders no longer trusted their own ideas and their own history. They no longer had the strength to go their own way in monetary matters. Some no longer wanted to. American ambitions had been reshaped by the money war.

PART ONE

The Atlantic Divergence

{⚜⚜⚜◉⚜⚜⚜}

FIG. 3. New England Shilling, 1652, Obverse.

CHAPTER ONE

An Invention

MASSACHUSETTS, 1620–1702

FIG. 4. New England Shilling, 1652, Reverse.

I. A Disaster

In 1690, New Englanders invaded Canada in search of gold. The first survivors arrived back in Boston Harbor on November 19. Fighting had continued for days beneath the fortified town of Quebec as clots of men surged back and forth up through the swamps, brooks, and wooded hills along the St. Charles River. But bad water, smallpox, starvation, and the cold had claimed more lives than the French. Each night under a full moon, the New England fleet bombarded the citadel but with little effect. Short on sleep, warned of French reinforcements, and afraid of a counter-attack, the invaders clustered in barns and farmhouses along the shore. On the night of October 12, four days after landing, soaked and cold they struggled into boats in the dark and paddled out to the fleet, leaving five field guns behind in what one participant called "the greatest Confusion imaginable." When they attempted to regroup downriver at Île d'Orléans two days later, a storm tore the fleet apart, snapping cables and scattering ships along the wide river. The only thing left was to head for home.[1]

The fleet, thirty-two strong when it sailed from Massachusetts Bay on August 9, struggled to return to Cape Breton and open water. Crosswinds drove some ships south and east out to sea, sending them as far as the Caribbean islands before they were able to turn back. One ship wrecked, but the crew was rescued. Another disappeared. One foundered and fell into the hands of France's Indigenous allies. When the French handed over a survivor much later, he told of men drowning in the waves and fighters who killed or captured any who reached the land.[2]

On October 28 Captain John Rainsford's brig ran aground off Anticosti Island in the Gulf of Saint Lawrence with sixty men aboard. Too afraid to move, they huddled on ship for several days as the storm continued to bear down outside. Finally, on November 7, they resolved to make for the island with what provisions they had left. The ship, without shifting from the rocks, was beginning to break apart. The men succeeded in building shelter on the strand, prying planks from the wreck for materials. They had one month of food left—salted pork and fish, biscuits, flour, and peas—and no hope of rescue. Traditional authority wore thin, but the men—mostly young conscripts drawn by promises of easy plunder in the north—resolved to hold together to preserve rations and their Puritan religion.

The first man died on December 20. He was the only one with medical training. Within a month, half of the others followed. As the ice thickened, hunger drove some to steal food, leading to debates between smoke-choked, bearded, filthy, frozen men over whether they would have to kill someone to make an example of. Starvation seemed inevitable. Desperate, the survivors made a plan. Salvaging a ship's boat, they cut it in half, adding boards until it was big enough to hold five men and supplies that would last, with luck, until they sighted the mainland.

Five volunteers left the island on March 25, promising to return with help from Boston. They sighted Cape Lawrence on April 11, where they killed a seal on the ice and continued south. Crosswinds pushed them out into the Atlantic, and massive icebergs—as big, some said, as the island they had left—threatened to grind them to pulp. They almost lost their way in a fog off Cape Breton on April 24, but the worst was over. Soon they killed a few birds and began to catch fish. A fishing boat found them off Cape Ann and hauled them through a storm into Boston Harbor on May 9, 1691. Everyone had given them up for dead. In fact, they were among the lucky ones.[3]

Out of the 2,500-odd conscripts who had set out, so many had perished, wrote the Boston minister Samuel Myles on December 12, 1690, that captains had misplaced bodies in the holds of their ships, some "having their eyes and cheeks eaten by cats before they were found." Others survived the trip, arriving at "Boston or elsewhere" only to "die up and down like rotten sheep" from infection. On the first ship to arrive, 65 out of 120 on board had died of smallpox and fever. On January 8, 1691, Boston merchant James Lloyd estimated another quarter would die before the new year was out. Some feared the survivors would bring contagion to the city and fled. They were right. Smallpox lingered until February. The dead were buried in salt marshes north of the city.[4]

For Massachusetts leaders, the repulse from Quebec was the climax of a financial and military crisis long in the making. Two years before, war had begun with Catholic France. For a year, the struggle was waged mostly in the native spaces between English trading posts on the Hudson River, the New England coastline, and the French strongholds of the St. Lawrence River valley, fought in large part by Indigenous fighters pursuing war for their own reasons. In the summer of 1689, though, a group of Haudenosaunee allied with the English attacked Lachine, just upriver from Montreal, killing and capturing over a hundred people, including French settlers. That fall, the new French governor, the Compte de Frontenac, devised a three-pronged winter assault that would range through the territory held by English allies to attack the colonists directly.

War parties hit three hundred miles of English frontier at once in the first months of 1690. In February, a combined French and Native American assault razed Schenectady, New York, killing all sixty men, including eleven African slaves, and capturing most of the women and children. Soon after, another party did the same to Casco, Maine. Still another ranged deep into Massachusetts, killing some eighty men, women, and children living near Salmon Falls along the Piscataqua River just seventy miles north of Boston. It had the help of Wohawa, a local Abenaki leader. According to Francis Montier, a Parisian captured in the English counterattack, Wohawa believed the English were responsible for Mohawk attacks the previous year. Mohawk raiders had "rosted & eaten off the fingers" of members of Wohawa's family, Montier claimed, setting them loose, maimed, with word that "the English sett them on."[5]

The French and their allies' plan, Massachusetts colonists suspected, was to push the English closer and closer to their coastal cities where, without farms to feed them, the colonists would starve, or civil unrest would tear them apart. "[The] Indians have a saying," James Lloyd wrote to the Board of Trade in London on January 8, 1691. "Drive the pigs to the great sows of Boston and New York, and they will suck her to death." The attacks threatened to shatter the English alliance. Mohawks complained that the English had grown complacent, that "They ate, drank, and slept much but left the war to them." Mohawk leaders demanded "a speedy attack on Canada" in retaliation. The Mohawks also called for a "general Embargo," cutting off all trade so the English might "apply themselves to be in readinesse for war against the French and Indians in all Quarters."[6] The Massachusetts fleet's journey north was the result. It was meant to pay for itself with plundered Catholic specie. Its return meant attacks would continue. It also meant a financial reckoning could no longer be avoided.

The colony faced uncomfortable facts. Massachusetts had stretched to send the expedition north, and its failure threatened to reveal limits to the colony's fiscal capacity for war. In the seventeenth-century British Atlantic, gold and silver were money, and on those terms, Massachusetts was poor. Meanwhile, financing the expedition had left the colony some £40,000 in debt, including some £7,000 needed just to cover the salaries of those who had risked their lives in the attempt. The question was, How to pay? The answer they arrived at—as daring in its way as the failed assault on Quebec—would reshape money in British North America for the better part of a century.

II. Money and Massachusetts: A Long-Standing Problem

The first English families who traveled to Massachusetts in the 1620s and 1630s had liquidated the bulk of their estates in Britain and the Netherlands, investing the proceeds in building sustainable households in a foreign, at times forbidding, environment. From the start, that meant hiring or purchasing laborers to augment the efforts of family members, in addition to livestock, land, and luxuries. These expenditures soon emptied the colonists' purses, but the arrival of new immigrants with fresh stocks of cash to trade for the livestock, land, and labor of the original colonists kept cash shortages from becoming acute until the English unrest of the 1640s.[7]

The English had significant advantages when it came to dealing with the cash shortages they faced in America. There had been few moments in the country's history where coin had been plentiful, and many when it had seemed to dry up altogether. In part as a result, Britons had developed a remarkable culture of credit that allowed most exchanges, particularly between people like the settlers, who knew each other very well, to be done without any money changing hands. Indeed, when viewed from a global perspective, seventeenth-century Britons and their colonial counterparts were peculiarly reliant on interpersonal credit to facilitate daily exchange. Whereas some places, like the Chinese and South Asian kingdoms, had developed multiple layers of complementary currencies of varying values, and others—like Native Americans and many African polities—had developed distinctive nonmonetary regimes for facilitating trade, the English had developed a system where credit, buying power, in effect, was located in a household's reputation, property, and ability to work.[8]

These were all nonmonetary qualities that nonetheless could be expressed in monetary terms as credits given and debits received. A young woman might watch a neighbors' children, or help with other household tasks, in exchange for the neighboring husband's work on a barrel or a wagon wheel. A shoemaker might take payment for a new set of boots by requesting part of a neighbor's slaughtered calf or mark their fee in a ledger in order to demand payment in the future. The result was a web of credit that one historian has called an "economy of obligation." It worked remarkably well when outside demands for monetary payment, either for taxes or imports, did not overly interfere. Such demands had begun shifting the English economy itself in the late sixteenth century further away from a neighborly credit basis. But settlers found that those same techniques, in America, remained remarkably effective—especially when coin all but disappeared.[9]

When war began in England in 1642, immigration all but ceased. Stopping the flow of coin to the colony was destabilizing, in part, because it exacerbated long-standing class conflicts. The colonies' Puritan founders had designed the system with themselves at its apex but couldn't function without cooks and carpenters, many of whom arrived as bound labor. These other colonists would not work for nothing and constantly demanded more. The Massachusetts General Court reacted to workers' hard bargaining, first, in 1633, by limiting wages for skilled stone and woodworkers to two shillings a day and those for unskilled labor to eighteen pence, all the while limiting commodity prices to one-third over the going rate in England. Those interventions were sufficient while coin lasted. But even before immigration slowed, in 1640, traders arrived with a "great store of provisions, both out of

England and Ireland," demanding the colonists' gold and silver in return. "[Now] all our money was drained from us," John Winthrop recalled.[10]

The colonists' first impulse was to replace gold and silver with some other thing, leading to a series of novel measures starting in 1640, which made goods other than gold or silver valid payment for financial debts. The court first set values for Indian corn, rye, wheat, and both blue and white wampumpeag, or "wampum," the clamshell beads so crucial to the fur trade with Indigenous nations. The beads, though, were only good for debts under 1 shilling. If a debtor couldn't find grain or coin, the court decreed that "the creditor might take what goods he pleased (or, if he had no goods, then his lands)." Debtors, too, were protected by the law, in that a creditor could only seize property once its value had been assessed by three men—one appointed by the creditor, one by the debtor, and another by the local marshal. But this led to further complications when it came to debts owed to free laborers.[11]

The same midcentury unrest that kept potential migrants and their money from crossing the Atlantic cut off the supply of bound laborers as well. Free laborers found themselves in high demand, but with new complexities due to the lack of coin. Few worked for pay on a day-to-day basis. Rather, as in the colonists' English homeland, workers typically joined the household of their employer—receiving pay, if any, at the end of their contract. The 1640 law meant if the master could not pay in coin, a servant could claim their master's property. Winthrop recalled that a householder named "Rowley" had been forced to sell two oxen in order to pay off his servant for the year. With little else to sell, and few coins available, he "told his servant he could keep him no longer, not knowing how to pay him the next year." The servant answered that he would serve Rowley in return for more of his cattle. "But how," Rowley replied, "shall I do . . . when all my cattle are gone?" The servant replied, "You shall then serve me, so you may have your cattle again." The threat to the colony's class hierarchy was evident; the last might become first.[12]

Some householders forced servants to take pay in kind against their will. In 1645 the Massachusetts General Court felt the need to pass a law that barred employers from forcing laborers to accept wages in alcohol, because "the forcing of laborers and other workmen to take wine in pay for wages is a great nursery or preparative to drunkenness." The law had little effect. New Englanders lamented in 1672 that alcohol had become an expected part of standard remuneration, "without which it is found, by too sad experience, many refuse to [work]." Payment in goods remained common throughout the seventeenth century and into the next. Even in 1694, a building contract specified that wages would be paid in bushels of rye or Indian corn, unless the contractor was able to find cash, in which case the builder "shall abate one-fourth part" of the price.[13]

The lack of coin also complicated the problem of attracting the wealthier migrants necessary to keep coin flowing to the colonial elite. The first migrants to New England came in search of religious freedom. But many who came after, too, sought wealth and—perhaps more importantly— independence. In 1630 Puritan minister John Cotton preached that the colonies would be a refuge from the relentless creditors of the Old World, who lent to borrowers in order to take advantage. "If men be over-burdened with debts and miseries," Cotton said, "they might retire out of the way," in America, "not to defraud their debtors (*for God is avenger of such things*) . . . but to [gain] further opportunity to discharge their debts, and to [satisfy] their Creditors."[14]

Many followed the call, but what wealth they found was not in coin, at least not primarily, and, in as much as debts were settled in coin, that presented difficulties. There were no mines in New England or further south. Gold and silver were as scarce in the New World as they had been, at times, in the old. Critics suggested that the lack of cash made immigrating to America the equivalent of a vow of poverty, an idea that some Puritans embraced. The "plantation in this part of *America*," Cotton Mather wrote in his 1702 ecclesiastical history of the colonies, "was indeed planted not on the account of any *Worldly Interest*, but on a Design of Enjoying and advancing the true *Reformed Religion*, in a *Practical Way*."[15]

Puritan publicist William Wood, though, wrote that America's critics mistook money for wealth, the real resources money could claim. The colonists might seem poor in comparison "with the rich Merchants or great landed men in *England*," after they laid "out monies for transporting of servants, and cattle, and goods, for houses and fences, and gardens." But their "increase comes in double." Immigration was an investment in a better, more equal life. "Howsoever they are accounted poor, they are well contented, and look not so much at abundance, as a competency," Wood wrote. "Can they be very poor, where for four thousand souls, there are fifteen hundred head of cattle, besides four thousand goats, and Swine innumerable?" Everyone had enough, and, if grain was scarce anyone could "have either fish or flesh for their labor." "So little is poverty in the Country," Wood continued, "that I am [persuaded] if many in *England* which are constrained to beg their bread were there, they would live better than many do here that have money to buy it." As for the American colonists, they might have "less money by them," Wood wrote, "but never less riches."[16]

III. The Problem of Taxes and Payment

Devastating conflicts in the 1670s, however, taught a painful lesson: that wealth was difficult to mobilize for war. For war, the Bay colony turned to taxes, and levying taxes meant wrestling again with the problem of money. Taxes in late seventeenth-century Massachusetts were levied in what were called rates. A rate had two parts, a poll tax of 1 shilling and 8 pence (one-twelfth of a pound) on all adult males who either headed a household or earned wages, and a property tax of 1 penny (one two-hundred-fortieth of a pound) per pound on each colonist's "personal & real estates." Usually, the General Court levied one "rate" a year. The court levied twenty-six rates in King Philip's War (1675–76), the cataclysmic yearlong battle with their Native American neighbors that left many New England towns burned and thousands on both sides dead, enslaved, or scattered.[17]

Most "rates" were charged in "country pay" or simply "pay," the non-perishable foodstuffs colonists produced, at prices set by the court. On November 8, 1689, for example, the General Court levied six rates. Five were payable in kind, with wheat, barley, barley malt, rye, Indian corn, or peas, at rates set by the court. For example, a bushel of wheat went for 5 shillings and 6 pence. That meant two bushels of wheat, roughly 112 pounds of grain, would cover the poll tax portion of six rates with 12 pence left over—enough to cover the in-kind property tax portion on just £2 worth of land or cattle. One rate, however, was "in Money," meaning each householder would have to come up with gold or silver for it by selling their goods at market. The colony offered a one-third discount if colonists paid in-kind taxes in coin.[18]

As we've seen, even in the best of times New England had little hard currency. That began to change, however, when Puritan traders opened trade with colonies in the Caribbean, who need the salt-fish, hardwood timbers, and livestock that New England produced in great numbers. By the seventeenth century, virtually all the silver in the world was produced by enslaved Indigenous laborers in Spanish mines. It passed from there into the Caribbean, where New Englanders found they could demand it, along with sugar and molasses, in trade. Beginning in 1652, Massachusetts had created its own mint in order to recoin foreign silver and establish a reliable standard that was compatible abroad—which is where most of the pine-tree shillings ultimately went, to settle debts in Europe. In the midst of a war that disrupted both trade and the harvest, things were worse. Silver supplies from Caribbean sources had dwindled through the 1670s, leading to the closure of the mint. Even grain was hard to procure, and many householders resisted warrants for the new taxes, forcing constables to "distrain the very many refusers." By spring 1690, the colony's soldiers were growing restive. Many had spent the past year patrolling the backwoods of Maine hoping, in vain, to waylay French patrols. They had not been paid for months. In order to silence their "clamors," the colony treasury paid some of them in IOU "debentures" that gave them a claim on the colony's tax returns in coin and grain as they came in. According to one observer, though, these debentures sold at market in Boston for just 25 percent to 50 percent of their face value, leaving the troops "in high disgust" and the colony at a loss for how to provide for the next campaign.[19]

The merchant John Nelson, who had been a key figure in ousting the hated Royal governor Edmund Andros, proposed an alternative funding structure on January 4, 1690. He, and other "private Gentlemen," would back the war effort "at their own charge," pooling their resources and credit to back offensive operations against the French and their allies—so long as the colony promised to pay them back.[20] The court agreed. For the Quebec expedition, backers appealed to Boston's merchant community—gathering up small pledges, or subscriptions of support, ranging from £50 to £200. "Subscribers are promised to be paid out the plunder if any got, Otherwise to be paid by the Country when able," John Usher noted on July 4, 1690. The merchants and other backers were generous. Expenses ran as high as £50,000, according to Myles. Others put the figure at £40,000. Regardless, when news arrived that the fleet was approaching, in early November, the colony immediately called for twenty new rates and created a ten-member committee of magistrates and merchants to borrow £3,000–4,000 in coin to pay off the soldiers and sailors as soon as they arrived. Investors could wait for tax receipts and plunder.[21]

The fleet that came over the horizon, however, presented a prospect far more dire than colony leaders had expected. There was no profit to be had, no loot, no conquest. And with no loot, soldiers and sailors would have to go without, stranded penniless in Boston through the winter. The attempt to borrow coin failed. Merchants were unwilling to lend hard currency to a colony already hopelessly in their debt. James Lloyd summarized the situation a week into the new year. "Since the revolution [to topple Andros] I judge that we have lost a thousand men by the Indians and I fear still more by the Canadian expedition. The money expended, debts, and money required may amount to £200,000," Lloyd wrote. "In fact, I fear we are almost run aground."[22]

IV. No Way Out: A Monetary "Invention"

There was no way of getting out with traditional means or half-measures. There was no gold or silver, and no hope of finding any. Borrowing had been tried and failed. Taxes could gather more grain or timber but not means of payment. The problem demanded an innovative solution and got one. Between the arrival of the first ships in November 1690 and May 1691, when the survivors arrived from Anticosti, Massachusetts leaders, in effect, had been forced to rethink what money was. The plan that resulted was an improvisation, stitched together in three acts over six months, but the thinking behind it was unconventional and consequential, offering a transformative view of money and its role in society.

In the midst of plague and war, Massachusetts leaders, in effect, brought a new understanding of money to life. In doing so, they set the parameters of a debate that would define economic thought and practice in British North America for nearly a century. Remarkably, it was not their own ideas, such as they were, that won out. Rather, in their desperation the colonial elders turned to the ideas of a remarkable outsider, whose strange ideas about money came with the weight and significance of years of service at the center of England's regicidal republican experiment. The result bore traces of the radicalism that had dethroned and beheaded a king. Americans would debate the validity of this monetary solution. Some thought it was brilliant, some fraudulent, radical or not radical enough, useful or hopelessly misguided. They would not, however, do without it. They would turn to it time and again to help fight their wars, to pay their debts, and to defend the economic primacy and political centrality of the colonies' propertied householders in Britain's maritime empire. In time, imperial officials in London would come to see American monetary innovation as a threat to empire itself. But at first, in 1690, before the founding of the Bank of England and the financial revolution that would transform the British state, they saw it as merely one, more or less viable, financial project among many. The American money was just what one of its prominent supporters called it, an "Invention." It was an invention that, in practice, would lead to its own kind of revolution.[23]

The ideas that colony leaders drew on when they created the first "Bills of Public Credit" were not entirely new, even if the outcome was. Some were as old as Aristotle, who, in some early modern readings, had emphasized money's political origins. Money was, as one of its first English translators rendered the key passage in book 5 of the *Nicomachean Ethics*, "founded, not on nature, but on convention; and . . . human laws, which have thought fit to employ it as a measure of value, may, at pleasure, set this use of it aside, and employ some other measure in its stead." Thomas More, the influential sixteenth-century English thinker, suggested that if money was made by "convention" and not the natural result of human interaction, it could be unmade, eliminated altogether, as it had been in the "utopia" he imagined arising across the Atlantic.[24]

"Once the use of money was abolished, and together with it all greed for it, what a mass of troubles was cut away, what a crop of crimes was pulled up from the roots!" More wrote. "Is there anyone who does not know that fraud, theft, plunder, strife, and turmoil, contention, rebellion, murder, treason, poisoning, crimes which are constantly punished but never held in check, would die away if money were eliminated? . . . Indeed, poverty itself, which seems to be merely the lack of money, would itself immediately fade away if money were everywhere totally abolished."[25]

For decades before 1690, seventeenth-century English utopians had plumbed the liberating potential of new concepts of money as well. In the 1650s and 1660s, English intellectual Samuel Hartlib and his associates had devised plans to overcome what they saw as an intractable scarcity of coin, ranging from seemingly prosaic merchants' collectives to arcane quests for the philosopher's stone. In the radical environment of Revolutionary Britain, the crown's power over monetary value was increasingly questioned, even ridiculed. Something new seemed not just possible but necessary—an economic revolution to the times.[26]

Some of these attempts had come to the attention of New Englanders. John Winthrop Jr., son and namesake of Massachusetts's founding governor, wrote Hartlib on December 16, 1659, asking after new ideas for a "banke," and inquiring as to whether there was any truth to tales of a process that had "transmuted nine pounds of quicksilver into pure gold" with only a little "powder taken upon the point" of a knife. Hartlib replied with a library of radical thinking, including works by William Potter and himself, along with assurances that a society "come from beyond the seas into England," though "most secret and hidden," did possess the trick of transmutation and in due course would reveal it to the world. In the meantime, however, Hartlib suggested that Winthrop read his enclosed plans for "the setting up of Bancos of Lands and Commodities." In thanks, Winthrop sent Hartlib a barrel of cranberries.[27]

Potter and Hartlib's insights proved intellectually fruitful among the New England elite, even if practical results were not immediately forthcoming. Winthrop proposed his own "way of trade & [bank without] money" to the Royal Society in London during a visit in 1662–63, following the model found in Potter's *Key of Wealth*, a 1650 pamphlet sent by Hartlib. The society, which had only been chartered a year before, passed on the project, however, and the plan was lost. Winthrop's friend and relative by marriage, the Oxford-educated Rev. John Woodbridge, who had settled in Newbury, Massachusetts, proposed something similar in March 1671, setting up a "bank of credit" that only lasted a few months. Woodbridge tried again in 1681 and succeeded in publishing his plan anonymously a year later. This time, his private bank of credit succeeded in issuing bills before it folded. Like Potter and Winthrop, Woodbridge saw the lack of coin in the colonies as a developmental defect, forcing colonists into troubling debt relationships they could avoid if gold and silver were more plentiful. Like Potter, he too argued that since gold and silver were unavoidably scarce, collective credit based on the value of colonial land and property must supply its place. However, both of these experiments were less relevant to the leaders in 1690 than the proposals of another recent immigrant from England, the republican refugee Captain John Blackwell.[28]

V. The Eventful Life and Strange Ideas of John Blackwell

Blackwell arrived in Boston for the second and final time on March 27, 1690, just two and a half weeks after his sixty-sixth birthday and after two bitter years as William Penn's on-site governor in Pennsylvania. A Pennsylvania Quaker, he wrote in his farewell letter to Penn, "prays for his neighbor on First Days and then preys upon him the other six." His arrival came near the end of a long, distinguished public career, albeit one that had been cut short twice by revolution. In 1690 he was, without doubt, the most experienced financier in British North America, and one of the most experienced with war and revolution in the whole Atlantic world. His words carried weight.[29]

When he was eighteen, Blackwell had followed his father, John Blackwell Sr., to war, joining the cavalry arm of the London militia, "Trained Bands," gathered to oppose the king's threatened assault. Blackwell Sr. was a wealthy London merchant who had served (and gone unpaid) as grocer to Charles I. Over the course of Blackwell's teens, his father grew increasingly radical. In June 1641 a warrant was issued for his arrest after he and several other men broke into the church of St. Thomas the Apostle in Southwark, tearing down altar rails and burning them in the yard while threating the parson that if he "came to read service in his surplice, they would burn him and his surplice too."[30]

Three years later, in June 1645, Blackwell—by then a junior officer—
fought at Naseby alongside Cromwell, who, when the battle was over,
brought Blackwell into his own cavalry regiment as a captain to replace
an officer killed in the battle. By the time the wars in England ended, in
1647, Blackwell was regimental treasurer. Soon, though, he got a more
significant commission: deputy treasurer at war to Cromwell's Commonwealth. In June 1648 he left the regiment, going into government
service full-time. His father, meanwhile, served as a judge, trying and
executing numerous royalists, and fronted expenses for the 1649 trial and
execution of the king himself. The younger Blackwell became an expert
at paying—or attempting to pay—the Commonwealth's troops, handling
more than six million pounds of army funds between 1651 and 1659, and,
in the meantime, amassing large estates around London confiscated from
royalists. He was instrumental in financing the invasion of Ireland using
a similar structure to the one Nelson proposed to Massachusetts some
forty years later. Using private "subscriptions," to be paid off in plundered
Irish estates, he raised £1,481,580 for war between 1649 and 1656, including his own investment of £2,350 for "Rebel Lands" in counties Dublin,
Kildare, and Cork.[31]

In 1656, at the age of thirty-two, Blackwell was elected to Parliament
from Surrey, where his father served as justice of the peace. It might have
been the start of a long career in power, but fate had other plans. On January 16, 1658, Blackwell's father died. That fall, Cromwell followed. In the
months after Cromwell's death, Blackwell fell in with a faction of disaffected former army officers led by General Charles Fleetwood who backed
the continuation of parliamentary rule. Fleetwood and his allies fell out
of favor, though, when Parliament began negotiations with Charles II to
restore the British monarchy. In February 1660 Blackwell lost his position
as treasurer of war. Three months later, the new king landed in Dover.
On June 12 Parliament named Blackwell in a list of Cromwellians who
would be forced to answer for their actions in the Civil War, including
the death of Charles II's father. Five days later, Blackwell was imprisoned
and stripped of his English estates. Unlike many of his peers, he escaped
with his life. With the help of a noble acquaintance, he was able to retain
the title to a small estate near Dublin. His career in public service, however, was over. His sentence included a lifetime ban from holding office in
England or Wales. He spent the next twenty years maintaining his small
fortune, raising a large family, and deploying financial expertise garnered
in his years with Cromwell in various financial schemes in the City of
London.[32]

In 1684 his career appeared over, when—according to Blackwell, who was then sixty—a group of fellow Puritans approached him, asking if he might travel on their behalf to New England. They wanted Blackwell to apply for lands to settle out of the territory seized from the Nipmuck of central Massachusetts seven years earlier, in the wake of King Philip's War. English Puritans seeking refuge from a Catholic monarch had reason to think new claims would be successful. On October 23, 1684, Charles II revoked the charter of Massachusetts and began the process of folding it into the Dominion of New England, a new supercolony meant to place the fractious settlements of British Northeast America under a single, royal administration. Settlers who had secured land under the previous regime would be forced to apply to the new government to confirm their title, and many, it was thought, would fail. Suddenly, it seemed, much of New England was up for grabs, and speculation in conquered lands, for better or worse, was Blackwell's profession. Blackwell took the chance, with his wife and daughter, and sailed to Boston in December 1684. He met with immediate success, securing a town plot on eight square miles of Nipmuck land on January 28, 1685. Blackwell might have left then were it not for what must have been, for him, a happy revelation. The Puritan connections that sidelined him in London had a rather different effect in the Mathers' besieged city-state. In Boston, his experience as a financier in peace and war, so long disregarded, was suddenly valuable again. Massachusetts would put those skills to use.[33]

In June 1686, after a year and a half in the colony, Joseph Dudley—president of the Dominion of New England—appointed Blackwell to head a committee for "the [improvement] and benefit" of the dominion's trade.[34] Banned back home, he was suddenly everywhere, associating with the leading families, with his advice sought after. He was "consulted with in all public affairs," despite being "a violent Commonwealth's man," one rival put it.[35] Three months later, Blackwell succeeded in founding the first chartered "bank" in North America and the last for nearly a century. Dudley declared the bank a "useful invention for this [country]," and Blackwell set about making arrangements for it—buying paper, a rolling press, and engraved plates for the bills as well as hiring a printer and clerks. The bank ultimately went nowhere, lost in the violence of the times. No one would give credit for land that might be overrun by an Abenaki or French raiding party at any moment, or for goods when privateering made the prospect of sale uncertain. Blackwell's prominent colonial partners abandoned him, "without a glass of wine for thankes," the bank plan collapsed, and in late 1688 he accepted Penn's offer to go to Pennsylvania. There, amid a sea of other difficulties, Blackwell encouraged a local plan for a bank of credit that also went nowhere and quarreled with Quakers who resented his appointment. The result was again frustration and failure. Blackwell must have been relieved to head north, the first leg on a journey home to Ireland and retirement.[36]

Back in Boston two years later, though, Blackwell's theories had never been more relevant. Ideas about money that may have seemed radical or unworkable just a couple of years before were getting a new hearing in light of the disastrous assault on Quebec. The collective and individual efforts involved had incurred debts that had to be paid fairly, an impossibility on conventional terms. But the seeming impossibility of payment, for some elite New Englanders, suggested that ideas behind earlier attempts were flawed. Their failures were as much conceptual as financial. Means of settlement existed, but they would have to be based on a new, more capacious notion of what money was—one that matched American conditions.

Woodbridge's bank, for example, was based on the idea that gold and silver were money, but given that precious metals were scarce, financiers should invent credit substitutes. Gold and silver's primary function, Woodbridge had reasoned, was a means to "avoid the hazard of Trusting." When gold and silver were scarce, as they almost always were, shopkeepers were forced to extend credit, putting their fortunes at risk. Payment in coin eliminated the problem. Since coin was indeed scarce, other substitutes were necessary. More impersonal *"Credit"* instruments, he argued, presented a superior alternative. Metal "was subject to *wear . . . fires, robberies, mistakes,* & the like contingencies," Woodbridge wrote. Like all movable wealth, it invited violence. Why not use an alternative that was just as valuable and far more secure? Why not deploy coin-substitutes based on something of "real, durable, & of secure value" that could not be picked from a pocket or clipped lighter with metal shears: a "Deposit in *Land.*" Depositors would leave deeds at the bank and receive bills or book credit in return. These *"Bank-Bills,* or payments therein, will effect, to all Intents, as well as plenty of Coin," Woodbridge concluded.[37]

In America, though, securities as substitutes for coin had significant weaknesses. Their value depended on creating a legal tie between the holder to an underlying property, entailing at least two difficulties. First, colonists would have to pledge what they owned, putting the properties themselves at risk. Many were unwilling to do so. Land was most colonial families' most valuable possession and, since a 1675 law that made land liable for personal debts, a major source of credit. Pledging it to a new, untried institution would not meet many families' criteria for prudent husbandry. After receiving Potter's plan for a land bank, John Winthrop Jr. wrote to Hartlib, that though many men "in their owne spirits, would be satisfied & willing" to pledge land to a bank, their "relations," "wives, children *that* are grown up, parents of some or, their wives parents & kindred or the childrens kindred in pretence of care of them & other friends, & friends all must be satisfied." That, Winthrop surmised, was "impossible . . . or will come hardly of, except in some few."38

Second, even if colonists pledged their land, its value as a security depended on the pledge being credible. Many settlers had used the 1675 law as an excuse to take Native American land, claiming Indigenous land in payment for debts, real or spurious. Indigenous resistance, meanwhile, in a kind of poetic justice, had destroyed the credibility of all land claims. Reprisals, massacres, and the sense, as the General Court wrote to King William on December 10, 1690, that "small party's Infest our Frontiers, and Remote Dwellings, Sculking about to wait an Opportunity for the Burnings of Houses, and Killing of persons unawares when at their imployment in the Fields, and Necessitate the English to Hunt them like wolves in the Wilderness, where the Trees, and Swamps are as forts to Secure them, having no Certain place of abode," made the security of Massachusetts land questionable at best.39

Even property in long-settled areas was hardly secure in 1690. James II had stripped Massachusetts's charter in 1684, and with it the legal basis for colonial land holding, in part because the king had learned that landholders in Massachusetts had been given clear legal title without the rent obligations owed to the king, or "quitrents," meant to both raise revenue for the crown and signify that all land ultimately belonged to the king. Edmund Andros, of the Dominion of New England, had been sent with instructions to make the colonists apply for new, confirmed land titles that would include quitrent obligations. Without a new title, which was difficult to obtain and impossible if the purchase could be traced back to illegal acquisition from Native Americans or colonial squatters, all land holdings were in question. One unnamed Boston woman testified in 1689 that Andros had told her personally that when she purchased her land from a man who had purchased it from Native Americans, she might as well have purchased all of Boston. She had just as much, and just as little, right to it. "Andros . . . explained that the land was the king's and they must take out patents [reconfirming their property rights] or the land would be granted [to] others who would do so." The result, Samuel Sewall observed in an April 1689 letter to London merchant Thomas Papillon, was that colonists'

"Lands, which were formerly the best part of their Estate, became of very little value, and consequently the Owners of very little Credit." Any coin substitute based on the value of land would face the same difficulty, fluctuating with the price of contested deeds.[40]

Blackwell's bank of 1686, while it had aims similar to Woodbridge's scheme, had a different set of ideas behind it. Money, for Blackwell, was the means of expressing value. Money was the figures in colonial ledger books, bonds, and bills of exchange, not any particular good or claim for goods. This idea had a number of useful implications. If money was a measure, it could never be scarce, like gold and silver. Likewise, it would not be tied to the fluctuating physical value of particular commodities, because, as a measure it was an expression of value itself. Money would be the means used to assess and express value; the metric of value in the same sense that the inch was the metric of length, not the measured thing itself.

Identifying money with commodities like gold, silver, or land was a historic mistake, Blackwell argued in his first plan for the bank. "Money, whether Gold or Silver, is nothing but a measure of the value of other things," Blackwell wrote. Yet "for a long succession of Ages," in the "civilized & trading part of the world," coin had become the "usuall & best known means of interchange." But coin's true importance was as a means to create a scale to measure value. Before "this Measure & way of interchange" was invented, Blackwell wrote, people had bartered commodities, leading to various injustices as "the [less] necessitous over-reached the greater."

> "The conveniencies of the way of Barter might have been much obviated, By a frequent setting [of] a just & equal value of the Price of all commodities, by [public] authority. According as the plenty or [scarcity] of them should require, and the market had ruled: But there being no such [common] standard, Money," a measure based on gold and silver, "hath [obtained] & been admitted as the best [balance] of Trade, both by wise & un-wise."

In adopting gold and silver as the "common measure" and a tradable good, though, the trading world had run into endless difficulties, Blackwell wrote. Mines failed. Traders shipped gold and silver away to parts unknown, never to return, even as trade increased. Now it seemed as if existing stocks of gold and silver were "insufficient in this age of the world," Blackwell wrote, circumstances that "hath put [diverse] persons" like himself "upon contrivances, how to supply that [deficiency], by other Mediums" including "Banks, Lumbards & Exchange of Moneys by Bills," like those Blackwell proposed. But his broader point, newly relevant in 1690, was that money was not a thing at all. It was a social relation that, under the right circumstances, with government support, might transcend its historical relationship to gold and silver. Blackwell's plan, which relied on merchants pledging to honor each other's credit, was a step in that direction.

> "By this," Blackwell concluded, "the trade and wealth of this Country is established on its [own] Foundation, & and upon a medium or Balance arising within [itself], vizt, The Land & Products of this Country; and not upon the Importation of Gold or Silver or the [scarcity] or plenty of them, or of any thing else from [foreign] Nations, which may be withheld, Prohibited or Enhanced, at their pleasures."

In other words, Blackwell argued that even radical arguments about money had confused the measure for a commodity and as a result had put people, unnecessarily, at the mercy of outside forces. If they could only realize that money was the measure of value—not one thing or another—they would see that their difficulty was conceptual rather than real. Money only appeared scarce, Blackwell argued, because of a misperception of what money was. Massachusetts leaders, like most of the world, were fixated on the objects that served as "money' in most of the trading world and ignoring the way that money actually worked in their day-to-day lives.

Blackwell's analysis was attractive in Massachusetts, in part, because it emphasized something important about the way that money worked in colonial life. Colonists were obviously aware of coin, but it was not central to their monetary practice. In day-to-day life, money was already a way of talking about value. A neighbor might value their labor at 2 shillings per day and get paid in bread, beer, butter, meat, rum or the promise of help years later, valued at the same amount. In these promises—which sometimes, but not always, found their way into the account books kept by colonial householders and, later, into probate inventories as a form of wealth—money was not a commodity. Years might and did go by where none changed hands. Rather, money was a way of measuring and expressing the value of goods and services, exchanged between householders over the course of their lifetimes. This practice, measuring and expressing value, was the essence of money, Blackwell wrote. Once the colonists recognized that, they could move away from their preoccupation with coin or promises for coin or goods that might serve as an equivalent of precious metal. Then, new possibilities would open up. The colonists could establish a financial apparatus independent of precious metals, relying instead on the institutionalization, on a colony scale, of the kind of promises they made to one another every day.[41]

Blackwell's ideas had roots in his experience of war in Ireland. When Blackwell was Cromwell's treasurer at war, he had signed the papers paying the salary of a young Oxford intellectual, William Petty, to value Irish lands. Petty's project resulted, in part, in a prolonged meditation on the nature of money and value, *A TREATISE OF Taxes & Contributions*, that Blackwell, with his interest and estates in Ireland, might have known of before it was published in 1662. Petty started his assessment with the intention of valuing Irish land in terms of their return in gold and silver, only to run into the very problem Blackwell alluded to twenty-six years later. Taxes and rents were rarely paid in actual coin, and when farmers were forced to do so, Petty observed, it was "somewhat hard" and definitely wasteful, as farmers "must first carry their Corn perhaps ten Miles to sell, and turn into money; which then being paid to the king, is again reconverted into Corn fetcht [sic] many miles further." But if the conversion to coin was wasteful, Petty continued, what was the purpose of coin in the first place, and how might its use be avoided?[42]

"The World measures things by Gold and Silver," Petty observed. That "measure" was coin's core function, but that did not mean coin was an ideal way to establish a measure of value. Metals were harder to assay for fineness than people thought, Petty observed, and "might rise and fall in its price, and be worth more at one place than another." If one was to design a system of "natural Standards and Measures" from scratch, "all things ought to have been valued by two natural Denominations, which is Land and Labour" rather than coin.[43] Silver and gold, then, could be done away with altogether.

Petty's and Blackwell's ideas both emerged out of a British world fundamentally rethinking what money meant in light of its seventeenth-century revolutions. If the monarchy was diminished, it seemed unlikely that the right to make money "inheres in the bones of princes," as early seventeenth-century jurists put it. Blackwell, a hardened Cromwellian, would certainly have rejected that claim, and he was not alone. Simultaneously, the effects of demand for silver for warfare and to feed Asian markets—shortages, arbitrage, and imperial competition in the Atlantic—made it increasingly clear that no government could hope to control its money as medieval rulers had, crying up and down the value of gold and silver, without dramatic consequences.[44]

Indeed, at virtually the same time Blackwell was writing, other British thinkers were laying plans for their own monetary transformations manifested in a profusion of schemes for banks of all sorts that marked the late seventeenth-century financial revolution. Rather than clarifying or changing the meaning of money, like Blackwell, or, as Petty advocated, adopting a theory value based on land or labor, most of these projectors hoped to create credit instruments that would serve as credible substitutes for silver in the domestic market. Some plans, like those that eventually informed the creation of the Bank of England, depended on creating bills exchangeable for gold and silver on demand. Others sought to issue exchangeable forms of government debt securities, ultimately payable in the coin that taxes would bring in. Blackwell himself, before coming to America, had been involved with a plan to transform the chartered Company of the Royal Fishery into a "bank of Credit, Lumbard, and Exchange of Moneys" that would serve as a model for his first proposal in Massachusetts.[45] All the proposals that found any traction, however, were plans to multiply monetary media. They took for granted that money *was* gold and silver, and all that was needed were substitutes. In the crisis of 1690, though, Blackwell was in a position to see his own, very different, ideas about money put into practice.

VI. Making Money in Law

America's temporary money was not made all at once. Rather, it was pieced together from existing legislation, in conversations and debates that only later made it into print. The first step was not radical at all. Before the first ships returning from Canada arrived in Boston, on November 6, 1690, the Massachusetts General Court had raised "Twenty Single Country rates." Twenty rates would amount to a property tax of close to 8 percent. But the November taxes came in addition to a further seventeen rates levied over the course of the previous year, for a combined property tax rate of a little over 15 percent (37/240). That was a hard ask but a necessary one, the General Court wrote, for "discharging of the Countries debts, and defraying the Public charges."[46]

Past "rates" were charged in either grain or coin, with a premium offered for the latter. Crucially, though, the November 6, 1690, law offered an alternative. The General Court ordered that "all persons that have Credit, with the Country," including presumably soldiers and war-bond subscribers, would be able "to pay by discount," suggesting that householders would be able pay at least part of their taxes with the colony's IOUs, less a "discount" based on their market value, assessed by the local officials collecting the taxes. As a financial matter, this made sense. A credit always canceled a debit. Taxes were a debt owed by the citizenry to the state, and it followed that a debt owed by the state could cancel a tax obligation.[47]

For some lawmakers, likely in conversation with Blackwell, this raised an intriguing possibility. What if all the state's outstanding debts could be canceled the same way, with credit issued by the state, offset by a new tax debt that they, as legislators, could impose on citizenry? On December 10, 1690, the General Court put that intuition into practice. It passed a law authorizing £7,000 in "Bills of Public Credit," in denominations ranging from 5 shillings to 5 pounds, to be granted to anyone "to whom the Colony is indebted" and otherwise would have received debentures in payment. "Every of which Bills according to the Summ therein expressed shall be of equal Value with Money, And the Treasurer and all Receivers Subordinate to him shall accept, and receive the Same Accordingly in all Public Payments," the Court declared. In other words, Massachusetts householders could use them to pay their "rates." The amount suggests that the bills were intended as a substitute for the failed attempt to borrow coin to pay soldiers and sailors off as they arrived in Boston, so that the town with a population of just 7,000 could avoid being overwhelmed by the returnees. The soldiers would go home promptly with the means to pay the taxes, and that, the council hoped, would help make the bills "of equal Value with Money." Householders struggling to pay their "rates" would, the council hoped, exchange land, cattle, and goods for the bills.[48]

The key connection between the new bills and Blackwell's thought lay in the word "expressed." Debt contracts like the colony's debentures, typically promised a sum of money or its equivalent in grain; the bills of public credit "expressed" a sum. Debts could not be held equal in value to any particular unit of account without, first, considering what the underlying commodity could fetch at market; second, when the contracts would come due; and finally, the likelihood that they would be paid on time. In other words, debt contracts inscribed on paper and signed by the debtor had to be "negotiable," worth only what someone was willing to pay for them. Different merchants might calculate those values differently, taking into account the prevailing rate of interest, the length of the contract, and the likelihood that the government would be able to pay when it said it would.

Bills of credit, on the other hand, were intended to be an expression of "the value of other things," as Blackwell had put it. They could be "of equal Value with Money," because money was an expression and thus always equal to itself. The gold, silver, and grain mentioned in the colony's country rates were commodities and fluctuated in value. An expression of value did not. The only thing at issue in a bill of credit was the seriousness and credibility of the colony's commitment to give that expression force.[49]

The General Court seems to have realized over the next several months that if the new law were taken seriously, "Bills of Public Credit" would be worth more than debentures promising a real return. Constables had to take the new the bills at face value, while for debentures they could charge a negotiable "discount."[50] The new "Bills" were already trading higher in return for coin in Boston than the debts that the state owed the merchant "subscribers" who had paid for the Canada expedition.[51] The Board of Trade's New England correspondents reported in January that under "the present way of money" debentures had "sunken to half price," while merchants were trading bills of credit a full 15 percent higher—at 13 shillings on the 20-shilling pound in relation to coin. This was still not ideal, of course. It would take wealthy Bostonians, including Sir William Phips, commander of the Quebec expedition, stepping in to buy the bills at their face value in silver, to establish the new instruments' value as an "expression."[52]

In the meantime, the General Court acted to remedy the disparity and do away with the debentures for good. On February 6, 1691, the court resolved to print and give bills to anyone who could produce "a debenture or Debentures." Three months later the court limited the whole amount printed to £40,000, which, the court observed, it was "Supposed will amount to the full of what the Country is indebted and will probably be Called in again by the rates already granted." The Court also acted to make sure that the relevant committee would "dispose of, and Secure" bills received in taxes "as there may be no Danger of their Coming forth into any private hands."[53]

The court also acknowledged that, even if they were better than debentures, the bills were still trading for less than their creators intended. It resolved that the bills issued in December 1690 and February 1691 would be worth 5 percent above face for paying taxes but were still good for the sum "exprest" in whatever gold, silver, or grain the treasury in Boston had on hand. The denominations, meanwhile, were lowered, suggesting the court hoped the new bills would see wider use as a medium of exchange. The second run would include bills worth as little as 2 shillings and as much as 10 pounds.[54]

Meanwhile, in the Boston community, opposition was growing against the bills, which were being called a plot to "cheat the men" who had fought in Canada and, presumably, the colony's other creditors. The problem lay squarely with the conceptual innovation that had made the bills possible. The bills, the Board of Trade's correspondents noted, were being called "paper money," a phrase intended to sound like a contradiction in terms. Many continued to believe that money always, ultimately, had to be a promise for gold and silver, and refused to understand how the notion of money as merely a measure, or an "expression" of value, could underpin a credible monetary regime.[55]

VII. Blackwell Explains the Logic of Temporary Money, and the Burning Begins

As pressure grew, the bills' designers were forced to explain themselves. This debate was where Blackwell's analysis came into its own. His best expression came later that year, in the first of two letters published in a pamphlet entitled *Some Considerations on the Bills of Credit*.[56] The designers intended to open up what had been a private debate. The pamphlet was "Published for the Information of the INHABITANTS." The bills of credit were new and strange. Little was likely understood outside of Boston, and even there the details were less than perfectly understood. The "*Gentlemen* who *Administer* the *Government*" were the "*Countries Agents*," Blackwell wrote. New Englanders were the "*Principals*," and they deserved to debate the ideas behind their new money.[57]

Blackwell opened the pamphlet by praising Phillips for his move earlier in the year to pay soldiers in the "debentures" that preceded the new bills of credit. "I am told, and am apt to believe it, that the Exchequer in *Silver* Runs very low; Nor can *I* think that the Country in General is much better furnished," Blackwell wrote, in his capacity as a "*friend to New England*." "'Twas an honest and good method you took to pay by *Bonds* what you could not by *Ready Cash*."[58]

Bills of credit, however, were different and more difficult to explain. They were not promissory notes like the bonds they replaced. Nor were they simply a new "money" given value by administrative fiat. They were instruments created on a new principle, that money need not be a commodity, a thing. The new bills, however, Blackwell wrote, were similar to debentures in at least one respect. Like bonds, bills were made of paper. That was why it was strange, Blackwell observed, to hear the bills objected to as "Paper-mony, as pay equal in value with the best Spanish Silver." Paper was a common enough way of representing value. "What? Is the word Paper a scandal to them? Is a Bond or Bill-of-Exchange for 1000 [pounds sterling], other than Paper? and yet is it not as valuable as so much Silver or Gold, supposing the Security of payment be sufficient?" The only difference between bills of credit and bonds, such as those Phillips had previously issued, was that the latter were ultimately promises to deliver something else. Bills of credit were not.[59]

Explaining the difference required a detour into monetary theory. The objections to "paper money" as paper money were based on the notion that money was gold and silver. This, Blackwell argued, was false. "You know Sir you and I have had some former Discourse about the Nature of Money," Blackwell wrote, "That (as such) it is but a Counter or Measure of [men's] properties and Instituted mean of permutation." This was precisely the assertion Blackwell had made in his first proposal for a bank, three years earlier. Here, though, the emphasis was on the word "Instituted." Blackwell wanted to reinforce the point that money was an institution, and like any institution, its rules were written by human, as opposed to natural, law. What was irreducible, for Blackwell, was the quality of money as a measure. But people could establish that measure in a variety of ways. For example, Blackwell acknowledged that a government could turn metal into money, as European states had done with their coins. "As metal indeed it is a commodity, Like all other things, that are Merchantable," Blackwell wrote. But this did not mean that money was necessarily metal. Money was only metal, a commodity, because money had been "instituted" as such. "But as Mony it is no more than what was said," he concluded, a measure of the value of other things, subject to rules people made for it.[60]

Why, then, did so many people believe that money was necessarily a commodity? Blackwell had a theory. Money, as a commodity, "had its Original from a general ignorance of Writing and Arithmetick," Blackwell wrote. "But now these arts being commonly well known may well Discharge mony from the conceited Necessity thereof in Humane Traffick. Is not Discount in Accounts good current pay? Do not Bills Transmit to Remote Parts, vast sums without the intervention of Silver?" The roots of the misunderstanding lay in the distant past, when people were ignorant of the techniques that, by the late seventeenth century, had allowed money to come into its own as a measure in political economy. People had made money out of silver, to be sure, but silver had nothing to do with its essence.[61]

What Massachusetts had done that winter, Blackwell continued, was to apply to political economy the same insight that allowed merchants to move value in the commercial world without coin—money mobilized as a measure. "Are not Taxes paid and received by mutual Credit between the Government and the People," a system of credits and debits like any other, Blackwell asked? Were taxes not a debt? Did they not, then, as a matter of logic, establish a credit relationship between the government and its citizens? Why not, then, mobilize that credit to "pay the Countries Debts, and then receive the same Credit of the country as good pay"? It would be strange, given that the credit originated "between the Governments paying the People, and the *Peoples* paying the Government," that "The Governments (or rather the *Countries*) *Bills* should not pass between *Man* and *Man*."[62]

People who doubted the values expressed in the bills failed to consider what it meant to be in debt to the Massachusetts government. Being in debt to the colony was a serious matter. The colony had the right and the ability to repossess "whole *Estates*" to collect what was owed, and it would if it had to. "Certainly Sir," Blackwell wrote,

> were not peoples Heads Idly bewizled with Conceits that we have no *Magistrates*, no *Government*, and by Consequence that we have no *Security* for any thing, which we call our own (a *Consequence* they will be Loth to allow, though they cannot help it, if once we are to [Hobbes's] state of *Nature*, which (says he) is a *state of War* and then the *strongest* must *take all*). I say if such foolish conceits were not Entertained, there would not be the least Scruple in accepting your Bills as Currant Pay.

The bills were an improvisation, Blackwell acknowledged, but one consistent with well-known practices of mutual credit. Asking for silver in taxes "were to require men to *Make Bricks without Straw*"—biblical shorthand for an impossible task, tyrannically imposed—or to go "Hog sheering, when there is no wool."[63] Mutual credit, on the other hand, "Government and the People," allowed the colony to do justice without waste. "If neither *Silver* can be had, nor *Corn* brought in without loss both to the Government and the People, what remains but *Accounts, Bills,* or such like *Paper-pay?* and certainly this necessity may (if I mistake not) bring to the whole Country no small advantage."

It was, after all, another way of giving life to the principles Blackwell had hoped to embody in his bank. That life was only possible if *Some Considerations'* readers were willing to make the intellectual leap with him. They had to believe it was possible to create a credit instrument that wasn't a promise for a commodity, to look in their account books and petty trades, neighbor to neighbor, at the everyday business of colonial life, and, in the figures they used to tally obligations due and services promised, see money as real as any from the Royal Mint. He had heard that French colonists already "pass such *Paper mony* without the least scruple." Blackwell was certain, he wrote, that the English colonists "Transcend the *French* in *Courage*." It was still unclear whether they would fall "short of them in *Wit* and *Understanding*." Blackwell, though, was heading home. He left Massachusetts sometime in late winter and arrived in London just before April 20, 1691.[64]

His ideas, though, would take root. In 1702, in his history of Britain's Puritan colonies, Cotton Mather called bills of credit an "*Invention . . .* of more use to *New Englanders,* than if all their *Copper Mines* had been opened, or the Mountains of *Peru* had been removed into these Parts of *America.*" Mather also supplied a formula for making them. First, the legislature passed "*an Act* for the Levying of such a Sum of *Money* as was wanted," imposing via taxes the debt that would serve as "a *Fund*" "on which the *Credit* of such a Sum should be rendered *passable* among the People." Second, a committee would be formed to print the bills and pay them to the colony's creditors. The taxes created demand for money to pay them; the new bills created supply. "The People knowing that the *Tax-Act* would, in the pace of Two Years at least, fetch into the Treasury as much as the *Bills of Credit,* thence emitted, would amount unto, were willing to be furnished with *Bills* wherein 'twas their Advantage to pay their *Taxes,* rather than in any other *Specie.*" The bills, meanwhile, "*Circulated* through all the Hands of the Colony pretty Comfortably" before coming to rest in the colony's treasury.

"And e're many Months were expired," Mather recalled, "the Governour and Council had the Pleasure of seeing the *Treasurer* burn before their Eyes many a Thousand Pounds Worth of the Bills, which had passed about until they were again returned unto the Treasury, but before their being returned, had happily and honestly, without a Farthing of *Silver Coin,* discharged the *Debts,* for which they were intended."[65]

The result would be consequential. Neither Blackwell nor Mather intended the new money to create a rupture with Britain, but the Massachusetts crisis of 1690 and the temporary money it inspired had set America on a different, alternative course. Bills of credit spread rapidly even as, as we shall see, an alternative, commodified vision of money became even more important on the other side of the Atlantic. Basic ideas about money, an institution so fundamental that most people just wanted to forget about it and get on with things, had created an internal divergence within the British Atlantic, a hidden fault. Money was dividing the empire. Thus, even as the colonists learned to mimic the manners and tastes of their British counterparts and traded with them in increasing volumes, even as wealthy families continued to send their sons to England or Scotland and talented Britons continued to settle in the colonies in large numbers, the distance between Britain and America in terms of political economy grew. In time, tensions would too.

CHAPTER TWO

Slavery and
the Financial Revolutions

LONDON AND VIRGINIA, 1690–1762

I. Meanwhile, in England, a Financial Revolution

America's temporary money would not have been out of place in seventeenth-century Britain, a place awash in all sorts of monetary experiments and bold new plans for financial institutions rooted in alchemical, mystical, mercantilist, even religious ideas. Within half a century, a single lifetime, that would change. One way to trace that change is to turn to the biography of a man whose life and interests would intersect with virtually every development of Britain's eighteenth-century financial revolution and its attempted extension to the colonies.[1]

Francis Fauquier was born in the summer of 1702 on Lime Street on the east side of the City of London and named after his father's brother. Fauquier's father, John Francis, was a Huguenot, a French Calvinist Protestant from the wine-country town of Clairac along the Garonne River east of Bordeaux. John and his brother fled to protestant England after Louis XIV revoked the Edict of Nantes, beginning a purge of French non-Catholics in 1685. Thousands of other French Protestants joined them. They did not come empty-handed. Collectively, these refugees converted some 3 million pounds' worth of prime real estate, mercantile stock, and business interests into portable valuables, tools, implements, coin, and bills of exchange, pouring virtually all of it into the British capital. London welcomed them. The directors of the English East India Company even

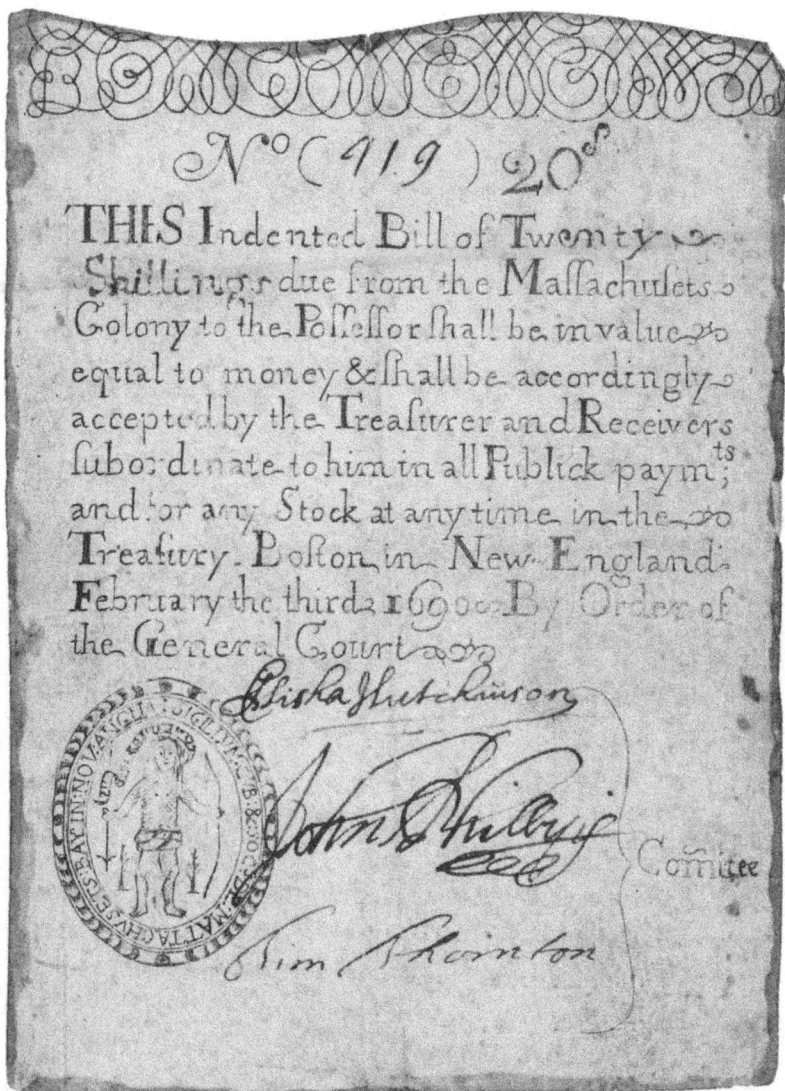

FIG. 5. Twenty Shillings, Massachusetts Bay, 1690, Obverse.

offered to hold their bullion, paying 3–4 percent interest until they were able to find more permanent investments.[2]

The money did not sit idle long. It helped jump-start a financial transformation that, within decades, would separate Britain fundamentally from its colonies, creating a divergence within the empire in terms of monetary organization. In America, bills of credit stabilized what had already been a chaotic situation; their invention helped them preserve practices of credit and household organization that had their roots in the England they had left and adapted to a new environment. In Britain, the financial revolution took the form of a massive, destabilizing jolt, knocking society as a whole off its monetary axis. Within a single generation it would upend British life and, unwittingly, harden an invisible rift over the ideas behind monetary wealth within the empire itself.

The transformation was multifaceted, but each piece, in its way, had to do with changing the relationship between British money—and the financial wealth founded on it—and time. It began, ironically, with a New Englander. In 1687, three years before he led Massachusetts's disastrous raid on Quebec, William Phips returned to London triumphant after a treasure-hunting expedition to the Caribbean. He and his crew had managed to locate a sunken Spanish treasure galleon wrecked off Puerto Plata on the north shore of Hispaniola, raising some thirty-two tons of Spanish silver and jewels from the bottom of the sea. The expedition was significant, in part, because of the novel investment vehicle Phips and his backers had employed to raise funds for the expedition: a joint-stock company based in the City of London. The expedition had cost £2,000. The loot was worth some £250,000. After expenses, taxes, and Phips's own share, investors earned more than one hundred times their initial investment. Phips got a knighthood out of it. The city learned a lesson. The expedition demonstrated that joint stock companies could generate huge profits. For newcomers like the Fauquiers and other Huguenots, without ancestral lands or titles, those returns proved irresistible. In 1689 there were just 14 joint-stock companies in England. By 1695 there were 140 worth £4,250,083, roughly as much as the annual revenue of the British state. French Protestant refugees had founded and invested in many of them.[3]

And they had not done so alone. Wealthy British men and women seized the chance to expand their fortunes as well. The vast expansion of private financial wealth gave financiers something they had usually lacked over the long seventeenth century: powerful political patronage. Its backers became known as the "monied interest," as opposed to the traditional "landed interest" of old-line aristocrats in Parliament and court. Unlike its rivals, the monied interest already had a taste for institutional transformation. Most were Whigs who had faced fierce opposition throughout the reign of James II. James's courtiers had been committed to notions of wealth as "natural," a product of the earth rather than human labor or organization, an attitude that came naturally to a landed elite. The revolution of 1689, however, decisively shifted the balance of power away from the land. The Whig parliamentarians, who expelled the Catholic James II and welcomed the Protestant Dutch prince William III as their new monarch, negotiated a vast increase in fiscal power for themselves at the expense of the crown. As one historian put it: "The tradition of ages was snapped." These were precisely the people with the most to benefit from London's new financial-izing economy. They were quick to put their new powers to work.[4]

As in Massachusetts, the justification was war. William III virtually came to the throne at war with Catholic Europe. By 1694 he had borrowed £6.1 million to pay for these wars, and he was seeking alternative modes of finance to spend on his armies abroad. The monied interest, meanwhile, were busy securing the value of their investments. The institutional program Parliament began in the mid-1690s was designed to satisfy them both.

The soul of this program was the Bank of England, founded in 1694 as a means of loaning money to the government without having to come up with the sum on loan in actual gold and silver. The bank promoters' plan had both a monetary and a fiscal component. On the monetary side, the country was running out of good coin. Britain had begun the 1690s with between £10 million and £14.5 million in gold and silver. That may seem like a lot, but virtually all taxes were only receivable in gold and silver, meaning at least a quarter of the monetary supply had to be mobilized each year just to satisfy the government. This took titanic and noticeable effort. Virtually everyone agreed that there was not enough money in the country to go around. Blackwell, back from New England, called for the government to distribute "Bills of Credit." Other plans were in circulation. The bank's backers, though, argued that its notes—notionally representing claims on the silver in its as-yet-unbuilt vaults—would serve best, offering a plentiful medium of exchange that could be transformed, at will, into metal currency.

The fiscal side of their plan was just as important. In return for its offi-cial charter, the bank agreed to loan £1.2 million to government in its first months of operation. For the favor, it charged 8 percent a year, with the promise of more loans to come. Cleverly, the bank arranged to pay its loan to the government before it had any gold or silver in its coffers, sending a combination of notes—claims for silver—and bills, its private corporate debt. The investors, quite literally, had worked out a system where the government paid them to print money on the government's behalf. Even-tually, actual gold and silver filled its vaults, but in the first decade, its gold and silver was never worth more than a third of what the bank owed. The bank, following Phips, organized as a joint-stock corporation. Its capital stock grew quickly, rising from £1.2 million to £6.6 million by 1696, as investors—including many of the nation's elite—clamored to join.[5]

It was not the bank but the mint that gave the Fauquier family a place in this new monied world. In January 1696 Parliament passed an "Act for Remedying the ill State of the Coin." The act's anodyne title masked its transformative ambition. The act mandated that the British state call in, melt, assay, and reissue every silver coin in the whole of Britain over just three years. The coinage, Bank of England architect Charles Montagu had argued in Parliament, was a disease infecting "the very Vitals of the Nation." Every pound collected in taxes was "diminish'd and devour'd by the unequal" exchange for underweight coin. Blackwell, in his pamphlet promoting English "Bills of Credit," called the coin "unserviceable," a reproach to the state that "should not be Suffered to Pass."[6] Parliament agreed. Eventually, £9.6 million in damaged silver coin made its way to the Mint, emerging as £5.1 million in new, full-weight shillings. British currency emerged from the process heavier and scarcer, both qualities prized by the monied interest, families whose fortunes took the form of bank shares and government debt rather than agricultural land.[7]

The physical effort required for the recoinage to work was remarkable. The labor was demanding and important, and it allowed immigrant families to rise quickly. These included the Fauquiers, who rode the Great Recoinage into Britain's financial elite. In 1695 John, then twenty-three, found a place at the Royal Mint in the Tower of London. The next year, the recoinage began. By Christmas 1699, when Sir Isaac Newton was promoted master of the mint, John oversaw all the precious metal flowing in and out of it, one of the most prominent and responsible positions in the tower. By 1707, he was Newton's personal deputy. By 1716, he was a director of the Bank of England. In twenty years, he had risen from refugee to wealthy statesman. The nation had changed with him. John's son, Francis, was raised in a world where financial wealth had taken on an importance all but unimaginable just two decades earlier.[8]

II. Money, Time, and Mr. John Locke

British money had also taken a new form. At its heart was a new relationship between money and time. Before the Great Recoinage, British money's value had been fundamentally tied to the power of the monarchy. Kings and queens had always had the power to set the value of existing coins, calling them up or down, as the mood or national interest demanded. They were also free to alter the coinage. They could change the official weight, the fineness of the metals at the mint at will. Elizabeth I, for instance, paid her soldiers in Ireland with a low-cost silver-alloy coin created especially for the expedition. When English merchants were forced to accept the low-quality coins at face value in London, they sued. If the silver content in the coins was less than advertised, they should be able to take a discount. Elizabeth disagreed. In 1605 James I's Privy Council ruled emphatically in the monarch's favor. "The King by his prerogative may make money of what matter and form he pleaseth," they wrote, "and establish the standard of it, so may he change his money in substance and impression and enhance or debase the value of it, or entirely decry or annul it, so that [gold and silver] shall be but bullion as his pleasure." In short, they concluded, *"principum jus ossibus inheret."* Money inheres in the bones of princes.[9] [10]

When Parliament set out to reform the coinage, it appointed William Lowndes, a newly elected MP and secretary to the Treasury, to develop a plan for what everyone knew would be a difficult task. Lowndes's report was a masterpiece of humane monetary analysis. He acknowledged the crown's traditional powers, noting that a monarch's historical reputation was usually tied to the care they took (or failed to take) in managing the coin. Parliament's goal, he argued, should be to do so while causing the least harm to the public. Under his plan, Britons would pay their battered coin into one of ten regional mints. In return, they would receive bills at the coins' face value paying 5 percent interest per year. This "useful and transferable credit" would serve as "Running cash" while the reminting continued. From a random sample of tax receipts, Lowndes determined that existing coins were roughly half the standard weight, worn by use and shorn by "clippers" who clipped the edges of stamped coins to sell as bullion. To discourage clipping, Lowndes decided to set each coin's value to silver bullion's actual market price. Thus, a new shilling would have a shilling's worth of silver in it, 20 percent less than existing full-weight coins. This would leave a 30 percent gap between the value of existing, half-weight coins and value of the mint bills. Lowndes proposed that the difference would be made up by a tax on land, the continuation of current import duties, and new taxes as necessary until the bills were repaid. The costs of the recoinage, in other words, would be shifted from the relatively poor, who owned the clipped currency, to the wealthiest landowners and merchants. His plan was to tax wealth, not the workers who made it.[11]

Lowndes was an establishment player. He had started in the Treasury twenty years earlier, as a clerk, and would serve in Parliament continuously for the next twenty-nine years. His goal was to preserve the status quo with a minimum of pain. His report, written on behalf of the Treasury board, was careful and historically informed. It said nothing especially new. It was not a treatise on money, per se. It made no theoretical claims.

It contained no explicit theory of money at all beyond its acknowledgment of the historical fact that the monarch—and now Parliament—could make of it what they chose. And yet it provoked one of the most famous and influential theoretical treatises in monetary history.[12]

The response came from John Locke, an aging invalid who had nonetheless established himself as court philosopher to the most powerful architects of the new Whig order, including John Somers, the lord chancellor, and Montagu, the chancellor of the Exchequer. Locke had done so, in part, with a philosophy that placed property prior to government. In Locke's analysis, government had been founded to protect property and little else. Somers and Montagu foresaw danger in Lowndes's realistic, humanitarian plan for the coinage. In as much as the new shillings would be worth less in international trade, the market-based devaluation Lowndes proposed might have had a negative effect on the value of their pound-denominated assets. In international trade, where silver content mattered more than local market value, every sterling debt would suddenly be worth 20 percent less. Lowndes's reasonable proposals, Locke wrote, would have a devastating effect on anyone who owned financial securities. These, he argued, would be losing "one Fifth of their Debts and Income." This, he noted, "will sit heavy on" the owners, such as his patrons. Locke himself had invested £500 in the Bank of England—a large proportion of his personal wealth. His income came in the form of annuities and rents. He too had something to protect. Market realism presented a danger to the financial edifice that his friends were busy constructing to finance William's wars while also enriching themselves. What was needed was a new idealism, and Locke gave it to them.[13]

Locke's answer had little of Lowndes's realism or humanitarianism. He had no time for his rival's practical concerns. The key question for Locke was one that Lowndes hadn't asked: what money actually was. According to Locke, money was nothing more than a specific weight of fine silver. Uniquely, Locke wrote, silver was both "the thing bargain'd for" and "the measure of the bargain." Denominations like the penny, shilling, or pound were just "sounds," Locke wrote. What people bargained for was "the intrinsick value; which is the quantity of Silver by publick Authority warranted to be in pieces of such denominations." Diminishing the quantity of silver in a shilling would only degrade the nominal value of the "shilling," because the two were inseparable. This was evidently not true. If it were, the price market price for silver would not fluctuate, because "An equal quantity of Silver is of equal value to an equal quantity of Silver." But the problem, for Locke, was not the market, where the demand for silver ebbed and flowed, but with politicians like Lowndes, who thought they could change the natural order. A shilling's worth of silver was only worth more than a shilling because no one could be sure what a shilling was in silver terms. The only answer was to solidify the relationship between British currency and a specific quantity of fine silver, and the only way to preserve the value of monied wealth, in that case, was to retain the old standard. Forget the actual market value of silver coins. The goal should be to immutably define the shilling in reference to a specific lump of silver. Thus the two would be inseparable. Creditors would no longer be forced to take payment in light coin, defrauded of their due.[14]

This was radical philosophy disguised as common sense. It denied market realities, like the price of silver, as well as centuries of tradition, but that was not its most radical component. It was radical because it presented money as a contradiction. Money, for Locke, was both concrete and abstract. It was meant to be a specific quantity of metal, yes, but not any actual physical piece of metal that existed in the real world. In the real world, the price of metals fluctuated. Silver shillings worth 12 pence traded for 15 pence in London markets. By Locke's logic, those 15 pence would have to somehow be redistributed between the abstract 12 in real time, an inversion of actually existing terms of trade. Silver would price the shilling rather than the other way round. But it made perfect sense applied to financial securities. By Locke's logic, a banknote worth £10 would always purchase the same amount of silver, regardless of market conditions. Its value, in other words, would have precisely the same physical manifestation regardless of time, politics, or conditions. At the same time, however, no physical amount of metal would ever be equal to the abstraction. *It* would have a price. *It* might degrade with handling over time. As such, the metal itself remained an abstraction, a claim that could never be realized. Locke's money found its perfect expression in a timeless representation of silver rather than silver itself.[15]

It was this timeless, abstract quality that reshaped British money. A timeless claim was just that: eternal, subject to nothing but itself. If British money was silver, the rule of the international market supplanted the rule of the sovereign—be it king or parliament. Monetary contracts would, in effect, be contracts for gold and silver, and thus, in a newly meaningful sense, beyond any other authority. As such, in addition to being timeless, British money might also defy place. Defining money in strictly metallic terms, in principle, made the meaning portable. As one critic put it, following Locke's logic in the recoinage, as Parliament did, only qualified English coins "for *Travel*." The recoinage amounted to "necessary Preparations for the journey they," the coins, "were design'd for."[16] Tellingly, the only other place on earth where silver passed, as money, by weight in the 1690s was Qing dynasty China. Defining the currency by weight also meant there would be far less of it to go around. Money would thus increase in value, a direct transfer of wealth to creditors, the holders of financial wealth. Everyone else would lose. Indeed, the Great Recoinage provoked a brutal and lasting depression. Food prices rose. Hundreds died of starvation. Perhaps the result was unintended, but the contrast between Lowndes's emphasis on the public good, and Locke's emphasis on preserving financial wealth at all odds, suggests it was not unanticipated. Locke, very consciously, had designed a money that was at once timeless, placeless, and heartless, a money fit for global empire.[17]

III. The Financial Revolution Reshapes British Life and the Fauquiers' Fortunes

The final plan for recoinage closely followed Locke's theoretical précis. Parliament gave the public just five months to spend underweight coins at face value. After that, they had to be sent to the Mint. No bills were offered in return. Nothing circulated in lieu of the coins as they were reminted. Mary Clarke, who owned a country house in Somerset, saw the effects firsthand as trade collapsed in line with the supply of coin. Her poor neighbors, who had been employed making woolen clothes, found themselves destitute, paid in the worthless underweight coin still in circulation. "The poor have noe bread nor noe worke noe fire nor noe cloths," she recorded in her diary in November 1696. The disaster was total, all the worse because it was manmade, the result of a deliberate policy.[18] The monied interest, meanwhile, profited handsomely. Wealthy men and women who had purchased securities in lightweight coins were being paid interest and dividends in full-weight coin that could be profitably traded for even more abroad. Locke himself had died in 1704, holding £12,037 in stocks and government debt, a wealthy man.[19]

The Fauquiers' fortune grew as well. When John Fauquier died in 1726, Francis inherited £5,000 sterling in Bank of England stock and £20,000 in the stock of the South Sea Company, securities worth roughly £4.22 million in 2025 values.[20] He would never have to work. The money worked for him. These financial securities, as the historian J. G. A. Pocock has observed, were, like Locke's money, a new kind of property. Before the financial revolution of the 1690s, a person's property was an extension of themselves, an expression of their legal and political "personality" as head of or a member within a productive household. When one inherited this kind of wealth, one also inherited a role, a person one had to be, whether lord or laborer. Fauquier's inheritance was different. His wealth was the residue of public action, stock in crown-chartered companies, whose major form of capital was government debt. With the new form of wealth, Pocock argued, came a new kind of identity, less about mastery of a household and more about the possession of individual rights. Heirs like Fauquier did not inherit titles; they gained financial rights guaranteed by the state and its commitment to Locke's immutable money.

Fauquier was far from alone in navigating this new world of heritable wealth. After losing his debate with Locke, Lowndes went on to pioneer a form of government debt that took the form of a "funded" permanent annuity, a bond that would make payments to the holder and their heirs in perpetuity from dedicated tax receipts. These proved extremely popular. Britain's national debt ballooned from £6.1 million in 1694 to £52.9 million in 1726. All but £3.8 million took the form of these new quasipermanent bonds. The value of stock in joint-stock companies, meanwhile, had doubled between 1695 and 1703, and doubled again by 1717. In Fauquier's fortune, the public and private were intertwined. When Whig leaders became concerned about the size of the public debt, they set up a scheme allowing bondholders to swap for shares in the South Sea Company, which held a monopoly on slave trading in Spanish America. The swap contributed to a stock-price bubble that burst in 1720, ruining many shareholders while neatly erasing government debt.[21]

The rise in new forms of heritable wealth based on individual rights accelerated ongoing transformations in British life. Perhaps the most striking transformation was in terms of gender. Unlike landed property, no law or custom prevented elite women from owning financial securities. By 1719, wealthy women owned up to a third of all government debt. Meanwhile, foreigners, barred from other kinds of property holding, took advantage of the expanding financial markets to invest abroad. The Dutch alone poured so much money into British public debt between 1739 and 1763 that they may have provided the margin of victory over France, securing the rise of the British Empire as a global enterprise.[22]

New forms of wealth also affected the way people lived and worked. Along the Thames, whole new occupations had bloomed overnight. There had long been brokers, traders, and speculators in London's cluttered counting houses, smoke-filled coffeeshops, and markets, but never before had those brokers commanded such wealth or existed in such numbers. In 1720 the nominal capitalization of London joint-stock companies alone equaled roughly 13 percent of the market value of every mine, forge, manufactory, sailing ship, warehouse, acre of land, head of cattle, townhouse, farmstead, and palace in the entire country. Meanwhile actual coin became even scarcer. Between 1700 and 1717 alone, the East India Company shipped 703 tons of fine silver out of Britain, mostly to finance investments in India, enough to mint £5.7 million at Locke's standard. By the 1760s, according to one estimate, there was only £800,000 in silver coin left in circulation.[23]

Expanding on their radical Whig roots in the 1690s, the people who owned and worked with financial wealth became a distinct community with a voice in national affairs. Occasionally, it was the loudest voice. The wealthiest investors and traders crowding London's back-alley coffeeshops gained a reputation as shrewd players in national politics. The state of the "funds," the price of public debt in the London market, could sink a government or give it the credit needed to maintain a particularly costly war. The work of trading funds, meanwhile, was a source of cultural discontent. "The public debt opened the iniquitous traffic of stock-jobbing, and introduced a spirit of gaming amongst all degrees of men," Malachy Postlethwayt observed in his *Universal Dictionary of Trade and Finance*, a popular guide to the trading world. Postlethwayt warned the unwary of being seduced by the seeming ease with which brokers made money. London's traders rigged the game for themselves, winning regardless of whether investors profited. The monied interest's true business, Postlethwayt argued, was "this scandalous commerce," where money was made and lost on a rumor and prices fixed between friends to defraud the unwary.[24]

Government, however, could not do without it. The funding structure had become fundamental to the British state. The market for state debt provided the means for conducting business in both war and peace. "There is no effectual way in the World to suppress us, but this," a bond trader supposedly told Daniel Defoe in 1719, "That the Government should first pay all the publick Debts, redeem all the Funds and dissolve all the Charters, *viz. Bank, South Sea,* and *East-India,* and buy nothing upon Trust." That was impossible. "Then, indeed, says he," Defoe wrote, "they need not hang the Stock-Jobbers, for they will be apt to hang themselves."[25]

Wealth did not automatically confer status in eighteenth-century Britain. However, since the seventeenth-century revolutions, British aristocrats and financiers shared an increasingly incestuous social milieu. Francis, like his siblings, aspired to more than the money he inherited. John had left his daughters, Mary and Elizabeth, £5,000 each in Bank of England and South Sea Company stock. Both used that wealth to marry landed gentry, as did Francis himself. A portrait by William Hogarth from the 1730s shows a party at Elizabeth's new townhouse. In it, Francis sat off to the side of a crowded sitting room, head erect, holding a golden-headed

FIG. 6. *William Wollaston and His Family in a Grand Interior*, 1730.

cane. Next to him was his new wife, Catherine Dalston, the daughter of a Yorkshire baronet.[26]

Introduction to genteel society brought with it access to new ideas, new pursuits, and new vices. Elizabeth's father-in-law, William Wollaston, was a philosopher of what he called "natural religion." Francis was intrigued, acquiring a copy of Wollaston's major work, *The Pursuit of Happiness by the Practice of Reason and Truth*, that he carried with him until the end of his life. Both Francis and his brother were also amateur scientists and joined the Royal Society in the 1750s. He did not have any regular occupation until his midforties, when, in 1748, he became a director of the South Sea Company. He was a noted philanthropist, however, serving as a governor at the Foundling Hospital in London, where his portrait still hangs. He was also a gambler. In the Hogarth portrait, Catherine is shown flashing Fauquier a hand of cards dominated by the ace of spades. He was known for gaming all night when the mood struck, playing for high stakes. Long after his death, some in Virginia said Fauquier only took up a post in the New World because he had lost his fortune to an admiral in a hand of cards.[27]

In truth, Fauquier seems to have abandoned his privileged life in England for adventure in Virginia because of an interest in fiscal policy. In 1756, just after war broke out with France in North America, Francis published *An Essay on Ways and Means for Raising Money for the Support of the Present War without Increasing the Public Debts*. He dedicated the work to Lord Anson, a naval hero who in 1743 had captured a Manila galleon carrying Mexican silver to China. By the 1750s, Anson was first lord of the admiralty, the head of the British Navy. In the *Essay*, Fauquier argues against raising taxes on consumer goods, which fell on the poor, observing that "A man that has nothing, can pay nothing." Instead, Fauquier advocates taxing people like himself, with new fees on grand houses and servants. In wartime Britain, everyone was interested in taxes. The pamphlet's first run sold out, and officials took notice. When Robert Dinwiddie retired as the acting governor of Virginia, Francis's name came up as a suitable replacement. The wartime government had heard that there were money problems in Virginia and approved Fauquier as an establishment figure who could reestablish financial orthodoxy. In January 1758 Fauquier got the offer. He would be appointed lieutenant governor of Virginia, a royal colony whose titular governor was practically never there. He would thus be ruler, in all but title, of the most important British colony in North America. This was success indeed. Fauquier placed his shares in trust, leaving them to Catherine and his sons in case he died abroad. Within weeks, he was on a warship heading west. That June he took up his position in Williamsburg amid a decidedly different financial revolution.[28]

IV. Meanwhile in America, a Monetary Revolution Strikes in Virginia

Massachusetts's temporary money had by then spread to every other British colony on the continent. The first colony to adopt a currency along Massachusetts's lines was South Carolina in 1703. New York and New Hampshire joined them in 1709. The others soon followed. The reaction from London to these developments was largely muted. Administrators understood that its wars needed to be paid for somehow. When Parliament did react, as in 1751, by restricting paper currencies in New England, it did so by limiting the time of years bills of credit could remain in circulation, rather than banning them altogether. Many colonies had expanded and improved on the Massachusetts system. In 1723 Pennsylvania established a "General Loan Office" allowing colonists to borrow half the tax-assessed value of their land in bills of credit. The office, or land bank, allowed coin-poor farmers to protect their land from creditors who might otherwise seize it for less than its worth. The bank proved so popular that Pennsylvania used the interest on its loans in lieu of taxes to pay for government activities, while burning the principal. The land bank idea proved popular, leading, in many colonies, to a two-tiered system of temporary money. Governments issued temporary bills of credit backed by temporary taxes in times of war, with both disappearing when the war was over. In peace, meanwhile, the government, in Benjamin Franklin's terms, "coined land," using the loan office to meet temporary demands for currency.[29]

Bills of credit had faced numerous challenges, both conceptual and practical. After overexuberant issuance in New England had led Parliament to intervene, Massachusetts itself, while not abandoning bills of credit entirely, had reestablished the value of its paper currency in silver terms in 1749 with the help of subsidies from Parliament. It issued its new bills, called "Treasurer's Certificates" or "notes," and paid 6 percent interest, leading many to be hoarded by investors, but the form was largely the same as it had been in 1690. The colony still used them to pay its creditors and still levied taxes; "notes" were still accepted in tax payments, counted, and burned.[30]

Perhaps surprisingly, the basic form of bills of exchange remained the same for decades. The colonies issued temporary bills, offset by tax obligations and, increasingly, mortgages on colonial land. In peacetime, most colonies were restrained. In wartime, however, the volume of money issued could reach staggering proportions. According to a report by the Board of Trade in January 1766, the colonies had issued £2.52 million in just ten years. They had also taxed and burned £1.75 million. But war was not their only purpose. The idea of using a temporary credit relationship instead of promises of gold and silver had opened up the possibility of a society freed from the scarcity caused by a lack of circulating coin. "It seems that the want of money, as well as the love of it, is in some sense the root of all evil," the Puritan minister John Wise observed in 1721. With bills of credit, there was no reason to push people into "unsolveable Penury and Vassalage, for want of a plentiful medium." Doing so would only benefit "Gentleman Hoarders," Wise wrote. A plentiful currency would allow farmers and tradesmen, working for themselves, to flourish. The bills were still radical, perhaps, but they worked.[31]

Some saw the new money as a means of shrugging off the strictures that Locke's system had placed on the idea of money. Was not the "Power to command the Industry of others real Wealth?" asked the Irish bishop and philosopher George Berkeley. The occasion was a pamphlet proposing a new Bank of Ireland. Berkeley had just returned from a visit to Rhode Island, where the colony's loan office, a land bank, issued £469,000 in currency between 1715 and 1750, leading—in Bishop's estimation—to impressive levels of wealth and equality. The colony had drawn official sanction from Parliament in 1751, when it set firm limits on New Englanders' peacetime monetary practices. However, whatever their fiscal probity, Berkeley noted, Rhode Islanders were well housed, fed, and clothed, "without a Beggar in the Streets, although there be not one Grain of Gold or Silver current among them[.]" This contrasted with conditions in Berkeley's native Ireland, and it was clear to him that money made the difference. Britain's American colonists had claimed the freedom to rearrange their basic institutions, and the result was a "flourishing Condition," Berkeley wrote. Ireland would do well to emulate it.[32]

By the early 1750s, Virginia was the only colony in British North America that had not made its own bills of credit. It did have its own paper money, though, known as tobacco notes. The notes were receipts from the colony's network of tobacco warehouses. Farmers who deposited tobacco could then use the notes to pay taxes, court fees, and anything else they owed the colony, in addition to local debts denominated in tobacco. However, they had one important limitation. The notes were only good within the county in which they were issued and its neighboring counties, meaning they would only circulate locally. In addition to tobacco notes, Virginia had its own unit of account. Its pounds, shillings, and pence were worth four-fifths of their British counterparts, and tobacco notes were convertible at 2 pence per pound. The whole system, established under Governor William Gooch in 1730, proved resilient and flexible, allowing for local payments and, through the warehouses, regulating the quality of tobacco shipped abroad.[33]

However, the notes proved inadequate for war finance. This became an issue in the fall of 1753, when Governor Dinwiddie sent George Washington, a young surveyor and slave-owner, to deliver a letter to Captain Jacques Legardeur de Saint-Pierre, the French commander at Fort LaBoeuf, near Lake Erie. Washington returned to Williamsburg in January 1754 with terrifying news. As soon as the rains came that spring, French soldiers planned to float down the Allegheny River into the Ohio River valley. By doing so, the French would assert control over a region already claimed by the Virginia-based land speculators of the Ohio Company, of which Washington was a member. Dinwiddie called for an expedition to secure the English fort at the fork where the Allegheny and

Monongahela rivers join to produce the Ohio River, promising volunteers a share of 200,000 acres on the east side of the Ohio for their service.[34]

Dinwiddie asked the House of Burgesses, Virginia's legislature, to equip the expedition. The Burgess agreed, but they were unsure how. The colony hadn't mounted a military expedition on its own since the seventeenth century and had no effective system of war finance. Tobacco notes didn't circulate on a colony-wide basis, and there was no other regular currency in the colony. Virginia's taxes consisted of a "poll tax" on enslaved adults and all free men over sixteen. There was also a 2 shilling tax on each barrel of exported tobacco and a small duty on liquor imports. The taxes could be paid either in coin or tobacco notes. Most, understandably, chose to pay with notes, meaning the colony had precious little in its treasury to pay soldiers with. Indeed, when the burgesses audited their accounts that spring, they discovered that the colony's popular treasurer, John Robinson, had loaned all of the coin in the colony's treasury—some £3,200 in sterling—to his friends and relatives, leaving virtually nothing to pay recruits or purchase supplies.[35]

Part of the issue was that Virginians did not use much currency in their day-to-day lives. Most manual labor was done by enslaved men and women. Wage labor was extremely rare. Even the complex iron smelters being built along the Chesapeake relied, largely, on the bound labor of African slaves. Alexander Spotswood had begun the ironworks in 1718 using German immigrants from the Sieg Valley, paying £150 for their passage across the Atlantic. The Germans, however, soon deserted the mines and furnaces they had built, founding a farming community of their own. Spotswood, in turn, invested in buying and training enslaved Africans and in doing so greatly reduced his expenses. By 1739, he could brag that other than himself, "the whole business of my Iron Works is carried on by Slaves who have no Wages."[36]

The same was true for the business of the colony. As in England, property was personality, only the property in colonial Virginia consisted of land and enslaved people, bounded within the slaving household instead of financial securities. Most trade in Virginia was done on household credit. Instead of borrowing money, people borrowed service—favors offered and favors given—a gallon of rum here, help at harvest there, counted up in a ledger book or committed to memory. Money was an exception. Even large purchases, like slaves or land, could be settled with credit or goods in kind. Virginians bought and sold little amongst themselves, preferring to produce what they needed on their own farms or order it from abroad. Credit with London merchants, land, and slaves, not coin, was the wealth they craved. Every wealthy planter had factors in London managing the sale of consigned tobacco and a line of credit from them for the purchase of luxuries and household goods. Planters could, in turn, extend that credit to their own neighbors, creating a web of claims and counterclaims that reached out into western woods. To extend credit, to allow someone to go into your debt, was a mark of friendship and, frequently, patronage. To withdraw credit was a sign of enmity and distrust. Communities organized around men with credit abroad, who offered credit in turn. Unsurprisingly, the most generous were the most likely to become judges, burgesses, and officers of the court—the colony's leaders.[37]

In other words, Virginia in the 1750s was much like Massachusetts in the 1690s and England a century earlier, a society wrapped in webs of credit. Virginian money was still, largely, a way of counting credit, a measure rather than a physical object, nothing like the Lockean vision of coinage. The *"Measure,"* as Blackwell had observed, was the important thing. Indeed, the burgesses set the value of the Virginia pound in relation to sterling in 1728, decades before their pounds, shillings, and pence were a physical currency. The measure, supplemented by tobacco notes issued by local warehouses, allowed Virginians to do business on their own terms, without looking for coin abroad.[38]

Which was all well and good until they had to pay and equip a militia. The burgesses were left trying to improvise. Their first thought was to borrow gold and silver from the wealthiest planters. In February 1754 the burgesses authorized Robinson to borrow up to £10,000 Virginian in gold and silver at between 6 and 8 percent interest. But it turned out that the men who had borrowed *from* Robinson were unwilling to lend to him. There were few takers and few volunteers for fighting in the West.[39]

Washington decided to go ahead with his expedition, in any case. It was a terrible mistake. In the mountains, about forty miles from the forks of the Ohio, he stumbled on a French scouting expedition. A skirmish ensued. In the aftermath, Tanaghrisson, a Seneca chief who had joined Washington after being expelled from the forks area by the French, murdered a wounded French officer. French survivors told the tale, and a retaliatory force dogged Washington's column as it attempted to retreat back to Virginia, killing or wounding nearly a third of them. News of violence soon reached capitals in Europe. France and Britain began mobilizing for a wider war.[40]

In May 1755 the burgesses arrived in Williamsburg to news that six French men-of-war had arrived at Louisburg at the mouth of the St. Lawrence River, carrying an army. This force planned to follow the Monongahela south to the Ohio, where it could fall on Virginia from across the mountains.

"Without an adequate Aid from the Colonies, I dread the Consequences," Governor Dinwiddie told the burgesses. "Men and Money" were needed. The burgesses agreed. The question, again, was how to find the latter.[41]

This time, they authorized Robinson to issue up to £20,000 Virginian in "Treasury Notes," paying 5 percent annual interest. These notes were meant to circulate as money before being paid off, as a "lawful tender in any payment, for any debt, demand or duty whatsoever." No Virginian could legally refuse them. If the colony could, it would have borrowed coin, Dinwiddie wrote to London on July 4, 1755, but scarcity made it "impossible to borrow."[42]

Another problem was competition for coin. British general Edward Braddock had landed on the Potomac with two full regiments of Irish regulars, intending to scatter the French and their Native American allies. Braddock and his troops had not come to Virginia alone. His expedition included loan agents promising generous London credit in return for Virginians' gold and silver plate. This offer proved irresistible to the same wealthy planters who had shunned the colony's own bond offering the year before. Treasury contractors Hanbury, Thomlinson, Colebrooke, and Nesbitt succeeded in purchasing some £120,000 of precious metal in Virginia alone, sending most of it north to pay for operations in Pennsylvania. Their spree left less than "£20,000 Cash in the whole Country," Dinwiddie reported at the beginning of 1756.[43]

Braddock, meanwhile, had failed to secure the Ohio. After arriving in Virginia, Braddock had told Shingas, a Delaware war leader whom he was courting as an ally, that the English would "Inhabit and Inherit the Land" along the Ohio River after their victory. Instead of joining the expedition, Shingas took word of British intentions back over the mountains, bringing new Indigenous allies to the French and leaving Braddock without Indigenous scouts. A few weeks later, on July 9, 1755, advancing with his army along the thickly wooded banks of the Monongahela River, Braddock stumbled on an advancing French force. The result was another debacle. A mixed force of some eight hundred Mingo, Delaware, Shawnee, Ottawa, Mississaugas, Wyandots, Potawatomis, and French fell on Braddock's column and shattered it. British regulars, in a panic, shot into their own ranks with volleys meant to kill warriors who ran firing from tree to tree. Roughly half of Braddock's force, more than eight hundred men, were killed, wounded, or captured. The rest retreated over the mountains, leaving their cannons behind on the wilderness road.[44]

With stragglers still trailing back over the Alleghenies, the burgesses met in an emergency session in August 1755. After an angry debate, they agreed to raise taxes and issue another £40,000 in treasury notes coming due in June 1760. The colony would owe £3,000 in interest a year, payable in gold and silver. It was an open question whether making those payments was physically possible.[45]

This, finally, raised the possibility of issuing bills of credit. In the spring of 1757 the Virginians decided they had no other choice. In their April session, the burgesses voted to recall all interest-bearing notes and replace them with notes that did not pay interest. Due to the "great scarcity of gold and silver in this colony, the taxes imposed by this act cannot be collected in time," the burgesses wrote, explaining the act. These new notes were accompanied by an equal slate of new taxes. When the taxes were paid, the notes would be burned.[46]

Thus, as the war between France and Britain swept across the Atlantic world, a true dichotomy had developed. The burgesses' decision to adopt bills of credit in 1757, unbeknownst to them, had completed bills of credit's conquest of British North America. Every colony used a temporary money extensively in peace and war. More importantly, perhaps, they did so in an unacknowledged repudiation of Locke and his Whig allies' accomplishment in Britain in the same decades. The colonies, as Virginia's struggle toward bills of credit demonstrated, still believed that social circumstances and politics determined the shape of money. Like Locke's rivals a century earlier, they did so not by invoking theory but through their actions, their willingness to iterate new institutions in the perceived face of great dangers. Moreover, they saw it as their duty as imperial subjects to do so, to keep their army in the field. They had no way of knowing that their decision, abetted by their new governor, would foment a debate over the nature of money whose outcome would split the British Empire.

V. Fauquier Arrives in Virginia
and Navigates the Money Problem

Fauquier arrived in Virginia in June 1758. At about four o'clock in the afternoon on Sunday, July 9, 1758, a cloud appeared over the York River, northeast of the colonial capital. The cloud was small, unremarkable at first, less than a mile across. As it came closer, it broke open, spitting thunder and lightning as it drove suddenly for the center of town. Just as it crested the ridge it began dropping hail, strange cuboids about an inch and half long and three-quarters of an inch deep, bristling with sharp, half-inch spikes. Fauquier's mansion, on the northern edge of town, took the brunt of it. Ice shattered every pane of glass on the north side of his house, pulverizing the garden behind it. The stones lasted on the ground until Monday night in ninety-five-degree heat.[47]

Hail was not the only surprise greeting Fauquier in his new post. He believed, as many of his peers increasingly did, in the significance of individual rights. Enslaved people, ubiquitous in Virginia, were a shock to his conscience. In London, as a wealthy heir, Fauquier had servants and paid them wages. In Virginia, as governor, he was obliged to own slaves, and he found the experience unsettling. Almost weekly, when the legislature was in session, the burgesses took testimony about the behavior of white slave patrollers who often tortured or killed the Black people they caught without passes on the colony's roads. He must have seen, too, the vicious beatings that slavers used to punish the people they claimed to own, the auctions that split families, and the grief that followed. He must have at least heard rumors of rape or other forms of sexual violence. He may have even participated.[48]

For the first time, he was surrounded by people of African descent, relying on them to meet every need. He was overwhelmed by a sense of collective and individual guilt. Fauquier found himself haunted by the fear that, after death, his slaves would "rise up in Judgement against" him. He knew his new friends would have much to answer for. Owning humans was "in its nature disagreeable to me," he would later write, "but which my situation made necessary for me." A fellow Huguenot, Peter Fontaine, the rector of Westover Parish, thirty-four miles up the James River from Williamsburg, put the matter more bluntly in a letter to his brother Moses in March 1757. "To live in Virginia without slaves is morally impossible," Fontaine wrote. Most free Virginians would not work for wages on any terms. None would work for less than a shilling a day. If someone was lucky enough to hire "a lazy fellow to get wood and water," Fontaine wrote, he would end up paying nearly £20 annually in wages. "Add to this seven or eight pounds more and you have a slave for life," Fontaine concluded. The decision to purchase enslaved people was obvious and unavoidable. It was economical.[49]

The first legislative challenge facing Fauquier was the colony's new, temporary currency. The Newcastle-Pitt ministry had appointed Fauquier, in part, because he was a man of the new system, a shareholder, a fiscal savant, a member of the monied class. They expected him to have no sympathy for a new currency. Fauquier, himself, wrote that he had convinced "the World," likely meaning the friends who had got him appointed, that he disapproved of all kinds of "paper Currency." But the fiscal realities of Virginia's war effort changed his mind. The colony's notes were the only way it had to purchase the blankets, tents, clothing, arms, ammunition, grain, salt meat, kettles, and pay the men needed to fight the French. Thus, instead of suppressing the currency, Fauquier found himself asking for more. Six months into his tenure, he explained this reversal to the Board of Trade.[50]

"The Act which provides for the payment of the Regiments and the Militia employed for the Defence of the Frontiers . . . is done by a new Emission of paper Currency; a Method which I have convinced the World I do not approve, and which has given an Alarm to the Merchants of great Britain," Fauquier wrote on January 5, 1759. "Yet, I do not see how it was to be avoided, as the Country is obliged to be at this Expense: for I must declare that if all the Specie of any kind, that I have seen since I came into this Colony were to be brought together in one Heap, it would not amount to £100 sterling. So much is the Colony drain'd at present by money sent to New York."[51]

The currency was temporary, with taxes serving as a "sinking Fund for the Redemption of every Emission," he wrote. Each note emitted would eventually be burned. British merchants, he knew, were nervous about being paid a paper currency instead of tobacco. But the Virginia legislature had passed a law ensuring that every debt with a British merchant would be settled for the price of a good bill of exchange payable in London for the sterling sum. Bills of exchange—in effect, cheques that allowed American merchants to draw on their London correspondents for payments due in Europe—had long been the preferred means of transferring money across the Atlantic in sterling. The "merchants of great Britain who are alarm'd at this, and have presented a Memorial against it, do not know the Law that is now in Force relating thereto," Fauquier wrote, "otherwise there could be no Ground for their Fears." There was no way for merchants to lose. American debtors would pay as much paper currency as it took to pay their debts on the other side of the Atlantic. Courts would enforce the rule. He asked the board to let the currency stand as a necessary war measure.[52]

When a further order from the Privy Council demanding that debts "dischargeable in Sterling Money only" arrived in July 1759, Fauquier ignored it. His earlier letters had already explained the problem. He believed that bills of credit were both fair pay and the only means of fighting a war in Virginia. With the war with France reaching a moment of crisis, the board appeared to give in. The burgesses, meanwhile, moved to adopt other colonies' monetary best practices. This meant ensuring that temporary bills would, in fact, be destroyed rather than recirculated. In 1760 the burgesses ordered Treasurer Robinson to count up bills received each year in taxes, certify the amount, and "so soon as they have given such certificate, to cause all such bills or notes to be burnt and destroyed."[53]

Within a few years it would become clear that the Board of Trade's insistence that Fauquier do something, anything, was a warning. It pointed to the broader monetary rift emerging within the empire. With Virginia's adoption of bills of credit, Britain's North American colonies had effectively become a monetary bloc. Moreover, it had become a bloc whose basic assumptions about money were at odds with those in Britain. At the same time, however, these assumptions reflected something fundamental about the American political economy: its lack of a permanent currency. This was a potentially explosive combination; it meant that Americans had adopted and needed a currency that British policymakers could neither accept nor, from their position in London, understand. Fauquier on the ground had immediately recognized the need for bills of credit, but his superiors in London, his patrons, continued to insist that something about the bills (they were still not quite sure what) and the way they interacted with sterling was wrong. It meant that any policy touching on money might lead to misunderstanding or worse.

In part, this reflected a generational shift. Within Whitehall, there were effectively two positions on American money. In the 1750s Britain's financial revolution was still on the edge of living memory. Some, like Fauquier, remembered that transformation for what it was, a political decision with social consequences, and thus viewed analogous decisions in the American colonies with sympathy. The attitude of the board, however, was an indication that the era of intellectual and institutional fluidity was coming to an end. In the halls of imperial power, an alternative perspective was gaining ground. Officials increasingly saw Locke's self-serving monetary intervention not as a choice but as an immutable truth. Ignorant of alternatives and hostile to what they did know, all these officials needed was an excuse to intervene.[54]

VI. The War Ends, Reviving Human Trafficking in the Atlantic

The excuse came with victory. On September 12, 1759, after four years of fighting, British regulars scaled cliffs behind Cape Diamant and defeated the French on the Plains of Abraham, seizing Quebec. Within a year, they had wrested all of the colonial settlements in the St. Lawrence River valley from French control. This posed a problem for Virginia's new bill of credit regime. When the French threat vanished, so too did wealthy colonists' willingness to pay taxes. Fauquier immediately felt a shift. The burgesses were always for "immediately disbanding Men . . . upon the least relaxation from their fears of an Enemy," Fauquier told the Board of Trade on June 2, 1760. The taxes needed to keep the bills in circulation were becoming a political problem.[55]

It took the revival of the Atlantic slave trade, however, to spur a group of the wealthiest Virginians to action against the currency. The reason was simple: the heaviest taxes supporting Virginia's bills of credit fell on imported slaves. In February 1752 the burgesses had reinstated a 5 percent tax on slaves imported into the colony. In 1755 they raised the duty to 15 percent. In 1757, to support the bills of credit, they raised it to 25 percent.[56] In 1757 no ships from Africa arrived, so few duties were paid. In 1758 slavers delivered only 372 African captives for sale across the entire Chesapeake region. However, with the threat of war receding, human trafficking to Virginia quadrupled in 1759.[57]

The herald of the change was the *Black Prince,* a two-masted, eighteen-gun, 100-ton ship that appeared in the James River, south of Williamsburg, in early July 1759. The *Prince* was a slaver out of Bristol, a cool, cliff-sheltered river-harbor on England's west coast that had prospered hugely by trading muskets, beads, chintzes, powder, shot, liquor, bars of iron and copper, and food, along with shackles, irons, and whips from forges and manufactories for captive Africans. In Angola, the Gold Coast, Guinea, and elsewhere, traders like the *Prince*'s Captain William Miller exchanged trade goods for men, women, and children exhausted by a long, deadly march to the seashore, where they were held in putrid exposed pens on the beach or the outskirts of trading towns. Roughly four in ten captives died before they even reached the coast, many more before ships could take them. After a stifling and terrifying voyage across the Atlantic where, on average, another one in ten perished, traders exchanged the survivors for tobacco, sugar, indigo, rice, coin, and, of course, London credit. The three-way profits generated gave the trade its name, the triangle. A complete circuit often took more than a year. Disease and rebellion were common. Rebels, like the dead, were forced overboard. Sharks followed ships in the hope of fresh bodies. The triangle trade took a physical as well as moral toll on the men who followed it. Death rates among British slaving crews were even higher than those of their human cargo.[58]

Few bothered to count the dead when there were profits to be had. The *Black Prince* had been built in London in 1739, registered in Bristol in 1749, and eventually purchased by James LaRoche. Like Fauquier, LaRoche was a son of successful Huguenot immigrants. By the 1760s, he was one of the biggest sugar importers in Bristol. By the 1770s, he would be a baronet and MP with a country estate in Gloucester. The *Prince,* which LaRoche acquired in his early twenties, operated as a joint-stock company on a smaller scale. LaRoche sold shares in it to merchants interested in breaking into slave-trading, sugar, and tobacco businesses. Profits were potentially immense. Captives purchased in Angola cost trade goods worth roughly £12 sterling apiece. They could be sold in Jamaica or Virginia for at least three times that, sometimes more. In 1757 after arrival in Jamaica LaRoche and the *Prince* sold 328 people, purchased in Anomabu, modern Ghana, for £43.45 sterling each, or about £14,252 altogether, netting close to £10,000 sterling—a substantial fortune—on just one leg of the voyage. On average, four crew members and some sixty African captives would have died en route, but LaRoche, of course, never saw them. He and his partners only saw the returns.[59]

In November 1758 the *Prince* left Bristol heading for Angola, the vast region south of the Congo River in central West Africa, with the intention of purchasing captives for Virginia in what promised to be the most profitable voyage of LaRoche's slaving career. By 1757, Angolan kingdoms had been trading with Europeans for centuries. In the sixteenth century Kongo had been a unified, ostensibly Catholic kingdom, with ambassadors in Amsterdam, Lisbon, Brazil, and the Vatican. By the mid-eighteenth century it had fractured into smaller enclaves, trading on the coast and raiding into the interior to meet the European demand for bound labor. "I know of no other way of making slaves there, but by robbery," Thomas Clarkson wrote of the Angola coast in 1789. He had accompanied a group of forty to fifty armed men over the coastal mountains in search of villages with young men likely to survive the trek back. One night, Clarkson woke to see flames leaping along the horizon from a village two miles away. The next morning, his partners returned with some fifty young men, captured in the confusion of arson, and began marching them to the coast.[60]

Few European vessels were there when the *Black Prince* arrived off Molembo, the trading port of merchant princes of Kakongo, just north of the mouth of the Congo River near modern-day Cabinda, Angola. The lack of ships, from Captain Miller's perspective, suggested that it would be easy to make a full cargo. Miller, indeed, was so overwhelmed by offers that he grossly overloaded his ship, taking on some 550 men, women, and children, where he had never before carried 400. Miller and his crew squeezed captive Africans into every corner of the vessel, rotating them regularly on deck so they didn't faint away and die. In early July, when Miller landed to take on water in Charleston, South Carolina, there were still 500 alive. The *Black Prince* entered the Chesapeake a week later, making for the James River. When Miller sold his captives on July 11, 1759, at an auction house across the James from Richmond, at an average price of £36 sterling or more, the Bantu-speaking Angolans became the newest forced migrants to British North America, as enslaved residents of colonial Virginia. LaRoche and his partners likely netted some £12,000 sterling on the sale. Virginia slavers, though, owed £5,625 Virginian (or £4,500 sterling) in taxes meant to retire the currency off the enslaved contents of one vessel alone.[61]

When slavers delivered 2,047 captives to Virginia from Africa the next year, resulting in a tax bill of roughly £20,470 sterling, the result was an elite tax revolt. In spring 1760, when Fauquier asked for troops, pro-importation Virginians attached a rider to the funding bill lowering the import duty by 10 percent, to 15 percent. In retaliation, planters favoring the bill came close to cutting off war funding altogether. Just one vote kept Virginia in the war. A year later, in March 1761, antitax burgesses succeeded in eliminating the other 10 percent wartime duty, leaving only the 5 percent duty from before the war.[62]

For some this was not enough. In an echo of the events in England six decades earlier, Virginia slave traders sought to rearrange the colony's money for their own advantage. Few were more perturbed by the tax on slave imports than Richard Corbin, a wealthy planter, commercial agent, royal quitrent collector, and member of Virginia's royal council. Corbin had opposed Virginia's currency from the beginning and the taxes that went with them. In 1757 he had instigated the complaints to London that had resulted in the Board of Trade's early attempt to quash bills of credit. Defeated, he bided his time. In 1762, though, he saw another opening, one that might eliminate the bills for good. His first step was to convince three of his fellow councilors, all appointed for their wealth and eminence, that the bills represented an ongoing threat to their interests. Crucially, Corbin was able to convince William Nelson, a wealthy Norfolk merchant and slave trader. Just three years earlier, Nelson had authored a defense of the currency on behalf of the colony. But with the French menace in abeyance, taxes seemed the greater threat. In the spring 1762 session alone, the burgesses proposed £4,625 in new taxes to offset the £30,000 in Virginia currency needed to pay troops serving in the West. A temporary wartime currency was beginning to feel like a permanent part of the Virginia system. Taxes earmarked for destroying the currency had more than doubled in five years, standing at £41,000 Virginia a year in 1762. Something had to be done.[63]

Nelson and Corbin began their campaign by demanding that Fauquier disband the colony's standing regiment—the troops kept under arms after France's surrender in North America. Fauquier demurred, so they decided to hand him a legislative setback. When the 1762 funding bill passed from the burgesses to the council, Corbin and the Nelsons narrowly defeated it, forcing Fauquier to delay a final vote until more councilors arrived. Their legislative maneuver, though, was a feint, a bid for time. Nelson and Corbin had already decided to take their complaints over Fauquier's head, to imperial administrators. Doing so, though, meant changing their argument. They were opposed to ongoing taxes, to supporting troops with no one to fight. But taxation and colonial defense were popular in London. Opposing them would not be a winning argument. However, they reasoned, opposing Virginia's currency, which amounted to the same thing, was.[64]

After his narrow victory in the council, Fauquier grew worried. He had heard Corbin was planning a strike against the currency (and the taxes that supported them), but with the legislature out of session, he did know what it might be. "I have been informed that several of the Merchants of this Colony have signed a Remonstrance to be presented to our right honorable Board in relation to future emissions of Paper Money; but I am entirely ignorant of its contents," Fauquier wrote the Board of Trade on July 10, 1762. Corbin and the Nelsons had worked "with great Industry" to conceal their next move. "The Drift and aim of [their opposition] was to get quit of the Expence of the Regiment," Fauquier warned, "well knowing that the Regiment cannot be supported without Emissions of Paper Money; there being neither Gold nor Silver in the Colony."[65]

Corbin and his friends were working to ensure that human trafficking stayed tax free and thus wildly profitable. They didn't care about gold or silver; they cared about slavery. Like Locke in the 1690s, they hoped to preserve and extend the legal basis of their wealth. Elite opposition to the currency was "a pretext," Fauquier wrote, a "plausible argument against the Bills, and that they would have opposed at any rate." If the colony was unable to support its regiment, Fauquier wrote Jeffrey Amherst on September 25, 1762, it would be due "to the Intrigues in relation to the Emission of more paper-Money." Corbin opposed the taxes that supported the colonial currency, not the currency itself. But if the currency was abolished, so would the taxes. They were two halves of the same system. After four years in Virginia and a successful frontier war to his credit, Fauquier thought he and the Board of Trade were on the same side. He was mistaken. The twin financial revolutions that had done so much to transform life on both sides of the Atlantic—the financial transformation in Britain that had fueled his family's rise and the monetary revolution just completed in Virginia—were about to collide.[66]

CHAPTER THREE

A "Strange and Deceitful System"

LONDON AND VIRGINIA, 1762–1764

I. Wills Hill Joins the Board of Trade

The two financial revolutions collided in the mind of one man. Wills Hill took over as head of the Board of Trade on September 28, 1763. Like many in his generation of British reformers, Hill was energetic and conscientious, passionate about perfecting the empire he had inherited and improving his position within it. He was born in 1718 in Gloucestershire near the Welsh border, joined Parliament in 1741, and joined the Privy Council—an influential group of ministers with direct access to the king—in 1754. He was fond of opera and his own opinion. His peers thought him a gifted orator, and he had a talent for ingratiating himself to whatever party was in power. He was also, as his contemporary Horace Walpole later wrote, "a pompous composition of ignorance and want of judgement." That pomposity was welded to grasping ambition.[1]

Hill's family's fortune had always been tied to the empire. His ancestor Moyses Hill came to Ireland as a low-ranking officer in an invading English army in 1573 and ended his life as a member of parliament and provost-marshall of the County of Ulster. Moyses made his fortune, in part, by extorting "rack rents" from English immigrants, on land leased cheaply from absentee British lords. The Hill motto was *Per Deum et ferrum obtinui*: I have obtained it by God and the sword. Hill inherited an Irish title, the Viscount of Hillsborough, and some 156 square miles of land around Belfast. Though Hill received many other titles over the course of his career, Hillsborough was the name that stuck.[2]

American agents, the men who represented North American colonies' interests in London, were cautiously optimistic about Hill's appointment. The new first lord of trade is "a man of business, alert, lively, ready, but too fond of his opinions and systems, and too apt to be inflexibly attached to them," Connecticut agent William Samuel Johnson reported. Johnson and other colonial representatives hoped Hill's Irish experience would give him a useful working perspective on "the rights and liberties of the distant branches of the empire." They had reason to be wary. Hill, like his friend and patron George Grenville, the new prime minister, was a man of finance. He had served in the Privy Council as its treasurer. And he came into office with a mandate to make the Britain's rapidly expanding external empire pay.[3]

One week after Hill took up his position, on October 5, 1763, he and the Privy Council announced a new policy towards America. As a kind of mission statement, it outlasted the Grenville administration itself. The Privy Council and its assistants had reviewed the customs receipts in North America and the West Indies and concluded that they, and the British public, were being cheated. After the salaries of the collectors were considered, the duties received did not cover a quarter of the costs of collecting them. The only possible explanation, the council concluded, was "Neglect, Connivance, and Fraud." The consequences went far beyond commerce alone, they wrote. The empire's coherence was at stake. "Not only the Revenue is impaired, but the Commerce of the Colonies is diverted from its natural Course," they wrote, that is, outside of the empire itself. Americans had been trading with French, Spanish, and Dutch rivals, even in times of war. A full program of reform was warranted, the council wrote, and immediately. "Maintaining these Colonies requires a large Revenue to support it, and when their vast Increase in Territory and Population makes the proper Regulation of their Trade of immediate Necessity, . . . the dangerous Evils above mentioned may render all Attempts to remedy them hereafter infinitely more difficult, if not utterly impracticable," the council wrote. Money, as it turned out, would be central to the problem.[4]

II. Hill Seeks to Create a Reempowered Executive Board of Trade

Hill's reforms started with the Board of Trade itself. The Board of Trade and Plantations came into existence in 1696, as part of the same wave of reforms and institution-building that produced the Bank of England and the Great Recoinage. John Montague, the Whig Zelig behind both the Bank of England and the Great Recoinage, was an early proponent. John Locke was an early board staffer. Locke had envisioned the board as of a piece with the recoinage. If "Money and Trade" were "inseparable," as he had argued, a board of trade would be necessary to regulate both. The board's original remit, as an arm of the Privy Council, included oversight of all of Britain's Atlantic colonies and their trade.[5]

Over the course of the board's history, though, its powers had waxed and waned. By the mid-eighteenth century, many colonists regarded it primarily as a forum for airing intercolonial disputes. In 1750, for example, Caribbean planters—slavers whose wealth was derived from the sugar produced by enslaved Africans—brought a case against the North American colonies before the British commissioners of the trade and plantations, in other words, the board. The lawyer for the planters, a Mr. Sharpe, presented a case showing that Americans had flagrantly violated the Molasses Act of 1733 during the War of Austrian Succession (1740–48).[6] The act placed a 6 pence sterling per gallon duty on non-British molasses, amounting to a prohibition on the trade. But that hadn't stopped American traders, particularly those from Rhode Island. These miscreants, Sharpe alleged, had gone as far as purchasing and trading French prisoners of war so that they would have legitimate reasons to visit French ports under a flag of truce to trade. Admiral Sir Charles Knowles testified that one of the captains under his command had been forced to fire fifty-two shots at one American vessel headed to Martinique before it would "bring to." The American smugglers carried flour, salted meat, and hardwood staves necessary to build casks required for the sugar and molasses trade. Without that trade, Knowles asserted, the French would have been forced to surrender Martinique or at the very least reduced "to extreme necessity." The Americans had been supplying the enemy.[7]

Neither punishment nor any sort of actual enforcement of the 1733 law was a goal of the Caribbean planters' suit. Rather, their aim was to leverage the Americans' flagrant disregard of the law to get their way in a monetary dispute.[8] The details emerged over the course of the trial, which stretched from November 13, 1750, to January 10, 1751. The key was money and who would be able to define it in intercolonial trade. According to the planters, American ships supplying the British sugar colonies had begun to demand gold and silver coin in return for the cattle, foodstuffs, and especially cask wood transported from the North American colonies. In return for precious metal, according to Knowles's testimony, Americans were willing to take "less than the real value of their Lumber." After leaving the British islands, the Americans, allegedly, took the specie to French colonies cut off by war from the Spanish American supplies of precious metal. There, they could buy cargoes of rum and molasses at a substantial discount to British prices. The problem was that British planters were cut off from the Spanish mints too. Traders in Jamaica and other British colonies had long traded enslaved men and women to Spanish coastal cities in return for specie from Spanish mines. War disrupted the traffic. Americans' demands for gold and silver were unreasonable because the sugar colonies were "drained of all their Specie," Knowles testified. Captain Richard Tyrell, whose ship had fired the fifty-two shots over a fleeing American ship's bow, testified that plantation owners, like himself, were "obliged to draw bills upon England in order to procure Specie when they," the Americans, "refused Rum and Sugar in Payment of Lumber," citing a particular instance where the "Master of a New England Vessel" had refused rum and sugar and was afterward seen loading both at the Dutch port of Eustatia.[9]

The resolution of the case is telling. On January 10 the parties reported to the board that the sugar planters agreed to drop their suit, so long as American captains pledged to take rum and molasses, instead of specie, in payment for their supplies. The Board of Trade, presumably satisfied with this conclusion, closed the case. No further action was taken. The board's role had been to serve as a forum for disputation, not to enforce the law. Enforcement was not the point. The 1733 law existed, in effect, to protect the rights of British subjects in the Caribbean from the trading practices of subjects in North America. The actual letter of the flagrantly violated law was irrelevant. What mattered was that the dispute had been adjudicated. British trade and the integrity of the empire, as a trading unity, had been maintained.

The judicial model of the board worked well. It soon became clear, however, that Hill had in mind a more aggressive, executive board. His ideal board president was George Dunk, Earl of Halifax, who took over the Board of Trade in 1748. Unlike most first lords of trade, Dunk had a vast, independent income and therefore no need to curry favor with Parliament. He soon became frustrated with what he saw as the board's limited powers, needled the government repeatedly, and threatened to resign if he didn't get more. By the mid-1750s he had annexed the executive powers usually reserved for secretaries of state, ministers who oversaw whole continents on behalf of the empire. There had been several short-term board presidents since, none with Dunk's flair or energy. Hill, though, had resolved to solidify an executive role for the board within Britain's imperial architecture.[10]

He had one significant advantage that Dunk lacked. In Dunk's era the empire had been reliant on colonial goodwill to enforce its rulings. It had no army in North America, and its navy was usually up to other things. But by Hill's appointment that had changed. On February 10, 1763, Britain and France signed a treaty in Paris that made Britain the dominant European power in eastern North America, making the North Atlantic, in effect, a British pond. As the historian John Brewer has put it, "Only in 1763 did Britannia truly rule the waves."[11] Meanwhile, in 1762, as first lord of the admiralty, Grenville, Hill's new boss, had sworn British naval officers in as customs officers, promising them a significant amount of the value of any seizures. For the first time, the board's rulings on trade would be backed by force. No longer a mere forum, the board would now be making policy, and Hill's allies in the parliamentary leadership and the Privy Council would see that policy carried out. The question was where to start. As chance would have it, the first thing to cross Hill's desk was a stack of papers relating to the monetary policy of Virginia.[12]

When Corbin and his friends sent joint letters to the Board of Trade, as well as to their friends in the merchant groups who had grown wealthy trafficking African captives to the Chesapeake and tobacco to Europeans, they evidently had the older, judicial model of the Board of Trade in mind. Certainly, none of them seems to have seriously contemplated the idea that the board would act on a scale larger than Virginia or even disallow the currency itself. Corbin had sent letters complaining about the currency back in 1757 with little effect. Fauquier's intervention on the ground had been decisive, preserving bills of credit as part of the war effort. Rather, Corbin had hoped to set up a kind of trial, where his concerns about currency and related taxes would be matched against the colony's interests in preserving it.

Corbin's war was waged on two fronts. On the first, he wrote to the Board of Trade on December 16, 1762, claiming that the king was being cheated out of his quitrents of 2 pence per hundred acres on Virginia land, because he (the commissioner in charge of collecting these taxes) had "been under a necessity of receiving the Quit-Rents in Treasury notes" because there was no more gold and silver in the colony. On the second, he had waged a war by proxy. Rather than petition the board again himself, Corbin sent a list of grievances to friends in the slave and tobacco trading firms of Glasgow, Bristol, London, and Liverpool. He asked these men to reword the complaints and forward them to the board as their own work. Crucially, neither letter mentioned their opposition to taxes. Money was the thing. The British merchants dutifully wrote the board that their contracts in America were in peril if Virginia's bills of credit were allowed to continue. The board, then, had forwarded petitions back to Virginia in February 1763, demanding a reply from the burgesses. The burgesses responded, at length, in May. The Virginians' reply was still unanswered on September 28, 1763, when Hill stepped in and began to work through colonial correspondence on his own.

III. Hill Takes the Initiative on the Problem of American Money

Hill's brilliant, perhaps perverse contribution was to read this yearslong sequence of claim and counterclaim as a philosophical debate about the nature of money. No one had asked him to do so. Corbin and his fellow councilors' original complaints about the currency, lodged in April 1762, on their face, rested on practical claims. The first was that Virginia's currency was not being burned fast enough—that there was "a deficiency of the taxes for sinking our paper currency." This was a remarkable act of misdirection or "Intrigue" in Fauquier's terms: opposing taxes by claiming they were not high enough. The second was that merchants who were forced to take Virginia bills of credit in return to settle their debts were losing money, the complaint Fauquier had already dismissed in 1759. The third was that Fauquier himself was remiss because he had failed to enforce the unenforceable royal order of 1759 that "Sterling debts" should be "only dischargeable in Sterling money." Corbin's friends among the British merchants extended these complaints only slightly, mostly by exaggerating for effect. The Glaswegian slave traders called laws forcing them to accept bills of credit "a stretch of power never practiced in any free Commercial Country." London merchants were perhaps the most expansive. They claimed that Virginia's laws forced them to exchange sterling money "of a fixed and certain value" for "Paper Bills of Credit of an uncertain and mere local value only," disregarding "Rules of Equity and Justice" and "introducing a mode and form of Justice unheard of in this Realm."[13]

The Virginians, in their reply penned at Fauquier's insistence in May 1763, were just as practical, meeting each charge with a statistical refutation. The charge that they had not levied enough taxes to gather up and burn the currency by 1769 was met with a commercial ledger setting each currency issue against the taxes meant to call them in. The bills of credit issued, £412,962 and 10 shillings in Virginia reckoning, made up one side of the ledger. This was balanced "By Notes burnt" since 1760. In all, Virginia had burned £85,655, 6 shillings, and 6 pence in notes by 1762. Another £25,574 and

18 shillings were ready to burn, and another £21,300 were in the Treasury, waiting to be tallied. Some £10,625 had never been spent and would be burned as well. This made £146,154, 19 shillings, and 7 pence burned, or slated for burning. More than a quarter of the total debt was already canceled. The burgesses expected to collect £40,850 a year in taxes for 1763–65, £39,919 after expenses and £45,000 a year through 1768, for a net of £41,895 a year. In 1769 there would be £21,366 in bills outstanding and £32,817 in taxes coming due. The taxes more than canceled out the debt.[14]

The burgesses' reply to the claim that the bills of credit had led to "great Loss and Injury" for British merchants was just as comprehensive. The Londoners claimed Virginian courts had forced them to take bills of credit at a loss, so Virginia's Committee of Correspondence tallied up the value of every court case since 1757. Over six years, the whole amount in question was £18,489 sterling, or just over one-tenth of 1 percent of the roughly £3.45 million sterling British in exports to Virginia for the same period. If every penny under dispute were sacrificed, the losses were hardly "great." In fact, British creditors in Virginia courts received currency with a face value of £27,194, or £21,755 sterling, for debts worth £18,489 sterling, more than enough to buy bills of exchange on London at prevailing rates. The committee had been unable to find a single instance where a merchant had been harmed by a court judgment settled in bills of credit. This was not to say that such harm was impossible, only that any harm done was tiny.[15]

But the practical debate held no interest for Hill. The balanced deals struck by previous boards were not what he was after. He was interested in systems, and the opposing systems of money presented in the documents were what evidently caught his attention. This too was strikingly original. There was no reason to think that the two systems, Britain's own based on a circulating currency of silver and gold, and the colonies', based ultimately on Blackwell's ideas about circulating credit, were opposed to each other. If anything, they were complementary.

Britain's financial revolution had created the fiscal and monetary basis for imperial expansion. Bills of credit had done the same thing for Britain's North American colonies, with a twist. Britain's financial revolution excelled at creating new forms of financial wealth: the joint-stock company shares, bank bills, government debt, and currency that, along with an expanding tax bill, were its lasting legacy. The colonial revolution, with its bills of credit, had gone the other way entirely. Bills of credit were temporary. They had an expiration date. They circulated like gold and silver, or British banknotes, but they did not last. Colonists looking for lasting, as opposed to circulating, forms of financial wealth would still have to look to Britain. The bills also served what was arguably the primary aim of the empire in the age of mercantilism: they allowed Britain's colonies in North America to ship what gold and silver they acquired directly to Britain. The two monies met different needs, moved in different circuits, between different people, for different reasons.[16]

Questions only arose at moments when one complementary currency had to be turned into the other, and it was at these moments that Hill's predecessors had intervened repeatedly. Their main concern always had been to make sure that the colonies' currencies remained complementary. The Board of Trade had intervened repeatedly since 1690 to make sure temporary monies were, in fact, temporary, setting strict limits on expiration dates in times of peace and times of war. They had also, as in Virginia, worked to make sure that any sterling debts settled in colonial currency were settled at a market rate of exchange. The only piece of parliamentary legislation limiting colonial currency issued prior to Hill's tenure, the Currency Act of 1751, set both limits in law, putting a two-year expiration debt on peacetime bill issues expanding to five years in times of war. This only applied to New England. Colonial bills of credit had never been banned, nor had a ban been contemplated for the precise reasons Fauquier ended up backing Virginia's bills in 1759. There was no viable alternative. "If I had attempted to have made any Alterations," Fauquier wrote in May 1763, referring to the paper-money bills he had encountered on his arrival in 1758, "I should not have been able to obtain a man."[17]

Hill did not accept that the two monies, sterling and Virginian bills of credit, might be complementary. His reaction disregarded most of the evidence presented to the board. It seems to have been partly instinctive and partly philosophical. In London, by 1763, the idea that gold and silver were money was widely accepted as a natural fact. "I can not alter the nature of things, find laws where they are not, thereby turn paper into gold and silver, nor can I make others convinced of the possibility of so doing," Virginia's London agent Richard Abercromby had written of his campaign to defend the new currency in 1759. The burgesses sacked him in response, but there was no doubt that Abercromby's sentiments were widespread. But Hill seems to have been provoked by the way that the Virginians had responded to the London merchants' claims about equity and justice.[18]

The Londoners' complaint centered on courts in defending British merchants' interests in Virginia. Giving colonial courts power to set the rate of exchange "however uprightly and impartially hitherto exercised" was itself unacceptable, the Londoners argued, because it involved "introducing a mode and form of Justice unheard of in this Realm." On its face, this was a bizarre charge. If two British or colonial merchants had a dispute over payment that they could not resolve themselves, "to whom can it be referred but, as all other disputes are, to the courts of Justice, the true constitutional resort?" the burgesses replied. How could that possibly be a "new mode of Justice?" they wrote. That was what courts were for.[19]

But the merchants' accusation had little to do with courts, per se. It had to do with the deep structure of the colonists' currency, the problem of time. From the Londoners' perspective, it was the way money had been conceived and written into law that made equity and justice impossible in Virginia. Equity was only possible when exchange was equal, and equality was only possible when the goods being exchanged could be reduced to a single value. Virginia's bills and pounds sterling, they asserted, could not be set equal to each other at any rate or on any terms. The very thing that made bills of credit complementary to sterling, the fact that they expired, while sterling coin, in theory, lasted forever, created the impossibility of a fair exchange. Virginia's notes, the merchants argued, were "Paper Bills of Credit of an uncertain fluctuating and mere local value only." Sterling money, on the other hand was "of a fixed and certain value." Nothing fluctuating, their analysis implied, could be set equal to something fixed. Virginia courts were forcing an unnatural exchange. The specific properties of Virginian money made "Equity and Justice" in Virginian courts impossible. The risks that merchants took in making the exchange, the small sums some may have lost, in other words, were incidental to the more fundamental injustice of accepting the bills on any terms whatsoever.[20]

The Londoners did not blame the courts themselves for creating this paradox. Instead, they blamed the burgesses for breaking with what, to their minds, was long-standing British practice. For almost a century, sterling money had been defined, in British law, as gold and silver. Gold and silver coins were the only things British merchants were obliged, by law, to accept in satisfaction of a debt. Everything else, even banknotes, navy bills, army bills, and exchequer bills "issued by Authority of Parliament" and paying interest, traded at a market rate.[21]

Virginia's money was an exception to the rule, in other words, that only gold and silver coins were to be accepted at face value. There, notes were accepted at face value as "legal tender" for all public and private debts, apart from royal quitrents. In other words, to British eyes, the colony had made paper equivalent to gold and silver, and thus "assumed to themselves . . . a power of making Paper Notes a legal tender in payment of Debts[,] a Sanction that no Law in this Kingdom has given" to anything but precious metal. For the London merchants, this was the height of colonial arrogance. In effect, they argued, the burgesses reclaimed a power that the British crown and Parliament had surrendered more than half a century before. It was this assumption of power, ultimately, that gave Virginia notes their "mere local value," creating the conditions of incommensurability between Virginian notes and the sterling money that made justice impossible at any price. The Londoners objected less to the currency itself than to the freedom to arrange money that the colony of Virginia claimed in making it.[22]

This raised a further difficulty, the question of power. Did Virginians, in fact, have the authority to reorganize their money? Virginians had no doubt. "Our dependence upon Great Britain we acknowledge and glory in as our greatest happiness and only security," the burgesses wrote, "but this is not the dependance [sic] of a People subjugated by the arms of a Conqueror, but of Sons sent out to explore and settle a new World, for the mutual benefit of themselves and their common Parent." It was self-evident that Virginia's currency, could not be issued along the same lines as in England. The Londoners, in complaining of this difference, had failed to consider "the true Distinction in the Cases," the burgesses wrote. The contrast between the two monies arose out of the difference between the two societies. "The Notes of the Bank of England, circulated upon Stocks of Specie," the burgesses wrote, but Virginia had no gold or silver to promise. "We had therefore no other Method than to emit these Notes to circulate as Money for a short limited Time, and to impose such taxes as should effectually procure their Return to the Treasury," the burgesses wrote. Virginian money was different because Virginia was different. The fact of that difference required a difference in institutions and the power to develop and implement them.[23]

There was no necessary link between "Justice to the British Merchants" and monies "circulated upon Stocks of Specie," the Virginians continued. "We have ever considered ourselves as under an Obligation to discharge our Debts contracted in *Great Britain* . . . at such a Rate of Exchange as would place the Money in *Great* Britain without loss." They acknowledged that sterling money, as a literal matter, meant gold and silver. But that did not mean that only gold and silver could settle sterling debts. In a world where gold and silver were rare to the point of being intermittently nonexistent, demanding specie payment was absurd. The Virginians could not understand how defining money as something other than the commodity that changed hands, out of need, and in service of the empire, could be a revolutionary act.[24]

At the core of the burgesses' argument was an assumption that they had the right, indeed, the duty, to create institutions "for the mutual Benefit of themselves and their common Parent." Perhaps the most cutting charge against them, they wrote, was that, in creating their currency they had failed to render "proper respect to the Crown" by "refusing to comply" with the 1759 royal order making sterling debts payable in sterling money. But the burgesses did not see compliance as their duty. Compliance must be subordinate to both practical and principled concerns. "We must be allowed to judge for ourselves, so far as our Sanction is necessary to any Law," the burgesses wrote. They had not been "convinced that the Measure proposed," making sterling debts payable in absent gold and silver "was proper," and thus "did indeed decline to pass such a Law." They had written a "humble" explanation of their conduct, to stave off any "Imputation of Disrespect to the Crown." But the fact was that the Americans believed that, in monetary matters, they had the right to judge for themselves.[25]

IV. The Board of Trade Begins an Investigation

On December 1, 1763, Hill and the Board of Trade took up the problem of Virginian money, officially, for the first time. After spending the day reviewing the burgesses' analysis, Hill ordered Edward Montague, the burgesses' agent, to appear the following Thursday, December 8, to answer the merchants directly. After both Montague and the merchants had made their presentations, the board asked the parties to leave the chambers. They did not have to wait long. The board, it seems, had already reached a conclusion. It was self-evident to the board that the merchants' demand that sterling debts must be paid in gold or silver, whether due "in Virginia or Great Britain," was essential to "doing justice." Anything else would be "neither just [n]or equitable." If the colony still "refused doing justice to the British merchants and did not comply" immediately, the board would take the matter to Parliament. He ordered a letter composed to the Virginians, including "the most positive instructions to Fauquier" to call an emergency assembly to order the burgesses to declare all sterling debts payable in gold and silver.[26]

This, however, was little more than had been done before. That fact seems to have nagged at Hill as the board went into winter recess. The abstract nature of the money problem, at the intersection between money as a practical institution and the power to define it, would likely have thrown Hill's predecessors off. The Board of Trade's long history of limited intervention in the monetary affairs of American colonies reflected both their practicality and a sense of their own limitations. Hill, though, was an exception. He loved "systems," abstract ideas, and making them work together. Grenville had given him a broad remit and sweeping powers to make change. If Virginia's monetary system was unjust, what of the other colonies? What were the implications of Virginia's monetary problem for the administration of trade in the North Atlantic as a whole? What ought the empire's position to be on what money actually was or should be?[27]

Hill's insight, over the holidays, seems to have arrived with a flash: If the only way of doing justice in payment of a sterling debt was to pay in sterling money or gold and silver, then that injustice must be ubiquitous in the American colonies. Notoriously, none of them had much gold or silver, and all of them, in one way or another, had incurred massive sterling debts while, at the same time, establishing alternative means of payment. If justice meant payment in gold and silver, then injustice in America, it followed, must be as common as breathing. The colonial monetary system, to Hill, suddenly took on the appearance of one great scandal, a conspiracy against the British mercantile interest. The Board of Trade's haphazard attempts at suppression had only abetted this gigantic swindle. Digging through colonial reports, Hill found what seemed like similar complaints from the merchants trading to North Carolina (though in fact they asked the board to rule that sterling debts in North Carolina be paid "ad valorem," according to their assessed value, as was already the case in Virginia). The fact that merchants trading to South Carolina, Maryland, New York, New Jersey, and Pennsylvania had not complained only meant that they too had failed to consider the matter systematically.[28]

Meanwhile, the need for reform had never been more urgent. The Privy Council had warned Hill, in October, that the many "wise Laws" binding the colonists of North America and the West Indies "to the Mother Country" were already "in great Measure defeated." Complaisance, they had cautioned, was only likely "to render all Attempts to remedy [the problem] hereafter infinitely more difficult, if not utterly impracticable." In their arguments against the Virginian currency before the board, one of the British merchants had likewise accused the colonists of "growing independency," around the money issue, a charge proven by lack of deference "paid to his Majesty's orders and even the contempt shewn them." Another had wondered aloud "to what purpose do we protect the Colonies and expend such sums in their defense if we are ultimately to be undone by them, and their trade instead of being beneficial to Great Britain is detrimental to, and only an incumbrance on its Merchants[?]" When it came to colonial reform, in other words, the money issue was the place to begin. The Privy Council had charged Hill with rooting out "Neglect, Connivance, and Fraud" in Britain's Atlantic colonies, and here, within mere weeks of his appointment, with only minor digging, he had uncovered a deception of seemingly incredible proportions.[29]

On January 10, 1764, Hill and the board took up the "state of the currency in the American colonies" as a whole. Hill called on colonial agents and British merchants trading to the colonies to assemble on January 19 for a grand debate on colonial money. The debate, while leaving no complete record, seems to have proved stimulating. Two days later, at a Saturday session, the board took up the matter again, and again on January 26. At last, the board ordered former governors, chief justices, and agents from New York, Pennsylvania, Massachusetts, Georgia, New Jersey, South Carolina, and Virginia to attend on February 2. Such a complete assembly of notables in the board's Whitehall offices was all but unprecedented. The board, as a typical matter, kept the concerns of each colony separate, filing letters and reports that only rarely intersected, and then, usually, only in the case of war. That separation made sense when the Board of Trade had been merely a forum for dispute between the empire's contending interests, but if it was to become the executive body envisioned by Hill and the Privy Council, transitioning, effectively, from a judicial to an executive role, those barriers would have to fall. By then it was clear that Hill had a sweeping intervention in mind.[30]

The February 2, 1764, session was productive. The colonies' former governors and justices, "all hands," the board's secretary recorded, agreed that a uniform regulation of the paper currency was desirable. Paper bills of credit, they decided, should not be legal tender after they had expired, and if any existing bills of credit did not have an expiration date, they should be given one. This amounted to cementing in place the American system that had been developing over the previous seventy years. All of America's paper money should be temporary; none of it taken to be a permanent form of wealth. For the former colonial leaders, the meeting seems to have been a moment of real collaboration and consensus. Their money, it seems, was something they had in common. Only the Pennsylvania delegation objected, seeking time to solicit comments from the colony.[31]

Colonial comment would take at least six months. That was time the empire did not have, Hill felt. Big things were afoot in colonial regulation, and currency had to be part of it. The next day, February 3, the board met again. They considered asking the colonies' input but, in the end, rejected any further delay, producing a proposed regulation for colonial agents' consideration. The proposal banned colonial bills from being legal tender without the board's prior approval. The only legal money otherwise would be gold and silver. The board gave colonial agents a few days to consider. On February 7 the agents returned, having digested the proposal. They rejected it. The agents were of "unanimous opinion," the board's secretary recorded, "that a certain quantity of paper currency ought to be allowed of in each colony, to be a legal tender in all contracts and dealings within the colonies." Hill and the board told them that they would take that refusal under consideration.[32]

In secret, though, he had already made up his mind. In between sessions, with staff help, he had been writing a history of the colonies' money and what, he believed, the empire's position on money should be. He completed the essay on February 9. Four days later, William Knox, the agent for Georgia, and Charles Garth, for South Carolina, visited the board, ostensibly, to discuss the "state of the silk culture in Georgia." The discussion soon turned to colonial money. While Knox and Garth had not seen Hill's essay, they had heard Hill was going forward with a new currency regulation against the colonies' objections. They wished to suggest that perhaps the bills could be legal tender in America, but not in reference to contracts "with any person or persons who at the time such debt was contracted, were residing, dwelling or inhabiting within the Kingdoms of Great Britain or Ireland." That would allay the merchants' fears while leaving colonies creative leeway. Hill, meanwhile, had already sent his essay on to colleagues at the Privy Council for approval.[33]

The February 13 meeting was the last time that the board sought colonial input on paper money. Its meeting rooms had begun to smell of raw sewage. On February 23 the board was forced from its chambers "by offensive smells, occasioned by some defect in the water closets." While the Board of Works fixed the problem, the Board of Trade sat adjourned, and Hill set about finishing his presentation to the Privy Council and George III, presenting his thoughts on money.[34]

V. Hill Tries His Hand at Monetary Theory

Hill's essay is critical to understanding how taxation without representation led to a revolution. Its basic thesis was that the entire system of American money was a deliberate fraud, which was bad enough. But the analysis did not end there. Hill had inquired deeply and concluded that bills of credit were reliant, in fact, on a different theory of money, a different idea of what money might be—how it moved and shaped interactions between individuals—than Britain's own system. And it was this theory that Hill objected to, what he called the bills' "Principles," the intellectual basis of bills of credit. Hill did not know Blackwell's name. He had not read deeply in the seventeenth-century pamphlet literature on alternative financial systems. And yet, that winter, he found himself wrestling with the old Puritan financier and ideas that Britain had long put to rest.

Hill admitted at the start that he did not have the best information on the colonies. He confessed to being "not sufficiently informed to say with certainty in what manner and from what Causes" bills of credit as a "legal Currency" had arisen, not being in the ancient records of the Massachusetts Bay colony. But he had the outlines, and these were correct. The bills had been created, he wrote, sometime between 1689 and 1692, "that Colony growing necessitous of the Expences incurred chiefly on Account of Sir William Phipps's Expedition against Canada." The colony had "borrowed Money in a method of which we are not particularly apprized" and repaid that debt with the new bills of credit, with the result that they "passed in Dealings and transactions with as little difficulty as Bank Bills do now in this Kingdom."[35]

Soon, he wrote, almost all the American colonies "had followed the example of the Province of Massachusetts Bay, in issuing Paper Bills of Credit, and making them legal Tender, though upon different principles and under different regulations." Nevertheless, Hill argued, they were founded on the same "reasons," the same basic set of ideas. These ideas, moreover, were false, and as a result American money was "unjust in it's [sic] foundation and Manifestly fraudulent in it's [sic] Operation." The ubiquity of these principles justified action on a continental scale. "Our Intention is not to convey censure upon any particular Colonies," Hill wrote, "but to Suggest a general Regulation upon full Conviction, that it is necessary as well for the Security and Interest of the Colonies themselves, as of the Trade and Commerce of this Kingdom."[36]

But to explain how American money had gone wrong, Hill first had to explain how Britain had gone right. For those answers, Hill turned to the man who was arguably Britain's greatest living authority on money, Joseph Harris, royal assay master at the London Mint. Born in rural Wales, Harris had been trained as an astronomer and scientific instrument maker, and, in his youth, had sailed on astronomical expeditions to Mexico and Jamaica. But, dogged by money troubles, in 1736 he joined the mint, where he became a powerful advocate for an unalterable metallic monetary standard. By the 1750s he was a much sought-after expert on monetary affairs, a parliamentary adviser, and had been awarded a £300 annual pension from George II for his services to the crown.[37]

Harris's definitive statement on British money came in 1757, when he published a pamphlet entitled *An Essay upon Money and Coins*. In it, he wrestled with precisely the issues that worried Hill. Indeed, Harris had even taken up the question of paper money in the American colonies. The bills' legal structure, and the ideas behind it, were less important than the physical stuff they were made of, in Harris's view. He was not in favor of bills of credit, he wrote, largely because they were printed on paper, and paper had "no real value." Harris was no dogmatist. He commended Pennsylvania, in particular, on its well-managed paper currency. He merely doubted its contribution to long-term prosperity. Colonial bills were "nothing, but mere promises, subject every day to be debased by the creation of more bills," Harris wrote—in sum, "weak, unjust and destructive."[38]

Harris was useful to Hill, though, because he was deeply interested in the problem of what money was in eighteenth-century Britain, the place, in Hill's view, that had it right. The answer, for Harris, was multifaceted. As a student of the seventeenth-century monetary debates that preceded the empire's twinned financial revolutions, Harris was particularly concerned with debunking the notion that money could be reduced to either one of what, in his view, were its two essential components. Both were essential to what made money money.

First, Harris wrote, money was a standard, or measure of value. "MONEY *is a* STANDARD MEASURE, *by which the values of all things, are regulated and ascertained*," Harris wrote. On that he agreed with Blackwell, and many other seventeenth-century monetary thinkers. But where Harris broke with those thinkers was in the idea that money was a measure first and last. Money could only be successful as a measure, in Harris's view, if it was also a commodity, a good in trade. Thus, money was, Harris wrote—paraphrasing what Locke had written in a similar position seventy years earlier—"both an equivalent and measure; being in all contracts, the very thing usually bargained for, as well as the measure of the bargain." Measure and equivalent had to go together. Money was a measure, Harris wrote, "*and is itself, at the same time, the* VALUE *or* EQUIVALENT, *by which, goods are exchanged, and in which, contracts are made payable*." That was why paper money, in Harris's view, was always doomed to failure. It might be a measure, but it could not be an "equivalent." Money, as an equivalent, had to have an "intrinsic value, arising from its usefulness, scarcity, and necessary expense of procuring it," Harris wrote. But it was unlike all other "commodities in this, that," as a commodity, "its value is permanent or unalterable; that is, money being the measure of the values of all other things, and that, like all other standard measures, by its quantity only; its own value is to be deemed invariable." The value of the money was always the value of the commodity itself. Its price could not rise because it was the measure of price.[39]

In Harris's view, metals—in particular, copper, silver, or gold—were the "fittest materials" for money because they fit requirements for what money was. Metal could serve as a measure because it was "divisible into minute parts" and had "an intrinsic value, in proportion to their quantity and weight." Gold and silver were particularly useful, Harris noted, because of their universal acceptability. They were the "money of the world," he wrote, echoing Locke. Harris acknowledged that money could be instituted or made in other ways. "But," he argued, "wherever that material, which passeth as or instead of money, hath no intrinsic value," it could not *be* money on Harris's terms. "There," Harris continued, "private property will be precarious so long as that continues to be the case, it will be next to impossible for such people to arrive at any degree of power and splendour." Britain's own eighteenth-century power and splendor, then, had a monetary basis. For Harris, that meant money as both a measure and an equivalent, both an instituted rule for value and a commodity in trade.[40]

Hill was looking for a general rule, something that could be applied to the empire as a whole, and Harris's analysis gave it to him. In Harris's terms, Virginian money was not money. It was a measure, to be sure, but not a commodity, not an "equivalent." Moreover, Harris's universal language of what money "*is itself*," everywhere, always, lent British complaints against American currency a new moral force. If money was necessarily both a measure and an equivalent, it must be so in Virginia as well as in all of North America. If that were true, Americans were not simply doing the best they could under difficult circumstances, making money from paper because they had no gold and silver. Rather, in taking the name of money in vain, they were engaged in a deliberate fraud.

"It would otherwise not be very difficult to shew, that a Medium of Trade must in its nature not only be a measure of Value; but an equivalent," Hill wrote. American colonists had erred, precisely, in this. The "Equivalent must be of a material, which is universally of intrinsic Value," Hill wrote. The Americans, fatally, had chosen paper, a thing "as unfit as anything can possibly be." That fact alone, he argued, should be "enough to evince the absurdity of this Measure." The result, Hill argued, was "absurd," because Americans could not, by government action, change the nature of money. Here was Hill's general rule, as true in Pennsylvania, New York, Virginia, or South Carolina as it was in Westminster.

But the American currencies were not merely absurd, Hill continued, they were fraudulent. This was, in part, because in Hill's view, the
absurdity of money without a commodity basis was obvious. Hill's key
example, drawn from the Board of Trade's American records, was a
measure passed in Massachusetts in 1711. The cost of sterling credit, in
1711, was rising, devaluing the bills in Atlantic trade. Massachusetts's General Court had acted to protect the value expressed in the bills, making
them a "legal tender" at the statutory rate of £133 pounds Massachusetts
to £100 pounds sterling. "The palpable fraud of the regulation in 1711 is
so glaring that it is impossible to suppose that the general Court, was not
sensible of it," Hill wrote. It was fraudulent, in effect, because of the assertion of power involved. What Massachusetts had done, in creating bills of
credit, was to assert, legislatively, that something that was not money was
money. Their legislation was either a contradiction or a lie, and the same
was true elsewhere in North America. British money was money because
it was a commodity. American money was not money because it was not
a commodity, not an equivalent. The whole amounted to a "strange and
deceitful system," Hill concluded. "Compelling Persons by Law to receive
these Bills at an Arbitrary and Nominal Value, is of the most pernicious
nature, destructive to Publick Credit, ruinous to the Colonies themselves,
and highly injurious to the Commerce of this country," Hill wrote. "We humbly presume the Art of Man cannot contrive any measure more ruinous and
destructive to the unhappy Country, where it was allowed to take place."[41]

In returning through Harris to the seventeenth-century debates, Hill
had unwittingly unearthed Blackwell's analysis, laying its radicalism
bare. Blackwell, in helping design the original bills of credit, had rested
his argument on what he called "the *Nature of Money*," that it was "but
a *Counter* or *Measure* of men's Properties," what he called an "Instituted
mean of permutation." For Blackwell, the idea that money might be a
commodity was contingent. It depended on how money was instituted
in law. "As *metal* indeed it is a commodity, Like all other things, that are
Merchantable," he had written, "but as *Mony* it is no more than what was
said," a measure or intermediate. For Hill, Harris, and the empire they
represented, the relationship question, whether or not money was a commodity, was fundamental. Money as a commodity had become, as Harris argued, a foundational part of the legal structure that underpinned
all property, the structure that underpinned Britain's "power and splendour." Moreover, Britain's success with its money as both commodity and
measure proved that both were necessary. Money's status as a commodity,
an equivalent, had become elemental to its nature. The existence of bills

of credit was, in effect, a denial of money's commodity nature. Because nature could not be denied, they were a deceit. And because that deceit took shape in trade, they were a fraud.[42]

The immediate question was how to oppose that fraud with imperial policy. Hill and his staff paired their intellectual memorandum with a new bill that would have the effect of limiting or prohibiting bills of credit, at least in their current form, everywhere in Britain's colonies. Hill proposed making it illegal to enforce a legal tender clause against anyone living or working in Britain—not just those owed "sterling debts." Any further new notes would only be legal tender if the Board of Trade approved them. Obviously, under Hill the board would not. He also proposed a punishment aimed directly at Fauquier and governors like him, who had encouraged the fraud by allowing colonies to fund themselves using the bills. Any imperial administrator tempted to allow bills to pass without royal approval would be fined £1,000 and banned from any position of responsibility in the imperial government. Their careers would be over.[43]

The deeper question, however, was how Hill's ideas about the nature of money might apply to British policy more broadly. Money as a standalone matter and its relation to empire were important enough, of course. Implicitly, though Hill did not acknowledge it, any policy based on his ideas would be a rejection of the old idea that all precious metal must go to Britain, a reimagination of empire itself. The new empire would be about enforcing rules concerning the nature of money outside of Britain, rather than ensuring it was all *in* Britain. The practical implications were more immediate, though. What money was, or could be, also had implications for tax policy, for the regulation of trade, and, more pointedly, on what powers could and could not be delegated to colonial legislatures. These matters would wait, but they would not, Hill knew, wait long.

Hill's plea for universal monetary reform suited the mood in the Grenville government. On March 9, 1764, two days after receiving it, the Privy Council forwarded Hill's draft regulation to Parliament, recommending it be passed into law. Parliament was less swayed by abstract ideas than the council was. The House of Commons ordered the Board of Trade to prove the damages Hill asserted. They wanted numbers: how many bills had been "created and issued" in the colonies, since January 1749, their value "in Money of *Great Britain*" both when they were issued and current, when they expired, and what taxes had been levied to redeem them. All were due in the next session of Parliament, with the strong presumption that the bill could wait until then. Similar tactics had preserved bills of credit in the colonies for three generations.[44]

Then a new MP stepped forward. Anthony Bacon had made a fortune in the Seven Years' War and just then was expanding his business in
Senegambia and the West Indies, leasing enslaved laborers to the British
government and armed services. He also was owed significant debts in
North Carolina, where new bills of credit had also caused consternation as what merchants called "a Notorious breach of public Faith contrary to justice and Equity." Bacon could see the value in Hill's regulation.
Rather than wait for the numbers, Bacon reintroduced the bill on his own
initiative. Over the next few days, he shepherded it, with several amend-
ments, through the House. The final legislation was perhaps less stringent than Hill would have liked, but on April 12, it passed. The House of
Lords agreed to it six days later, and the king gave his assent the day after
that. On April 19 the Currency Act of 1764 became law—before Virginia's
assembly had even received Hill's threat.[45]

VI. Virginians Struggle to Understand
the New Imperial Mood

Winter wheat was in the ground at Mt. Vernon, and Virginians, enslaved
and free, were laying up tobacco in warehouses along the creeks and rivers of the tidewater on October 30, 1764, when Fauquier called the colony's political representatives upstairs to the long, oval council chamber at
the top of the Williamsburg capitol.

With the burgesses assembled, Fauquier quickly got to business. The
burgesses, yet again, had been tasked with responding satisfactorily to
the "Proposition made by the Merchants of Great Britain trading to this
Colony to the Right Honourable Board of Trade, relating to their having
Sterling Debts secured them by a Payment in Sterling Money." The burgesses were understandably tired of the debate, and Fauquier had delayed
bringing the Board of Trade's latest demands to them for as long as he
dared. The previous winter the board had demanded that Fauquier call an
emergency session on the money topic. He had not. He also avoided mentioning money in the spring session, writing the Board of Trade in May to
say he hoped to give "the Members time to consider cooly [sic] the Business laid before them," to make sure the board received the burgesses' fresh
response before Parliament's spring session the next year.

The next week, on Friday, November 9, Edmund Pendleton, a
forty-three-year-old lawyer, magistrate, and burgess from Caroline County
on the Rappahannock River, reported back to Fauquier. The money
question had been put to the legislators before, Pendleton said, and their

answer was the same. The empire's essential demand was to eliminate the clause making Virginia's treasury notes a "legal Tender in Payment of all Debts" and replace them with gold and silver. That was unacceptable, if not impossible. Legal tender, Pendleton said, was "the essential Part" of money. It was what made the Virginian notes—the colony's variant on bills of credit—work. Soldiers and suppliers had accepted the notes, in part, because their creditors would have to accept them in turn. Altering it was impossible "without violating the Principles of natural Equity" and "might be attended with Oppression as well as injustice."

The board's proposal, "only that we should secure the payment of Sterling Debts in Sterling Money, here, or in *Great Britain*," was absurd, Pendleton said, "as we have not Sterling Specie to pay here, which the Merchants well know." Moreover, it had become clear in Virginia, as it had in Massachusetts and in all the colonies, that a paper currency had advantages. "A Payment in Paper, was preferable to one in Specie here, if such we had to pay," Pendleton continued, because a slip of paper was free to transport on the ships already carrying Virginia produce to British ports. Meanwhile, "Specie could not be sent to Britain with a loss of Freight and Ensurance," never mind the cost of procuring it in trade.

Fauquier's reply on Monday was ominous but irrelevant. He would report their "Non-Compliance" to London, he wrote. "You can blame no one but yourselves for any Consequences." There was little more to be said in Virginia. Three thousand miles away, in London, the imperial system had already changed in ways no individual colony would be able to contain. Hill's regulations, like his ideas, were bigger than Virginia. Individual colonies were no longer the arenas where battles about money would be fought. The central monetary question since 1690 had been how individual colonies, without gold and silver, might make a money to match their circumstances. The new question would be what colonial powers to preserve, to fight for, when those circumstances no longer mattered to the people making imperial laws. When money was a local matter, its relationship to imperial power could be ignored. When money was an imperial matter, it could not be. Hill's memo would provoke, in essence, a fight about the power to shape economic reality. The shape of that fight was already clear by the end of 1764's legislative session, when on top of the sugar and currency acts, Parliament declared it intended to levy a stamp tax in North America.[46]

PART TWO

The Conflict Begins

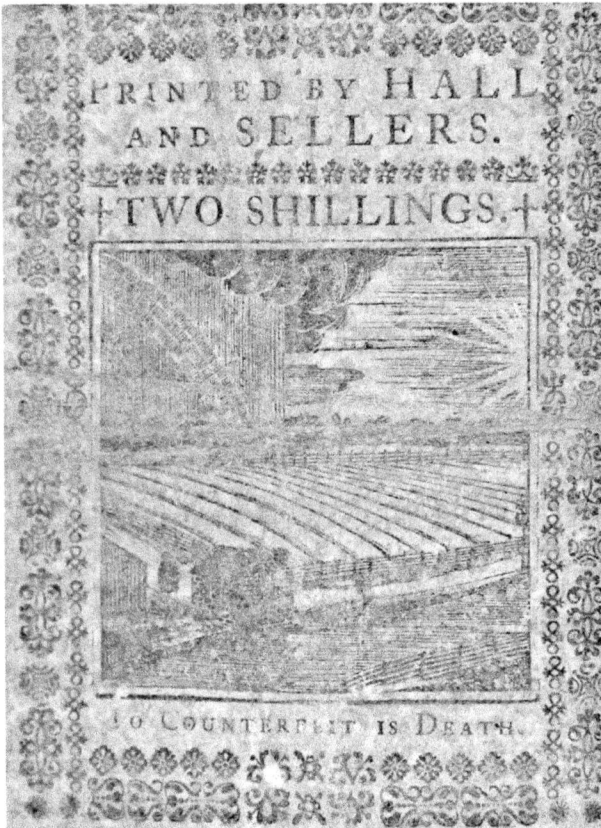

FIG. 7. Two Shillings, Pennsylvania, Reverse.

CHAPTER FOUR

The Stamp Act Crisis

LONDON AND AMERICA, 1765–1766

I. Grenville's Global Machine

The Stamp Act, proposed in 1764 and passed in 1765, precipitated a crisis. The problem was money and the way it worked in a reforming empire. Hill believed that Britain and its North American colonies had incompatible monetary systems. That was certain. But for most of British imperial history, Hill's position on bills of credit would have counted for little, if anything. Other officials had come to similar conclusions, only to find their ideas bent by intransigent reality. The colonies—for understandable structural reasons—did not have gold and silver. Bills of credit allowed them to fight for Britain as if they did. Other creditors had complained. Other officials had ruled. In 1709 the Board of Trade had declared New York's new bills of credit "an intolerable hardship upon creditors who have already lent their money or sold their goods upon covenants." However, the bills were necessary for the war effort and were allowed to stand. Hill's ideas would probably have met with a similar fate had it not been for unfortunate events and one prime minister's mandate to reconstruct the empire after its success in the Seven Years' War. These had the effect of forcing the issue and turning a monetary dispute into an imperial disaster.[1]

It started with the rise of a new generation of British money men. "The extension of commerce . . . , the improvement of the advantages we have obtained, and the increase in public revenue," the new prime minister, George Grenville, wrote in 1763, "are the proper works of peace." Grenville had tasked his aides, younger men who had followed his rise from fiscal gadfly on the naval board to a position of ultimate power within the empire, with developing a vision for what that "improvement" might look like. What they envisioned was a global machine, stretching from Boston to Bengal, with each part fitting neatly into the next. In that context, Hill's insights about the nature of money became crucial. Grenville, in accepting Hill's conclusions, had decided that whatever else it might be, a global empire must also be a currency union. For empire to work, wealth on one side of the world had to be commensurate—easily exchangeable—with wealth on the other, easily transferable from place to place. For that to happen, there had to be common understandings for what was meant by the term "money." Virginia's money problem had raised the issue. There had been no question before and thus little specificity in the laws that Parliament used to bind its empire. But the colonies' currency, their bills of credit, Grenville's close aid Thomas Whately wrote in 1765, had created a dangerous sense of unpredictability in the North Atlantic. "All Contracts became uncertain; all Returns in Trade precarious." The colonies had confused neglect for permission to do what they pleased, making of money what they willed. Specificity would not be lacking again.[2]

Hill's memo soon found its way into seemingly unrelated legislation. The Currency Act was Parliament's direct, initial response to Hill's labors. But his insight—that colonial currencies had been created on a fundamentally different, fraudulent basis—had implications for virtually every piece of colonial regulation, because it meant that when Parliament mentioned a fine, fee, or tax, it would also have to specify precisely what would be acceptable as a medium of exchange. Hill's victory, then, was conceptual. Though he had not succeeded in banning American paper currencies or eliminating the American colonies' "strange and deceitful system," he had succeeded in defining money within the bounds of Britain's empire. Laws governing that empire would be written with this new understanding of money in mind. Whatever local variations there might still be, "money," within the empire's sphere of influence, as a matter of imperial law, would mean precious metal.

The first evidence of Hill's influence appeared in the second major American bill that passed in Parliament that spring, a collection of new taxes and regulations that became known as the Sugar Act. Most of the changes related to Britain's North American colonies' trade with the Caribbean islands, which specialized in the growing and industrial processing of sugarcane using enslaved and brutally exploited African laborers. Previous imperial levies of various kinds had quoted fees in sterling, leaving to local authorities any necessary conversions. But Hill's report had proved to Whately and other parliamentary draftsmen that Whitehall's previous faith in the universal meaning of their money had been misplaced. Something stricter was necessary.[3]

The answer came in the Sugar Act's forty-fifth clause. It declared not only that the duties, penalties, and forfeitures in the act were payable in the "sterling money of *Great Britain*" but further, that by "sterling," Parliament meant metal. Whatever "monies" came in, Parliament declared, "shall and may be received and taken according to the proportion and value of five shillings and six pence the ounce in silver." Drafters borrowed the language from a 1733 law meant to prohibit molasses smuggling that colonists had deemed unworkable and largely ignored. It was a plausible precedent but entirely untested as a means of actually securing payment in North America. Fees that Americans actually paid, like those for the postal system established by Queen Anne in 1710, were levied in what the laws called "British money." In practice that meant payment could take any form, so long as postal officers were able to use them to buy bills of exchange to make payment good in London.[4] No law before 1764 had made a serious demand for silver bullion in North America. Hill's antipathy to colonial currency had begun to reshape imperial policy.[5]

The actual contents of Hill's memo approved by the Privy Council were still effectively unknown beyond a small circle of ministerial advisers to George III. The power that the memo represented—the power to reshape basic economic institutions as a foundation for a reformed British Empire—would soon be felt by millions. In the absence of direct knowledge of the memo's contents, however, the task of understanding that power, of naming it and crafting a response to it, would fall to colonial leaders. The colonists were acting at a huge disadvantage. Unaware of the ideas and assumptions behind the policies, they could only attempt to intuit them. They were feeling forward towards the unknown.

II. Henry McCulloh's Plan for Issuing Bills of Credit on a Continental Scale Goes Seriously Wrong

So too were the imperial administrators themselves. The Stamp Act began, ironically, as a proposal to produce bills of credit on a continental scale. The author was Henry McCulloh, a retired sixty-three-year-old Irish adventurer, sometime administrator "Supervising, Inspecting and Controlling His Majesty's Revenue and Grants of Lands" in North Carolina. He was also a land speculator and self-styled expert on the North American colonies. In the summer of 1763 McCulloh turned his house on

Turnham Green, on the western edges of London's sprawl, into a freelance shop writing proposals on colonial policy with little expectation of success. He had pressed administration after administration for influence, with pamphlets bearing such titles as "A miscellaneous essay concerning the courses pursued by Great Britain in the affairs of her colonies with some observations on the great importance of our settlements in America, and the trade thereof" and "The wisdom and policy of the French in the construction of their great offices, so as best to answer the purposes of extending their trade and commerce, and enlarging their foreign settlements." But McCulloh's timing, like Hill's, was perfect. This time, one of his proposals would become law.[6]

On February 10, 1763, Great Britain, France, Spain, and Portugal signed the Treaty of Paris, ending the Seven Years' War. In April the prime minister, John Stuart, the Third Earl of Bute, resigned. George III's advisers selected George Grenville to replace him because of his reputation as an expert financier. Grenville, at fifty-two, was a member of a powerful Whig family, happily married, famously frugal, and, after seven years at the Treasury and six years as treasurer of the navy, accounted as a master of British budgets. In July, Grenville and his aides were already looking for ways to tax America, when McCulloh's two latest proposals arrived in the post: The first was a plan "For creating and issuing bills of credit, under the denomination of Exchequer Bills of Union, for the general use of His Majesty's Colonies in America." The second was entitled "Proposals with respect to a Stamp Duty on America."[7]

To McCulloh's mind, the main problem with bills of credit was that they were local. Soldiers marching from one colony to another would suddenly find their wages useless, or meaningless, because the taxes that backed them only applied in their home colony. McCulloh's proposed solution was twofold. Britain, he wrote, should levy a set of taxes on all the colonies, while "creating and issuing bills of credit," which he called "Exchequer Bills of Union," that could be used to pay them. The taxes, he argued, should take the form of a "stamp tax" much like the one Britons themselves had been paying since the seventeenth century, in addition to an 18 pence levy on each enslaved person. The continental bills of credit would be printed in London and issued by officers in each colony, circulating on the basis of the tax. McCulloh expected the two taxes to pull in some £60,000 sterling worth of "bills of union" per year, allowing them to "remain a perpetual Resource for . . . Relief of the Mother Country."[8]

Grenville's aide, Charles Jenkinson, forwarded the proposal for a colonial stamp tax to Grenville himself as soon as he received it. Grenville, in turn, ordered Jenkinson and Thomas Whately, Grenville's friend, secretary, and closest adviser on imperial finance, to make further inquiries as to whether such a tax was possible. The proposal had arrived just in time. Grenville and Jenkinson had spent the previous months focused, in part, on tightening customs regulations, collecting and modernizing the duties that already existed. Their "ideas upon this Great National Concern of Establishing & collecting in a more Effectual Manner the Public Revenue in America," however—as a London Custom House official wrote that summer when asked for advice on taxing America—were still "Imperfect." Here, though, was an entirely new branch of revenue proposed by an expert on the colonies.[9]

Grenville was interested in taxing the colonies for several reasons. First and most pressing was the £249,160 hole in the British budget in 1764. This was a larger problem than its scale, against the government's £10.7 million budget for 1764, suggests. The government was used to running a deficit, but in 1764 the government had not borrowed enough to pay what it owed, leading to problems in processing payments, particularly to army contractors, who were becoming increasingly desperate. These difficulties had contributed to reasonable doubts in the new government's so-called fiscal expertise, leading to a fall in the price of British bonds in the London stock market and to the widespread belief that new taxes were coming in Britain the following year.[10]

More broadly, there were strategic and ideological imperatives at play. The first was to support the new standing army in North America, which was desperately (and ineffectively) trying to control the Native American territory ceded by the French. First, a standing army required a stable revenue, and sending money from Britain had proved ruinously expensive—a justified expense in wartime, perhaps, but inexcusable during the peace. Frustrated American paymaster George Colbrooke explained to Grenville in October 1764 that "one Hundred Pounds issued to us, at the pay office did not yield one hundred pounds in America," because "a great many per cents" were lost along the way.[11] A source of revenue in America would solve that problem. As Grenville put it in his March 1764 address to the Commons, "We have expended much in America. Let us now avail ourselves of the fruits of that expense." Second, Britain itself was suffering from a crushing debt burden that had, indeed, required heavier taxes than ever from a populace starved for coin. The national debt had risen from £73.8 million in 1756 to £129.2 million in 1764, and debt charges—mostly interest—accounted for 45 percent of the national budget. The nation was, as one commentator put it, "sufficiently exhausted already."[12]

Finally, there was a concern arising from the permanent nature of both British money and the overwhelming solidity of its national debt. The permanent nature of the British national debt, 97 percent of which, or £129.2 million, took the form of "funded" perpetual annuities, which would pay interest—derived from specific taxes—forever, seemed to necessitate some sort of permanent revenue in North America. There was no specific call, just a general sense noted by many commentators, that the permanent burden of Britain's monied interest justified some sort of American counterpart. This urge was exacerbated by what the Treasury saw as the Americans' shocking ability to pay off their own wartime debts. American colonies, according to the Board of Trade's staff analysis, had borrowed £2.52 million to support the Seven Years' War and by 1764 had paid off all but £767,865. This record suggested to Treasury officials that the colonies had hidden financial resources which could be exploited for perpetual annuities of their own, but it was based on a misconception. The "debt" that the colonies had paid off virtually all took the form of bills of credit, which the colonies "discharged" when the bills were burned. The colonies' hidden financial resource, in other words, was the temporary money that Hill at the Board of Trade and Grenville on the Privy Council had just declared a notorious fraud.[13]

The Treasury, with new experts in hand, sought to tax America in any case. McCulloh, who was in poor health, does not seem to have been well prepared for his change in circumstances. After years of irrelevance, he had stumbled into the center ring. He found himself suddenly summoned to Whitehall, where Whately wanted to know everything. Over the next year, McCulloh found himself bombarded with questions about the stamp taxes. Which legal instruments did the colonies use? Why a stamp tax and not just a tax on slaves? What rates should the government impose in the colonies as opposed to at home?[14]

Unbeknownst to McCulloh, Whately was also hounding his contacts in the colonies. The bulk of English stamp taxes fell on legal documents. Levying a similar tax in America required finding out what forms Americans used. He was finding it difficult to acquire accurate information on what those forms were. Letters to colonial governors and attorneys general wielded a blizzard of confusing, and hardly authoritative, lists. Each colony was different, each more confusing than the last. Whately decided to go around them. Years earlier, when he had worked as a lawyer, he had mingled with colonial émigrés and radical intellectuals at the Crown and Anchor, a pub on the Strand across the street from the Church of St. Clement Danes in Westminster. One of his acquaintances from those days was John Temple, a young, American-born relative of Grenville and Lord Temple who later secured a post as the customs collector for New England. On June 8, 1764, Whately wrote to Temple begging for insight into the situation and offering insider information in return. His questions revealed just how at a loss he was. McCulloh had told him that American colonies did not use the same legal forms used in Great Britain. But he didn't know which ones. "Have you any fines & recoveries?" Whately asked, "Have you any inferior Courts that hold plea to a certain sum only? What appeals have you from one Court to another? . . . What of the English duties will be burthensome? which should be omitted? Which should be lightened and why?" This was basic information, and Whately had none of it.[15]

Eventually, with the help of New York's absentee attorney general, John Taylor Kempe, he settled on sixty-three separate taxes, including fees on every pleading in civil law, new taxes on customs certificates and ship clearances, wills, deeds, bonds, and a series of brutally heavy duties on the colonial press, including a 2 shilling tax on every newspaper advertisement—the main source of American printers' revenue. The result was not really one tax but many calculated to work together, ranging from a halfpenny on half-sheet pamphlets to £10 sterling to join the colonial bar. The taxes were intentionally designed to be impossible to avoid. From an imperial perspective, George Grenville told gathered members of Parliament after introducing the taxes on February 6, 1765, the advantage of a stamp tax was that "to a great degree [it] executes itself." No new officials would be needed, aside from distributors in each colony, who would shepherd the paper, produced in official printshops in London, to the courts and customhouses that would use them. As in England, the legal nature of the stamped documents—deeds, legal pleadings, customs clearances, and debt instruments among them—would enforce compliance. "The instruments not stamped are null and void, and no person will trust" unstamped paper, Grenville observed, "especially as the case may be brought by appeal to this country" to unsympathetic courts in Great Britain. The only real concern, in terms of compliance, was fraud. "Forgery is the only fright to be apprehended, but severe penalties may prevent it," Grenville concluded. "The punishment in this country is death."[16]

With the taxes themselves settled, the question was how they might be paid. Grenville, while apparently deeply concerned that the nominal fees were not set too high, does not seem to have concerned himself with the problem directly. Whately and Jenkinson were left to figure out that detail for themselves. McCulloh's original plan, of course, had been to issue bills of credit on a continental scale that could be used to pay the tax. That was why he had come up with the stamp tax proposal in the first place. "If Funds are established to answer the Expence of Government in America, it will also be necessary to regulate the Currency in the respective Colonies, to have it the same in all," he had written. In other words, there was no point in charging taxes without providing a currency for doing so. But McCulloh's analysis does not seem to have made any impression. The idea that the tax debt itself might be used to produce a credit currency was seemingly too extreme to merit Whately's consideration, and McCulloh could not make the point in a way Whately could understand. Kempe's work made no reference to alternative currencies, and he was kept on. Whately dismissed McCulloh in November 1763.[17]

III. Grenville's Aides Work to Propose a New Means of Payment for New Stamp Taxes

With McCulloh's plan for a new currency eliminated, the options for tax payments in America were limited, and Hill's memo limited them still further. Again, the issue was time: how to find a permanent means of payment in colonies where temporary money was the norm. Again, practicality had no place in the search for an ideal solution. Those in the imperial bureaucracy who, like McCulloh, understood American monetary practices found themselves shut out of the process. The Treasury's auditor general, Robert Cholmondeley, who handled colonial quitrent payments but had no access to Hill's analysis, suggested in July 1764 that the colonies be allowed to pay in their own paper currencies at whatever rate of exchange would bring the fees back to Britain at their full sterling value. Payment in coin was impossible, because prior to the Seven Years' War, "Virginia was the only Province in North America where the circulation of foreign silver or any silver took place." Afterward, none of the colonies used silver coin. Thus "paper money" should be accepted, "in the case of all his Majesty's Quitrents & casual revenue in America," so long as it was "rated according to the current rate of bills of Exchange [payable in] England." Cholmondeley's proposal made perfect sense and was based on deep practical knowledge. He was in effect the Lowndes of his era, a powerful figure seeking to advance ministerial aims while doing the least harm. All the colonies had issued bills of credit, and all had access to bills of exchange payable in London. If Cholmondeley's plans had been adopted, there would have been no practical reason for Americans not to pay the tax. Their main objection would likely have been that imperial taxes required them to make more paper money, while their own were dedicated to burning whatever

temporary wartime bills remained. Still, were it not for Hill's determination that American paper money, with its "fraudulent" foundation, had to
be eliminated, his plan might have been accepted in London and proven
unobjectionable in America. But it was not.[18]

Unlike Cholmondeley, Whatley was well aware of the Board of Trade's
belief that American paper money was a fraud afflicting the empire. That
meant bills of credit, as a means of payment, had to be ruled out. His
concern, Whately later explained, was that any tax charged by Parliament
must have a fixed meaning, a certain value fixed to "an equal Standard,
not varying as Currencies may vary in different Colonies." He had first
encountered the problem in formulating the 1764 Sugar Act. Searching
for a precedent in colonial legislation, he had hit upon the language used
thirty years earlier, which had charged duties in "sterling money . . . to the
proportion and value of five shillings and six pence the ounce in silver."
He had copied the language, first into the amended act regulating colonial sugar trade in 1764, and then directly into the legislation that would
become known as the Stamp Act.[19] "I will venture to say," Whately wrote,
"that in every Revenue Law for *America*, some similar Clause must be
inserted." Anything else, he argued, would be "absurd." Cholmondeley's
warning, that none of the colonies actually had silver in circulation to pay
a tax, apparently carried less weight than Hill's ideas.[20]

The silver clause in the Stamp Act seems innocuous. Yet there are few
moments in American or British history more momentous than Whatley's
decision, with the stroke of a pen, to reject everything that the most knowl-
edgeable people in the British government knew about American money.
He must have known that it was a risk, as his later defensiveness strongly
implied. In order to take it, he must have on some level believed that Hill's
analysis was correct. If American money was a fraud, not an institutional
response to colonial needs, it stood to reason that they were hiding their
real money, their silver and gold. If that was right, his taxes would coax
it out. Moreover, as Whatley later explained in great detail, he and the ministry had no plans to ship whatever coin they acquired through the stamp
taxes to Britain. Sending it home would only mean having "to send it back
again" at great expense. Tax receipts would stay in America where they
would be used to pay for the troops occupying formerly French territory.
The only question was whether Americans had the silver in the first place.[21]

McCulloh knew better. His plan had combined new taxes with new
means to pay them. To move forward with one and not the other was
senseless. "Several other matters ought to have been taken into Consideration previous to passing the late Stamp Duty Act," McCulloh wrote to

Thomas Townshend after the final act was published, "especially as there is not Specie in most of the said Colonies to Enable the people Settled there to Pay in Specie the several Duties required from them So that under their present Circumstances it is impossible for many of the Colonists to pay obedience to the said Law," whether they wanted to or not. McCulloh could see an eruption coming, an insurrection against taxes that would prove impossible to pay. As a whole, McCulloh concluded in his last statement before returning to retirement, the Stamp Act amounted to "a dress of Horror."[22]

IV. Benjamin Franklin Intuits Incorrectly That the Stamp Taxes Are Part of a Larger Plan

When Pennsylvania's agent in London, Richard Jackson, wrote Benjamin Franklin about Grenville's plan for a Stamp Act in June 1764, Franklin intuited that the plan might be the beginning of a continent-wide currency. That would make sense given Parliament's new paper currency regulations. Restrictions on American currency might be a prelude to an imperial replacement. A continent-wide tax, though, was not the best method, he thought. "I think I could propose a better Mode by far, both for us and for you," Franklin wrote Jackson on June 25, 1764.[23]

A full discussion, however, would have to wait for Franklin's arrival in London in December. But by the time he arrived, London's American circles were abuzz with discussion of the proposed stamp taxes. Franklin shifted focus. Grenville, typical for a first minister, had refused to provide details. All was mystery. Franklin, though, managed to secure a meeting with Grenville on February 2, 1765, at his chambers in Whitehall along with Jackson; Charles Garth, who represented Georgia and South Carolina; and Jared Ingersoll, the just-arrived agent for Connecticut sent to protest molasses taxes passed the previous year. Garth and Jackson were both MPs.

At the meeting, Grenville was politely apologetic about the secrecy around his tax plans, telling the agents that "he took no Pleasure in giving the Americans so much Uneasiness as he found he did," Ingersoll recalled. Grenville told the Americans' representatives that he considered taxing the colonies a matter of duty. He had given his word to Parliament the previous year, promising a new tax to defray the costs of stationing troops in North America. Now, he was doing his best to come up with a way of doing so that was efficient and equitable.[24]

In Franklin's recollection, Grenville had asked for help. "Can you Gentlemen that are Agents name any Mode of Raising Money for Publick

Service that the People would have less Objection to, if we should agree to drop this bill?" Grenville asked the agents. Franklin took this as a confirmation of his suspicions. The new taxes, like the Currency Act, were part of a new plan for creating an imperial currency for North America. Franklin's confusion, for all his intelligence, experience, and savvy, is easy to understand. For Franklin, "Raising Money" in America meant creating bills of credit. He had suspected something similar before, and now his intuition was confirmed. What else could Grenville mean? There was no gold and silver in North America or, in any case, not enough that it could be raised in sufficient quantity to support the troops. He took Grenville's question as a confirmation that the stamp tax was meant to serve as a "debit" that would allow the ministry to create continental bills of credit—exactly what McCulloh, unbeknownst to Franklin, had proposed. Franklin took Grenville's request for help as an admission that the prime minister did not know precisely how a new currency would work. This was not surprising. Few, if any, British ministers understood how bills of credit worked as a practical matter. Thus, Franklin felt "encourag'd," he later wrote, "to present him," Grenville, "with a plan for [a] General Loan Office in America."[25]

Franklin also took his happy suspicion to Thomas Pownall, a former governor of Massachusetts now serving as the Treasury's London paymaster for British forces in Germany. The two set to work. Ten days later they had a draft based on Pennsylvania's 1739 plan to expand its own loan office. Their plan was to open loan offices in every colony in North America, offering new, imperial bills of credit in return for mortgages on colonial land. On February 12 they sent it to Grenville. This, they wrote, was just the alternative Grenville was looking for. By "supplying the Colonies with a Paper Currency" as was "absolutely necessary," the loan offices would also provide a "certain and very considerable Revenue" to the crown. Grenville would be "Raising Money," indeed.[26]

The next day, February 13, the Stamp Act received its first full reading in Parliament, with each clause specifying that the duties would be levied in sterling money. Grenville, it seemed, was not, in fact, open to bold colonial ideas. Still, details were lacking, and Franklin was optimistic that the Stamp Act was part of a larger "Scheme" to provide a paper currency. On February 14 he wrote John Ross, an ally in the Pennsylvania Assembly, that while he was certain a stamp act would pass, "The Parliament will however ease us in some Particulars relating to our Commerce; a Scheme is under Consideration, to furnish us a Currency, without which we can neither pay Debts nor Duties." He was hopeful because it was the only option. Without a currency, he knew, Americans could not pay the tax. The truth was still inconceivable: that Franklin had misunderstood Grenville on February 2. For Grenville, "Raising Money" meant raising gold and silver. Franklin knew that was impossible in Pennsylvania. He could not believe that Grenville, with all his power, did not know it as well. Also, he needed Grenville to be wise. Franklin's purpose in coming to London was to submit a petition that would remove Pennsylvania from control of the Penn family and place it under Grenville's control. It would be two long years before Franklin learned the reason why he was mistaken, how the Privy Council, with Grenville at its head, had approved Hill's memo, ruling that Pennsylvania's monetary system was a fraud.[27]

V. Parliament Passes the Stamp Act with Little Opposition

The House of Commons passed the Stamp Act on February 27, 1765. The debate that preceded it was one of the most memorable in that body's long history. William Beckford, an MP who had made his fortune by enslaving and working to death hundreds of African transportees in his sugar factories in Jamaica, worried that the tax had "no precedent." Others worried that Grenville, ultimately, had no sense of the forces he was playing with. When Grenville had met with the American representatives weeks earlier, Ingersoll recalled, they had suggested that the colonies were too poor to pay the tax. "He said we told him we were poor, and unable to bear such Tax," while "others told him were we well able," Ingersoll recalled. "Now, says he, take the Business into your own Hands, you will see how and where it pinches, and will certainly let us know it, in which Case it shall be eased." Grenville likely meant his statement as a sop to his guests, but it was revealing. It suggested that he too was unsure of the outcome. He was willing to bet, but as several MPs rose to point out, he seemed unaware of what he and the empire might lose.[28]

Col. Isaac Barré rose to say that he worried that the ministry was "working in the dark." The son of Huguenot refugees, like Fauquier, Barré had lost an eye in the final assault on Quebec in 1759 before being elected to Parliament two years later and still had a lead ball lodged in his cheek. His voice carried weight. We have the power to tax and the right to do so, Barré continued, but he worried that if "the power be abused, the right" might be "subverted." Charles Townshend objected that if the colonies were excluded from taxation, then Parliament "must give up the word 'colony'" for North America, "for that implies subordination." The power to tax was an index of imperium in North America. Grenville replied that he agreed with Townshend. The taxes were about the principle that "Privileges and burdens must go together."[29]

Barré objected that the question was not one of "sovereignty" but of whether levying a tax on people that Parliament did not understand was a good idea in the first place. The empire was placing a huge bet, in effect, on the notion that Hill was right, that the colonies' currency was a "deliberate fraud" and that they, in fact, had the means to pay taxes in the silver bullion Parliament wanted. Grenville himself had admitted as much to Franklin and the other agents the week before. Townshend rose to defend Grenville. There was no doubt that the Americans were prosperous enough to contribute to the empire, Townshend argued. The question was whether Parliament had the nerve to make them. "And now these Americans, children planted by our care, nourished by our indulgence . . . and protected by our arms, will they grudge to contribute their mite to relieve us from the heavy weight of the burden which we lie under?" But that was not the point. The question was one of knowledge, essentially, whether the colonies could in fact pay the taxes on terms Grenville's team had devised. The money question was still unanswered. Townshend's remarks, to Barré, revealed just how ignorant his fellow ministers were. His angry, improvised response would become famous.[30]

"They planted by your care? No! Your oppressions planted them in America. They fled from your tyranny to a then uncultivated and inhospitable country—where they exposed themselves to almost all the hardships to which human nature is liable, and among others the cruelties of a savage foe, the most subtle and I take upon me to say the most formidable of any people upon the face of God's Earth. And yet, actuated by the principles of true English liberty, they met all these hardships with pleasure, compared with those they suffered in their own country, from the hands of those who should have been their friends.

"They nourished by your care? No! They grew by your neglect of them: as soon as you began to care about them, that care was exercised by sending persons to rule over them . . . to spy out their liberty, to misrepresent their actions and to prey upon them; men whose behaviour on many occasions has caused the blood of those Sons of Liberty to recoil within them." The House was stunned. and Barré still wasn't done. "They protected by your arms? They have nobly taken up arms in your defense, have exerted a valour amidst their constant and laborious industry for the defense of a country, whose frontier, while drenched in blood, its interior parts have yielded all its little savings to your emolument.

"And believe me," Barré concluded, "remember I this day told you so, that same spirit of freedom which actuated that people at first, will accompany them still." Other ministers might understand policy better, Barré continued, but they did not understand America as well as he, who had traveled and "been conversant in that country. The people I believe are as truly loyal as any subjects the King has, but a people jealous of their liberties and who will vindicate them, if ever they should be violated, but the subject is too delicate and I will say no more." Other members congratulated Barré afterward on his speech. Some, violating the secrecy of parliamentary debate, made sure that Barré's speech made it to printers in America. It mattered little in Whitehall. The next morning, ministers voted 250 to 50 to approve the tax. The House of Lords approved it on March 8, and King George III granted it his assent on March 22. The empire was moving ahead "in the dark."[31]

VI. An Unforeseen Monetary Crisis of Empire

When the Stamp Act was finally published, it accomplished something quite unlike any imperial legislation that preceded it. Most parliamentary legislation was based, at some basic level, on shared premises. People on both sides of the British Atlantic had much in common: a common language, legal tradition, religious convictions, and political allegiances. What became known in later years as the radical republican tradition in American thought was, in fact, a shared tradition—at least as popular in London and Liverpool as it was in Charleston or Philadelphia. The same could be said of clothing, foodways, accounting methods, and much, much more. Americans, if pressed, thought of themselves as British or Englishmen abroad. In virtually all ways, Americans in 1765 had far more in common with their average British counterparts than they had in the seventeenth century, when many migrants to North America had fled because of heterodox religious beliefs and arrived as would-be conquerors, homeless and hated, in a foreign world. They used the same tools, read the same books, spoke the same language. "On the eve of the American Revolution" they were, more than one historian has argued, "more English than they had been in the past since the first years of the colonies." Thus, when Parliament passed a law, it expected it to have the same meaning, the same appearance and efficacy, on one side of the Atlantic as it had on the other.[32]

Money was the great exception. American money and British money had diverged in the 1690s and never reconverged in the decades since.

Despite the efforts of Hill at the Board of Trade and local reformers like Thomas Hutchinson in Massachusetts, if anything, American and British monetary cultures had grown more distinct, not less, as the century wore onward. By 1765, money—as a way of maintaining and establishing relationships between people and between citizens and the state—had come to have distinctly different meanings on either side of the Atlantic, with distinct vocabularies, institutions, and folkways to match. Moreover, as the career of the Fauquier family shows in miniature, the process was not one-sided. Britain had strayed as far or farther from its seventeenth-century roots as a monetary society as its American colonies had. And they had both been pulling in different directions.

Merchants who traded in the Atlantic knew this. In 1765 the accountancy teacher John Wright devoted a very popular book to the topic called *The American Negotiator*. Despite the "flourishing" trade between Britain and North America, Wright wrote, merchants were still shocked to learn that money was not the same on one side of the Atlantic as on the other. The colonies, he observed, with some understatement, "varied greatly in the way of Reckoning their Monies, or Currencies, from what has been by Law established in *England* or *Great-Britain*."[33]

But, as we have seen, the British government—at its ministerial core—was either unaware of or hostile to this great commercial fact. To be sure, the parts of the government that dealt directly with colonial money, the customs bureaucracy and quitrent collectors, knew the American situation very well. But their advice was either ignored or twisted to suit the Grenville and Hill agenda for a united imperial monetary standard. They did so not through a purposeful extension of British institutions—banks, mints, or the creation of a truly imperial currency (a policy that, as Franklin's and McCulloh's work suggests, might have been popular with some, perhaps most colonists)—but by denying the basic validity of its colonies' temporary monetary form, coupled with a systematic misreading of colonial fiscal practice. The combination of ignorance and philosophical hostility suggests a policy of currency union through conceptual conversion. One gets no sense from Grenville's or Whatley's letters or position papers that there was any real malice involved. Quite the opposite. They were doing their best to make the taxes as painless and easy as possible. Like missionaries of a jealous god, they simply did not understand what they were doing.[34]

What they had done was to produce a document that would be read completely differently on one side of the Atlantic than it would be on the other. In Britain, the Stamp Act read as a reasonable list of relatively light taxes on printed literature and legal fees. The silver clause, charging the fees in silver bullion valued by the ounce, read as pro forma. Silver, or at least an ideal representation of silver, *was* money in Britain. In America, silver was a barrier. There, the same law looked like a list of prohibitions, fees barring anyone without access to precious metal from some of the most basic institutions of empire, the courts, the land, and the press. It read to many as a wall set between British subjects in North America and Britishness itself, and, as such, an almost unbelievable provocation.

VII. Virginia Judge John Mercer Gets One of the First Copies of the Stamp Act

In Virginia, the burgesses were still in session when the first copy of the Stamp Act arrived on April 8. A British correspondent had copied the act's text into a private letter to John Mercer. Mercer, the sixty-year-old chief justice of Stafford County, had been born in Dublin and immigrated to Virginia in 1720. There, he had become an expert on legal procedure, editing the first published collection of Virginia's laws. He immediately understood the threat that the Stamp Act represented. Within two days, amid the carousing, horse racing, and bickering of the legislative session, when Williamsburg's population swelled to twice its usual size, Mercer had written up an alphabetical list of the new taxes, hoping to make them "more intelligible" than the confusing list of duties contained in the actual act.[35]

Mercer summarized his position in a preface that consisted of three barking paragraphs. By the war and by British contractors, Virginians had been "stripped of our Gold and Silver, and . . . obliged to substitute Paper in it's [*sic*] Room." And now, "reduced to the extremest Necessity, we are expected yearly to find a larger Sum of Sterling Money, for procuring common Justice in our Courts of Law and Equity, than this Colony could ever have raised in their most flourishing Circumstances." The Magna Carta, Mercer wrote, promised that the British would never sell, deny, or delay right or justice. But the Stamp Act, by placing new fees on courts, meant that justice would indeed be sold, and "at a Price that not one in a Hundred will be able to pay the Purchase Money; poor Americans!" He advised the *Virginia Gazette* and every other press in the colonies to raise the alarm: "Before your Press is stopped, which I doubt [not] will shortly be the Case," by the new fees.[36]

The taxes "reduced" Americans "to a worse Condition than the Israelites" in Egypt, Mercer wrote. In Exodus 5, pharaoh ordered the Israelites to bake bricks without providing straw, an impossible task. Imposing it was the definition of tyranny. But Parliament had done something worse. "There was Straw in Egypt, but no Sterling Money to be gathered in Virginia, and I am afraid no *Moses* or *Aaron* on Hand to Deliver us."[37]

Mercer believed that the Stamp Act represented tyranny. He had no problem with being taxed by Parliament per se. The problem was silver. He was a hemp farmer. If he had been taxed in hemp, he wrote, he would not have protested the law. What he objected to was a tax so wrongheaded, so ignorant, so pharaonic that it would bring all of colonial government, along with its presses and its courts, to a halt.[38]

Mercer's essay was soon the talk of the town. His letter was passed around, read, and reread. Most seemed confused about what exactly to do. Perhaps Mercer's correspondent was wrong. Perhaps he overstated the problem. That changed at the end of the session, at the instigation of a twenty-eight-year-old country lawyer who had only been elected a few weeks earlier named Patrick Henry. Though inexperienced as a legislator, Henry was already adept at rendering currency problems in political terms.

Henry had made a name for himself by pulling a similar trick in the locally celebrated case of the Parson's Cause, the year before. There, the issue was the shift from tobacco notes to bills of credit for preachers' pay. In 1758 the burgesses voted to pay Anglican ministers in Virginia bills of credit rather than a set weight of tobacco. They set the conversion at the low but reasonably accurate market price of 2 pence Virginian per pound. Each parson would get roughly £133 in bills rather than notes representing 16,000 pounds of tobacco. The Virginia clergy objected both because they had misgivings about Virginia currency and because wartime prices for tobacco had soared. The king's Privy Council had ruled in the parsons' favor. The case, the Parson's Cause, was set to determine what, if any, damages were owed the parson of Hanover County.[39]

The issue, for Henry, was whether the king had the right to annul Virginian laws. In Henry's opinion, he did not: "A King, by disallowing Acts of this salutary nature, from being the father of his people, degenerated into a Tyrant, and forfeits all rights to his subjects' obedience," Henry told the jury. An opposing lawyer yelled "treason!" but Henry kept right on "in the same treasonable and licentious strain," a witness recalled. The jury agreed with Henry. It awarded the aggrieved parson one penny in damages, and Henry became a local hero. Little more than a year later, he became a burgess.[40]

In late May, Henry set about applying the same logic to the Stamp Act. Working with other younger members of the House, including George Johnston, John Fleming, and Robert Munford, he worked up a list of resolves that sifted the most politically volatile elements from Mercer's analysis. Gone were the central but ultimately quotidian references to precious metals. Gone too the biblical references. For Henry, the Stamp Act's demand for the impossible justified a positive assertion of Virginian power to resist such an imposition. The burgesses, Henry and his friends wrote, "have the only and sole exclusive right and power to lay taxes and impositions upon the inhabitants of this colony." Any outside interference with that right, by "any person or persons whatsoever," they wrote, "have a manifest tendency to destroy *British* as well as *American* freedom." Henry waited until most of the burgesses, including Mercer, had left town before, on May 29, bringing his resolves to the floor. The House passed the five resolves—the last and most radical by just one vote. Thomas Jefferson and a crowd of other young Virginians swarmed at the door as Henry, over cries of "treason!" shouted, "If this be treason, make the most of it!" When Henry left the next day, the remaining burgesses repealed the resolve mentioning American freedom, but the point had been made. The impossibility of paying the new taxes had pried open colonial politics, creating space for a new, as yet inchoate radicalism. Henry's resolves gave that radicalism a voice.[41]

VIII. Virginia's Analysis Spreads North

News of Virginia's resolves spread north, overland through Maryland, Pennsylvania, and by ship to New England. The Northern Colonies were just emerging from what, from their perspective, had been a brutal postwar depression. Treasury payments for troops and supplies had visibly increased the wealth of trading cities like New York, Providence, Philadelphia, and Boston, but its traders had overextended themselves in the process, borrowing heavily from British traders in the expectation of ongoing Treasury payments. "By the Ceasing of War several Sources of the current Wealth of this Province will be shut up," Massachusetts governor Francis Bernard warned his constituents on May 25, 1762. It would prove necessary, he continued, "to revive and promote a Spirit of Industry, Frugality and Oeconomy, all of which have been of late too much relaxed, by an unusual flow of Money," parliamentary silver, "much exceeding what could naturally arise."[42]

His warning proved prescient. When those payments dried up, due to the new administration's belt-tightening measures and the actual lack of ongoing hostilities, it created a massive demand for means of overseas payment: bills of exchange for London credit and foreign coin. Bills of exchange were the cheapest to send abroad and disappeared first. Gold and silver went next. Internally, the taxing and burning of most bills of credit worked to parallel effect. Merchants who managed to pay their debts could relax, trading on credit with known partners for goods in kind. Those who could not, failed.[43]

As supply dried up, demand for silver abroad was growing. American merchants were fielding increasingly strident orders from Europe. The case of Samuel Abbot, a Boston-based merchant, was typical. In the last years of the war, when Parliament was showering the colonies in specie, Abbot had extended credit generously across New England and prospered doing so. In 1764 Abbot's British creditors began to press him for coin—a serious matter, as his business depended on their credit and goodwill.[44] But by 1765 his cash supply was nearly gone. He was worth £35,000 in Old Tenor—an accounting standard that had been popular in his youth—but had only £210, or £21 sterling, in gold and silver. This was a dangerous position. He could neither send silver abroad nor purchase increasingly expensive London credit at home. The only solution was to press his debtors in turn, wheedling, cajoling, and threatening them to pay up.[45] Others were similarly threatened. "Money we have not in specie; that is all gone to England in remittances," Daniel Coxe, a merchant in Trenton, New Jersey, wrote to an American friend in London on April 12, 1764. "[The British] need not send tax gatherers, for they can gather nothing—never was money so very scarce as now."[46] When Rhode Island governor Stephen Hopkins heard that a Stamp Act was planned, his immediate thought was of the debts already coming due. In his colony, "as fast the money can be collected, 'tis immediately sent out of the country." But debts, like bills of credit, were temporary. British taxes, like British money, were for always. "Think then, what must be the condition of these miserable colonies, when all the money proposed to be raised in them, by high duties . . . is sent quite away, as fast as it can be collected; and this to be repeated continually forever!"[47]

For those who dealt in precious metals on a regular basis like New York merchant John Watts, the shortage of specie in 1765 was a pressing matter of fact. As early as the fall of 1763, Watts was informing his correspondents that gold and silver, which had been relatively abundant in the last years of the war, had become "extremely scarce."[48] By December he reported regretfully, "the Trade has swept off all the Gold & Silver for remittances."[49] Bills of exchange on London were in such high demand, Watts reported, that all merchants were collecting specie to send instead, but there was little to be had.[50]

Watts was shocked, then, by the demand for silver in the Stamp Act. For him, the oppression it represented was a matter of professional expertise. In April 1765 he wrote to a correspondent that while he acknowledged "The Supreme Authority of the Legislature" in Parliament, trade was such that Americans had "No Money to carry us thro." Again, money could have only meant silver. Watts grew increasingly frustrated with parliamentary demands, which he labeled "so unintelligible . . . it would puzzle a Newton." There was a "real Scarcity of Money," he protested, but British "wise ones who know Nothing of the Colonies . . . and are regardless of what they do know, not content with what the Colonys have got, want to ruin them for what they have not got."[51]

For many in the northern colonies, then, the news of the Stamp Act induced something like disbelief. Few could believe that Parliament intended what it seemed to intend with the Stamp Act: to take something from them that they didn't have, much less respond to it. In this relative vacuum, Henry's resolves provided a framework for thought. The story was garbled in the retelling. The *Newport Mercury* reprinted six resolves on June 24, omitting the third, including the repealed fifth, and adding two more that had not been approved. But Henry's thinking lost none of its force. Within days, copies were circulating in Boston where, Governor Bernard lamented, it was "inconceivable how they have roused up the Boston Politicians." In Annapolis on July 9, an Irish spy at dinner with a Philadelphia merchant noted that the first toast of the night was to the Virginia Assembly rather than George III. The resolves were less significant for what they said than for the fact that they said them first. Many colonists were independently reaching similar conclusions: that the Stamp Act justified a reconsideration of the relationship between the colonies and parliamentary authority.[52]

Slowly, though, shock gave way to a search for allies. On June 6, 1765, the Massachusetts House of Representatives concluded that there was little point in acting on its own, without the support of the other continental colonies. Rather, they concluded, the best course of action was to ask other colonies "to consult together on the present Circumstances of the Colonies, and the Difficulties to which they are and must be reduced by the operation of the late Acts of Parliament for levying Duties and Taxes on the Colonies." They proposed inviting representatives from all the colonies to meet in New York City in early October, to compare perspectives and write a combined statement of their concerns to Parliament and the king. The British ministry had made clear it would not listen to individual colonies, they reasoned. It would not be able to ignore all of them.[53]

IX. Pennsylvania Lawyer John Dickinson's Career Crashes alongside the Postwar Economy

Riding through Reading, Carlisle, Bethlehem, York, and Lancaster that summer, the lawyer, writer, and occasional politician John Dickinson gained a firsthand glimpse at the consequences of what was an already extreme shortage of money. Dickinson was born in Talbot County, Maryland, in 1732 and raised in Kent County, Delaware. He was the oldest son of wealthy, slave-owning Quakers. He was thin and frail as a child but obviously gifted. When he was twenty-two, after four years of study in Philadelphia, his family sent him to study law in London at the Middle Temple, one of the most prestigious law schools in Britain. The Middle Temple had once been the London headquarters of the Knights Templar, and it retained some of its medieval grandeur. Dickinson would walk the yards, dine in its lofty, hammer-beamed hall, and read in the libraries, dreaming of becoming another Edward Coke or one of the other lofty English jurists that had preceded him. He spent nights in London pubs and clubs meeting radical thinkers with ambitions like his own. After returning to America, he was elected to the Delaware legislature at twenty-six, became its speaker at twenty-eight, and at thirty joined the Pennsylvania Assembly as a leading voice of the Proprietary Party, a major rival to Franklin himself.[54]

By 1765, though, his career in politics had flamed out. Monetary politics were to blame. The colony had more than doubled its supply of bills of credit during the Seven Years' War. It had funded this expansion with a tax on land. As it turned out, some of the taxes fell on unimproved lands owned by John Penn, the colony's hereditary absentee proprietor. Penn refused to pay. His bill would have come to less than £500 a year, but there was a principle at stake. As proprietor, Penn received taxes. He did not pay them. He also refused to accept bills of credit in payment for his quitrents, quasifeudal dues that colonists still owed his family. Franklin and his friends argued that Penn's refusal justified throwing the proprietor out and assenting to royal rule. Dickinson, who had long claimed Penn as a patron, disagreed. Royal rule would mean rule by Parliament, and Parliament could not be trusted to sympathize with Pennsylvania institutions any more than Penn did. "Certainly the *British* parliament will not do what they think an unjust act," Dickinson told his fellow legislators, "but I cannot persuade myself, that *they* will think it unjust, to place us on the same footing with themselves." In other words, royal rule would mean that the legislature would be stripped of its power over Pennsylvania. The colonists would be subject to the same laws, the same taxes, the same rules and regulations as the British. Dickinson admitted that Penn was imperfect, but Parliament, he argued, would be worse. Even Dickinson's enemies conceded that it was a good speech, but it made no friends. Franklin was unmoved, and Penn, miffed, cut off his patronage. Without allies he was unelectable. Rather than face a humiliating defeat, Dickinson withdrew his name from consideration for the legislature in early 1765 and retired to his law practice.[55]

That July found him riding from courthouse to courthouse, county seat to county seat, choked by the dust from drying fields of barley, oats, and flax. No rain had fallen since May, except, he wrote his mother "a little Sprinkling while I was in Bethlehem." His horse was starving; the grass was dried to stubble. His cases were depressing.[56] Debts contracted during the Seven Years' War were coming due, and many were in default because debtors couldn't find enough in coin or bills of credit to pay them. The result was a "terrible crush."[57]

Everyone felt it. Merchants in Philadelphia and London hired lawyers like Dickinson to pursue their creditors in county courts. If their creditors couldn't pay, their assets would be auctioned to the highest bidder. Big merchants pressed country stores, who pressed farmers with few cash reserves. The colony's loan office had been invented to prevent just such an eventuality. But the Currency Act prevented the loan office from operating, just as Penn's personal tax revolt prevented the colony from creating new bills of credit. The result was a wave of bankruptcies and sheriff's auctions, a boon to a lawyer like Dickinson, but a worrying one. As a legislator, he had thought of parliamentary mismanagement as a distant possibility. Now his fears were becoming reality. And on top of those concerns came the Stamp Act.[58]

X. Popular Violence Spreads in American Seaports

Americans were already frustrated when the Stamp Act arrived. The postwar slump had frayed nerves, and Parliament's ham-fisted attempts at reform had hurt, not helped. The taxes were a final straw, impossibility added to insult. As the monetary details of the proposed tax spread, the colonists became enraged. But by late summer, the stamp distributors in each colonial capital were known. They soon became targets of mob action. By late summer, crowds protesting the act dominated the streets of colonial capitals. Officials describing the events in hurried letters to London emphasized the way that taxes charged in silver had stirred every segment of the colonial population. The crowds included sailors, whose ships would remain docked as long as silver fees went unpaid, merchants who couldn't collect debts without courts charging silver fees, and propertyless men caught in the postwar slump. Colonists who would otherwise regard one another warily across divides of class or religion had found a common cause.

The taxes also had the effect of bringing together colonies that had little in common beyond their shared membership in the North American monetary bloc. Notables such as John Hancock in Massachusetts and George Washington in Virginia suddenly had a vital common interest. Both warned correspondents in London that the taxes would be devastating. "No, Gentlemen," Hancock wrote his British creditors, "there is not cash enough here to support it, and pray where are we when our Cash is gone or indeed where will you obtain your remittances?" Washington worried that the new fees on court cases would make it impossible for local magistrates to function. "Our Courts of Judicature must inevitably be shut up," George Washington wrote to Francis Dandridge, "for it is impossible (or next of kin to it) under our present Circumstances that the Act of Parliamt (sic) can be complyd with were we ever so willing to enforce the execution." Colonists did not have the silver to pay the tax, but they would not be the only ones affected by it, Washington noted: "if a stop be put to our Judicial proceedings I fancy the Merchants of G. Britain trading to the Colonies will not be among the last to wish for a Repeal of it." The remarkable thing about the Stamp Act was the way it dissolved barriers of class and position, uniting the colonists in opposition, because none of them had the silver.[59]

In Boston, on two nights in August, crowds gathered to protest the act. Their targets were the act's supposed supporters, though in fact even colonial leaders were opposed to it. On August 14, after gathering under a broad elm near Boston Common they dubbed the Liberty Tree, the crowd headed for the port. First they tore down a new building meant, they believed, to house the stamped paper. Then they turned on stamp distributor Andrew Oliver's house. The crowd ransacked it, burning its picket fence along with effigies of Oliver and Lord Bute, in a bonfire intended as "a burnt offering . . . for the sins of the people which had caused such heavy judgments as the Stamp Act, etc. to be laid upon them," and drinking the contents of Oliver's cellar. Oliver publicly resigned his post three days later. He and other officials had seen both wealthy and poor in the mobs. The crowds in Boston, the governor wrote, were "so general . . . so supported that all Civil Power ceased in an Instant."

From there the crowd turned on officials who were rumored to have brought the Stamp Act upon them. On August 26 a crowd attacked the house of Thomas Hutchinson, chief justice and lieutenant governor, and gutted it, smashing doors and windows, and confiscating Hutchinson's silver plate along with some £900 sterling in coin. The crowd was still busy tearing the slate shingles from Hutchinson's roof as the sun rose. Hutchinson, it later turned out, had tried to prevent the Stamp Act, but the mob's point was made. Mere wealth would not be enough to protect the few who could afford to pay the new taxes.[60]

In New London, Connecticut, protesters gathered under their liberty tree, sang songs, and performed homemade skits that played on the now-ubiquitous imagery of the stamps as "Egyptian bondage" pioneered by Mercer. Their local target was Jared Ingersoll, who had reluctantly agreed to serve as stamp distributor after going to London to protest the Sugar Act. "Instead of coming home with answers of peace, lenity, and good-will towards us, he, comes inhumanly with a variety of Stamp duties . . . proclaiming sacrifice, sacrifice unto me," local poet Benjamin Church declaimed in front of Ingersoll's flaming effigy. "Bring your silver and gold (for I know not the paper money of your colony)," Church continued. Later, horsemen confronted Ingersoll on his way to the Connecticut Assembly. They forced him to resign, forfeiting a £3,000 sterling bond he had given in England in the process. Their protests were justified, Ingersoll admitted. The tax might rase £4,000 in Connecticut, he reported to London in September, but "it was a doubt with me, whether we even had that Sum in the Colony, in what we call Hard Money, i.e. Gold and Silver Coin."[61]

In Maryland, stamp distributor Zachariah Hood was forced to flee to Long Island, New York, where a group of "volunteers" soon caught up with him and forced him to resign. Local protesters had already pulled his house to the ground. In Pennsylvania, Franklin's opponents, believing he had backed the act or even planned it, schemed to pull down his house as well; they were only stopped by another mob of his friends. When stamps finally arrived in the city on a British warship on October 5, muffled bells tolled, and flags hung at half-mast. A crowd led by some of the most prominent city leaders, including Franklin's allies, forced the stamped paper to remain on the ships that brought it, effectively nullifying the act.[62]

In Virginia, things reached a head in October when the stamp distributor George Mercer arrived in Williamsburg with a cargo of stamped paper. He arrived three days before the act was to go into effect on November 1. As he walked from his lodgings toward the capitol, a crowd that had gathered at Christiana Campbell's Tavern on Waller Street confronted him. They asked what he planned to do. John Mercer, George's father, had already stated publicly that he would resign as a judge rather than enforce the act. Like Ingersoll, Mercer had given a £3,000 bond on accepting the post. He would forfeit a fortune if he resigned.

The question implied a threat. Mercer retreated toward the tavern and the crowd followed, showering him with demands. Fauquier and a group of the wealthiest men in the colony had emerged onto a porch to see the commotion. Seeing Fauquier, the crowd backed away. Fauquier personally escorted Mercer to the governor's mansion, where they discussed possible next steps. Fauquier told Mercer that his father and brother were "frighted out of their Senses for him." He relented. At five o'clock the next day, Mercer mounted the steps of the capitol and vowed not to enforce the act without "the assent of the General Assembly of this colony." On November 1 both Virginia courts and ports shut down rather than pay the duties. Debt collections were suspended indefinitely. All was in "a State of general Outlawry," Fauquier wrote, and he was "at a Loss to form a Judgment of how to proceed."[63]

In Wilmington, North Carolina, an evening of bonfires, toasts, effigy burnings, and a mock funeral gave way to action after Dr. William Houston, to his surprise, discovered he had been appointed to distribute the stamps. A mob escorted him to the courthouse, where he was forced to resign. Afterward, the crowd placed Houston in an armchair on their shoulders and paraded around the building, offering three cheers at each corner before returning to the tavern for drinks.[64]

In Charleston, Governor William Bull hid the stamps on a naval vessel. On October 23 several hundred protesters armed with clubs and cutlasses surrounded the house of stamp distributor Henry Laurens, where he was asleep with his ill and pregnant wife, Eleanor Ball. They shouted "LIBERTY, LIBERTY, STAMPED PAPER" and demanded access to his house. Laurens, after recognizing men in the crowd, eventually let them search it. Not finding the stamps, the crowd gave Laurens three cheers and went home calling, "God bless your honor, Good night Colonel, We hope the poor lady will do well."[65]

XI. Massachusetts's Early Call for a Colonial Congress Bears Fruit

Massachusetts's call for a colonial "congress" in New York gathered momentum along with the protests. Every colonial legislature that was able to meet that summer sent delegates. Only Georgia, North Carolina, and Virginia were missing because their governors had not allowed emergency meetings to choose representatives. New Hampshire could not afford to send anyone. In Philadelphia, the Pennsylvania Assembly gathered in September to select delegates. Someone suggested Dickinson. It is not hard to imagine why. The money issue was front and center, and he was available. All but three of the colonies that sent delegates explicitly justified the congress as a chance to consult on "the present Circumstances of the Colonies and the Difficulties to which they are and must be reduced" by a tax that was impossible to pay.[66]

The delegates from nine colonies met in Federal Hall on Wall Street, lodging with friends and family or in local taverns. They immediately faced a problem. South Carolina's delegates arrived with news that Grenville had already informed the colonies that "Objections of inability . . . would have very little weight with Parliament."[67] But inability was the point. The delegates' first realization was they were trapped in a paradox. It was as if Parliament had disallowed them from protesting the very thing that made the taxes objectionable.[68]

The second realization followed from this paradox. If "Objections of inability" were not going to have any effect, the delegates would be forced to go deeper—to the constitutional assumptions that had allowed the Stamp Act in the first place. Rather than objecting to the sheer inanity of the stamp taxes, they would have to consider what kind of power that stamp duties charged in silver implied, and what kind of powers they, as representatives of the affected colonies, might need to claim so that Parliament could not assert it again. The task required them to work on a higher level of abstraction than they, perhaps, had anticipated.

Dickinson was given the task of writing the first draft of the resolves that every member of the congress could agree on. The Virginia resolves provided a template, but Henry had spoken for a colony. Dickinson was speaking for a continent. His guiding question, he wrote in the first of thirteen resolves, was what the colonies in America held "the same." They held the same "allegiance to the crown of Great-Britain," he wrote in the first resolve. They had the same "inherent rights and liberties" owed to all who shared that allegiance. That liberty required the power that "no tax be imposed on them, but with their own consent, given, or by their representatives." And none of them could "be represented in the house of commons." The Stamp Act, he argued, not only abridged that right but also showed why it existed in the first place. The right to representation existed, he argued, because "the increase, prosperity, and happiness of these colonies depend on them." The Stamp Act had proved the case. This brushed close to the inability of the colonists to pay, the issue precluded by Grenville. Accordingly, the delegates made Dickinson sharpen his language. In his original draft,

Dickinson wrote that "due to the peculiar Circumstances of these colonies," paying the stamp duties would be "extremely grievous and burthensome." His fellow delegates amended it. They could not let their inability to pay go unmentioned. The ninth and final resolve of the Stamp Act congress read in full: "That the duties imposed by several late acts of parliament, from the peculiar circumstances of these colonies, will be extremely burthensome and grievous, and from the scarcity of specie, the payment of them absolutely impracticable." The congress sent its resolves to Britain, along with separate letters to the king and the Houses of Lords and Commons, and returned home hoping for the best.[69]

XII. American Colonies Refuse the Stamps en Masse

One by one, each colony in North America committed to refusing the stamps. Merchants associations in all the major ports banded together to cancel their orders for British manufactures if the bill wasn't repealed. The Stamp Act, a committee of Philadelphia merchants wrote in a letter to their British counterparts, "must inevitably drain us, in a very short Time, of our Specie, disable us from discharging our present Debts to *England*, and effectually cut off the beneficial intercourse."[70] The only North American colonies where the act went into effect on November 1 were Georgia and Quebec, where governors had troops to enforce order. Even there, without silver to buy or even stamped paper until more than a month after the law went into effect, things lapsed into what the *Quebec Gazette* called "involuntary inactivity" and an "unavoidable Intermission" of seven months.[71]

For the first time, a rift had appeared within the empire, and money had caused it. Hill's insight into the fundamental character of bills of credit—that they were fundamentally not a commodity, an "equivalent" in trade—was not itself an imperial program. He had intended it as a statement of facts *about* money, facts that proved the American system was a fraud. The plurality of money within the empire stood as an obvious refutation of his "facts." But with money, assertions that money is one thing or another, no matter how spurious, become real if the person asserting it is in a position to write those assertions into law. Hill had the dubious privilege of having his notion of money written into laws that constituted an empire. As it creeped into other aspects of imperial governance, Hill's ideas became policy in effect. The devastating consequences of the Stamp Act did not cause Hill or anyone else to rethink the problem of money. They forced colonists, however, to rethink their assumptions about the extent of imperial law.

The colonies might have protested the Stamp Act regardless of how it was charged. They had protested the Currency and Sugar Acts before it and would protest the Mutiny Act arriving soon after. But the protests would not have been as unified or penetrated as deeply through all levels of free American society. Many would have paid the taxes if they could have. As Mercer argued, if the taxes had been charged in hemp, he would have been happy to pay them, and many colonial leaders would likely have agreed. If the tax had been accompanied by a new currency, as Franklin and McCulloh had hoped, there would have been no practical reason to refuse it. There would have been a choice, to pay or not, and many would likely have chosen the former.

Silver took volition off the table. Historians have long wondered how it was that thirteen colonies, so different in virtually every other respect, could have come together, united against Britain a few short months after an extraordinarily successful war. The money problem, and Britain's tacit drive toward a currency union, explains the birth of American resistance in what became known as the Stamp Act Crisis. The colonies were unified precisely because none of them could pay it. They had no choice but to resist.[72]

The question for political leaders like Dickinson, who had been elevated in the crisis, was how to use that unanimity to the greatest effect. The revival of the ancient principle of no taxation without representation was rooted, however, in a consistent and unforgettable error about money, taxes that could not be paid. But to what end? The question that haunted Dickinson, as he rode across New Jersey to Philadelphia from the congress in New York, was whether that error, alone, was enough to keep the colonies together, to maintain the unity they'd just forged, and to work together to implement the necessary constitutional reforms on the imperial level that would prevent Parliament from passing anything like the Stamp Act ever again. It was the only way, as he saw it, that an empire, divided by money, could remain united.

With the Stamp Act, what had been a debate about the nature of money was becoming a debate about the constitution of the British Empire. There was nothing inevitable about this change. A more subtle and better-informed tax policy, a less confrontational approach to reforming imperial currency, or a ministry that prized difference within the empire over conformity to its internally idiosyncratic notions of what money might be could have pulled American colonists closer. Instead, by writing a hostile philosophical pronouncement into imperial law, Grenville and his allies made the long-standing amicable monetary differences between the colonies and the metropole into the flashpoint for an intra-imperial confrontation. They did so in such a ham-fisted manner that Americans had no choice but to resist and to rethink their role within the empire going forward. They would spend the next several years doing just that, even as Grenville's imperial machine, working on a global scale, gained momentum abroad.

CHAPTER FIVE

The Right to Be Wrong about Money

I. Grenville Loses Power after Boring the King and Insulting His Mother

George III despised Grenville and always had. At the core of the king's antipathy was Grenville's sense that he was destined to be, not just prime minister, but the young monarch's chief adviser and educator. Grenville, meanwhile, loathed the king's childhood tutor and mentor, John Stuart, the Third Earl of Bute. This would have come as a surprise in America, where Grenville and Bute were generally thought to be working together to pervert the monarch's natural love for his colonial subjects. In fact, Grenville was so jealous of Bute's influence, he tried to bar even Bute's friends at court from seeing the king or advising him. Meanwhile, as often as he could, Grenville forced the king to sit through endless private lectures on policy. "When he has wearied me for two hours," the king confided to Bute, "he looks at his watch to see if he may not tire me for an hour more."[1]

By May 1765, the king was done. George's primary role in his Parliament-dominated government was to legitimate the ruling ministry—to make or unmake the men who would actually rule the empire. And he would unmake Grenville. "Every time, I meet with some insult from these people," he wrote to Bute that spring, and began interviewing potential replacements. Grenville's most prominent rival, William Pitt the Elder, the dominant parliamentary figure of the 1750s, refused the job. The other "Old Whigs" who made up Grenville's ineffective opposition failed to even put forward a viable candidate. By June, Grenville was stronger than ever. Parliament seemed poised at the brink of a new dynastic era dominated by Grenville, his family, and his friends.[2]

Then Grenville found a way to insult the king's mother. In the spring, George III became sick, begging the question who might serve as regent if he became incapacitated. The king demanded permission to choose his own regent, including the right to consider his mother for the role. Grenville refused, seeing Bute's hand in the demands. When a regency bill came to Parliament in June with a list of potential candidates, Grenville deliberately excluded her.

George was infuriated. He reached out again to Grenville's rivals, who finally agreed to form a government around Charles Watson-Wentworth, the Second Marquess of Rockingham. Watson-Wentworth was an amiable thirty-five-year-old horse fancier from rural Yorkshire with practically no relevant experience. Under Rockingham, the young historian Edward Gibbon wrote, none of the leading ministers, the prime minister, the chancellor of the Exchequer, and both secretaries of state had any experience in public office. "I believe the case is unparalleled in our history," Gibbon wrote. "It is to be hope[d] that genius will supply the place of experience." There was little reason to think it would. The only thing most ministers knew about him was that he loved gambling. Mostly, he was not Grenville. He took office on Wednesday, July 10, 1765.[3]

As the summer wore on, it was increasingly clear that George's objections to Grenville's pedantry had distracted Parliament's leaders from a growing crisis in North America. Desperate private letters and public reports of protest arrived with the first ships from the other side of the Atlantic. Ministers mostly ignored them. No one liked to be taxed, they reasoned. But by the early fall, the sheer volume had grown unbearable. The dissenters were also difficult people to ignore. Letter writers included royal councilors, judges, governors, and wealthy merchants with relatives in Parliament. They uniformly hated the tax, not as a tax but as a monetary imposition. Over and over, they wrote, silver was the problem. There simply was not enough precious metal in circulation to keep courts, land transfers, newspapers, and ports going. Anyone who knew anything about America knew it.

"All their money consists of paper currency," former Massachusetts agent William Bollan wrote in a pamphlet published in London that summer. Parliamentary taxes would render them "still poorer, more unable to pay" their debts in London, he wrote. "But what is most extraordinary is, that the act requires such duties to be paid in sterling money at 5s. 6d. per ounce. It might as well have ordained, that every man in the colonies should be seven foot high, since they are both equally impossible to be inforced [*sic*], for the people have no money."[4]

Private letters were, perhaps, less disturbing than growing reports that American merchants were planning to cut off trade with London until Parliament repealed the Stamp Act. The merchants' movement grew out of a sense of desperation. In Boston, traders who had always been enthusiastic if less than perfectly law-abiding members of the establishment were growing frantic. Legally speaking, Massachusetts's currency was silver and, as we've already seen, had been since 1749. In reality, however, the colony had less coin in circulation, even, than its neighbors to the south.[5] Massachusetts merchants sent vast quantities of silver out to settle debts after the war. Then came the Stamp Act's demands for silver. While many colonists worried that the act's legal fees would shut down colonial courts, Massachusetts merchants saw a danger to colonial ports, where stamps were required to clear ships out of harbor. "If the Stamp Act takes place we are a gone people," the wealthy merchant John Hancock wrote to his London correspondents on September 11, 1765, citing the danger to shipping if, as seemed likely, no stamps would be available for ships needing to clear port.[6]

The difficulties in paying stamp taxes on shipping paperwork, in turn, inspired Hancock and others to mount a commercial appeal for repeal. The next month, Hancock notified his correspondents that he and his fellow Boston merchants would not import "a shilling" from Britain until the act was repealed. "Nothing but the Repeal of the Act can Retrieve our trade again," he wrote. "If not Repeal'd you may bid Adieu to Remittances for past goods, and Trade in future. Your Debts cannot be Recover'd here for we shall have no Courts of Justice after 1st November." If his correspondents' captains, Marshall and Scott, arrived before the act went into effect, he would "clear them out . . . not loaded." If they arrived after, he would "haul them up [for] we have no Stamp Master nor Stamps Suffer'd to be Distributed," and any vessel without stamped papers was "liable to be Seiz'd besides," he wrote. "I am free & Determined to be so & will not willingly submit myself to Slavery: We are a people worth a Saveing." A week later he sent a final plea to his London partners to help repeal the act. His appeal and others like it had a dramatic effect. A movement began, spearheaded by the same London merchants who had fought against Virginia's currency, to have the Stamp Act repealed. Rockingham and his ministry faced a choice: stick with Grenville's system, against all evidence, or pull up its central American plank. They would not have long to decide.[7]

II. Dickinson Begins to Think Like
a Continental Politician

John Dickinson, meanwhile, had returned to Philadelphia and his law practice after the congress in New York. For the first time in almost a decade, he held no elected position. Still, he could not put politics away. The congress had given him a new sense of possibility. Before, his politics had been local, tied up with disputes in Delaware and Pennsylvania and with his relationship to the Penns. The congress, though, had framed politics from the perspective of a united continent. Continental politics suggested the need for ideas that applied as much to South Carolina, where Dickinson had made a friend in the influential delegate Christopher Gadsden, as to the Middle Colonies and New England.

His first attempt at continental politics came out simultaneously in London and Philadelphia later that year, to immediate effect. The result, as befitted the author of the Stamp Act congress's continental resolves, was the most thorough and searching analysis of the Stamp Act in print. Dickinson chose to frame his analysis as "a letter from a gentleman in Philadelphia to his friend in London." It was closer, though, to a letter from America as a whole to the new ministry.

Dickinson began his analysis with his observations drawn that summer from his experience as a traveling lawyer, riding from court to court. What he had seen, he wrote, was a colony and a continent in crisis. That fall, Philadelphia courts alone had seen thirty-five bankruptcies, as colonists had applied for relief "by our [Pennsylvania] insolvent act." The problem was a shortage of paper money as well as coin. "If these effects are produced already, what can we expect when the same causes shall have operated longer?" Dickinson asked. But his thoughts were not limited to Philadelphia. He sought at every turn to extrapolate from what was happening in one of the wealthiest cities in one of the wealthiest colonies to what *must* be happening in every colony on the continent. "What can we expect," he continued, "when the exhausted colonies shall feel the *Stamp Act* drawing off, as it were, the last drops of their blood? From whence is the silver to come, with which the taxes imposed by this act, and the other duties imposed by other late acts are to be paid?"[8]

The demand for silver was important, Dickinson wrote, because of what it taught, and what it had forced colonial leaders like himself to think through. Dickinson had been educated in England and built his political career around loyalty to an English landholder. And yet, he wrote, he had never before considered the interests of British politicians as any different than his own. The money problem, however, had forced him to reconsider.

Dickinson argued that the Stamp Act was something new. The Sugar and Currency Acts of 1764 were "restraints," Dickinson wrote, but Americans "have not until lately been unhappy. Our spirits were not depressed. We apprehended no design formed against our liberty."[9] But postwar taxes were burning through the colonies' paper currency at a rapid rate, while commercial debt "sweeps off our silver and gold in a torrent to Great Britain." In this "exhausted condition," Americans were obliged "to take up and totter under the additional burden of the *Stamp Act*." The demand for silver had become a pivot for colonial politics.[10]

"It is unnecessary to endeavor to prove, by reasoning on these things, that we shall suffer, for we already suffer," Dickinson wrote. "Money is become so extremely scarce, that reputable freeholders find it impossible to pay debts which are trifling in comparison with their estates. If creditors sue and take out executions, the lands and personal estate, as the sale must be for ready money, are sold for a small part of what they were worth when the debts were contracted. The debtors are ruined. The creditors get paid but part of their debts, and that ruins them. Thus, the consumers break the shop-keepers; they break the merchants; and the shock must be felt as far as London."[11]

"How may we mitigate the miseries of our country?" Dickinson asked. "*Great-Britain* gives us an example to guide us. SHE TEACHES US TO MAKE A DISTINCTION BETWEEN HER INTERESTS AND OUR OWN. Teaches! She requires, commands—insists upon it—threatens—compels—and even distresses us into it." If Parliament was unable or unwilling to take American institutions into consideration, they would have to advocate for themselves.[12]

For Dickinson, Great Britain, with the Stamp Act, had created America. It had found a way of forcing the leading citizens in every colony to see themselves as a political whole. There had been little sense, before the Stamp Act that the colonies had common institutions, much less a common basis for resistance. Again, the money problem had made combinations that were previously unimaginable inescapable. Even if America's own interests were ignored, the Stamp Act made empire in America on the old mercantile basis, sustained by monetary imbalances with British trades, untenable. "Suppose the STAMP ACT, enforced by uncommon penalties and unheard of jurisdictions should pick up every piece of gold or silver that shall wander into the plantations, what would *Great-Britain* gain by this measure? Or rather what would she not lose, by attempting to advance her revenue by means so distressing to commerce?" Americans did not seek independence, only "kindness and generous confidence," Dickinson concluded. "In short we can never be made an independent people, except it be by *Great-Britain* herself; and the only way for her to do it, is to make us frugal, ingenious, united and discontented." With something like the Stamp Act.[13]

III. Grenville Retreats to the Firm Ground of Parliament's Right to Err

The merchants' combination and powerful pamphlets like Dickinson's had the effect of putting Grenville and his allies, still in Parliament if not in power, into a defensive crouch. The result was the first radicalization caused by the Stamp Act. The struggle had perhaps a more significant effect on the ministers who had proposed it and lost than the Americans who had fought it. Out of power and faced with the failure of their plan, they chose to see the defeat as proof that a more radical approach was needed. Their fall, after all, had nothing to do with the imperial machine. The king's enmity was no reason to quit fighting for reforms they believed were necessary.

The first thing they had to face was the administration that had succeeded them in power. Rockingham had little experience, but he did have several key advantages. First, he had no taste for abstractions. He had no interest in the philosophical systems that had created the money problem in the first place. Second, Rockingham had no stake in Grenville's "great system" and thus no reason to disbelieve the deluge of letters explaining just how insane it was. Stacks of them were coming in. None supported Grenville. Governor John Wentworth of New Hampshire spoke for many when he told Rockingham that Grenville's system made "payments impossible" while the taxes would "consume every shilling of Specie in New England within two years . . . effectually draining them as if it was annihilated." The "evil does not rest there," Wentworth continued. Trade would decay, credit diminish, and British manufacturers, too, would suffer. "The British Merchants will soon find the Errors of crediting a Country whose moneys are consumed by public taxes."[14]

Grenville knew the challenges facing his system were serious. He seems to have understood that colonial complaints about silver were valid, but their validity had perhaps the opposite effect one might expect. He was not chastened. The American complaints, he came to believe, only reflected the fact because his system had never, in fact, been put in place.

If Americans had been forced to find silver, they would have found a way. Sure, they would have had to transform the way they did business, the way they organized their politics, their courts, their trade, their wealth, but what of it? The end result would have been an imperial system where the colonies were safe from monetary heterodoxy, subordinate to British financial interests, and a safe consumer of British-traded goods.

What was not valid, he came to see, was any challenge to the authority that allowed him to make change in the first place. The right to be wrong was the power to reshape the empire. It must be preserved. Colonial officials like Wentworth, in Grenville's view, had too little perspective to understand their own complaints. They were too close to the facts to see the system. In its defense, Grenville devolved. Where he had been a decorous, almost courtly debater, he was now a gadfly, inserting his position into every exchange, pressing repeatedly for every advantage.[15]

This approach had little effect on Rockingham. Whatever his other faults, he had an unwavering interest in actually listening to the colonies, whereas Grenville would have merely directed. The more Rockingham and his allies listened, the more objections they found. Worst of all was a contradiction that Grenville himself seemed to have introduced into the system as it was designed to work. The most important thing he had overlooked, according to his critics at home and in the colonies, was the Spanish trade—the source of all American silver in the first place.

The problem with the Spanish trade began in the early 1760s, when Grenville was still working in the admiralty. With the Seven Years' War ending, there were debates within the British government over what to do with its swollen wartime navy. Grenville's answer as first lord of the admiralty was typical of his peculiar genius. He had grown increasingly enraged at the trade that colonists carried on with Britain's foes, the French and the Spanish, in the Caribbean. Rather than waiting for the next war, he reasoned, the fleet might be empowered to capture, seize, and profit from the sale of smugglers' ships. He enlisted the navy as customs enforcers via three acts. The first, in 1762, greatly increased payouts to captains and crews that successfully seized smugglers. The second extended long-standing "hovering" regulations, designed to prevent small ships from lingering, "hovering," just offshore, running goods by night into small inlets and rivers without paying the customs duties they would be charged in ports. The third (like the second incorporated into the Sugar Act of 1764) ordered all naval officers stationed in American ports to take the custom-house oath, a move Grenville believed necessary to curb the "dangerous Evils" of smuggling.[16]

The problem with this new, martial vigilance, as Grenville's enemies in Parliament kept pointing out, was that trade with Spanish colonies in the Caribbean was North America's (and ultimately Britain's) main source of silver coin. This oversight became a key argument in favor of repealing the Stamp Act. When Parliament reconvened on January 14, 1766, Pitt, standing one chair away from Grenville in the Commons, turned to him and declared that "every capital measure" he had taken as prime minister had "been entirely wrong!" Grenville, Pitt continued, had set out "to prevent the *Spanish* trade, and thereby stopping the channel, by which alone *North America* used to be supplied with cash for remittances to this country," while taking in the very "cash"—silver—he had prevented them from procuring.

Grenville stood by, furious. Why were the Americans consulted at all about imperial practices? Were they not subject to Parliament, like everyone else in the empire? "Where were the Americans emancipated?" Grenville interjected. At what point, he meant, had Parliament given them the right to decide their own future? "When were they made slaves?" Pitt replied. The exchange would become famous in America. But it was the Spanish criticism that stung. Grenville returned to the Spanish trade a few days later, without direct provocation, denying that he had ever sent "cutters" to the West Indies to interdict Spanish ships. No one in Parliament had mentioned cutters. Henry Conway, secretary of state for the Southern Department, which included North America and the Caribbean, had merely repeated Pitt's claim that Grenville's regulations had stopped "the dollar trade with Spain." It seems clear that Grenville, the systemic thinker, was sensitive to claims that, in demanding silver from the American colonies, he had failed to consider where it might come from.[17]

Technically, Grenville protested, he had "discouraged no trade but what was illicit, what was prohibited by act of Parliament." A Spanish ship from Mexico or Cuba bringing silver to a British port to trade for cattle, mules, wheat, saltfish, hardwoods, or enslaved people would have no problems. The problem was the port part. Spanish traders had traditionally traded with small settlements or even individual plantations along the coast, "hovering," as the act put it. These coastal traders were now the navy's chief prey. If caught, they would find both ships and cargo "forfeited and lost." As a result, Spanish traders had disappeared.

On April 2, 1764, Jamaica governor William Lyttelton reported that the crackdown had completely stopped the bullion trade, an embargo made worse by the fact that the island had no currency apart from Spanish silver. "As the orders I have received do not appear to me to allow any latitude,"

Lyttelton wrote to the Board of Trade, "this particular trade stands prohibited." George Johnstone, governor of the new colony of West Florida, likened the situation to being "besieged by our own fleet."[18] "Not a *Spanish* vessel can now come with money to this island, but what is seized," a British merchant in Jamaica wrote in May 1764 in a letter published in London's *Gentleman's Magazine*. "We have been prevented receiving in this island (since I arrived) near a million dollars," he continued. "What can be the reason for suppressing so beneficial a part of commerce, is a mystery to all people here." Grenville tried to amend regulations to allow the silver trade as soon as he heard about the difficulties, ordering in May 1764 that Spanish vessels putting in for "assistance and refreshment" would not be molested "provided they do not bring or carry any foreign goods or merchandise." But according to Jamaica traders, the damage had already been done. Pitt's point when he claimed that everything Grenville had done was "entirely wrong" was simply that Grenville, the systemic thinker, either knew or should have known that his crackdown in the Caribbean would affect his tax plans in America. The rebuke stung because Grenville prided himself on his knowledge, and with the Spanish trade he had overlooked the obvious.[19]

Silver continued to haunt Grenville as Parliament got down to the serious business of questioning witnesses on whether the Stamp Act should be amended or repealed. Grenville often took a leading role in the opposition, attacking pro-Rockingham witnesses by suggesting they were plants paid or threatened into testifying against him. "Do you think yourself safe if you go back to Virginia [having] given evidence in favour of the Stamp Act?" Grenville asked Virginia stamp distributor George Mercer in front of the House on February 12, 1765, after Mercer testified that the act would bring ruin to his colony. "I should never think myself in danger in any part of the world from speaking the truth," Mercer replied.[20]

Grenville could not admit that he had been wrong, even as witness after witness confirmed he had been. "Do you think the colonies are in a state of inability if willing to comply?" one MP asked Barlow Trecothick, a prominent Boston-born merchant who had become a leading voice in American affairs in London. "Yes. Utterly for want of specie in many of them," Trecothick replied. There was "little specie" in any part of America, Trecothick continued, "not much in Massachusetts, [and in] Rhode Island, [and] Connecticut scarce any." Americans could perhaps pay "in the commodity of the country . . . or paper," Trecothick concluded, but not silver.[21]

When asked about whether the colonists could pay, Capel Hanbury, a merchant trafficking in Maryland and Virginia, told the members,

"[I can't] conceive they are able to pay the tax. It is desired/directed to be paid in specie." That was proof enough.

"Does this inability arise from that?" an MP pressed.

"I can't apprehend the paper can be of use," Hanbury replied. "[There is] Very little specie in Virginia and Maryland." The taxes might be paid in tobacco but not silver. Stamp distributors "might turn merchants and sell tobacco" to fill government coffers, but "they would be in a hard situation."[22]

Benjamin Franklin, interviewed on February 13, was just as frank. "In my opinion," Franklin told the panel, "there is not gold and silver enough in the Colonies to pay the stamp duty for one year." Franklin's testimony made him a hero in America when it was published soon after. He made no mention of his own dashed hopes that the Stamp Act would result in a new colonial currency, or his error in appointing a friend, John Hughes, stamp distributor in Pennsylvania because of them.[23]

As the debates concluded in February, the colonists' inability to pay in silver was clear. A parliamentary consensus was growing for repeal. Charles Townshend, an influential MP who was sympathetic to Grenville's plans, had opened the session by arguing that "he could not repeal the act on account of the right," nor "on account of the violence that had been used against it, but only if at all, in impracticability, or inexpedience of it, or the inability of the colonies to pay the tax." This, of course, reversed Grenville's advice to colonial agents a year before, the advice that had shaped the congress's approach in New York. But the inconsistency did not bother Townshend nor the rest of the house. It was obvious, by then, that the taxes would be impossible to pay.[24] But Townshend's invocation of "right" gave Grenville an opening, a chance to retreat to firmer ground. With the silver question all but conceded, Grenville and his allies sought to prove that Parliament's right to err was indispensable.

Their method was to claim that every statement about colonists' inability to pay was a rights argument in disguise. It failed. When Trecothick asserted that "no modification" of the Stamp Act would satisfy Americans because "the people from one end of the continent/country to the other have set their faces against it," Grenville was quick to ask, "On what principle" had they done so?

"They think it oppressive in its nature and an infringement on their right. From both," Trecothick replied.

"If the oppression was removed would they submit?" Grenville asked.

"They consider the whole as oppressive, both the quantity and quality," Trecothick said.

"Do you think that if this Stamp Act was repealed and another internal tax laid would they not oppose it equally?"

"I [don't], but they might," Trecothick replied.

"Do you think they would oppose an internal tax merely as such?"

"I think there is no danger that they should," Trecothick said. It was the particulars of the tax, not preexisting beliefs about the powers of Parliament, that had forced Americans to appeal to their rights.[25]

Mercer, when facing a similar line of questioning, was equally clear.

"What was the disposition of Virginians three years ago?" an MP asked.

"Not the least breath of disloyalty," Mercer replied.

"Did it use to be their opinion that British Acts of Parliament ought [not] to be received?"

"No," Mercer replied. "Nor now except the Stamp Act."

"Has not the idea of oppression awakened the idea of right?"

"I believe so," Mercer said.

"The sooner that oppression is removed will not the idea of right be quieted?"

"The sooner the cause is removed to be sure the effect will cease," he said.[26]

Witness after witness made the same point, that it was the sheer unreasonableness of the Stamp Act that had forced Americans to appeal to their constitutional rights. Even Martin Howard, who was hanged in effigy and had his house ransacked by Stamp Act rioters, agreed.[27] "They made no objection while they [were] only taxed by customs," Howard told the committee, adding, until recently, "I never heard any opposition to the right of Parliament."[28]

Grenville's final chance to discredit his opponents came when Richard Oswald rose before Parliament, the last witness before the vote on repeal. Oswald, a fifty-one-year-old slave trader from the northernmost tip of Scotland, had made his first fortune in Glasgow, Jamaica, and the Southern Colonies trading tobacco, sugar, and wine for his cousins' firm. He had moved to London to marry Mary Ramsay, of another fortune built on the labor of enslaved Africans. Robert Burns, the Scottish poet, would later call Mrs. Ramsay "a purse-proud Priestess of Mammon ... pinioned in everlasting fetters by illgotten gold." Her new husband soon made another fortune by purchasing and reinvigorating the all-but-abandoned slave-trading base of Bance Island on the Windward Coast of Africa. Thousands passed through his hands each year. In 1766 alone Oswald was responsible for the purchase, transport, and sale of 1,718

African men and women. By 1764, Oswald had expanded into government contracting, selling bread to the British Army in Germany during
the Seven Years' War. Oswald was a friend of government, and of Grenville in particular. He had not seen America in twenty years. He had no
fresh information. He only seems to have testified as a personal favor to
Grenville himself.[29]

Asked whether the Americans were able to pay the stamp duties,
Oswald replied with assurance, "I think them very able." He had numbers
to back it up. The colonies contained some 800,000 white men. If the
tax brought in £60,000, he speculated, that amounted to 1 shilling and
6 pence per head.

That was ignoring the silver problem, and Oswald's questioners pressed
the point. Oswald confirmed that the colonists used paper money. "[Why]
did paper money have a currency?" his examiners asked. "For want of bullion," he replied. "I speak only from what I hear," he told the committee.

Suddenly, Oswald was on the defensive. Questions became increasingly
sharp. "If [the tax] is to be paid in specie there will be some expense the
first time to procure it," he admitted. The silver trade, though, would be a
business opportunity. "If I was there," he continued, "I would undertake
to supply all the colonies with silver and if I had none would bring it from
the West Indies." This was just as easy, he added, "as sending it from here to
Berwick."

But here the Spanish trade problem arose again. No silver was coming to Jamaica, so none would flow to America. Had he heard of its
interruption?

> "Yes, from foreign vessels coming to our ports being apprehensive of
>   being seized," Oswald replied.
> "Why then do you say they are capable of paying this duty?"
> To that Oswald managed only to make a stumbling denial.
> "Do you of your own knowledge know of the present state of any one
>   colony and their ability to pay the tax?" he was asked.
> "No," was all he could reply.

Finally, the opposition was able to ask its questions. Grenville or one
of his allies asked the key question. "Would the present disturbances have
happened if they had not questioned the right?" Oswald said, "No." And
when they asked, "Are not all the complaints of the disturbances from
disputing the principle of the Stamp Act?" He said, "Yes." But by then
Oswald had no real credibility. Grenville's best witness had been reduced
to monosyllables.[30]

IV. Parliament Repeals the Stamp Act
but Gives Grenville a Victory Too

Parliament repealed the Stamp Act on February 21, 1766. The final vote was 275 to 167. According to Horace Walpole, Grenville's friends made one last effort, claiming that several colonies, including New York, might actually be submitting to the act. "But this was treated as the lie of the day; and had no effect." The lobby of St. Stephen's Chapel was packed with British merchants who gave Secretary of State Henry Conway, leader of the repeal effort, three "huzzahs" when he appeared. When Grenville emerged, George Walpole recalled, "the crowd pressed on him with scorn and hisses." Grenville grabbed the man nearest to him by the collar, "swelling with rage and mortification." "Well, if I may not hiss," the collared man said, "at least I may laugh," and laughed in Grenville's face.[31]

The news arrived in Boston on May 16, 1766, on a ship from London with a copy of the Act for Repeal. In Massachusetts, the colony declared a day of public remembrance and celebration. In Boston's First Church at the head of King Street, the thoroughfare leading up from Boston's Long Wharf, Charles Chauncy, the sixty-one-year-old veteran of decades of religious controversy and town politics, preached a sermon on Proverbs 25:25, "As cold Waters to a thirsty Soul; so is good News from a far Country."[32]

"Such is the 'good news' lately brought us from the other side of the great waters," Chauncy told his holiday congregation. "No news ever handed to us from Great-Britain, ever gave us a quicker sense, or a higher degree, of pleasure," than the news of the Stamp Act's repeal that spring. "It rapidly spread through the Colonies, and, as it passed along, opened in all hearts the springs of joy. The emotion of a soul just famished with thirst, upon taking down a full draught of cold water, is but a fain emblem of the superior gladness with which we were universally filled upon this great occasion."[33]

Within three days the news had reached New York and Philadelphia. In Burlington, New Jersey, the colonists toasted the king, the queen, the royal family, Parliament, the Rockingham ministry, their governor, their province, Pitt, Lord Camden, the Marquis of Rockingham, Henry Conway, Lord Dartmouth, General Howard, Colonel Barré (who had coined the phrase "Sons of Liberty" in his speech against the Stamp Act), Benjamin Franklin, Barlow Trecothick, and that "the Stamp Act be buried in oblivion." In New York, residents celebrated by ringing bells and firing cannons, followed by bonfires at sunset, a public illumination—with candles placed on every windowsill to light the way for revelers—and "Sons of Liberty" "assembling at their usual house of public resort" for drinking, music and toasts to Pitt and George III. In Hartford, Connecticut, the celebrations got out of hand on May 23. A crowd of twenty-eight young men, including two African Americans, playing with fireworks, accidentally blew up a brick schoolhouse, sending two young men flying out of the glass-paned windows and killing three.[34]

The news reached Virginia in early June, when many leaders were in Williamsburg for the stamp-free Courts of Oyer and Terminer. The result, on June 13, was a ball at the capital "and elegant entertainments" attended by Fauquier himself, along with "a large and genteel company of Ladies and Gentlemen, who spent the evening with much mirth and decorum, and drank all the loyal and patriotick toasts" promenading with their enslaved attendants through the candlelit streets. Fauquier reported to his superiors that "Loyalty and Gratitude shone forth on every Occasion."[35]

The joy was infectious. An impossible weight had been lifted due to American unity. "Besides all which, 'tis undoubtedly true, that the circulating money in all the Colonies would not have been sufficient to have paid the Stamp-duty for two years; and an effectual bar was put in the way of the introduction of more, by the restraints that were laid upon our trade in those instances wherein it might, in some measure, have been procured," Chauncy observed at the rhetorical peak of his celebratory sermon. "We should have been stupid, had not a spirit been excited in us to apply, in all reasonable ways, for the removal of so insupportable a burden."[36]

Hastily drawn up non-importation pacts were revoked. Ports reopened, newspapers ran special editions and printed reports of celebrations across the continent. The status quo seemed to have been restored, leaving many to wonder what normal could be after a decade of war, followed by almost two years of protest and the successful repeal of an act of Parliament. Few, in their relief, noticed the Declaratory Act, passed in the same session as the repeal of the Stamp Act as a salve for the Grenville faction. The Declaratory Act cemented Grenville's right to be wrong into imperial law. The Stamp Act may have been a mistake, but the right, the power, to pass such a law must remain with Parliament. In 1766 it refused to concede the precedent, despite its own opinion that the power had been abused. Parliament was the only legitimate judge of its own misconduct. The act declared that whereas the colonies, using Dickinson's words at the New York congress, had "claimed the sole and exclusive right of imposing duties and taxes upon [themselves]." Parliament "declared" that it "had, hath, and of right ought to have, full power and authority to make laws and statutes of sufficient force and validity to bind the colonies and people of *America,* subjects of the crown of *Great Britain,* in all cases whatsoever."[37]

V. Politics Briefly Returns to Normal in Virginia and Pennsylvania

In May 1766 John Robinson, Virginia's longtime treasurer, died. He had been extremely well liked, and when the interim treasurer, Robert Carter Nicholas, began auditing his accounts, it became clear why. There was a lag between when the colony's wartime bills of credit were taxed in by county sheriffs and the time, usually no more than once a year, when the tax receipts were gathered together and burned. After the last wartime bills of credit were issued, in March 1762, Robinson, on his own initiative, took to loaning out the bills in his possession that were not yet expired in addition to whatever coin he had on hand. That meant all of them. The first expiration date for bills still in circulation was on March 1, 1765. The word seems to have quickly got around among Robinson's friends. When he died, some £100,761 Virginia worth of tax receipts were missing. His private papers, meanwhile, made clear that Robinson himself was due £105,000 for personal loans made in the years he was in office. The auditors put one and one together, concluding that the "taxes received by him" had been "re-emitted and lent out to sundry Persons," though it was still unclear who. Robinson seems to have done deals by handshake, leaving few records of who owed what, and eventually forcing the colony to make up the difference by selling virtually all of the enslaved people, houses, and land Robinson had accumulated in his sixty-one years of life. Robinson only "illegaly [*sic*] reemitted to supply the Necessities of Friends, to whom he could never give a Denial," Fauquier told the board of trade on December 18, 1766. "Such was the Sensibility of his too benevolent heart." Fauquier's main concern, though, was stopping settlers crossing the mountains to settle on the "[extremely] fine" Native American land between the Allegheny hills and the Ohio River, an illegal pilgrimage that seemed likely to start another Indian war and incur expenses that the burgesses, deprived of bills of credit, had no means to pay for.[38]

Dickinson, meanwhile, returned to the law and ran a busy office in Philadelphia. He even felt the need to take on more help, hiring and training a young Scottish lawyer called James Wilson, who had immigrated to Philadelphia from central Fife at the age of twenty-three. The gradual disappearance of bills of credit was having strange effects. In one case, the London agent of Lord Baltimore, Edward Hoyt, hired Dickinson to sue

John Vining of Dover, Delaware, for paying him in silver. The bond Hoyt was executing had called, explicitly, for Maryland's paper currency instead. He wanted the paper, not coin. The reason was simple. Once its wartime taxes expired, any of Maryland's leftover bills of credit could be exchanged for stock in the Bank of England. Silver, after the cost of transport and insurance, would be worth far less in London than the stock. Baltimore, through Hoyt, insisted on payment in paper. Vining was just as insistent that silver was good money. The litigation dragged on for years.[39]

Dickinson's legal work was lucrative but unfulfilling. He was restless. He seemed hungry to prove that 1765, the year in which he had taken a leading role not only in Pennsylvania and Delaware but in imperial affairs, was no fluke. Letters from friends he had met at the New York congress reminded him that he had more to offer. An ocean away, Parliament's 1767 spring session would give Dickinson his chance.[40]

VI. Grenville and His Allies Seize Another Chance to Tax

Grenville was nothing if not tenacious. He and his friends had determined that the American colonies must be taxed if they were to be made part of the grand imperial design he had pushed for in public and in private since the final months of the Seven Years' War. When the Rockingham ministry dissolved after barely a year in office under pressure from the king, Grenville saw another opportunity. Rockingham's replacement was the ever-reluctant Pitt. Pitt's mental health was fading and with it his ability to dominate Parliament by personality alone. Within a year, he would retire to the country retreat of Bath near Bristol, wracked by dementia. His retreat left Grenville as the loudest voice in the Commons. He used his platform to argue for new taxes, taking a hard line on the American colonies, whose pleas for consideration had produced the profoundest defeat of his public career.[41]

Without a stable center, the ministry became a jumble of competing interests and ideas, drawn from a loose coalition of Rockingham's enemies. Many of these were Grenville's old allies. Hill was back at the Board of Trade, though stripped of his powers over currency and appointments. The key figure was Charles Townshend, who, after leading the opposition to repeal, became chancellor of the Exchequer. He too hoped to exploit America. In short, he hoped to establish a precedent of Parliament's right to be wrong when it pleased about money, taxation, and imperial policy. He would push the bounds that Grenville had allegedly overstepped.

Townshend's imperial program required first boosting his popularity in Britain. The first step, then, was reducing the taxes on British landholders by a quarter. Nothing could have been more popular in land-rich Parliament. Second, he began casting about for colonial revenue to make up the difference.[42] The first and perhaps most viable candidate for taxation was India, where the East India Company had just secured new possessions. But many MPs, including Townshend, were also shareholders in the East India Company. Consequently, Townshend mounted an at best half-hearted attempt to take over the company's new revenues. Unsurprisingly, it failed to gain support, with the government accepting £400,000 a year from the company for two years to settle its claims.[43]

That left America, whose perceived lack of gratitude had rankled many of the repeal's more reluctant supporters. "Great Britain having yielded [on the Stamp Act], the tribunes of America flattered themselves that new concessions might be extorted," Horace Walpole wrote in his memoirs. Townshend thus felt empowered to call for a new American tax. The size did not matter. His goal was to prove that the Stamp Act's repeal was an exception, not a precedent. The right to tax, Townshend told Parliament, "was indubitable"; the only question was how to exercise it. He had an idea.

Townshend's plan was to use the Americans' own words against them. Colonists protesting the Stamp Act had made a distinction between "internal" taxes like the Stamp Act and the "external" taxes that regulated imperial trade. External taxes, they seemed to imply, were acceptable. The Townshend Acts passed that year, then, took the form of import duties on British goods including lead, paint, glass, paper, and tea. The duties were small, and the trades affected, except tea, were insignificant. The taxes on red and white lead and pigments, Townshend told Parliament on June 1, 1767, would bring just £3,000. But they would at least serve to establish the principle of parliamentary supremacy and the legitimacy of its power to tax the colonies, and thus the power to eventually reshape them in the way that Grenville had previously proposed. The new taxes were charged in silver bullion, to be sure, but the Spanish trade had been restored, and payments were limited to the merchant community with access to it. Anyone who objected could do without. It was almost as if the taxes had been designed to be ignored.[44]

However, the taxes were ill-timed. Not only did they immediately follow the Stamp Act, an ancillary dispute made them more important than might otherwise have been the case. Along with the Stamp Act, in 1765 Parliament had ordered colonial legislatures to house British soldiers stationed in or passing through their colonies as well as provide them with

basic provisions, including "fire, candles, vinegar and salt, bedding uten-
sils for dressing victuals, and small beer, cyder, or rum." Most had com-
plied in full, but the New York legislature—still smarting from restrictions
on its paper currency—had skimped, providing shelter, bedding, and fire-
wood but declining to offer salt, vinegar, or alcohol on the pretense that
troops barracked in Britain had to provide these for themselves. The reason, again, was Parliament's hostility to bills of credit. New York's legislature could not support British troops without issuing new bills of credit. It
could not do so, however, without violating the Currency Act of 1764. The
colony's new governor, Baronet Henry Moore, had written to the Board
of Trade just months before, begging permission to issue new bills, "as all
the present Bills in the [province] will be sunk next year, and the Country
left without any medium of commerce, for there has been very little silver
to be met with since the interruption of the Trade with the Spaniards."
After the assembly voted to deny salt, vinegar, and alcohol, Moore wrote
an outraged letter to Secretary Conway. "It is my opinion that every act of
Parliament, when not backed by a sufficient Power to enforce it will meet
with the same Fate here."[45]

Moore's letter could be read one of two ways. On one hand, it seemed to
claim that the New Yorkers were refusing to support the troops on principle, and that they could only be brought around by force. The irony with
that reading is that the army (i.e., force) was right there. On the other, it
might be read as an appeal for new bills of credit. Perhaps the "sufficient
Power" he referred to was the colony's power to maintain its monetary
institutions. None of his subsequent letters that year showed the same
degree of apparent moral panic, and the same New York assembly that
voted against salt, vinegar, and booze wrote a near-poetic ode of thanks
to George III for repealing the Stamp Act, celebrating the colony's "just
Dependence upon, and due subordination . . . to the Mother County."
Moreover, most of the legislature's attention was on other matters: land
disputes with other colonies, and the growing and well-justified concerns
of neighboring Native American nations over colonists' illegal and violent
push into the Mohawk Valley.[46]

Parliament chose the former interpretation. The result was outrage.
Townshend, with Grenville acting in support, sought to make an example
of New York. He framed a law that barred New York's legislature from leg-
islating until they agreed to comply. Moore's letters, Townshend told Parliament on May 14, 1767, "called loudly upon the majesty of this country to
assert itself." The key question, how New York might pay, was overlooked.
In Parliament on May 15, 1767, Thomas Pownall called the act "dangerous"

and "not necessary," predicated on momentary anger and confusion. It passed regardless. Parliament suspended the New York legislature in the same session that it passed new, relatively unobjectionable taxes. The goal, Townsend declared, was to "strike an awe into the factious and turbulent" North Americans. If anything, it had the opposite effect.[47]

VII. Dickinson Reverses Locke in His Letters from a Farmer

Dickinson's response to Parliament's assault on the New York legislature would make him the most celebrated writer in North America. His *Letters from a Farmer in Pennsylvania* were popular because they crystallized in clear and measured prose an issue that had worried colonial thinkers for three years. The question, in its simplest form, was how the mainland colonies of North America, with their different religious, political, and economic institutions, should express their concerns over the imperial reformation heralded by the Stamp Act.

The difficulty with British leaders, Dickinson had observed years earlier in his first public work, the speech in favor of proprietary rule in Pennsylvania, was that they "never deviate from a precedent of power." The previous three years of debate had proved the point, as Grenville and his friends tried again and again to assert the empire's power in North America. Dickinson's goal was to provide an alternative precedent, one that Americans in all the colonies could grasp with equal fervor.[48]

The imperial challenge had taken the form, as one historian has noted, of an assault on the colonies' "customary constitutions." The problem was that each constitution was different. There were royal colonies, like Virginia, and proprietary colonies, like Pennsylvania and Maryland, colonies founded by religious exiles, like Massachusetts, and by aristocratic adventurers like South Carolina. With the Stamp Act, the money problem had cut through the noise, revealing a fundamental similarity in monetary arrangements, that few colonists themselves had likely been previously aware of. But other aspects of their constitutions, economies, and political arrangements were better known and posed abiding sources of tension between them. The question Dickinson took up in his letters was how—faced with a direct challenge to just one colony, New York—and with taxes that were designed to be invisible, colonies might maintain and build upon the unity they had felt during the Stamp Act crisis. Only unity, he was sure, would pressure Parliament, whose plan, Townshend's reaction to New York had made clear, was to pick on them one by one.[49]

The moment of near-universal resistance during the Stamp Act crisis rang out over and over through his twelve letters. It had been a moment of obvious and unarguable, if perhaps unintended, oppression. Now it could serve as a touchstone. How, Dickinson asked in the first letter, published on December 2, 1767, in the *Pennsylvania Chronicle*, was Parliament's demand for military support, the demand that the New York legislature had almost offhandedly defied, any "more tolerable than the STAMP-ACT?" In the second letter, published on December 7, he leveled the same critique at the new taxes, arguing that both Townshend's duties and the Stamp Act "used the same mode of expression," justifying the American taxes as "just and necessary" because of the necessity of "RAISING A FURTHER REVENUE" in North America. In terms of intent, "*substance* and *right*," both acts aimed at the same thing: "*to raise a revenue from us only*." What was the difference, then, between the new "external" duties and the "internal" duties of the Stamp Act? "No more than this," Dickinson wrote, "that the injury resulting to these colonies, from the total disuse of British paper and glass, will not be *so afflicting*." The new taxes were light, but that did not mean they were just. To believe that, he argued, was to believe that colonial rights consisted "not in exemption from *injury*, but from a certain *degree of injury*." Any tax for a "revenue," a stream of money realized on British terms, in silver, might serve as a precedent, a funnel emptying into the madhouse of 1765. The Stamp Act was becoming less an active concern so much as a test case, an example of how far Parliament might go, and an example of what was necessary if Parliament was to be resisted. In the fourth letter, he went so far as to describe the resolves of the New York Stamp Act congress—authored by him—as an "American 'bill of rights.'"[50]

But Dickinson knew that his invocation of the dangers of the Stamp Act created a contradiction. Parliament had repealed the Stamp Act because it was "inexpedient," because of the silver clause, the Spanish trade, and the obvious madness of charging for a universal tax in a currency that most people did not have. The repeal had come because even Parliament realized the taxes would be impossible to pay. Dickinson himself had written the clearest and most successful example of the inability argument, when he had described the Stamp Act's demands for silver as "drawing off, as it were, the last drops of [the colonies'] blood." Meanwhile, a clear majority in Parliament, including many of the colonies' British allies, had rejected any argument implying that Parliament did not have the "right" to tax Americans. For these allies, Americans' rights under the British constitution—their local, relatively democratic powers—were not the issue. Prudence—a due regard for the differences that developed between the colonies and their imperial cousins—was the key. Property, money, silver, the material bases of a commercial empire—these were the things that mattered.[51]

But the problem with this way of thinking, Dickinson wrote in his twelfth and final letter, published on February 15, 1768, was that the law of empire, and especially the law of money, inextricably linked material life and governance. This threatened the great diversity of interests, laws, and financial institutions within individual colonies and colonists. The empire had become too large, too diverse, too unknowable for any autocratic system, no matter how prudent, to work. And if it did, it would only work for some, the lucky few who would be heard. This seemed to be Parliament's plan in singling out New York. To focus on material interests alone, in other words, was to focus on the differences between the colonies in a way that invited colonial division. On a property basis, Massachusetts had little in common with New York and Pennsylvania, and virtually nothing with the South. If they did not stick together, each region could be played off against the other indefinitely. "Our vigilance and our union are success and safety," Dickinson wrote. "Our negligence and our division are distress and death."

The question was how to justify unity. Dickinson's answer had several parts. First, the colonies had to focus on what had allowed them to flourish in the first place: their distance from imperial power and the local institutions that distance made possible. They needed to value the resulting diversity as an essential element of a shared British heritage. "Let us banish and discourage all illiberal distinctions, which may arise from differences in situation, forms of government, or modes of religion," he continued. "Let us consider ourselves as men—Freemen—Christian men—separated from the rest of the world, and firmly bound together by the same rights, interests, and dangers." In an era where sectarian violence was well remembered, this was a call for a politics that transcended narrow identities.[52]

The second element, for Dickinson, was to give a name and political weight to the imperial structure that had enabled the colonies' diversity. These he labeled "rights." Rights were something Americans could hold in common regardless of their beliefs, who they were, or where they were from. In the contest against parliamentary power, the intercolonial differences were a weakness, especially because the power to maintain those differences—the different ways colonies had determined to tax themselves, to make money for themselves, and to order themselves, distinct from Britain and from one another—was precisely what Dickinson and other American leaders sought to maintain. The notion of differences preserved through shared rights provided a language for describing a realm of liberty that allowed for different modes of government along with different ways for ordering wealth, money, political power, labor, and religion. Rights could be invoked in defense of difference. "For this reason, every man amongst us, who, in any manner, would encourage either dissention, diffidence, or indifference between these colonies, is an enemy to himself and to his country," Dickinson wrote. "Let us take care of our rights," he concluded, "and we therein take care of our property."[53]

The letters were a sensation, reprinted in nineteen of the twenty-three newspapers in anglophone North America, and within months in collected editions in Philadelphia that sold out more than seven separate printings. But it can be difficult to understand why. Dickinson was not a charismatic politician. His tone was neither incendiary nor inspirational. He did not have many set opinions. He seems to think things through in real time, contradicting himself in the process. But given his career trajectory, from failed legislator to continental scribbler to economic analyst, it is possible to grasp what Dickinson was trying to convey and why it resonated so powerfully.

What Dickinson had achieved that winter was to reconcile conflicting strands within the American resistance over the money question. What he denied, most forcibly, was Parliament's right to be wrong about money. What he supported was an imperial structure that left control over money—in whatever form—in local hands. He did this by turning the equivocal response to the Stamp Act into what was, in effect, a new order of precedence in political life; giving primacy to political power over property, rather than the other way round. His insight emerged out of what he perceived as the imperial reaction to arguments he had already made. On the one hand, Dickinson and his allies in London had insisted on the material impossibility of paying Parliament's taxes in silver. On the other, they had objected to Parliament's infringement of their right to tax themselves. The two strands worked together in practice, but logically they were at odds. To object to a tax that was impossible to pay on the grounds of impossibility implied that a less impossible tax might be permissible. Similarly, the idea that Parliament had no right to tax the colonies at all implied that any tax, in any form, was objectionable. Neither conclusion was acceptable. The first, which Parliament had adopted under Townsend, practically begged the empire to test colonial limits. The second suggested that the colonies were cut off from the imperial project. On what grounds, then, should the colonists object to a tax they could not pay?[54]

These contradictions were evident in Dickinson's own work. He had initially been reluctant to include the silver clause in the declarations of the Stamp Act congress, partly, it seems, because of the way in which the jackboots of impracticability muddied the ground of rights. Similarly, in his political writings he tended to draw a clear line between constitutional issues, such as the right to tax, and the everyday issues of trade, planting, taxation, money, and property. There was a sense, common to the world of the British agrarian or "country" tradition to which Dickinson alluded in creating the character of "the Farmer," that rights and material facts were somehow opposed, that talk of property, silver, or money sullied finer constitutional analysis.

What Dickinson realized that winter, however, was that these contradictions concealed a deeper principle, an order of precedence. Politics, Dickinson argued, preceded property. There was no way of securing the latter while ignoring the former. This was both a call to action and a new ground for unity. "Let these truths be indelibly impressed on our minds," he wrote, "that we cannot be happy without being free—that we cannot be free without being secure in our property—that we cannot be secure in our property, if, without our consent, others may, as by right, take it away— that taxes imposed on us by parliament, do thus take it away—that duties laid for the sole purpose of raising money, are taxes—that attempts to lay such duties should be instantly and firmly opposed—that this opposition can never be effectual, unless it is the united effort of these provinces— that, therefore, benevolence of temper toward each other, and unanimity of counsels are essential to the welfare of the whole—and lastly, that, for this reason, every man amongst us, who in any manner, would encourage either dissention, diffidence, or indifference between these colonies, is an enemy to himself and to his country." In other words, property had no real existence, no security, without government and the rights it enforced. Thus, there was no contradiction between defenses of colonial property and defenses of colonial rights. There was an order of operations. Rights had to be defended if property was to be preserved. The colonies, he wrote, "form one political body, of which each colony is a member. Their happiness is founded on their constitution; and it is to be promoted by preserving that constitution in unabated vigor."[55]

Dickinson's argument was revolutionary in ways that were not immediately apparent. To begin with, it was a radical statement against the commodification of political life, the notion that institutions like money were essentially commodities and thus beyond political control. Conversely, it suggested that all property was political, making politics, rather than a market, the root of commercial, and thus imperial, governance. Second, the idea that politics preceded property ran counter to a century of anglophone political theory, beginning with Locke. English writers, following Locke, had long argued that property preceded government. In his *Treatise of Civil Government*, Locke had argued that property rights were natural rights, providing a firm foundation for political association. Property began with man himself. God "gave Adam property," Locke argued, when he gave Adam "private dominion over the earth." Government came later "for the preservation of every man's right and property, by preserving him from the violence or injury of others." This was in part the argument that had made Locke attractive to the Whig financiers of the Glorious Revolution. It was also the philosophical basis for Locke's search for a natural money, a "money of the world," to underpin the new Whig financial system: the banks, the loans, the vast increase in financial property that had led to the financing of the revolution. If property existed before the state, outside the state, then surely money, as a form of property, was beyond political control. And it was precisely this appeal to abstraction, to money as a unifying ideal rather than an actually existing institutional multiplicity, that Grenville, following Hill, had deployed in the money clause of the Stamp Act.[56]

For Dickinson, the events of the previous three years made it clear that government alone gave meaning to property. Property did not precede government; government was the basis of all property. The money problem, through taxation without representation, had proved the point. Governments produced and protected property, just as colonial governments produced bills of credit. Thus, when it came to resistance, focusing on local property interests, whether slavery or currency, was a strategic error. Without rights such as the power to tax, there was no property. Thus, it was the right to self-government, not the right to property, that mattered. When it came to organizing a continent-wide resistance movement, this was a powerful argument. It challenged Dickinson's fellow leaders to find ways of speaking for the whole continent. He had solved a problem that most American leaders did not even know they had. Few outside London argued that each colony should go its own way, but no one had effectively articulated an alternative ideal. Dickinson had. He had accomplished a kind of transmutation. He had taken universal resistance to Parliament's demand for silver and transposed it, finding a unified "political body" in an impossible demand for precious metal.

His ideas would soon have immense consequences. On December 5, 1767, three days after the first of the letters was published in the *Pennsylvania Chronicle*—the mouthpiece of Dickinson's political enemies—Dickinson wrote a letter to James Otis, the Boston firebrand who had served with Dickinson in the Stamp Act congress. "The Liberties of our Common Country appear to me to be at this moment exposed to the most imminent Danger," Dickinson wrote. He enclosed a complete run of the "Farmer's Letters." Otis shared them with Samuel Adams, and together Otis and Adams composed a circular letter to other colonial legislators calling for a unanimous response to acts made "with the sole and express purpose of raising a revenue," a line pulled directly from Dickinson. The Massachusetts House approved the letter on February 11, 1768, and it was eventually adopted by legislatures up and down the continent. A renewed spirit of unanimity, inspired, in part by Dickinson's Farmer, his anti-Locke, was growing, and the opposition took note. In London, Wills Hill, since January again head of the Board of Trade, read the Massachusetts circular on April 15 and a week later, on April 22, ordered Massachusetts governor Francis Bernard to dissolve the legislature if they would not "rescind the Resolution" and "declare their Disapprobation" of it. The House refused, voting 92 to 17. Bernard dissolved it and requested troops to restore order. On October 1, 1768, the first two regiments of British troops arrived to occupy Boston by force.[57]

On April 21, 1768, Hill wrote Fauquier in Virginia, warning him that the circular letter was coming his way and suggesting that he instruct the burgesses to "take no Notice of it, which will be treating it with the Contempt it deserves." Hill, though, was too late. On March 3, 1768, Fauquier had died in Williamsburg from an illness picked up that winter. He was the last acting governor of Virginia who would be remembered fondly by his constituents. Speaker Peyton Randolph had delivered the circular to the burgesses on March 31, 1768. They approved their own version of it, protesting Parliament's purported "Right to raise money upon them without their Consent" in letters to Parliament, George III, and the House of Lords on April 14 and 15, before Hill was even able to write. Dickinson's *Letters from a Farmer* had been appearing in the *Williamsburg Gazette* since January, with the twelfth published on March 31, the same day the circular arrived. Hill's hope, he wrote on April 22 in a letter to Governor Bernard, was to avoid "unwarrantable Combinations" between colonies that might "excite an unjustifiable Opposition." With Dickinson's help, opposition was already coalescing. Within a year, non-importation and non-exportation agreements would sweep the colonies, beginning the radical phase of what some were already calling a revolution in colonial affairs.[58]

Dickinson's arguments had crystallized a case for "combination" across colonies for which others had been searching. It altered the political terrain of colonial America. The *Letters* marked the dawn of a truly continental politics barely imaginable three years earlier. "We should stand upon the broad common ground of those natural rights that we all feel and know as men, and as descendants of Englishmen," Dickinson's friend and South Carolina radical Christopher Gadsden wrote Connecticut leader William Samuel Johnson in December 1765. The particularities of colonial charters, whether royal or not, must "not ensnare us at last, by drawing different colonies to act differently in this great cause," Gadsden wrote. Difference was a trap. "Whenever that is the case, all will be over with the whole," Gadsden wrote. "There ought to be no New England man, no New-Yorker, known on the continent, but all of us Americans." Dickinson's letters with their wide appeal and radical implications had helped bring Gadsden's dream a step closer to reality. Just as Grenville's dogged defense of the power to create his colonial system had entrenched a British imperial account of the colonies' "rights" in London, Dickinson's three-year effort to incorporate and transcend the problems posed by taxation in silver had finally landed on an argument that worked. It acknowledged that local differences meant as threats to property would only rarely align as obviously they had with the Stamp Act's demands for silver. Rights came first. And it used the Stamp Act to show that a threat to one was a threat to all because, as Dickinson had argued years before, it set a "precedent of power" that Parliament—as the troop ships arriving in Boston attested—would not willingly surrender.[59]

Dickinson's argument, however, had another implication that was not immediately apparent. The idea that politics took precedence over property implied to some that politics was the only thing that mattered. Indeed, as negotiations between the colonies and Great Britain continued, it became possible to imagine that rights and property existed in different spheres, that political rights might be desirable at the expense of other material claims. Moreover, Dickinson's assertion that politics trumped property could leave outside observers, whether in London or writing centuries later, with the impression that politics and rights were the only things that mattered in the colonial resistance movement, when in fact politics mattered precisely because it governed property. It also had the effect of opening up a gap between intensely held ideas about colonial rights and the institutions—like bills of credit—that, in the 1760s, it was clear those rights were needed to protect. That gap would prove immensely important when the strains that began with the Stamp Act crisis led to war.

CHAPTER SIX

Silver, Famine, and Tea

BENGAL, MASSACHUSETTS,
AND LONDON, 1769–1774

I. When the Monsoon Fails in Bengal, the East India Company Makes Matters Worse

One of the great ironies of the imperial debates of the early 1770s is how little America features in them. By the late 1760s, it was becoming clear that the most dynamic, profitable, and significant part of the empire was in South Asia, in the fabulously rich provinces of Bengal, Orissa, and Bihar. Incorporating these territories without bankrupting the East India Company that administered them was the order of the day. Even when America came up, it was always in the context of how it might relate to the larger whole, of which India was an increasingly important part. So, to understand the final stage of the colonial conflict, it is necessary to take a detour to India.

Money was central to ideas about how America fit into the expanded empire. As we have seen, by 1769, Hill's money memo had found its way into imperial policy, radicalizing both a select group of powerful British ministers—who believed new imperial powers were necessary to make their currency union work—and emerging continental nationalists like Dickinson, Otis, and Adams. The reason Hill's memo had been adopted in the first place, however, was the Privy Council's strong ideas about what the American colonies were for, again in relation to India. The American colonies were meant to serve the empire as an expansion market for imperial goods. Changing their money would make the American market safe, its payments secure. The reason a new market was needed, in turn, was a vast, anticipated increase in the goods coming from the Indian Ocean, Asia, and the Pacific. American demand would rise to meet Asian supply.

At the productive heart of this new arrangement sat Bengal. As part of the Treaty of Paris signed in 1763, France had agreed to withdraw all of its troops from the mouth of the Ganges, solidifying gains won at the Battle of Plassey in 1757 between British and French-backed forces, and securing British influence within this massive, wealthy region. It had some 30 million inhabitants, roughly three times the population of Great Britain, when George Grenville's friend Robert Clive secured the right to tax it from the Mughal emperor in 1765.

Clive, like Grenville, had gone for silver. The Bengali rupee, the region's central currency, had been in use for centuries. Bengal would be the East India Company's silver mine, its answer to Spain's holdings in America and the Netherlands' monopoly in Japan. Clive believed controlling Bengal's independent tax base would provide the silver needed to purchase all of the muslins, calicos, silks, and other manufactured goods it currently traded for in India and to fund new investments in Chinese tea. The region was able to use silver as a currency, in part, because it had long served as one of the Asian sinks of American and Japanese silver. Europeans, Arabs, and others had brought the precious metal to India in order to purchase the brilliantly colored, light cotton and silk textiles woven by the region's highly skilled manufacturers. "The world's wealth accumulates in India," an Ottoman official wrote in 1647. In 1765 the East India Company sought to tap it.[1]

Four years went by, with revenues increasing each year under the company's administration, until a flaw appeared in the program. In Bengal, the hottest time of year is the spring, which brings a baking heat that peaks in April. In late May, the winds strengthen and shift to the south or southeast, bringing humidity, cloud cover, and rain that last into October—the monsoon. The combination of rivers, rain, and intense heat had long made Bengal, at the mouth of the Ganges; Bihar, further upstream to the west; and Orissa, further south along the Bay of Bengal, one of the most fertile, populous, productive, and wealthy regions in the world, based as it was on the production of silk, cotton textiles, and opium. The region was largely agricultural and thus dependent on the rains. Without the rain, the rivers that threaded the region would not flood, riverside crops would fail, and the poorest families—landless laborers, small artisans, and sharecroppers— would be forced to purchase food from elsewhere or starve.

In 1769 the rains did not come. On November 23, 1769, long since the rains should have already arrived, Henry Verelst, the governor of Bengal, wrote from Calcutta to the East India Company's directors in London. Verelst warned "of universal distress from want of grain owing to an uncommon Drought that that prevailed over every part of the Country—In so much that the oldest Inhabitants never remember to have known any thing like it." Verelst assured his bosses, "We have taken and shall pursue every measure in our power to relieve the miserable Situation the poor Inhabitants must be involved from this [dreadful] Calamity—But we cannot flatter ourselves that all our Endeavours will prevent very fatal Effects being felt or that Human means can check its baneful Influence."[2]

Food was still available in November, but scarcity was coming. Verelst had two main concerns. First was the company's income in India, which he had spent years growing from £2.26 million for the fiscal year ending in 1766 to £3.79 million in 1769. "The Consequences of so General a Calamity can not be confined to Individuals—though they may most severely feel them. The Publick must suffer likewise, & we have too much reason to apprehend, it will occasion a very considerable [diminution] in your Revenue," he wrote. This might be the occasion, he suggested, to ask the British government to forgo its "Demands," including its £400,000 yearly subsidy and customs payments. Second was the company's army, which might starve along with everyone else before another crop of rice ripened the following September. Verelst directed the company's agents to purchase six months' worth of grain for his soldiers "laid up in proper storehouses" and, in December, left Bengal for a new post in London.[3]

The famine of 1769 was not the first that had faced Bengal or Northeastern India. Major famines had occurred in 1752 and 1761, resulting, witnesses recalled, in "multitudes" of dead. Still, the region had prospered. But this was the first famine that occurred when the East India Company was in charge of the land tax revenue.[4] The traditional response to famine was to slash taxes and buy food. In 1630 the Mughal emperor, Shah Jahan, ordered granaries built to distribute food, gave money to the poor, and forgave all taxes for two years. In 1661 the emperor, Aurangzeb, ordered massive imports of grain, selling it at reduced prices or giving it to the neediest, while forgoing ground rents owed by farmers, who, after all, were most affected. During the same famine, the mahrana of Udaipur in Rajasthan employed the poor to build a massive artificial lake to contain the water from diminished rivers, beginning a system of still-existing waterworks in earth and marble that transformed his city into a lakeside paradise.[5]

The East India Company, though, neither fed the people nor stopped collecting taxes. It kept sending its silver to China. On January 25, 1770,

John Cartier, Verelst's successor as governor, wrote London that the rajah of Burdwan, west of Calcutta, had asked for rents to be remitted, or postponed a year, and he had "been induced to grant" this "indulgence" so that the region suffered only a "temporary inconvenience and not a total loss." But the real concern was revenue. In Bihar, Governor Cartier wrote on February 4, there were such "scenes of misery and wretchedness, such general poverty and despondency that we cannot expect to see a revenue equal to former years." He even suggested that some tax abatements, if "not wantonly allowed," might be necessary. Few were granted. When tax receipts were tallied in September 1770, the Bengal council reported returns of 13,802,693 rupees. Only 803,321 rupees had been forgiven, less than 6 percent of the total. The final tally, Quaker MP Henry Beaufoy later observed, meant that "the Company's collectors compelled the living to pay the taxes of the dead." Almost none was spent on food.[6]

Many of the young men working for the company were horrified by what they saw on the ground as the foreseen disaster reached its peak. George Bogle was twenty-three years old when he landed at Calcutta in the *Vansittart* on August 19, 1770, near the height of the famine, after crops had been planted but before they could be harvested. On many days, 150 dead bodies were disposed of in the river. "Whole families perished of hunger, or fed upon leaves of trees, or, contrary to religion, ate animal food; some even subsisted on dead carcasses," Bogle wrote to his father in September. Another young EIC clerk, John Shore, later Baron Teignmouth and governor-general of India, still recalled the scene vividly forty years later. He was eighteen when the famine hit. "Still fresh in memory's eye I view," he wrote, the "shriveled limbs, sunk eyes, and lifeless hue; Still hear the mother's shrieks and infant's moans," jackals, vultures, and bodies in a "wild confusion dead and dying." Company servants' conscience-stricken attempts to purchase more grain were pitifully small and far too late. According to Bogle, Cartier personally opened the company's granary, feeding 15,000 people per day before the food gave out. But that charity nowhere approached the scale of the problem. Total relief spending came to just £9,000, one-fifth of 1 percent of the company's local revenue in 1769.[7]

Rather than prepare for famine, one anonymous British trader wrote to the *Gentleman's Magazine*, many of the company's junior "writers" saw a path to fortune. "As soon as the dryness of the season foretold the approaching dearness of rice," he wrote, "our Gentlemen . . . were as early as possible buying all they could lay hold of," presumably using the same money they had collected from the farmers themselves. This was in the fall of 1769, a year before the famine began in earnest. Soon, the writer continued, merchants in Bihar were complaining that "the English had engrossed all the rice," only to be dismissed by the company's representatives in Calcutta. These "writers," whose position overseeing the land tax gave them direct access to regional markets, were able to purchase rice, the witness wrote, at between 224 pounds to 265 pounds per silver rupee. They sold it for roughly 29 pounds per rupee in the spring, a nearly 900 percent markup. The profits were astonishing. One "writer" in Bihar, the witness wrote, was reputed to have made £60,000 sterling in a single season. Those who held out made even more.[8]

Several granaries burned in Calcutta in April and May, just as the extent of the famine was becoming apparent far from the parched Bihari rice fields. At this point, the company set out to buy all the grain it could, setting the price at 8.5 kilos per rupee, thirteen times the price one year earlier. It requisitioned all the grain stored in Calcutta for workers on local fortifications "who were threatening to desert for lack of victuals." Little grain was left for the local market at any price, and people began to die en masse. The *Gentleman's Magazine* correspondent recalled the results. "I have counted from my bed-chamber window in the morning when I got up forty dead bodies laying within twenty yards of the wall, besides many hundred laying in the agonies of death for want, bending double, with their stomachs quite close contracted to their backbones," he wrote. "I have sent my servant to desire those who had strength to move farther off, whilst the poor creatures looking up arms extended, have cried out, Baba! Baba! my Father! my Father! This affliction comes from the hands of your countrymen and I am come here to die, if it please God, in your presence." When a census was taken several years later, a third of the population of Bengal had disappeared, roughly 10 million women, children, and men— slightly less than the population of Britain. At least 2 million, equivalent to the entire population of British North America, were dead. Others were forced to flee starvation as tax collection continued unabated. As Alexander Dow, who witnessed the famine as an East India Company officer, put it: "Fortune, though unfavourable, was less fatal, than the rapacity of avaricious men."[9]

Private greed, though, was less important than power and profit. The East India Company as a whole, Adam Smith observed, was "perfectly indifferent about the happiness or misery of their subjects, the improvement or waste of their dominions, the glory or disgrace of their administration." They were interested in revenue. When Cartier explained the toll of the famine to his superiors in London, he presented mass death as a revenue problem because revenue was what mattered: silver for China, sterling for London. This was what Dickinson had warned of when he wrote about "taxation for the sole purpose of a revenue." Revenue knew no natural limit, if its effects could not be felt or understood. Americans had some allies in Parliament. Bengalis had none. Under his administration, Verelst later recalled, between 1765 and 1770, EIC officials had exported £4,941,611 in bullion and goods from Bengal and surrounding districts, £3,037,266 of which—mostly silver bullion—went "to supply the China market with silver." This would have been impossible to achieve, Verelst admitted, "without some degree of violence." In that way, the famine year was no different. Little wonder the MP Horace Walpole took to calling the company a "crew of monsters."[10]

II. The East India Company's Panic and Greed Leads to Bankruptcy in London

The violence of the East India Company's exploitative famine regime, however, opened the doors to another kind of disaster: bankruptcy. Historians have tended to overlook the link between the famine and the disaster that befell the company a few years later in London, but the roots of the company's disastrous 1770s extend directly to the famine in Bengal. Verelst and his council in Bengal worried that diminished tax receipts would not cover the EIC's expenses in India in addition to the China trade. Thus, on October 23, 1769, they agreed to "open the Treasury Doors to Remittances," taking deposits in bullion from company employees—like those making a killing in the grain trade—and other Europeans in return for bills of exchange payable by the company in London. The bills solved a real problem for the company's most rapacious servants: how to get their ill-gotten wealth back to Britain. Rather than paying for insurance, transportation, and other fees, they would be able to deposit whatever they'd gained with the company in Calcutta, receiving a bill of exchange that the company would have to honor in London. The East India Company's servants took advantage. The amount of private bills of exchange that the company was liable for in London jumped from £296,562 in the fiscal year ending in 1771 to £1.58 million for the year ending in 1772, an amount equal to roughly half the company's annual revenue.[11]

Meanwhile, the East India Company was having trouble selling its wares. Ironically, its main problem was tea. Tea was the reason that the company, under the direction of Robert Clive, had taken over the right to tax in Bengal in the first place, and the reason that company leaders in Bengal felt the need to accept private deposits in bullion when Bengali

revenue promised to fall short. Pound for pound, tea was the most profitable cargo in the world. Company silver invested in goods produced
in India, like the famous cotton textiles of Bengal, on average yielded a
profit of 10 percent after expenses. Silver invested in Chinese tea yielded
30 percent—doubling the company's money every two and a half years.
Outsized profits enabled the British government to charge outsized
taxes, roughly 90 percent of the tea's wholesale price, or roughly a quarter of all customs receipts in the 1760s. "The large investment which
we are enabled now to send home by means of the supplies we remit to
China and the cargoes from hence render the revenues of this country,
an object of the most utmost importance not only to the Company but
to the British nation," Clive wrote in late 1765. Indian silver for Chinese
tea was the connection.[12]

But profits required buyers, and those were drying up precisely at the
moment they were most needed. Total sales of East India Company goods
fell from £3,564,385 to £3,254,124 in 1771. By 1772, £3,260,072 in goods
were sitting in East India Company warehouses unsold, including, crucially, 17,775,000 pounds of Chinese tea worth a little over £2 million at
the wholesale price of 2 shillings and 3.75 pence a pound set at company
auctions.[13]

The shortfall in revenues coupled with a sharp increase in liabilities
prompted the East India Company to seek new loans from the Bank of
England, £400,000 in July 1772 and £300,000 more two weeks later.
When the bank—which had its own financial troubles—balked at the second loan, advancing just £200,000 and asking for security in advance,
the East India Company turned to the government. In a meeting on
August 11, 1772, with Frederick North, who had served as prime minister
for two years, the company made it clear that it would need more than £1
million in cash "to carry on circulation of its affairs." Even if all of its debtors settled on time, by March 1773 the company would be £500,000 in
arrears—bankrupt.[14]

III. Lord North and Company Thinkers Retool
North America's Role in the Empire

Lord North was a good speaker and an able administrator. He was not
particularly interested in America and was not particularly disliked by the
colonists. Compared to Grenville, he was a saint. One of his first acts as
prime minister was to repeal most of the Townshend tax program, leaving only the reduced duties on tea. The repeal defanged the American

opposition movement by conceding to almost all of their demands. American merchants who had resolved not to import goods from Britain until the dispute was resolved, many inspired by Dickinson and similar appeals for American solidarity, found themselves ordering more than ever. All seemed on the mend. North, though, was a devotee of the East India Company's interests, which he saw as central to the maintenance of the empire itself. On a purely financial basis, the point was hard to argue. The company directly supplied more than £1 million a year in direct subsidies (£400,000 a year since 1769) and customs revenue, or roughly 10 percent of the government's 1772 income of £11 million. Over the previous three years, an internal EIC report estimated, the company had paid £2.15 million in tea duties alone.[15]

North was concerned and set out that fall to both bail out the company with a £1.4 million loan and to reform it such that it would never need saving again. One of those reforms had been proposed by a company contractor named James Steuart, a one-time radical Jacobite intellectual based in Edinburgh, whose *Principles of Political Oeconomy*, published in 1767, had established him as an expert in both the theory of money and public finance. In Steuart's view, the company's revenue problems in India—and the mass devastation of the famine—were both, at least partially, a result of its inability to see money as something other than bullion. Steuart acknowledged that bullion was necessary for the China trade and other company efforts, but, in his view, the company's complete control over the economy of Bengal meant that there was no need to limit the definition of money to bullion there. The EIC, he wrote, could form a bank in Bengal much like the Bank of England, circulating notes exchangeable for the bullion it collected in taxes, and issuing loans to the company in advance of tax receipts. Such a bank might not have saved the millions who had died, but it would save the company from its maniacal focus on bullion and give it, ultimately, new financial flexibility by establishing "a paper credit." It would also, Steuart suggested, create a new financial incentive to keep farmers, who might apply to the bank for credit, on their land, alive, and productive, which the current government did not have. Moreover, the bank, as Steuart proposed, would be run, at least in part, by the Indians themselves. Bengali *shroffs*, Steuart wrote, would become bank directors and, through the bank, "the protector of the labouring man! Interest does all."[16]

Steuart's analysis was complicated by the fact that the China trade made the only real measure of company revenue "the weight of silver."[17] The demand for high-quality silver in weight ordered the company's rationality in the same way that the concept of money derived from it, as a measure and equivalent, ordered the rationality of Britain's imperial monetary regime. Whatever the complicating local exigencies, silver was the company's primary motivation for maintaining a territorial empire—even at the cost of millions of lives. The equation between the North American and Indian Empires was made in silver; both company and Parliament were committed to extracting revenue on specie terms. In India, this meant resistance to measures, like a bank, that Steuart hoped would ease monetary scarcity while allowing the company to still export precious metal, just as the Bank of England had enabled the company to export much of the silver from Britain.

Henry Verelst, the governor who, in Bengal, had overseen the company's plunge into bankruptcy, dismissed Steuart's plan for a Bank of Bengal and a "paper credit" that might have allowed food purchases for virtually the same reasons that Hill and the Board of Trade had rejected American paper currencies in 1764. He may not have read Hill's memo, but he was a product of the system that had made it plausible as imperial policy. "As all our ideas are derived from the impression of material substance," Verelst wrote, affirming the concept of empiricism associated with Locke and David Hume, "he who uses a term not expressing some such impression, discourses without an idea."[18] A monetary "standard," Verelst wrote, could not "have any other signification than to express a certain quantity *of current coin.*"[19] And the natural way to ascertain the value of a coin, in turn, was "the price of bullion in the market."[20] In Bengal, for example, when a coin is received in trade, "it is necessary to estimate the intrinsic value of each piece, and calculate the whole mass by relation to" the fineness and weight of a well-known local coinage.[21] Silver is "the only measure of commerce in Bengal," Verelst wrote.[22] Thus, Verelst reasoned, the only solution was either a new gold coin or more silver, either through trade with the Middle East or by sending less to China. "Dreaming of banks and paper credit," as Steuart had done, was folly, Verelst wrote. Real "wealth," silver, had to be acquired if Britain's extractive empire was to bear fruit.[23] Without silver from India, there would be no tea. Without silver for tea from America, the company's profits could not be realized in Britain. Anything else, Verelst wrote, meant "rendering the revenues of a distant country useless to Great Britain." Verelst's analysis was a report from the coalface of empire as a currency union as it had manifested in India rather than America. The results were far grimmer and yet nothing had been learned. Philosophy masquerading as necessity still dominated the discussion. "Bengal, like other subjected provinces, must yield its tribute," Verelst concluded. The same, or similar, would soon be said of America.[24]

Regarding the East India Company's solvency in London, Steuart suggested that the British government should look to America. Four million pounds of tea were smuggled into British possessions annually, Steuart wrote, most of it paid for in bullion. Smuggled tea was popular because it avoided taxes and was thus roughly half the cost of the legal stuff. Since there was no way, fiscally speaking, to cut the tea taxes charged in Britain itself, it made sense instead to reimburse the EIC for the taxes on tea it intended to export to Europe and America. That reimbursement, or "drawback," would allow the company to sell its tea in America and elsewhere for either the same or slightly less than the prices offered by the smugglers, thus driving them out of the market and increasing the market for East India Company tea proportionably. The company could use the silver earned in America and Europe, meanwhile, to either supply China or supplement its stocks in Bengal. "And if the Custom-House duty upon tea exported be sacrificed for obtaining this great end," Steuart concluded, "the balance of the trade of the nation will be proportionally augmented."[25]

In late 1772 a company official named Robert Herries fleshed out Steuart's proposal, framing it as a way of eliminating the vast stockpiles of tea currently just taking up space, which, if sold, would generate £1,425,000 and solve all the company's problems in a stroke. Selling that tea in Europe, the company's directors concluded, would only encourage Europeans to smuggle duty-free tea back into Britain. The answer, then, would reside in America, which officials estimated, at the right price, might consume £2 million in tea a year. The question was whether to carry over the 3 pence per pound tax on tea, the last remaining vestige of the Townshend duties repealed three years earlier. The Townshend tea tax had proved an impediment to tea sales when it came on top of British customs duties, but if these were removed, so was any impediment to paying the taxes in America. Company officials expected to be able to sell their tea at 2 shillings a pound including the tax, 7 pence less, even, than Dutch smugglers. They had no reason to suspect that Americans would object to the tax alone. Many American merchants had weathered public opprobrium and paid the taxes. John Hancock alone had imported 120,000 pounds in taxed tea in the years since 1770. There was seemingly little need to worry.[26]

Some commentators warned that the American market would never prove as lucrative, in silver terms, as the company expected. If Americans bought the tea, it would be at the expense of other "merchants in England, and thereby tend to increase the distress which is already too severely felt for want of remittances," one merchant wrote to Henry Crabb Boulton, the company's chairman, in the wake of the Tea Act passing in 1773. And that was assuming the Americans could find silver to pay for it in the first place, as "there is not enough specie in the country to pay for the quantity of [the tea] intended to be exported."[27] As before during the Stamp Act crisis, these voices were ignored.

IV. A Brief but Suggestive Interlude at Sea

The North Atlantic was an "angry flood," Josiah Quincy Jr. wrote, sailing south from Boston in February 1773. Two weeks out of Boston, he was between continents. The weather was fierce. At night, "distant flashes of lightning gleamed all around the horizon," and the "waves seemed to curl with flames, just sufficient to keep the darkness visible." Bundled and strapped onto a hencoop for air as his ship charged south, Quincy experienced an exultant calm. "What a transition have I made, and am still making!" he wrote. His plan had been to leave during the winter in New England, to land in South Carolina and follow the spring north, spreading the gospel of insurrection in his wake. Quincy was twenty-nine years old and dying of tuberculosis.[28] He was also, reputedly, one of the greatest legal orators in Boston, a confirmed patriot, and a radical. He compared the storms to his own work in the Massachusetts courts. The ripping northeast wind, distant thunderheads, and spray across the deck "conspired to make deep impressions and fit the mind for meditation," Quincy wrote. "The little hall of right and wrong," the courthouse, "is changed for the wide, immeasurable ocean." The ship was "scarce a speck in this wide expanse," yet it still braved "this world of night and chaos." In resisting Great Britain, he felt, the colonies were doing the same.

Quincy had left a city electric with politics, a time, Quincy's grandson recalled, of "stern agitations and profound anxieties" that Quincy and his wife "shared deeply and passionately." Each year since 1770, at Quincy's suggestion, the city had held a vigil gathering in meeting houses and churches to commemorate the five men and boys shot down by occupying British troops, and the anniversary was barely a month away when he sailed. Quincy and his family had been at the heart of the controversy. As a young lawyer, he had joined the radical faction in Massachusetts and by 1770 was reportedly calling himself "Wilkes Quincy," after the famous

English dissenter. In 1770 he had helped John Adams, his cousin through marriage, defend British soldiers on trial for the killings, while his older brother Samuel served as prosecutor. Afterward, Quincy emerged as a vital patriot voice, battling Governor Thomas Hutchinson in the newspaper columns and passionately reasoned pamphlets that fed the controversy between North America and the "mother" country. Just a few months before traveling south, he had been elected to the Boston Committee of Correspondence. His journey, in part, was meant to put northern radicals in contact with their southern counterparts. He was a young man at the center of an engrossing controversy. Even sweating and brittle with fever, he could think of little else.

Two weeks into the voyage, Quincy overheard a fellow passenger expressing outrage at the "arbitrary" and "unjust" imperial government and sought to draw him into a conversation on American rights. It turned out he was a British naval officer named John Alexander Hunter, a purser with fifteen years' service in charge of funds and accounts on a twenty-gun warship stationed in Boston Harbor and now sailing south in disgrace. He had been caught embezzling, having turned a £45 salary into an income of £400 a year, and thrown out of the service.

"Mr. Quincy, we all know this, Great Britain has no right to tax you," Hunter said. "The ministry know it as well as you, but money must be had somewhere. Every thing is strained to the utmost at home. The people of England see as well as you, that North America must one day be independent, and it is her interest, and most certainly that of the present administration, to prevent this, for a much longer time than you imagine." Britain would not relent, Hunter argued, and as long as its navy dominated the Atlantic Ocean, Americans would eventually be forced to submit. "Why all the world are slaves," Hunter concluded, "and N[orth] America can't hope to be free."[29]

V. The East India Company Sends Tea to America and Finds Itself Unwelcome

The East India Company's initial consignment to America consisted of 599,000 pounds of tea heading for four colonial ports: Boston, New York, Philadelphia, and Charleston. The tea would be delivered to colonists who had applied to be the company's consignees, warehousing it in America and auctioning it off four times a year, as was done in London. For some, Bengal's fate foretold the colonies' future if the East India Company got a foothold in America. A New York pamphleteer in "Alarm No. 2" noted on

October 9, 1773, that the company stood accused in the London press of having "monopolized the absolute necessities of Life in India, at a Time of apprehended Scarcity," even as "Thousands perished by this black, sordid, and cruel Avarice." Others, initially, could not understand the fuss. Dickinson, asked for his opinion on the slate of East India Company reforms that continued the tea levy, at first thought it had to do with the American colonies. It changed taxes on tea in Britain, while retaining the 3 pence per pound tax to be levied in specie on landing in America. This maintained the status quo. To be sure, he wrote in an analysis dated October 30, 1773, the act "is made expressly for the benefit and advantage of the East-India Company," but it left American affairs unchanged.[30] This was before Dickinson, or many other Americans, knew about the full extent of the company's conduct in India.

After hearing that the company ships loaded with tea had set sail for America in November, Dickinson revised his view. In the interim, he had read up on the company's behavior in India and surmised America's role in securing its profits in London. Now the company's new role in American tax collection seemed ominous: "Insolence . . . joined with Oppression," Dickinson wrote. In giving the company the right to sell tea and collect taxes in North America, Parliament had treated its North American colonies like the spoils of war, to be "divided among themselves as lawful Booty." The law made clear that in the British empire, "Subjects" were "considered as Property," Dickinson wrote. The company, he now knew, was not a neutral factor. "They have levied War, excited Rebellions, dethroned lawful Princes, and sacrificed Millions for the Sake of Gain," Dickinson wrote. He had read about the death toll in India. "The Revenues of mighty Kingdoms have centered in their Coffers. And these not being sufficient to glut their Avarice, they have, by the most unparalleled Barbarities, Extortions and Monopolies, stripped the miserable Inhabitants of their Property, and reduced whole Provinces to Indigence and Ruin. Fifteen hundred Thousand, it is said, perished by Famine in one Year, Not because the Earth denied its Fruits, but this Company and its Servants engrossed all the Necessaries of Life, and set them at so high a Rate, that the Poor could not purchase them." Now, beggared by demands from creditors returning from abroad, many of them its own employees, its directors had "cast their Eyes on *America*, as a new Theatre, whereon to exercise their Talents of Rapine, Oppression and Cruelty."[31]

The question, still, was not the taxes themselves but the economic sovereignty, the power they implied. The consignment system was nothing like the near-total control that the company exercised in Bengal. What mattered was that Parliament had apparently surrendered its own interest in the tea tax merely to secure the right to tax in America. "It is not the paltry Sum of Three-Pence which is now demanded, but the Principle upon which it is demanded, that we are contending against," Dickinson wrote about the last of the Townshend taxes, on the tea purchased with Indian silver, still standing after years of protests. The events in India, the violence and indifference, the helplessness and greed, confirmed Dickinson's analysis: politics preceded property, constituted it, made it real: an analysis the Stamp Act, parliamentary taxation, and the link between money and taxes in North America made not only clear but necessary. *"Before we pay any Thing,"* he concluded, *"let us see whether we have any Thing we can call our own to pay."* In fact, America and the right to tax it had barely figured in parliamentary debates. The debates had centered on preserving the solvency of the East India Company and with it the benefits those revenues brought the state. The British reaction to American resistance would fall along those same lines.[32]

On the evening of December 16, 1773, a group of Bostonians dressed as Native Americans stole aboard the *Dartmouth, Eleanor,* and *Beaver* and emptied their 340 chests of East India Company tea into Boston Harbor. The whole amounted to 90,000 pounds of tea, worth roughly £9,000 including £1,125 due in taxes. New York and Philadelphia avoided similar scenes by forcing the ships carrying East India Company tea to return to England before landing. In Charleston, the tea was landed but went unsold and the duties unpaid. It rotted in a warehouse until 1775. It was a short episode, relatively unimportant on its own. The tea, however, was not the point.[33]

The point, as soon became apparent in London, was that America had interfered with Parliament's ability to bail out the East India Company, doing so in any way it saw fit. The danger to the East India Company in 1773 had focused parliamentary minds in a manner that no event in America before, perhaps, the Declaration of Independence ever would. The danger to the company, and the threat its insolvency posed to national finances, had suddenly and explosively expanded the average parliamentarian's sense of the empire in India's real significance, Thomas Pownall wrote. "People now at last begin to view those Indian affairs, not simply as beneficial appendages connected to the empire; but . . . [as] indissolubly interwoven with our whole system of commerce." The commerce was the empire and vice versa. In response, "people in general from these views begin to see such a union of interest, such a co-existence between the two," the company and the nation, "that they tremble with horror even at the imagination of the downfall of this Indian part our system; knowing that it must necessarily involve with its fall, the ruin of the whole edifice of the British empire."[34]

VI. America Responds with Unified Resistance to Parliament's Action

When Parliament began to marshal a response to the events in Boston in March 1774, North and his allies were clear that the issue was not tea or even the power to tax. The issue was whether or not Parliament would have the ability to fit America into its empire in the way it saw fit. "I very much fear the question now brought to issue will be nothing less than whether the colonies of America are, or are not the colonies of Great Britain," George Rice said at opening the parliamentary debate on March 7, 1774. America was a British "dominion," and Parliament's role was to make of it "an useful dominion," a part fitting into the whole. The key was "union," North argued, opening the next week's debate. "We must control them or submit to them."[35]

North's plan was to punish Boston, to make an example of the city with the highest profile as a center of resistance. He proposed a three-part system of retribution: closing the port of Boston, suspending the charter of Massachusetts Bay Colony, much as it had done to New York several years earlier, and the Administration of Justice Act, which stipulated that officials charged with crimes in Massachusetts could have their trials relocated to Britain, if it seemed unlikely that they could get a fair trial. Most of the pushback he received was from members of Parliament who reminded North that the Americans were objecting to taxes because of the precedent set with the Stamp Act. If his desire was to control America, to make it useful, the best thing to do was to repeal the tax on tea and then go ahead, opening up the North American market to the East India Company.

"Tea," the Anglo-Irish parliamentarian Edmund Burke said, opposing the measures on April 19, 1774, "is perhaps the most important object, taking it with its necessary connections, of any in the mighty circle of commerce. If commercial principles had been the true motives to the repeal, or had they been at all attended to, tea would have been the last article we should have left taxed for a subject of controversy."

Rather, a year earlier Parliament was faced with what Burke called "the precipice of general bankruptcy" with the famine-induced failure of the East India Company. Parliament's East India committees, Burke continued, had learned that "without a more extensive sale of that article, our

East India revenues and acquisitions can have no certain connection with this country." With the reimbursement of duties on tea sold to America, Burke continued, Parliament had made its dependence on the American market plain, especially as it looked to the future. "It is through the American trade of tea that your East India conquests are to be prevented from crushing you with their burthen: They are ponderous indeed; and they must have that great country to lean upon, or they tumble upon your head." Yet the matter of the tax had not been attended to. "It is the same folly that has lost you at once the benefit of both the west and of the east," Burke said.[36]

After Burke finished, an argument burst out on the floor of St. Stephen's Chapel. Some accused Burke of maligning George Grenville. Others argued that Grenville had confused the issue. Parliament was not punishing Boston because Boston had resisted the tax on tea. Parliament was punishing Boston because it resisted the act that reformed and saved the East India Company. North rose at the end of the evening to second this broader view, ironically echoing Dickinson and others who argued for colonial unity. The tax was less important, North argued, than the power that the taxation implied, the power to arrange the colonial institutions for Britain's (and the East India Company's) benefit. If "at this time the tea tax cannot be advantageously repealed; there is not one reason existing for repealing it," North told the ministers. "If resistance is intended to the Act we have passed and those we have in contemplation, can anyone suppose this repeal would prevent it. No. The mere tax is not their objection." What the colonists rejected was parliamentary power to order its empire. In North's view, the Americans had not resisted the tea tax but the India bill itself and the empire-building power it implied, just as they had resisted the silver clause in the Stamp Act. "I don't believe that had this tax been laid before the Stamp Act it would have met with any objection." The lesson North had taken from the Stamp Act's saga was not lenity. Like Grenville, he had learned that it was the power the Stamp Act implied that had to be preserved. "In order effectually to serve your colonies you must show them you are both able and resolved to maintain your power over and to control them. I don't know what the event of the measures I have proposed may be, but I am sure that resolution and firmness will be a great means of making them effectual."[37]

The reaction to his firmness in America, though, was another round of debates about colonial rights and plans to make them plain to Parliament. The connection to India and the broader imperial system was largely ignored. The point, taken up by Dickinson in a new series of letters and by many others in newspapers across the continent, was that if Parliament could do these things to Boston and Massachusetts, it could do them anywhere. That other places had acted differently than Boston, that Boston merchants had different interests in the tea, and different trading relationships with Britain more generally, were not important. The fact that Boston had been singled out mattered less than the precedent. Dickinson's closing argument in the *Farmer* letters, in other words, was finally bearing real fruit. Principles were more important than property. What those principles were, though, required further deliberation. The colonies took the opportunity to make those deliberations later that same year, in Carpenters' Hall in Philadelphia, in what became known as the First Continental Congress. But the Philadelphia congress would have even more significant consequences. When the congress's October 1774 address to the House of Lords and the king reached London early in 1775, calling for the repeal of virtually every piece of colonial legislation from the Declaratory Act of 1765 through the recent assault on the liberties of Massachusetts, and threatening to cut off all exports to Britain if Parliament did not concede, Lord North saw it as a further threat to the imperial system.[38] He decided to declare war.

VII. The Timing and Causes of the American Revolution Reconsidered

The American War of Independence is usually said to have begun on April 19, 1775, with the battles at Lexington and Concord. In reality, it began months earlier in Westminster. Quincy, still desperately ill, had arrived in London from Massachusetts in November 1774 in the quixotic hope of brokering a deal that would prevent the conflict. On January 13, 1775, he visited with Thomas Pownall, the beloved former governor of Massachusetts. War, Pownall told him, was already sure. "The matter is decided," Pownall said. He was right. Early the next month, North introduced a resolution declaring that Massachusetts, "countenanced and encouraged" by other colonies, was in "rebellion." North knew what he was doing. Lord John Cavendish called the resolution a "declaration of civil war." John Wilkes, mayor of London, said that North's aim was to "engage our officers and troops to act against them as against rebels." Burke said North's decision was destined to "to dye the rivers of America with the blood of her inhabitants." The *London Evening Post* too said "civil war" was being declared.[39]

To be sure, North and his allies did not intend to bring the whole continent into a conflict, only Massachusetts. They hoped a sharp, violent campaign would serve as a deterrent, restoring Britain's authority on the continent. The model they had in mind was the campaign against the Jacobite rebels who had risen in Scotland in 1745. There, the appearance of a British army had led to squabbles between the rebels themselves and, eventually, to near total defeat at Culloden field. After their victory, the British had scoured the Highlands, pillaging and burning, while banning Highland dress and weaponry, in an attempt to crush all organized resistance. The results had been more than acceptable to London and might be repeatable in Massachusetts. "The people of Scotland were better humoured since the rebellion," Attorney General Alexander Wedderburn, a Scot who had been Clive's personal attorney before he entered government, told Thomas Hutchinson on January 19, 1775. The resolution declaring Massachusetts in rebellion passed with large majorities in Parliament on February 6 and the House of Lords on the following day. North immediately sent a letter to Boston, authorizing General Thomas Gage to begin offensive operations. The ships carrying Gage's orders to meet "force with force" in Massachusetts arrived on April 16, 1775. Fighting began three days later.[40]

This timing is important if we want to understand the causes of the American Revolution. It matters because it shifts where we might look. The roots of actual Revolutionary violence in America have always been somewhat difficult to discern. Practically speaking, there was no organized rebellion in February 1775, no colonial army massing to besiege Boston or repel British forces, no navy being built, no funds being raised. New Englanders had made ad hoc preparations to be sure, filching British gunpowder and attempting to buy more abroad, as the arms and powder rumored to be gathered in arsenals like Concord attested. But the preparations were inadequate for a war because none was planned. The First Continental Congress, like virtually every official gathering in the colonies before it, had been anxious to declare its allegiance to the king and to Great Britain. The delegates' goal was to reform the connection between the colonies and Parliament, not to end it. The means they chose were mercantile, not military. Individual peacemakers, like Quincy, still hoped to see escalating tensions resolved. It was Parliament that had decided force was necessary. The American reaction to that force, days after Gage's orders were received, was perfectly understandable. The Massachusetts militiamen who flocked toward Concord and Lexington on April 19 were simply defending themselves. Parliament was the war-making body of the British state, and Parliament began the Revolutionary War.[41]

Still, the broader American reaction to the fighting was immediate and unified and must be explained. Accounts of the Revolutionary struggle, the ten years between the Stamp Act Crisis of 1765 and the first shots being fired, have long wrestled with a paradox. On one hand, American thinkers like Dickinson, Adams, and others writing in newspapers, pamphlets, sermons, and songs articulated a deeply political, rights-based account of their resistance, directed toward an imperial constitution they hoped to reform. This American constitutionalism was matched by British insistence on the sovereign supremacy of Parliament, making it possible—indeed compelling—to view the entire saga of America's pre-Revolutionary decade as defined, largely, by an intellectual debate about the nature of rulership, over whether Parliament's power could ever be limited or divided. It was precisely these kinds of questions and debates that animated American resistance in the press, in colonial legislatures, finding its way, indirectly, into the debates of Parliament itself.[42]

On the other hand, the actual working business of American resistance was far from abstract. It took place in a quotidian, mercantile register, expressed in terms of a moral, patriotic character given to British or American goods in trade, like the tea that had been thrown into Boston Harbor. For all the oppression that Americans rightly felt, and the character of the rights they drew from it, the parliamentary diktats that caused their concerns were taxes on court fees, paints, glass, and tea, objects of everyday use. Likewise, for all the outrage and talk of constitutionalism and rights, the primary form of American resistance from 1765 to 1775 was the non-importation agreement. This was a boycott on British goods, and, with the Second Continental Congress, a non-exportation agreement that threatened to shift America's trade into other channels, selling to the Dutch, the Spanish, or the French. Thus, in telling the story of America's Revolutionary period, we are left a seeming contradiction between universal ideals and pocketbook politics, abstract theories and their mundane expression in the colonial marketplace.[43]

If, however, we survey the global dimensions of the crisis facing the British Empire, the difficulty resolves. The British Empire's aim in the 1760s was to remake what we might call its commercial constitution, a task that, in the view of its political class, required precisely the new powers identified by Grenville in the aftermath of the Stamp Act crisis. Those powers were important because they were deemed necessary to make American colonists more tractably reliable consumers of British goods. The American project, from the Stamp Act on, was how to limit imperial power such that precisely the kind of interference Parliament deemed necessary would be impossible to pursue—in other words, unconstitutional. American resistance came to be articulated in a constitutional register, then, because it was the imperial constitution that they hoped to affect—and, to their minds, preserve. Yet their resistance movement took the form of mercantile protest because the contested terrain was precisely the empire's commercial constitution, its emergent world system.

If the American story has seemed paradoxical, meanwhile, the British side of it has remained mysterious, touched with tragic inevitability. Why would Parliament declare war on its colonies, when all it had to do was to show a willingness to compromise? Was it its members' sense of honor? A lack of imagination? A bloody-minded belief in the efficacy of violence? A combination of all three? As one historian has recently observed, the British course seems to have been set from the moment America refused the East India Company's tea. By late 1774 there was seemingly no chance that violence could be avoided as "too much had already occurred."[44] American historians have also seen war as "all but inevitable" by 1774, given both sides' preparation for armed conflict.[45]

This sense of inevitability fades, however, in the face of perceived imperial necessity. From the British perspective, to avoid war was to negate the empire itself. The empire, as Grenville and his peers perceived it from the 1760s on, was a system meant to drive wealth toward the imperial center. This was nothing new. However, dominant notions of how that might be done had changed. They had shifted from relatively simplistic ideas of maximizing imports of gold and silver via the balance of trade to an idea of regular subordination defined by the ability to command the terms of trade, of value, within the imperial sphere. Rather than mercantilist hoarding, their focus was on the power to create a coherent world system, what Giovanni Arrighi has termed "free trade imperialism." The goal, as Verelst had put it with regard to Bengal, was to avoid "rendering the revenues of a distant country useless to Great Britain." If the empire in North America was useless, in other words, it was not an empire at all. If America could not contribute to that system because it was unwilling to change, then it would have left the empire. This was unacceptable.

The only question left was whether the change would be slow or fast. After the Stamp Act, Britain had decided on a slow approach, but the famine and the East India Company's bankruptcy forced their hand. The underlying cause of Parliament's decision to go to war in America was its apparent need, in the broadest sense, for economic sovereignty in

North America. In an increasingly global empire, it needed to make sure that Americans would be able to buy what the empire was ready to sell, and it needed to ensure that the terms of trade would make the proceeds from those sales immediately intelligible in London. It needed Hill's currency union. If Americans were not willing to give it to them—resisted, indeed, the slightest steps toward the union that empire demanded—they were willing to kill in order to secure the point.[46]

A decade after the Stamp Act, ideas about the relationship between money and power were still at the root of the crisis. If anything, the institutional contradiction identified by Hill had deepened as both sides shifted the debate. In Britain, American resistance to the Stamp Act had radicalized the ministers most committed to a global vision of empire. They demanded greater imperial power in response to American resistance, with the ultimate aim of erasing difference, of flattening the monetary landscape. In America, the sheer variety evident in colonial political economy had led thinkers like Dickinson to create a vision of divvied sovereignty, an imperial federalism bound by "rights" rather than claims to property, which was provocative because it denied precisely the power that Parliament demanded as a necessity. The Bengal famine and its aftermath had clarified the conflict, making it immediate and acute. In 1773 American buyers were needed to save the empire. There was no avoiding or postponing. And they had rejected the role they had been assigned because of the way legislation like the Tea Act threatened their perceived rights, the space they had identified within the prewar constitution to make institutions of their own.

In retrospect, British leaders probably could have avoided the conflict altogether if they had been willing to imagine an empire like the one they actually had, where a variety of money systems and other local economies could work together as complementary rather than competing forms. The reason they did not, in the end, seems to have been a fundamental insecurity tinged with hubris, a fear of disintegration coupled with a desperate desire to make the world conform to their vision of it, regardless of the human cost. As we have seen, similar forces were already at work in Bengal with devastating results, for, as Verelst wrote, Parliament had to go to war not because of what was happening in America, per se, but because of the implications of American resistance for an empire that stretched from Boston to Bengal. Hunt, the disgraced purser on Quincy's voyage to South Carolina, was right. Not just America, but the world as the British Empire ordered it, was becoming enslaved, not to a particular king, but to a set of ideas about the nature of economic reality. Britain itself was not exempt from this process. Its empire in North America had fallen prey to its leaders' preconceptions. The system became its own cage.[47]

The money question that had precipitated the crisis nearly a decade earlier was no longer explicit in the debate, but it had not disappeared. It had shaped both Parliament's notions of its own power and, with the Stamp Act, Americans' sense of the totalizing changes that accepting such power might entail. The famine in Bengal had shown how far a British government would go in pursuit of its financial goals. The ensuing debate revealed the extent to which those ends were explicitly tied to philosophical claims about the nature of money—claims that Parliament believed applied equally to Americans. But they did not. Not yet. The next few months would show just how free America still was.

PART THREE

The Double Revolution

FIG. 8. Six Shillings, Pennsylvania, 1775, Reverse.

CHAPTER SEVEN

The Double Revolution

AMERICA, 1775–1776

FIG. 9. Continental Dollar Design, "Fugido: I have Left," United States, 1776, Obverse.

FIG. 10. Continental Dollar Design, "Fugido: I have Left," United States, 1776, Reverse.

I. A Double Revolution Begins

The American Revolution, as it began in 1775, consisted of two interrelated projects. We might call this America's double revolution. The first was political, a push for local, democratic control brought on by a combination of imperial overreach and brilliant organizing by colonists like Dickinson and hundreds of others. American colonies asserted that they were "states," independent sovereign bodies "united" only in the sense that they had come together to achieve common goals of, first, protecting their rights within the empire and, second, after the summer of 1776, achieving independence.

The second project was monetary. Within days after the fighting began, colonies, now states, began shucking off the strictures that the Board of

Trade and imperial government had placed on their monetary powers and began financing the war using bills of credit. It was this second revolution that made the first real. Making a state meant making war, and making war meant making money. Political freedom in the first instance was predicated on financial capacity, and that on the freedom to conceptualize money to match American circumstances. If Americans had accepted that money was gold and silver, as the empire avowed, they would have lost the war before Parliament began it. Instead, they started the war on their own terms.

By making money, the colonists made their Revolution real. This was perhaps most obvious on the level of the states, where many new Revolutionary governments sought to secure their legitimacy with elections before issuing new, tax-grounded bills of credit. These bills of credit, in turn, were a confirmation of the legitimacy of new political arrangements. Every time a colonist used them, accepting or giving them in payment, they confirmed their faith in the revolution as a popular project. But the monetary revolution's most powerful contribution was the role it played in creating the United States itself. Money was the new nation's first project. The idea of creating a continental currency, in itself, implied a continental government, whose form was as yet unclear, to be sure, but nonetheless one with powers analogous to the states themselves. The creation of the continental dollar, the currency of the American Revolution, was the creation of the United States. This connection is even, albeit obliquely, mentioned in the Declaration of Independence. When Thomas Jefferson wrote that Americans "mutually pledge to each other our Lives, our Fortunes and our sacred Honor," he likely had the new nations' bills of credit in mind. The dollar was the physical embodiment of their pledge.

II. The Tax Man Cometh

For one new arrival, American money would come to define the conflict. On November 30, 1774, a thirty-seven-year-old retired tax collector named Thomas Paine was carried on a stretcher onto the docks of Philadelphia. Trained by his Quaker father as a corset-maker, Paine had spent much of the past two decades as a circuit rider for the British excise service. These had been exhausting years, riding from hamlet to hamlet, brewer to distiller, chasing smugglers and collecting dues in the rich countryside of southern England, as a member of perhaps its most hated profession. When "the devil's away with the exciseman . . . we'll laugh, sing, and rejoice man," Paine's contemporary Robert Burns, and fellow exciseman, was to write a few years later in one of his most popular songs. Men like Burns and Paine made a living collecting the taxes that had turned Britain into a formidable state. It was militarily powerful, in part, because of its ability to extract taxes, leveraging them to go ever deeper into debt to drive naval and military production. Over the previous century, British taxes had grown to new heights, making tax collection an increasingly oner- ous task. Collectors' pay, however, had not increased, making them vul- nerable to bribes and incentives to look the other way. Paine himself had been briefly dismissed from the service in 1765 for "stamping" as inspected warehouses he had never visited.[1]

In 1772 his fellow officers nominated Paine to write up their concerns. The result was *The Case of the Officers of the Excise,* Paine's first public work, a tightly argued essay on the expenses and temptations of tax collection signed by three thousand fellow excise officers. It made little impression in London, but it was the end of Paine's first career. Faced with dismissal, bankruptcy, and, in May 1774, divorce from his second wife, Elizabeth, Paine turned to friends he had made in London's scientific and radical circles, where he had become an avid lecture-attender and self-educator. One of these acquaintances was Benjamin Franklin, still serving as Penn- sylvania's representative in the imperial capital. Recommendation from Franklin in hand, Paine sold everything he owned and set sail as a com- mon passenger to Philadelphia.

The passage was a trial. Disease struck in the mid-Atlantic, killing pas- sengers and crew alike. Paine arrived in Pennsylvania's metropolis still feverish and weak but alive. The power of Franklin's recommendation was soon evident. Within months Paine had secured work editing the *Pennsyl- vania Magazine* with bookseller Robert Aikin and tutoring the children of the city's merchants. His essays against slavery and on the suicide of Robert Clive attracted attention and opened more doors. In Britain, he had been a minor hanger-on in a city where wealth and birth, or proxim- ity to both, were the only path to significance. In Philadelphia, he was increasingly a respected intellectual. Every circle, every conversation, was open to him. For the first time, he felt heard, valued for his ability rather than judged for his failures. It was a heady time, appreciated and unex- pected. And it was at this moment that, as Paine later recalled, the coun- try was "set on fire about my ears." "Bad as I believed the ministry to be, I never conceived them capable of a measure so rash and wicked as the commencing of hostilities," Paine recalled in the seventh essay of his series

The American Crisis. After February 1775, "it was time to stir. It was time for every man to stir."[2]

III. The Double Revolution Comes to New England

After the clash at Lexington and Concord the colonies surrounding Boston had both revolutions forced on them with shocking immediacy. Preparations on the local level in Massachusetts had been ongoing for months. But open conflict brought a new set of commitments, a new need for money to meet them in every colony, and, for the members of the Second Continental Congress, meeting of Paine's new home of Philadelphia that May, for the colonies as a whole. The need for new money was convulsive. It forced Americans to revive monetary institutions that they had either mothballed or strictly limited because of parliamentary policy since 1764. New Englanders, whose money had been restricted since 1751, had arguably the most revolutionary response. Massachusetts, Connecticut, Rhode Island, and New Hampshire threw aside a quarter century of restrictions on their currencies in order to meet the British threat. As a new, American army gathered at Boston, drawn from surrounding farms, fishing villages, and interior hamlets, these restrictions were abandoned in favor of monies based on the credit of the new states and their people.[3]

By midsummer, Massachusetts abandoned restrictions on its currency set by Governor Thomas Hutchinson and his allies a quarter century before, alongside parliamentary restrictions on bills of credit. The Currency Act of 1751 had barred New Englanders from issuing a currency that was a "legal tender" acceptable in all payments. The only legal tender was silver. Thus, Massachusetts currency since 1751 had been based on silver, but silver that they didn't have—having once again shipped it all abroad. This created a crushing contradiction. On May 3, 1775, the Massachusetts Provincial Congress at Watertown, nine miles up the Charles River from the besieged city, authorized borrowing £100,000 "lawful money," in gold and silver, at 6 percent interest. But the plan failed almost immediately, proving a "slow uncertain method of supplying the treasury," for the obvious reason that there was practically no circulating silver. The need for silver, though, they soon realized, was only there because Parliament had demanded it. Ideas about money, quite literally, were tied up with political sovereignty. The terms of the failed loan, in May, referenced "King *George* the Second." The Massachusetts bills of credit issued two and a half months later, printed by an exiled Paul Revere, bore the motto *"Issued in defense of* AMERICAN *liberty.*" In July, Massachusetts authorized £100,000 lawful money in bills of credit printed in denominations as small as one shilling. The transition had been made.[4]

In the colonies within marching distance of Boston, the pattern was similar. New Hampshire showed the same initial hesitation as Massachusetts. New Hampshire, too, was in the peculiar position of having a money based on gold and silver it didn't have. After the Seven Years' War, the colony had taxed in and burnt all of its outstanding "Old Tenor" bills of credit and went on the hard-money standard prescribed by Parliament. The May 25, 1765, law establishing New Hampshire's lawful money used the value of a variety of foreign gold and silver coins to establish what the value of a New Hampshire pound would be. That new standard, according to law, would apply to "all debts Bargains Contracts & dues . . . wherein money is to be paid or is made the measure & value of the things under consideration," and book "accts shall be kept and regulated accordingly" if they were to be valid in court. In its minutes, the assembly called the law "A Bill for Establishing the value of money."[5]

On the day New Hampshire governor John Wentworth approved the assembly's valuation bill, June 28, 1765, the assembly passed the year's tax bill, for £1,305, to be paid "in specie." "Specie," in this case, did not mean gold and silver. It meant "in kind." The text of the law made it explicit: "Whereas there are but small sums of paper Bills of Credit now circulating in the Province in proportion to the largeness of the Taxes by reason of his Majesty's good subjects may be put to great difficulty to procure any particular sort of money to pay their Taxes," the assembly stipulated that it would accept bills, gold or silver, or—and more to the point—a list of New Hampshire produce in taxes. Bar iron, hemp, Indian corn, rye, peas, winter wheat, barley, pork, beef, flax, bees or bayberry wax, "Well tanned sole leather," tallow, "Winter & Spring Codfish," pitch, tar, turpentine, white pine joists and boards, and two-inch white oak planks were all accepted at rates established in the *"New Tenor"* valuation, "in specie" but not in coin.[6]

Payment in kind continued until 1775, when, on Saturday, May 20, the Fourth Provincial Congress stated that in order to avoid the "most abject Slavery" and "preserve our most darling Rights and inestimable Privileges" and having been "Reduced therefore by this most Terrible necessity," it would raise an army of two thousand men.[7] It could not pay troops with wax or white pine boards. But what was the alternative? Bills of credit were known, but few in the legislature remembered the mechanics of issuing them. They hesitated.

The New Hampshirites' vacillation was understandable. Massachusetts, their much larger neighbor to the south, was still trying to make a loan plan work. Moreover, at that point New Hampshire had done without an official, physical money for nearly a decade and had been under the official parliamentary restriction on paper currency for a quarter century. The restrictions had consequences. As a colony, New Hampshire had had to fight the governor and Board of Trade for each money bill and faced constant comparison with their supposedly more successful neighbors to the south. In May 1775 those same legislators were faced with a conundrum: they had to pay for troops, and they had no coin. With Parliament an enemy they could make bills of credit, but New Hampshirites were unsure as to how, and uncertain about whether they should. So, they reached out to the Second Continental Congress for help.

"We have resolved to raise forthwith two thousand men," the New Hampshire Congress wrote John Sullivan and John Langdon, its representatives in Philadelphia, on May 23, 1775. "How we shall pay them, you are sensible must now be one question. We trust as you know the state of the Colony that you will enter into the full importance of the question." Just in case, they described that "state" for them: "The little cash we ever had, is by one means or another, almost entirely drained off. . . . Yet we seem to have no method left but borrowing, and we don't know that we can borrow, unless we issue a proper currency ourselves, or have a currency on a general plan, or can borrow in some of the other colonies."[8] They were, in essence, wrestling with the same problem their ancestors had in 1690, a set of ideas about money that produced a sense of helplessness induced by imperial policy. In a separate letter to its continental counterpart, the New Hampshire Congress asked for a "general plan for bills of credit."[9] In the meantime, the congress decided to shoulder the burden personally. They resolved that "every member pledge his Honour & Estate in the name of his Constituents to pay their proportion of maintaining and paying the officers & soldiers," letting their personal credit stand in for the obligation of the whole.[10]

The problem with that plan, however, was that even the personal credit of members of New Hampshire's Congress was of little use to volunteers struggling to keep themselves fed in the camps outside of Boston. At virtually the first hints of violence in the hinterlands, men and boys from the rock-scraped coasts of coastal New England to the far river valleys abutting Canada had converged on British-occupied Boston. From the beginning, American leaders believed that the siege would turn on whether or not these volunteers could be paid and fed. The two were practically the same problem. Much of what troops received in pay was understood to go toward "subsistence," supplementing whatever rations they received.[11]

With the port of Boston effectively closed, farmers and tradesmen along the Charles and Mystic Rivers had welcomed the soldiers, both as a relief from the British force and as a market for crops that might have gone to waste with the city closed. Many farmers had a side business carting produce to the city in the summer and sledding it in the winter, and the American army was a logical market to seek out. For the farmers streaming into camp with food for sale, most of the soldiers would have been strangers—fellow New Englanders, to be sure, but not people whom it would be wise to do business with on credit the way they would have with a neighbor or the settled proprietor of a store. No, pay would have to come in some form of money, a fact that the officers leading the army soon came to recognize.[12]

Barely a month after the first shots were fired on May 29, 1775, Colonel John Stark wrote the New Hampshire Congress that there was a "great want of money" because "neither the officers or soldiers can subsist without it, much longer by any means." A stranger's credit would only go so far. Stark wrote that he was receiving "daily complaints" that unless money was advanced to the army directly, soldiers' "courage will fail, and they will return; and by that means, we shall work our own destruction." Money had to be procured "by some means or other," Stark wrote.[13]

For Archelaus Lewis, a private in Captain John Bartlett's company of Falmouth militia who marched to Boston in the summer of 1775, the campaign was a lark. It was a chance to risk something for a cause, to go to war, but also to earn something to bring home. For Lewis that meant, between marching for exercise and spying on the British regulars he saw with their "guns & Baynets" glinting across the bay, he would participate in the monetary economy of the camp.[14]

Lewis had come prepared. Almost immediately, he set himself up as a purveyor of clove water and rum within the encampment, selling punch to soldiers who were bored or afraid. But Lewis's business depended on soldiers being paid. The British attacked at irregular intervals, taking boats from Boston or, ranging across the fortifications on Charlestown Neck set up after the June 17 battle on Breed's Hill, burning houses and firing on American positions before returning to their lines. Lewis's unit, he wrote, was often there to meet them, where "the Bulots flew like hail."[15]

But they had limits. On Sunday morning, July 23, 1775, Lewis and others were getting ready to go to meeting when they received orders to go on a "fatigue" march to keep them in military trim. According to Lewis, the men resented missing their weekly religious services, particularly when they were not being compensated in more mundane matters. Lewis's captain, John Bartlett, accordingly went to headquarters that afternoon, Lewis recorded, and "Pititioned to th general for the money for the Shoders." The general responded quickly, coming "up the camps" to tell the soldiers "thatt they was Sertain of their money as they had it." After that reassurance, Lewis wrote, "the Regiment was well Sattifyd and was willing to go upon fatigue."[16] They were paid two days later. Even two soldiers who "Refused to [pass] muster," Lewis noted, "came tow and Received their money."[17] Within the week, Lewis noted, with some satisfaction, he had sold out of alcohol.

Lewis used his pay and earnings to stock up on spirits and, when he skipped a Sunday meeting, to go into Cambridge for coffee and sugar and a hot meal of fish and potatoes. Soon, he had saved enough to provide small financial services for soldiers who had to settle accounts in camp before returning home. On August 13, 1775, he accepted a sword in pawn from a Sergeant Clark in return for a quarter wedge of a Spanish silver dollar, which Lewis then paid John Portifield—presumably to settle Clark's debt.[18] Settling debts before physically leaving the army was a serious matter, Lewis knew. He would later note to himself that Thomas Hughes, the paymaster of the Seventh Virginia, was dismissed from the army for leaving camp without returning to "settel his accompt."[19] Soldiers expected the governments that paid them to do the same.

Thus, under pressure, New Hampshire acted before receiving word from the Continental Congress. On June 9, 1775, New Hampshire voted to make £10,050 in "Notes of hand on the faith of the Colony" "struck" with copper plates and to be taxed in and burnt by 1778.[20] Bills of credit, unlike personal credit, could be carried across the province line and spent on clove water and rum.[21]

The other New England colonies did the same. In July the Connecticut Assembly authorized £50,000 "in the Bills of Credit of this Colony equal to lawful money," accompanied by a 7 pence per pound poll and estate tax providing "an ample and sufficient fund, to call in, sink, and discharge the aforesaid sum."[22] Rhode Island ordered bills of credit valued at £20,000, Lawful Money, printed on May 3, 1775, to support a force of 1,500 men "for the defence of the colony." The bills were to be destroyed within five years.[23] Rhode Island's elderly governor, Joseph Wanton, refused to approve the act, arguing that it would "unavoidably bring on universal bankruptcy throughout this colony," but the assembly ignored him.[24] Wanton was apparently already invested in the metal-money order. When the Newport County sheriff Jabez Champlin raided Wanton's house in March 1776, searching for Rhode Island's original charter, he also found "seventeen dies for counterfeiting dollars and half Johannes, instruments for edge-milling, and other implements of counterfeiting" specie currency.[25] Wanton had planned to benefit from the old monetary regime only to have it swept out from under him.

IV. The Revolution Spreads to New Jersey

News of the clashes at Lexington and Concord reached New Jersey within days. On May 2, 1775, Hendrick Fisher, head of the New Jersey Committee of Correspondence, called for a new Provincial Congress at Trenton to confer on the crisis. As in other colonies, the first order of business was arming and organizing the militia and figuring out how to pay for it. Money was a focus from the start. "Money has aptly been called the sinews of war; so it may also [be] the *anima* that enlivens, that braces and gives firmness to the nerves of our Constitution," the Newark Township's General Committee of Association wrote in its instructions to delegates to the Trenton Congress on May 18, 1775. On May 23, 1775, its first day in session, the New Jersey Congress voted a £10,000 tax, to be paid in "Proclamation Money," New Jersey's paper currency. The tax was distinct from the province's other taxes in that its goal was not to "sink" or destroy the currency. Rather, local tax collectors and assessors were to gather the bills so that they could be spent again to put New Jersey on a war footing. Taxes to destroy existing bills would continue working. When it met again in August, the congress resolved explicitly that any surplus bills after expenses would be "applied towards discharging the quotas of such counties in the public taxes of the Province" and destroyed.[26]

The Trenton Congress was an unofficial adjunct of the regular colonial government still meeting in Burlington a short ride south, under royal Governor William Franklin. The rebel congress had grafted its insurrectionary finance onto New Jersey's existing system without official approval. As such, the New Jersey Congress was deeply concerned about establishing legitimacy before it made a new money and increased "the burthen of taxes already laid upon the good people of this colony for the just defense of their invaluable rights and privileges" to balance it.[27] On August 5 the provincial congress voted to hold fresh elections. Only when it reconvened in

October with new delegates did it invoke its citizens' credit explicitly and make its own Revolutionary currency.

The key to maintaining the "credit" of New Jersey's new, insurrectionary bills of credit was to make sure people would use them. Using the bills was an implicit endorsement of their legitimacy and the legitimacy of the new government. On October 23, 1775, tax officials reported that some property holders had "refused to pay their quotas," to purchase the bills of credit the congress demanded in taxes.[28] The congress's solution was to create a forced market. If New Jerseyans were reluctant to sell their property to purchase proclamation money, the Revolutionary government would sell it for them. On Tuesday, October 24, 1775, the New Jersey Congress ordered that anyone who "refused paying the sum assessed" would be warned, and if they still refused, that their "goods and chattels" would be sold at public auction. Any money left over, after the sheriff's fee of 1 shilling and 6 pence "for each distress and sale," would be "returned to the owner or owners of the goods so distrained as aforesaid."[29] Tenants whose landlords refused to pay could sell their own produce, pay the tax, and subtract the balance from their rent. Either way, the goods would go to market.[30]

With the principle of coercion established, the provincial congress proceeded, that same day, to elaborate a detailed plan for making the new money. Its first task was to tally up needs, "the expence necessary for the defence of this Colony." In order to defend New Jersey, the delegates decided, the state would need 3,000 "stand of arms"—muskets and steel bayonets—10 tons of gunpowder, 20 tons of lead, 1,000 cartoucheboxes, two medicine chests, four hundred tents with "the necessary furniture, canteens and knapsacks," £4,000 in proclamation money to pay volunteers, 2,000 blankets, £300 worth of "axes, spades and entrenching tools," £500 worth of artillery, and £1,000 for a bounty on saltpeter, one of the ingredients necessary for gunpowder. In all, they reckoned that £30,000 proclamation money would cover it and appointed a commission to print the bills and "to make a provision to sink" and burn them. One of the commissioners was a Hunterdon County miller, landowner, and local justice named John Hart, one of the New Jersey signers of the Declaration of Independence. After five days of work, on Saturday, October 28, 1775, Hart's commission brought the completed ordinance to the congress for "striking" the whole sum.[31]

Their plan is the most comprehensive official account of how paper became money in the Revolutionary era. Turning paper into money involved two processes. First was the physical process of purchasing paper, etching, pressing, cutting, blotting, and signing—all laborious operations, given that it meant printing and signing 18,700 individual bills with values ranging from £3 to 6 shillings. The second was ceremonial, a complex invocation of provincial and personal honor that gave the bills official value, showing how New Jerseyans invoked the honor and credit of the state, its printers, and its commissioners before emitting it in paper form.

Before receiving the bills, Hart and the other three commissioners, John Carey from Salem County in the southwest of the state, and Azariah Dunham and Hendrick Fisher from the northeast, had to appear before a justice of the peace, the local official who enforced the power of the court, and "take an oath, or affirmation if Quakers, for the true signing of the said bills of credit." The oath affirmed that commissioners would sign "to the best of their skill" and maintains the integrity of the process as a matter of "duty." When printers delivered unsigned bills, the signers themselves were ordered to make each printer swear that, "from the time the letters were set and fit to be put into the press . . . until the same bills were printed and the letters unset and put into boxes again, that I went at no time out of the room in which the letters were without locking them up so as they could not be come at without violence, a false key, or other art then unknown to me," and furthermore that "all the blotters, and other papers whatsoever printed by the said letters, to the best of my knowledge, are here delivered, together with the stamps and indents and devices." Each printer got a copy of the oath to take home with him, "that he may govern himself accordingly." Next, the signers were to "burn and destroy" blotting papers used to remove excess ink from the bills, divide the stacks of printed notes, agree to a system for numbering them, secure the stamps containing the state's coat of arms, and carry the bills home.[32]

Hart himself probably had the shortest trip from Trenton, riding fifteen miles north into the hills to his 611-acre farm and milling operation overlooking Beden Brook in southwest Hunterdon County. He would have given his oaths before men he knew. Hart was the son and son-in-law of justices of the peace and served as Hunterdon's judge of common pleas. His family had immigrated from Long Island at the turn of the eighteenth century. Before he married Deborah Scudder, the daughter of a wealthy local landowner, in 1740, he purchased 193 acres in the valley. In 1775 he was the largest landowner in the area, owning mills for grinding grain and preparing cloth, and racing horses, along with three enslaved men and women.[33] He would have delivered the bills to his brick house, on a hill overlooking the valley, and there sign them, day after day, "with all possible expedition" as the leaves changed and fell.[34] On an appointed day he would have taken the road back to Trenton, met with the other signers, compared numbers, and burned any extraneous bills together. The signers would continue exchanging bills, taking them home, signing them, and meeting again, until all 18,700 were ready for delivery to the treasurer. But, as a property owner, Hart's duties were just beginning. He would have to purchase the bills and use them. The bills were sunk by a property tax on all "goods and chattels, lands and tenements" of £10,000 a year beginning in 1784 and running to 1786. Hart's Hunterdon County paid the highest proportion of the taxes in the state. Hart and his committee not only made the bills. In the end, they had pledged to destroy them.[35] Making the bills would take months—they were not fully printed, in February 1776, when the provincial congress ordered £20,000 more.[36] Destroying them would take years.

Hart, like the other members of the New Jersey finance committee, was not a financier. The men who made the revolution's money were often among the wealthiest in their counties, but they were not "monied" and did not have any particular monetary expertise. But that is part of what is so striking about America's first Revolutionary monies. They did not require a particular expertise to make because they were a logical extension of common practice. Households, like Hart's, created the private equivalent of bills of credit all the time, in notes, bonds, and in neighbors' books of account. These obligations might take years, or a lifetime, to "sink." As Blackwell observed almost a century earlier, a bill of credit was essentially the same thing on a broader scale.

In making new monies, the revolutionaries once again applied the rules of credit and debt embodied in the colonial household to an entire colony. They were able to because American resistance, on money, on taxes, had preserved both the institution—bills of credit—and a world where the household was still the locus of virtually all labor and wealth. Since the seventeenth century, American colonists had conducted almost all of their business without the intervention of what Blackwell had called a "commodity" money. Money for them had remained a measure, a way of expressing worth and value, of quantifying wealth. Money had not become an objective in itself—it was still a means to other ends. In that sense, the Revolution, as the war with Britain was already becoming known, was just another way that the colonists arranged money and credit to build their own wealth and that of their kin communities. Only this time, the aim was not land for a grown son or daughter's family, or any of the many varieties of nonmonetary colonial wealth. The aim was collective independence. When the money was sunk, the old order would—they assumed—reassert itself.[37]

Hart, like other delegates to the Second Continental Congress convened that May, was sure to have made the connection between American bills of credit and the American Declaration of Independence. He signed both. On July 1, 1776, Hart arrived in Philadelphia as a New Jersey delegate to the congress. The next day he voted for independence, pledging his life, fortune, and sacred honor. As a signer of New Jersey's bills, he had already pledged all three. He had performed and administered oaths of honor. He had pledged his property to sink New Jersey's bills. And, by taking a leadership role in the provincial congress and putting his signature on its bills, he had pledged his life. Soon after signing the Declaration, Hart returned home where he was elected speaker of New Jersey's Revolutionary legislature. But Deborah was sick, and he spent much of his time attending to her. She died on October 8, 1776. In December, with British forces close on the Continental Army's heels, he was hiding with the cattle in the hills above his home as British foragers sacked it, looking for him.[38]

V. Pennsylvania, Maryland, and Virginia Join the Double Revolution

The colonies south of New Jersey followed their northern neighbors, printing bills of credit on similar terms. On June 30, 1775, the Pennsylvania Assembly resolved to resist any "invasion or landing of British troops" in "this or the adjacent colonies" and voted "bills of credit to the value of thirty-five thousand pounds" to pay for it "prepared and printed on good strong paper."[39] "For the more certain paying, redeeming, discharging, and sinking of the said bills of credit," the Pennsylvanians continued an existing provincial tax, and "enjoined" tax officials to "to raise, levy, recover and pay" the taxes "as they regard the freedom, welfare and safety of their country."[40] On November 18, 1775, they authorized another £80,000 to be destroyed by the same tax.[41] The Maryland Convention did the same on July 26, 1775, authorizing $266,666 worth of "Bills of Credit of the denomination of Dollars" for "the defence of this Province."[42] The Convention pledged the bills would be "redeemed or sunk on or before the first day of January 1786 by Taxes, or other legislative provision," and bound "their Constituents and pledge the faith of this Province for the Redemption."[43] In 1775 Delaware contented itself with authorizing £30,000 in bills of credit for its loan office—the interest would be used to pay government expenses. But on February 22, 1777, after loan-office commissioner, Boaz Manlove, defected to the British with £10,000 of the new money, the assembly voted another £25,000, with £10,000 going "for the defence and use of this state" to be "sunk and destroyed within the term of five years."[44]

In Virginia, in June 1775 members of the last colonial House of Burgesses were already arguing over money with their increasingly isolated royal governor, John Murray, the Fourth Earl of Dunmore. The burgesses passed an act on June 19, authorizing new treasury notes to pay Virginia militia who had fought in Dunmore's western war against the Mingo and Shawnee in the Ohio country the previous year.[45] In order to destroy the notes, the burgesses proposed reimposing a 10 percent duty on slave sales. Dunmore, having fled the colony after successfully seizing its gunpowder stores in April, was on a warship anchored twelve miles away in the York River. From his berth, he rejected both the money and the tax, stating that without a "suspending clause"—suspending the bill until imperial officials signed off in London—he could not approve it.[46]

"I made it my business to intimate by several Members, to the House, that without such Clause I could not pass an Act for emitting paper Money," Dunmore wrote the Virginians.[47] The burgesses replied on Friday, June 23, that there was no other kind of "Money" in Virginia to pay troops with, necessitating "a speedy Emission of Paper Money." Moreover, they argued that since some tax would be necessary for the money to be destroyed, a "duty of ten per cent on Slaves would be least burthensome to the People."[48] It was a memorable occasion. Thomas Jefferson would cite Dunmore's refusal to allow a tax on slave sales—"to restrain this execrable commerce"—in his first draft of the Declaration of Independence a year later.[49]

With a popular Virginian congress meeting in Richmond just a few days later, the burgesses also informed Dunmore that they planned to adjourn. Dunmore's reply was indignant: the burgesses, implicitly, seemed to claim they could convene and adjourn at will, "as if you had such Power," he wrote from his warship. On Saturday, June 24, the burgesses took Dunmore's letter into consideration and resolved to "prepare for the preservation of their property, and their inestimable rights and liberties." They dissolved themselves and never met again under British rule.[50]

Instead, most of the members reconvened in Richmond on July 17, 1775, in the third Virginia Convention. Their first resolution, on July 19, was to organize an army and to form a committee to do so. Two days later, they added to the committee's brief: to write "a Clause or Clauses for the Pay of the Forces to be raised."[51] On July 24, 1775, George Mason, who was on the committee, remarked that despite keeping long hours—meeting every morning at seven a.m. and working, minus meal breaks and "a little

Refreshment" until nine or ten at night—they were making little progress. "This is hard Duty," Mason wrote, explaining: the "Extent & Importance of the Business before us . . . to provide arms, ammunition &c, and to point out ways & means of raising money. These are Difficultys indeed!"[52]

In mid-August the convention authorized Virginia treasurer Robert Carter Nicholas to issue £350,000 in treasury notes to pay and supply its soldiers—including those who had served in Dunmore's war. The convention levied a battery of taxes to destroy the notes, including taxes on "every coach chariot, or four-wheeled carriage, except common wagons" and "every two-wheel chaise," "tithable persons" including slaves and infants, and a variety of licenses and legal actions—taxes reminiscent of the Stamp Act—minus the silver clause.[53]

The convention "unavoidably suspended" the taxes for a year "to suit the distressed circumstances." In the meantime, the convention stressed, "the whole estates, real and personal, of the inhabitants of this colony, shall be, and are hereby pledged as a security" in case taxes were unable, for whatever reason, to sink and destroy them.[54] Mason wrote George Washington that the convention expected the new taxes to "sink 50,000£" a year, though he worried they might not be destroyed fast enough to secure their credit, given the mass of new monies from other provinces and the Continental Congress.[55] The convention gave the legislation issuing new notes and establishing taxes the same title as the bill Dunmore had rejected several weeks before. Dunmore, for his part, was still anchored in the York River. When the governor had rejected their right to make temporary money, Virginians had abandoned him—and asserted their right to invoke their constituents' credit on their own.

Both North Carolina and Georgia followed Virginia. In North Carolina, where colonists had long clashed over money and the lack thereof, the Hillsborough Congress voted $125,000 worth of bills of credit on September 7, 1775, and "Resolved, That this Province be pledged for the redemption of the Bills of Credit now directed to be emitted." Taxes to destroy the bills were scheduled to begin in 1777 and continue for nine years "unless the money should be sooner sunk."[56] In Georgia, on Wednesday, July 12, 1775, the Provincial Congress meeting in Savannah unanimously resolved that "being a full representation of its constituents" it could authorize an "equal and general tax" toward "sinking" £10,000 sterling, and authorized itself or the Georgia Council of Safety to issue certificates up to that amount, signed by their treasurers.[57]

South Carolina was different. Like the Virginians, South Carolina's legislators worried about the ability of their citizens to pay taxes in the midst of a war with Britain. Like their northern neighbors, they asserted the right to exercise their credit with the citizenry as a trusted trading partner might, without specifying when exactly they would meet their obligations. On the morning of Wednesday, June 14, 1775, the South Carolina Provincial Congress authorized £1 million in "current money," printed on a total of 103,000 paper certificates worth up to £50 each, for a defensive effort.[58] The South Carolinians did not specify a tax to destroy the bills. Instead, the congress pledged "the faith of the Public to provide funds for calling in, and sinking" the currency, called "certificates of public debt," "in a reasonable time."[59]

The South Carolinians intended to destroy the certificates. They were unsure when. "It was much pressed by some, to lay a tax, and sink a certain proportion of the paper currency, which was, but such a proposition was refused," wrote John Drayton, who lived through the events. "And in justification of the measure, it was urged that the *Association*, by which, the whole property of the Colony was bound to make good the contracts of the Provincial Congress, was, a sufficient security."[60] According to Drayton, objections to taxing included worries that if the British invaded, the congress wouldn't be able to collect it due to "the confusion of the times," after which, "the circulation of the money would be entirely destroyed." It was only prudent, Drayton concluded, to avoid that risk, for "no tax ought to be laid on the people for sinking the paper currency, during the civil convulsions."[61]

South Carolinians' ultimate resolve was not in question. The opposite was closer to the truth. The colony's wealthy planters and merchants actively sought to limit expenses because as large property holders, they expected to pay the taxes that would ultimately destroy them. "What is most vexatious," Henry Laurens wrote to his son John on June 18, 1775, "is that the Gentlemen who have precipitated the people into this vast expence, are of Such fortunes as contribute very little toward the discharge of public debts."[62] Men like the Laurens, on the other hand, would have to part with their property in order to do so. When the taxes came, they would need to sell to those with the money to buy, only to turn around and destroy it.

VI. New York Has Another Idea

New York was the sole exception to the universal march toward Revolutionary monies in 1775. New Yorkers already had paper currency. In 1771 the colonial legislature passed an act authorizing £120,000 in bills of credit. After years of back and forth with imperial officials on the restrictions of the 1764 Currency Act, Parliament had allowed them a dispensation. The new bills would be acceptable to pay off mortgage loans issued in bills of credit by the New York loan office and in taxes. The interest on the loans—which could also be paid in gold and silver—was supposed to cover government expenses. But as it turned out, after years of monetary limbo, few who did not already have a mortgage to pay off would accept the bills. As a result, New York legislators admitted in 1774, their local bills were not as valuable, even in New York City, as bills from neighboring colonies. As a solution, they passed a bill making it illegal to value other colonies' bills at a higher rate than New York bills "upon pain of Forfeiting a Sum equal to the Value of the Bills so passed, exchanged, paid or received at the Rate payable therefore at the Treasury of the Colony issuing the same." New York's attempt to regulate the value of its currency spoke to a fundamental insecurity that would prove difficult to overcome when fighting began in Boston.[63]

In 1775, when it came time to consider their contribution to the continental defense, New York legislators did two things. First, they checked the feasibility of collecting enough in silver and gold to pay and equip their militia. After consulting with New York merchants, they declared it was "impossible to raise a sufficient sum" in specie. This was a feint but a necessary one because of what the New York legislators intended to do next. Instead of issuing their own bills of credit, on May 27, 1775, the New Yorkers formed a committee to ask the Second Continental Congress to do it for them.[64]

The New Yorkers' analysis made it clear that continental bills of credit were the only possible way of financing the war. Specie might have been preferable for the same reasons that the British ministry had decided to charge its taxes in silver bullion, the New Yorkers acknowledged. There had been no continental currency before. Each colony had its own subtly different system for issuing bills of credit and way of valuing them, and specie would be the easiest thing to send across borders to pay for transportation and supplies because of its "universal estimation."[65] But if, as the committee soon concluded, there was not enough gold and silver in the colonies to pay for a war against Britain, the solution was precisely what Henry McCulloh had proposed in his initial plan for the Stamp Act: a continental currency that all of the colonies would be responsible for taxing out of existence together. "Whenever a paper currency has been emitted and obtained a general credit, it will be a new bond of union to the associated Colonies," the New Yorkers concluded, "and every inhabitant thereof will be bound in interest to endeavor that ways and means be fallen upon for sinking of it." The currency would incorporate the united colonies into a body with credit of its own, bringing all the citizens of the rebellious colonies together and, in effect, making them one political people. The New Yorkers proposed the new currencies should be printed in each of the colonies separately, with each province's coat of arms on one side and a general device representing the union on the other. The symbolism was clear; each colony would retain its individual identity, but their strength was in their union.[66]

The New Yorkers also hoped that if their plan worked, New York would become the financial center in North America. If a continental currency existed, the New York Committee wrote in their May 30 report to the Provincial Congress, it would provide significant advantages to the province. "The neighbouring Colonies of Connecticut and New-Jersey are indebted to this colony in very considerable sums," the committee reported, and "in prosecution of measures necessary for our defence, large sums of money levied or issued for that purpose must undoubtedly centre in this Colony." In light of those two facts, "it follows clearly that this Colony will at first possess a much greater proportion of the general currency than her sister Colonies."[67] With this advantage came dangers: if the "commercial equality of money" dipped, the province holding it would lose most. They had a solution, though. They advised the Continental Congress to create a paper currency while binding each colony "to sink its proportionable part."[68] That way, New Yorkers wouldn't be stuck holding the currency. New York, with its deep harbors and long Hudson River valley, would serve as a natural conduit for goods and currency moving between the Middle and Southern Colonies and their northern neighbors. They would be able to trade the dollars they earned to other colonies, which would need them to tax in and destroy their part of the continental currency.[69]

The Second Continental Congress took up New York's proposal regarding "the ways and means of raising Money" on Tuesday, June 13, 1775. It deliberated for three days.[70] The first question was how to denominate the bills. Unlike the colonies, the continent did not have a monetary tradition, a common measure, to support or employ. Yet without one, or at least the semblance of one, the bills of credit Congress printed might be unintelligible. Whatever the Continental Congress chose had to be universally known, referring to a well understood measure of value. In order to make the continental currency intelligible, it would have to be issued in terms of something all the colonies would recognize and understand. To use the pounds, shilling, and pence of one colony or another as a standard would be for "one Colony to interpose its credit for the others" and was thus rejected. The obvious choice, the pound sterling, was never considered.[71]

By the second day of deliberations, the Congress had settled on a well-known silver coin as the unit: the dollar.[72] The Congress decided on making bills "each expressing to be of the value of a certain Number of Spanish

Dollars," Benjamin Franklin recalled five years later.[73] Silver was rare, but the value of Spanish dollars, traditionally collected in the colonies' trade with the Caribbean and southern Europe, was well known and easy to express in all of the colonial currencies. Most already had laws giving the dollar an official valuation. The translation worked. On Thursday, June 22, 1775, the Continental Congress authorized printing "a sum not exceeding two millions of Spanish milled dollars," printed in denominations from $1 to $20, on 403,800 paper bills.[74] Almost immediately, dollar-denominated securities were being traded in terms of each provinces' own pounds, shillings, and pence. On June 20, 1775, the New York Provincial Congress agreed to advance £2,000 New York worth of the "Continental currency" to saltpeter-makers to secure a local source of gunpowder. This was before the Continental Congress in Philadelphia had even agreed to print the currency. But the decision was more momentous than the committee knew. The dollar would be the official unit of account of the United States from that moment forward.[75]

After settling on a unit, the Continental Congress faced what New York delegate James Duane called "the stability of the fund": maintaining the value of the new "Continental dollar." Like all the individual colonies, Congress's plan was to destroy the temporary monies created for the war, in accord with New Yorkers' suggestion, with a continental system of requisition or taxation. When it authorized the bills, the Continental Congress resolved that "the twelve confederated colonies be pledged for the redemption of the bills of credit, now directed to be emitted." As in each individual province, Congress's "pledge" was to use law and force, if necessary, to tax the dollars out of existence.[76]

VII. Making the Double Revolution Legible on a Continental Scale

Unleashing fourteen different monies simultaneously in 1775 invited myriad interpretations of what the money meant. The most pressing question was how the new dollars would be equated with foreign currencies in the new states and in the hands of the brave merchants who were already working to secure arms from Britain's rivals in Europe.

The facing inscription of the continental currency authorized in July 1775 stated that each bill "entitles the bearer to receive" some number of "Spanish milled Dollars, or the value thereof in gold or silver."[77] It was difficult for many, even in the colonies, to understand how a "dollar" on paper could be anything other than a promise for a "dollar" in coin.

This was part of the confusion the notion of a continental "dollar" created: the dollar was intelligible because it was a valuable object, like a bushel of grain—and yet taxes were supposed to be used to maintain it. Symbolically, this was a contradiction. The value of a silver dollar was abstracted from the coin itself, attached to the national currency, which was then put in the hands, ultimately, of each state, each with its own traditions, systems, and relationship to the broader conflict. The younger members of the new Revolutionary movement had never been taught the American monetary tradition and had to learn on the job. That practical experience, meanwhile, usually stood at odds with their formal educations. They had read Locke, Hume, and others who were the intellectual basis of the British position. Blackwell and Cotton Mather were all but forgotten. What remained were the laws, the institution of bills of credit themselves, and the war itself, which would stretch them all to the limit. Still, the temptation was there to exploit the ambiguity between the "dollar" as an "expression" of value and the dollar as a physical object, to ask people to treat a continental dollar as if it were one made out of silver, to believe it would be "redeemed" not by taxes but by payment, in specie, from the congressional treasury.[78]

On May 22, 1776, one year into the war, Congress created a committee to establish the value of various foreign coins in relation to the continental dollar. The committee, which included John Adams and Thomas Jefferson, declared that "holders of the bills of credit emitted by authority of Congress will be entitled, at certain periods, appointed for redemption thereof to receive out of the treasury of the united colonies [they were not yet states] the amount of the said bills in Spanish milled dollars, or the value thereof in gold and silver."[79] They knew, of course, that the "treasury of the united colonies" contained virtually no gold and silver, and that any such period would be far in the future. On July 29, 1775, just after Congress authorized the first continentals, it had declared that the bills were designed to be destroyed, with "each colony [to] provide ways and means to sink its proportion of the bills ordered to be emitted by Congress, in such manner as may be most effectual and best adapted to the condition, circumstances and usual mode of levying taxes in such a colony."[80] The sunk bills were then to be marked and burned. Gold and silver were only mentioned as a substitute for continental bills, which could be used to make up tax quotas for a given year as it had in the colonies, particularly when—after years of taxation and burning—the bills got scarce. When the tax debts that balanced out the bills of credit in the colonies' account were satisfied, if colonial treasurers had silver and gold, they would "advertise" it in colonial newspapers, allowing holders to bring the bills in and exchange them for metal. Afterward, treasurers were directed to "burn and destroy" these last bills too. The "period" where continental dollars might be exchanged for gold and silver was in that distant future when the bills themselves would have been taxed out of existence.[81]

In the meantime, however, the 1776 committee wanted its dollars to be accepted as equal to the physical silver coins that embodied the value each continental dollar was supposed to express. Thus, rather than issuing traditional legal tender laws, which made money, by law, pass at face value in payment of a public or private debt, Congress decreed that its "dollars" should pass as if they were gold and silver, leaving the actual tender laws to the states. On their face, the bills declared that they entitled the bearer to "*SPANISH MILLED DOLLARS,* or the Value thereof in GOLD or SILVER."[82] With the redemption entitlement as a justification, Congress declared on May 22, 1776, that Americans had to accept bills as if they were gold and silver in all exchanges, regardless of any other circumstance, or be "deemed an enemy to the liberties of the colonies."[83] Congress could justify the equivalence between bills of credit and precious metal on the grounds that the continental dollar had the same value, by definition, as its metallic counterpart—and that it was this equation that made the dollar intelligible in all the different state currencies. But doing so also created confusion about whether the dollar was, in fact, a promise for gold and silver at some distant date.

In effect, the confusion was a mark of how well, if imperfectly, the British attempt to corral American money in the years since 1764 had worked. Few colonies had issued bills of credit for a decade. Merchants, forced to do without the bills, had increased their stocks of silver—anticipating dues like the Stamp Act coming back around. But more importantly, without the habit of issuing and managing temporary money, many defaulted to British notions of what money should be. As a result, even in the moment of bills of credit's greatest triumph, there was a growing confusion about what the bills represented, amounting to confusion about what might be expected (or not) from a new, independent, continental government.

VIII. Britain Sets Its Permanent Money against the Revolution

In Britain, meanwhile, there was no doubt. On April 24, 1776, North's voice rang out across the ministers assembled in St. Stephen's Chapel in Westminster. "The British nation," North said, "would not let its most valuable and important rights be wrested by force, violence, and rebellion, out of its hand." But in order to "exert that strength, which, when properly exerted, never failed to prevail," North needed to borrow sterling money. Parliament approved the loan. By the end of the year, the government had borrowed £1.94 million.[84]

Every pound, meanwhile, was understood to represent gold and silver. The notion that British money equated to gold and silver was obviously an ideological position rather than a real one. It was well known and often asserted at the time that much of Britain's monetary wealth had no plausible metallic basis, was in effect "paper wealth," and that this paper wealth was "a ministerial engine of state."[85] There was nothing, perhaps, beyond a popular prejudice for coin over paper stopping Parliament from issuing bills of exchequer to fund the war in America. Indeed, in the speech announcing the loan for the American war, North announced that the ministry planned to increase the number of exchequer bills by £250,000, to £1.5 million. But that prejudice had real consequences for the legal architecture of British money.[86]

In 1776, when Parliament needed to spend, it felt the need to find ways to coax investors to give it the paper and metal "monies" it desired in return for compensation. The implication was that monetary wealth both preexisted and existed outside of the state demands and needed to be coaxed back in. Doing so required striking a bargain with those who had money and might be willing to invest. Funding the war, North argued, meant navigating between two aims: "to make the best bargain he could for the public" and "to give a stockholder a reasonable profit and encouragement to subscribe." It also entailed offering variety. For every £100 they put in, investors would get two things. The first £70 would get each investor 3 percent bonds worth £77.50, a top-up North justified as reflecting the "fair market-price" of the stock "subject to redemption" at will by Parliament. The next £30 would get them three lottery tickets. Of the 60,000 tickets, 19,992 were winners, or "fortunate tickets," as the law put it. The two biggest were worth £20,000; the smallest prize was £20. All £600,000 took the form of 3 percent annuities. "Monies" to be invested were payable to the cashier of the Bank of England, with a 15 percent deposit due up front. Side bets, "sale of chances," and "wagering" on winners was prohibited. Subscriptions not paid in full were forfeited to the public, who, not for the first time, had rolled gambling and investing into a lucrative whole.[87]

The interest on these annuities would be paid by new taxes on wheeled carriages and stagecoaches, along with stamp duties on playing cards, dice, newsprint, and indentures. These taxes might be paid in any British money, including bills of exchequer. But North, in his speech, was invested in proving that Great Britain contained enough physical, metallic wealth to pay for the new fees with ease. North had apparently heard rumors that there was not enough gold and silver in Britain to meet the financial demands that the new borrowing would place on the bank, but he observed that if "the bank was a bubble, so was the world." The nation, moreover, he argued, was teeming with gold and silver—"not much short of twenty million pounds" in his estimation, plenty to meet any demand.[88]

Great Britain's "internal opulence [was] almost beyond conception." North repeated the words several times over the course of his speech, as if repeating them would make them true. The wealth of Britain's mercantile and landed elite was apparent. But even the British poor, he asserted, were the wealthiest poor in the world. "Examine the labourer's stile and manner of living; examine his food, his cloathing, his house, and even his little luxuries," North continued, "and compare him with men of the same class in Ireland, or any other part of the empire, or Europe; and it would amount to this demonstrative proof, that although our taxes were great, our burthens were heavy, that yet the means of procuring the necessities, nay, even the comforts of life, were easier attainable in this country, than in any other, under the sun." The point was that Britain's preexisting monetary wealth would suffice to meet any needs the exchequer put upon it until America's loyalty was restored. The rebellion would be overwhelmed.[89]

In return for this wealth, the government offered securities that were themselves moneylike, albeit paying interest. These assets were divisible, transferable, and perpetual. "Every contributor, his, her, or their executors, successors, and assigns" was entitled to 3 percent interest, payable twice yearly at the Bank of England. In the meantime, owners were allowed to transfer the annuities like any other piece of property, to "any person or persons, body or bodies politick or corporate, whatsoever, in the books of the Bank of England." Moreover, once a subscriber had completed their investment, the bank would place the whole £77.50 to the subscriber's credit, allowing them to "assign and transfer the same, or any part, share, or proportion thereof," to anyone the investor desired. Payments on the annuities, however divided, would continue until "the redemption thereof," when the government returned the principal invested, placing it once again outside the state.[90] A complete repayment, observers noted, was unlikely. All the coin in Great Britain, even if it could be collected and North's starry estimates were credible, would barely scratch the principle. Instead, the national debt had become a quasipermanent "monied property," in "opposition to the landed," and the basis for a new class: the "monied interest" defined by its access to and interest in coin, credit, and the securities that paid it.[91]

By 1776, it was clear that the widening war would be a contest between these two systems. Britain had money—and had it on terms it had sought, and was still seeking, to define as universal. The rebellious colonies had the system they had developed on their own, one whose implications they did not fully understand. They had been forced by circumstances to make a test of it. The British, for the most part, still believed that the American system was a fraud waiting to be discovered by the men fighting the war. "In time the rebels will be tired out," the merchant parliamentarian William Innes said, in a long speech on America's prospects in the building contest. "Their guilt, folly, and expense, must breed intestine dissension [and] the common men must soon be convinced of the fraud of being paid in paper money." They would even, he predicted, come over to the British side because "money," meaning real, British money, "will engage them to enlist."[92]

IX. God, the Double Revolution, and Tom Paine

For many new Americans, though, the bills were seen as a kind of divine providence. For Paine, whose monetary education in the intellectual clubs of London had centered on the British system, they were little less than a miracle. As a writer, Paine had more than risen to the occasion of the rebellion. His initial fears about having found himself in a war that he did not start, fighting for a cause that was not his own, subsided. America's cause, he concluded, was not just his cause but the cause of "a continent—of at least one eighth part of the habitable globe," he wrote in *Common Sense*, a radically antimonarchist and deeply religious pamphlet, that secured his reputation as a dissident writer without parallel since Dickinson's *Farmer*. All future generations, he wrote, are "involved in this contest." "Now," he wrote, "is the seed time."[93]

In terms of money, Paine believed that the lack of precious metal might be an advantage. Without mines, there would be no incentive for other European powers to supplant Britain. An independent anglophone North America, he wrote, would be a "*free port*. Her trade will always be a protection, and her barrenness of gold and silver secure her from invaders." Like the British, they would have nothing to steal.[94]

On June 7, 1776, Richard Henry Lee of Virginia tabled a resolution with the Second Continental Congress, declaring that the colonies "are and of right ought to be free and independent states." The Congress, in turn, appointed a committee of five to compose a declaration of independence. They gave Thomas Jefferson, a young, wealthy, and ambitious slaveowner from Virginia the task of writing the first draft. Jefferson was already famous as the author of the *Summary View of the Rights of British America*, a polemic published in 1774 and directed at George III. His analysis revealed a keen sense of the issues at stake. "No longer persevere in sacrificing the rights of one part of the empire to the inordinate desires of another," he advised, in reference to Parliament's long-term efforts to shift the empire's commercial constitution. The *Summary View* also revealed an impressive rhetorical style; Jefferson was emerging as Virginia's answer to Dickinson. Indeed, Dickinson, with Jefferson, had been the key author of Congress's first attempt to justify its resistance, its *Declaration of the Cause and Necessity of Taking Up Arms*, almost precisely a year earlier. But Dickinson was not in favor of independence, leaving Jefferson alone. In scant weeks, Jefferson produced the first draft of the Declaration of Independence. Congress, minus Dickinson, adopted it after several quick rounds of revision—removing a clause that blamed England for slavery in America, for instance—and officially voted to adopt it on July 2, 1776. Final printed copies were distributed, and independence proclaimed, two days later.[95]

In a little more than a year, the American colonies had thrown off two sets of British impositions. Within months, they had thrown off imperial restrictions on their currency, using temporary bills of credit to mobilize their property for war. And in the summer of 1776, they had declared themselves independent, "united States," as the declaration put it, with their own army, their own currency, and they hoped soon their own government, which would draw on the lessons of Britain's imperial overreach to create what Lee had called "the form of a confederation." Its fate was still in doubt, but the double revolution was complete. Two monies, one temporary and one permanent, as well as two nations, were at war.

CHAPTER EIGHT

The Money War

I. The Two Wars of the American Revolution

The American Revolution was two wars, one evident, one hidden. The first was Britain's attempt to reestablish sovereignty within North America. The second, less obvious but no less significant, was the war to disestablish American economic sovereignty, the war on American money. In the first, virtually everything the British did went wrong. In the second, they succeeded in spite of themselves.

The British plan to reestablish sovereignty in North America was never practical, largely because it was based on false information. British leaders had believed that the revolutionaries were a minority and that everywhere the British army went, loyal American forces would spring up to support a return to imperial rule. Refugees like Pennsylvania's Joseph Galloway, who had fled to London, built support for the war by arguing that four-fifths of Americans "would prefer a union with Great-Britain." The only thing needed was a British force to peel back America's Revolutionary veneer to reveal this hidden majority. The British planned sweeping expeditions through the American countryside, from Long Island into New Jersey in 1776, down from Canada into the Hudson River valley and up the Chesapeake to Philadelphia in 1777, and, beginning in 1778, an ambitious three-year swoop through the South from Georgia northward into Virginia to do so.

At each turn the goal was "supporting friends," as General Henry Clinton put it in his memoirs. "The number and zeal of those colonists who remained attached to the sovereignty of Great Britain undoubtedly formed the firmest ground we could rest our hopes on for extinguishing the rebellion," Clinton wrote. The results were not what they expected. Loyalists did appear, but only when Britain had already subdued a region. Rarely, if ever, did they help on their own in any numbers. Even when they did, British commanders complained, few America-born colonists volunteered. Loyalist regiments, where they existed, were most often filled with recent migrants from Great Britain.[1]

The result was a military failure. The New Jersey campaign ended in retreat, after Washington's counterattack at Trenton. The Hudson campaign saw an entire professional army captured by militiamen at the Battle of Saratoga. The British were forced to leave Philadelphia after less than a year, when a French fleet cut off supplies from the Delaware. Initial successes in the South, including the capture of Savannah and Charleston, led to overreach and another army lost at Yorktown in 1781. But these failures had significant knock-on effects. Everywhere the British army went, American governments fell into disarray, and with it their ability to finance the war.

The same British strategy thus had radically different effects on the second war—the war that British commanders seemed to only half know they were waging against American economic sovereignty. Apart from being difficult for the uninitiated to understand, bills of credit like the continental dollar had one major weakness. They were meaningless wherever the issuer didn't have the power to tax, either directly—as in the states—or by proxy, as was the case with the Continental Congress. Taxes, meanwhile, were all but impossible to collect when governments were disrupted, and disruption was precisely what the otherwise hapless plan of the British army in North America produced. The British who failed to restore imperial rule in any of the rebellious colonies succeeded brilliantly, and unwittingly, in unsettling bills of credit in all of them.[2]

Considering its success, the British commentary on the second war is surprisingly muted. British and loyalist writers tended to see the failure of the American currency as a consequence of the same sorts of flaws that the Privy Council had identified a decade earlier. They treated American paper money as self-evidently fraudulent from the start. Tory poets labeled the bills "worthless paper" and "a fine device of Congress" in early 1776, when they were trading in Philadelphia at par with gold and silver. And they repeated similar slurs, albeit more plausibly, when the bills actually did decline in value.[3]

The American reaction to British success in the second war, though, was transformational. America's own money would be abandoned in part because of its temporary nature. American radicals and revolutionaries while agreeing on little else, converged around their desire to cut the value of bills of credit loose from time, to make them a permanent store of value. The irony, of course, was that the reason bills existed, the logic of the form itself, was that they were not: they were a temporary means to other ends, a credit against a tax debt. The attempt to make a temporary credit permanent would prove explosive, threatening the cause of independence itself.

II. The First Challenge: The Invasion of Canada

The basic challenge to American bills of credit—that they were useless where the states could not tax—emerged as an issue in the first American offensive of the war. After the attack on Lexington and Concord, an American army had assembled to besiege occupied Boston. However, the American leadership knew that a British counterattack was only a matter of time. In particular, Congress knew that Canada would likely serve as a staging ground for British attacks, just as it had for the French two decades earlier. Congress hoped to preemptively liberate it with an assault on Quebec aimed at bringing the northern colony into the United States.

On August 1, 1775, the Continental Congress sent General Philip Schuyler $100,000 in continental currency and authorized him to spend up to $200,000 more to organize the expedition.[4] With that money in New York, Schuyler had been able to pay his forces, hire carpenters, operate a mill, build boats large and small, and equip his army for the journey north. But on the first long stretch of the Richelieu River leading from Lake Champlain toward Montreal, the money stopped working.[5]

On the evening of September 6, 1775, after a hard day of fighting in the swamps near Fort Saint-Jean, Schuyler greeted a local farmer who had made his way into the patriot camp to deliver the terms on which they would supply the American army. The "gentleman, whose name I am not at liberty to commit to paper," suggested to Schuyler that the Canadians wished to remain neutral in the fight between the Americans and the British. "But if we should penetrate into *Canada* it would not displease them, provided their persons and properties were safe, and we paid them in gold and silver for what we had," Schuyler wrote John Hancock, the president of the Continental Congress, on September 8, 1775.[6]

Canadians would not accept bills of credit. Schuyler had no gold and silver. He also became terribly sick as the ill-equipped Americans settled in for a siege of Fort Saint-Jean and the weather turned cold. While there were supplies in Canada, they were impossible to purchase with the paper money he had employed at Ticonderoga: "Paper of any kind, not having the least currency in *Canada*," Schuyler wrote on September 19 from his sickbed. The only recourse was a different form of money. "I wish a considerable sum, in specie, was immediately sent to Mr. *Trumbull*, the Paymaster," Schuyler wrote.[7] The urgency of Schuyler's request increased a week later. By then, he had attempted to purchase his own stock of specie in Albany, only to find there was virtually none available. He needed metal from further south. "The urgent necessity of an immediate supply of gold and silver strikes me so forcibly, that Congress will pardon me if I seem importunate, and entreat them to send what can be got at *Philadelphia* by express." Without it, he suggested, the invasion would fail for want of support from Canadian farmers who refused to accept continental dollars.[8]

It took nearly two weeks for Schuyler's plea to reach Philadelphia by express riders. As soon as the Continental Congress read it, the search was on for specie. On Friday, October 6, 1775, Congress sent out a call to the states for a total of £20,000 Pennsylvania worth of "silver and gold," or about 53,200 Spanish silver dollars. Over the weekend, Congress learned that there was some specie still in the Pennsylvania state treasury, left over from its land bank program. On Monday, October 9, Congress ordered the Pennsylvania treasurer to hand it over in exchange for Pennsylvania currency or continental bills, "[as] the success of the expedition to *Canada* depends upon supplying General *Schuyler* with a quantity of Gold and Silver." The next day, October 10, 1775, Hancock dispatched four members of the Philadelphia Light Horse with $16,970⅔ in silver and gold for Schuyler's use, less than half of what he had requested.[9] Meanwhile, in Ticonderoga, Schuyler's demands continued. "I fear the want of specie will be fatal to us, should everything else go well," Schuyler wrote on October 18.[10] The Pennsylvania specie arrived two days later. It soon ran out, and the American expedition foundered.[11] Congress repeated its call for coin on January 20, 1776, asking each colony to "collect all the gold and silver coin they can," because the Canadian invasion "cannot be successfully carried on without that article." By then the American forces in Canada were shattered. Starving and broke, they had mounted a near-suicidal blizzard assault on the Canadian fortress at Quebec City. The Americans lost nearly half their 1,200-man force, including General Richard Montgomery, who was shredded by grapeshot in front of his men. Montgomery had been forced to attack, Schuyler argued, because the money had failed.[12]

There was no strictly financial reason for Canadians to refuse an American currency. In 1775 the continental dollar was worth practically as much as silver coin, and presumably they could have been traded south, as bills of credit had before. The question was one of economic sovereignty. Inside the states, bills of credit were a credit against a tax debt, an instrument with real value to whoever might have to pay those taxes. Outside, the bills were just paper. Canadian farmers understood, or at least suspected, that their value depended on control the invaders would never establish.[13]

III. Causation and Timing in the Demise of the Continental Dollar

Historians have tended to see the failure of the continental dollar as a straightforward problem of oversupply. In this view, the problem with bills of credit is that Congress simply printed too many, increasing the quantity of bills so quickly that hyperinflation was sure to follow. But as more recent work on the continental dollar has suggested, this confuses cause for effect. The first significant declines in the dollar's buying power came in late 1776, before there were any issues with oversupply. Increases in the volume of continental dollars were Congress's understandable reaction to this earlier shift, a response to higher prices and declining values rather than the other way around.[14]

Some historians have located the decline of the continental dollar in the Congress's inability to tax in the states, "a consequence of the perverse allocation of the power to tax before and under the Articles of Confederation," the plan of union that the states finally approved in 1781. But this analysis, too, falls short in terms of the timing. By 1781, the continental dollar had long since been abandoned, and, again, the taxes meant to bring in and destroy congressional bills began in 1779—years after the first declines in the dollar's value, which began long before Congress, or anyone else, knew that the taxes meant to anchor the dollar might prove impossible to collect.[15]

However, the basic analysis—that the power to tax was at the root of the continental dollar's troubles—is well founded. The value of the continental dollar declined because of the accidental British success in the second war, the one to disestablish American money. The problem America had was territorial control. From the first, declines in value that marked the career of the continental dollar were caused by the British army's success in making large parts of America into the functional equivalent of Canada, where the economic sovereignty of the new nation did not hold.

In other words, the basic instinctive reaction of many Americans, in all the colonies—that the bills were failing because of a lack of patriotism—was essentially correct. As Dickinson had argued in his *Farmer* letters, all property, including money, was the product of government, of sovereignty. Thus, the existence of money extended from the will of the people. The issue was whether the people's will, and the power of the Revolutionary state, could extend to regions where a hostile army was on the march. Loyalty might be equated with faith in the essential durability of the Revolution, and faith was the arena within which the war over American money, would be won or lost.

IV. Britain Deals the First Blow against Continental Bills of Credit

The British army abandoned Boston in March 1776 and retreated to Nova Scotia. After Congress issued the Declaration of Independence in July, it became clear that British commanders had another, more defensible area in mind as a North American base: the islands of Manhattan and Long Island. Their attack in August was devastating. Soon, the remnants of the Continental army were retreating across New Jersey, and Philadelphia was evacuating. By early September, soldiers were throwing up defensive lines on the outskirts of the city. Further north along the Delaware, the American army was catching its breath and struggling to secure supplies. Pennsylvania men poled flatboats up the river loaded with food into the hills toward Easton. Wagons followed the roads north on the west side of the river. On December 16, 1776, Nathanael Greene, a thirty-four-year-old Quaker from Rhode Island and an officer in the Continental army, followed them.

Greene rode the skeletal forests and fields of Bucks County, surveying ragged troops camped and quartered along the upper Delaware. They had retreated ninety miles in nineteen days, Thomas Paine recalled, "sometimes within shot and sight" of the enemy, tearing up bridges only to see them rebuilt in their wake, and leaving behind a shocked and devastated province. That summer, Paine had volunteered to serve with the Pennsylvania Associators as a secretary before being transferred to Greene's command in Fort Lee, New Jersey. He had retreated across the state along with them. The army had found rest behind the Delaware as British soldiers and their mercenary allies settled into quarters on the New Jersey side. It was widely believed that the British would press on to Philadelphia when the river froze, and the metropolis of the Middle Colonies would be lost. Greene and the other officers were planning a desperate attempt to push them back.[16]

Greene met a small group of other officers on the road north. For Washington, headquartered on a farm near two likely Delaware crossings, the coming campaign was a final test, with "all that is dear & valuable" depending on it, he wrote. The question was whether the states allied against Britain could field "a respectable Army . . . such as will be competent to every exigency," he wrote John Hancock before setting out that morning.[17]

Greene's mind that day was on the practical problems of getting the army ready for the winter campaign. The barrels of salted pork, salted beef, beer, vinegar, and flour, the shot and powder each soldier would carry in their cartridge boxes, the woolens and linens they would wear through the winter, all had to be paid for or simply taken. Either way, they must be had. For Greene, that meant the continental dollar and the army's ability to fight were intertwined. That night, bivouacked on the bank above Corryell's Ferry on the western side of the Delaware north of Trenton, Greene wrote his wife, Catharine, that the only way to maintain the states' money, which was "almost lost in the Jerseys, and much injured in this State," was military success. "A good army will soon repair the credit, and nothing else."[18]

Greene's fear was that the money would fail before the army did. People were "refusing to supply the Army under various pretenses, but evidently from a disaffection to the Cause and to the Currency," he wrote Hancock on December 21. Faith and loyalty were failing. Congress should give Washington the power to "punish the disaffected if necessary," for refusing the "Continental Money" and "withholding the necessary supplies" for "the one will put it out of our power to pay, the other to support the Troops," he wrote. Greene's own people, the Quakers, he wrote, were most likely to have "the effrontery to refuse the continental currency," which "cannot fail of drawing down the resentment of the People upon them."[19] This was treason, no matter how hard-pressed Americans were, and Greene believed that violence was justified in response.[20]

Other Revolutionary leaders were equally concerned. The Continental Congress, preparing for the worst, fled south to meet at a tavern in Baltimore. Robert Morris, who stayed behind, sent his family to the country along with his books and papers. Many other Philadelphians had done the same, leaving a "dismal and melancholy" city inhabited by sick soldiers and Quakers committed to nonresistance.[21] The evacuation, Congress's flight, "devastation" and betrayals in New Jersey, and the British general Clinton's invasion of Rhode Island all painted a "gloomy picture," Morris wrote Silas Deane, Congress's representative in Paris, on December 21, 1776. The flight of Congress, the evacuation, and the army waiting for ice floes to solidify were less frightening than the money's sudden collapse. "The depreciation of the continental currency," Morris wrote, was the "one circumstance, more distressing than all the rest, because it threatens instant and total ruin to the American cause, unless some radical is applied and speedily."[22] Morris believed the nation's only hope, other than a French diversion, was "some fortunate event or other."[23]

Few colonists understood the situation as well as John Dickinson. The years since his triumph with the *Farmer* letters had been difficult. He had hoped for reform and found himself in a revolution. In July, he voted against the Declaration of Independence before, like Paine, volunteering to fight with the Continental army in New York. In the retreat across New Jersey, he had seen firsthand how the money failed in the face of a pursuing enemy force. When the retreat ended, on the far side of the Delaware he knew that the Congress's bills' reach would extend no farther than Congress's control. He feared further conquests, moving his wife and family from Philadelphia to a farm in Dover, Delaware.[24]

On December 14, 1776, Dickinson wrote to his brother Philemon from New Castle, Delaware, at the mouth of the river, warning him to "Receive no more Continental Money on your Bonds or Mortgages" from New Jersey debtors. Dickinson sent the letter with one of the men his brother enslaved, who was captured by Philadelphia's Council of Safety and forced to give up the letter.

The Council of Safety, the body charged by the new state with investigating possible subversive influences, suspected that the intercepted letter was evidence of disloyalty and, eventually, brought Dickinson in to explain himself. Dickinson, who had spent months fighting in New York, disagreed that loyalty had anything to do with it. His concern was practical. Philemon was a general in the New Jersey militia. His home, Dickinson later explained, "was in that part of the country actually possessed by the British army." Philemon's debtors might gather up the then-worthless bills, cross the Delaware, and "pay off their debts" with bills useless where Philemon actually lived. He had merely sought to warn his brother of the bills' structural flaw, their relationship to economic sovereignty. At the time, Dickinson later explained, there were rumors that virtually all of New Jersey was prepared to accept British general William Howe's November 30 pardon offer, in return for swearing not to bear arms against the king's troops. Others had the same fear. Samuel Adams wrote John Warren that he believed Philadelphia itself was "lost" with the conquest of the Jerseys until "recovered by other Americans." If Revolutionary governments fell, Dickinson knew, the currency would collapse. Even if it didn't, the contrast in valuation between neighboring regions, one where the bills were contracts honored by the state and another where the bills were worthless paper, would create perverse effects—debtors hunting creditors and fortunes made by trading across the line where paper either became money or ceased to be. Dickinson's sophistication may not have concealed a lack of faith. The Council of Safety exonerated him, but the incident would haunt his political career for years.[25]

Paine, too, had money on his mind at the end of 1776. In Newark, New Jersey, on a brief break during the army's pell-mell retreat, he had begun composing the essay that would become *The Crisis No. 1*. It began, "These are the times that try men's souls" but quickly switched to a monetary metaphor. "What we obtain too cheap, we esteem too lightly; it is dearness only that gives every thing its value," Paine wrote. "Heaven knows how to put a proper price upon its goods; and it would be strange indeed if so celestial an article as FREEDOM should not be highly rated." The essay appeared in the *Pennsylvania Journal* on December 19 and as a pamphlet on December 23. It was circulating in Washington's camp before his Christmas attack on Trenton, across the Delaware.[26]

Washington's attack had the intended effect. It forced the British army into retreat and stabilized the continental dollar's precipitous decline. But damage had already been done. Before Howe's invasion of New Jersey, the continental dollar, like many successful bills of credit, had traded at higher value than the taxes designed to draw them in and burn them were worth. As noted earlier, those taxes only began in 1779, suggesting that the rational value of the bills—when time is factored in—was roughly 70 percent of their face value. That 30 percent, the difference between the face value and rational value of the continental dollar, its loyalty premium, had been all but wiped out in the economic reaction to Britain's invasion. Events shifted the calculus. Before the conquest of New Jersey, no one had quite believed that a whole state could be stricken from the union. After, few could afford to imagine otherwise. American economic sovereignty had faced its first significant challenge.[27]

V. The First Decline in the Dollar's Value and the "Patriot Economy"

The dip in the American continental dollar's value at the end of 1776 catalyzed what many historians consider to be the most radical movement of the Revolutionary period, the movement behind what the historian Barbara Clark Smith has termed "the Patriot Economy." This movement was opposite to the liberal, laissez-faire elite who found themselves ascendant after the Revolution. These revolutionaries, Smith argued, "asserted public power to counteract the coercions of the market," locating their notion of freedom itself "in a popular capacity to determine the use and value of property within a framework of social purpose and human need." The value of the continental dollar, which affected masses of people associated with the war, was their cause célèbre. Bills of credit, by their very existence, announced the government's role in the creation and regulation of property and wealth. When someone refused them, or refused to trade them at face value, it suggested a lack of faith that might be countered by political or military means, either through representatives or in the streets.[28]

It became a popular cause, but the patriot economy began with acts of the Continental Congress. The drop in the continental dollar's value created a heightened sense of paranoia. On January 11, 1776, Congress passed a resolution warning of "evil disposed persons," the "disaffected" it called them, who were trying "to obstruct and defeat the efforts of the United Colonies in defense of their just rights" by attempting to "depreciate the bills of credit emitted by authority" or refusing "to take the continental currency." Congress urged states to treat anyone refusing the bills "as an enemy of his country." On December 27, 1776, meeting in Henry Fite's house in Baltimore with the British threatening Philadelphia, Congress took this logic further. On Greene's advice, it gave General Washington the power "to take, wherever he may be, whatever he may want" from inhabitants who either refused to sell or refused to sell at a "reasonable price." Moreover, Congress gave Washington authority to arrest "persons who refuse to take the continental currency, or are otherwise disaffected to the American cause." Disloyalty justified force. Market forces would yield to patriotic demands.[29]

Congress called for renewed support from the states, to shore up faith in the money through collective action. In January 1777 Congress urged states to make continental bills a "lawful tender," allowing them to "pass current in all payments, trade, and dealings in these States," with the idea that making the bills a legal tender at the same value as the silver dollar would help stabilize the value that the bills expressed.[30] On February 15, 1777, it called on the states to regulate "fluctuating and exorbitant prices" for labor and household products that had destabilized the meaning of the dollar in some regions at the expense of others. Simultaneously, the Congress also sent a call for two regional conventions to coordinate stabilizing the dollar; a convention in Yorktown, Pennsylvania, for states north of Virginia, and a southern one in Charleston, South

Carolina. Both were to coordinate pricing policy to cut down the possibilities for arbitrage, trading on different prices given for continental money between states.[31]

The Charleston convention does not seem to have met. The northern convention, however, met at Yorktown, Pennsylvania, on March 23, 1777, for eight days of debate on ways to support the currency. Chairman Lewis Burwell of Virginia wrote Congress on April 3, 1777, that delegates from Pennsylvania, Delaware, Maryland, New York, New Jersey, and Virginia were unable "to proceed with unanimity" on the money problem. They did, however, succeed in injecting a new concept into an ongoing congressional discussion of the currency that complicated its regulation as a measure. For the first time, the convention raised the idea that the sheer quantity of the congressional currency was becoming a problem, in part because most normal trade had come to a halt. There was a mismatch, Burwell wrote, between the "great quantity of paper currency" and the "quantity of transferrable property, especially in the states in the neighborhood of the army." Demand, in the form of wages and commissary payments, was outstripping what farm households and merchants could supply.[32]

Farmers had "no further use for [the currency]," Burwell observed. They could not buy things with it because of the decline in trade. Unlike the war against France, when British goods had flooded into the American market, the only things available for purchase during the Revolution were the "necessaries and conveniences of life," which most farm families produced themselves. Distant taxes, meanwhile, could only create just so much demand. Farmers had already started producing less because there was nothing to buy. The Revolution was finding that temporary money put a limit on accumulation.

Meanwhile, states disagreed about whether the real drop in farm production justified higher prices, which might make them more interested in producing for the army. The delegates from states closest to the ongoing fighting insisted that higher prices were justified until these circumstances changed. Without higher prices to entice them, farmers would simply withdraw from the market or trade only for goods, producing "the most fatal consequences to these states," the northerly delegates warned.

The convention also noted a new factor at work: the speculators Dickinson had already observed making fortunes trading currency from war zones into areas where American economic sovereignty held. These were the "disaffected and inimical" seeking to invest in "in silver, gold, and other commodities, which have an intrinsic value" and willing to pay "high and exorbitant prices for the same."[33] Some delegates favored limiting the number of bills or increasing the availability of imports so that farmers would have something to buy. Others were in favor of just setting prices and punishing people who ignored them. All seemed to agree that the all-but-cashless credit culture of American farmers, the root of bills of credit as a money form, had become a wartime liability. The main disagreement was over whether or not to limit prices with new legislation, and they left that dilemma for Congress.[34]

VI. The Empire Strikes Back

Meanwhile, military developments again intervened. The fall of 1777 set the scene for the new states' greatest defeat and their greatest triumph. First came disaster. A British expeditionary force, landing at the head of the Elk River in Chesapeake Bay after a short campaign in the Brandywine River valley, managed to take Philadelphia, marching into the city on September 26, 1777. Pennsylvania itself had become a Canada. "Nothing will pass at this time, (unless with a Few), but Gold and Silver, which is hard upon those who have a quantity of the old paper money by them," Philadelphia resident Elizabeth Drinker wrote in her diary on December 9, 1777. "Nothing but hard money will pass," she noted two days later.[35] Washington's defeated army, meanwhile, was camped on the outskirts of Philadelphia, struggling to secure supplies to last them through the winter. The cause seemed hopeless.

Less than a month after Philadelphia fell, however, on October 17, the British general John Burgoyne surrendered his entire army after the battle of Saratoga in the Hudson River valley. Burgoyne had attempted the assault that Congress had hoped to preclude with Schuyler's attack on Quebec. He had led six thousand men, mostly Hessian mercenaries, down the Hudson River valley from Canada in an attempt to cut New England off from New York. Instead of loyalists, his army stirred up a nest of American militia, who cut him off and forced his surrender. Burgoyne's loss brought France into the war on the struggling republic's side. The Americans had, within a month, traded a city for an army and a new, hugely powerful ally. It seemed a fair exchange.

Burgoyne's surrendered army, meanwhile, began an expedition across New England that would leave an illuminating monetary record. The account of Brunswicker captain Heinrich Urban Cleve, written after the Americans captured him at the battle of Saratoga, is particularly revealing.[36] On November 4, 1777, Cleve arrived in Worcester, Massachusetts, as a prisoner of war. There, he and his fellow officers were forced to sell their golden British guineas for American bills of credit to pay for supplies. Cleve and his fellow officers paid 1 guinea, worth 21 shillings sterling, for 15 continental dollars. This was more than triple the official exchange rate: a guinea was only worth 4⅔ dollars at the rate Congress established in 1776.[37] Ironically, Cleve bought dollars because merchants were firmly against giving more food or clothing in return for gold and silver than they would for an equivalent in dollars—which was against the law. By buying paper with gold and silver, Cleve had more than tripled the amount he could buy. Cleve received even more paper for his gold further west, closer to the fighting in New York. There, Hessian officers traded each guinea for 18 dollars.[38]

There were two reasons that Americans were anxious to get rid of paper dollars, Cleve wrote. The first was loyalty—or lack thereof. "Many Tories seek to get rid of their paper money and goods so that they may flee the more readily with cash if the party spirit should turn into a spirit of persecution," Cleve wrote. These traders wanted money that would be good behind British lines.[39] The second reason was the desire for European luxuries. The merchants who had managed to shift trades from Britain to mainland Europe demanded gold and silver for goods slipped past the British blockade. "The merchants, who get their wares from the French and Dutch, can only pay in real coin, because, I hear, American money is not accepted in Europe," Cleve wrote. This made sense. Europeans would never pay the taxes. Loyalty was less important, however, than wartime exigencies. In his experience, Cleve wrote, "Republicans" were just as eager to get rid of their paper as Tories looking to slip away. "Whole barrels full of paper money come in from distant places," either the actual war zone or from perhaps counterfeiters in New York, "to take advantage of the chance to exchange" with the Hessians, he wrote.[40]

America's new allies, meanwhile, were struggling to understand the American monetary system, and American diplomats were having difficulty explaining it to them. After Burgoyne's surrender at Saratoga, France, which had previously contented itself with providing clandestine but crucial support through a front company run by the aristocrat and playwright Pierre-Augustin Caron de Beaumarchais, entered the war on the side of the United States. In particular, it brought its fleet to bear on the previously unchallenged British naval blockade and met with conspicuous success. French victories near the mouth of the Delaware River forced the British army out of Philadelphia in the summer of 1778, a grand coup for the American cause. But France's new role also forced it to come to grips with its new ally's finances. All, it seems, was not well.[41]

In 1778 the French government commissioned a report on the continental dollar from Charles-Geneviève-Louis-Auguste-André-Timothée d'Éon de Beaumont, known as the Chevalier d'Éon, a sometime spy and diplomat who had lived as a woman since 1777, claiming she had only been raised as a man to secure the line of inheritance. D'Éon's report analyzed how the dollar had performed over the previous three years of war. Her conclusions were not encouraging. Because of their long-standing balance of trade "in favor of the metropole," it had been impossible for the Americans, as colonists, to secure enough "pieces of gold and silver in sufficient quantity for their use," d'Éon wrote. As a result, the Americans had been obliged to issue "Continental paper," which had suffered a "great blow" in the British invasion of 1776. The need to print more and more ever since had made matters worse, she wrote. "National credit had been great at first, but now had no effect." In other words, the British were winning the money war. The actual mechanisms or ideas behind bills of credit, meanwhile, were still a mystery to French officials, and the bills remained a source of tension throughout the war.[42]

VII. The Empire Splits the Patriot Economy

In 1778 a split appeared within the previously unified patriot coalition between those who continued to believe that bills of credit were linked to sovereignty and thus loyalty, and a small but increasingly influential group of thinkers who believed that British successes pointed to a theoretical flaw in bills of credit themselves. The contest between theory and loyalty would continue to divide the patriot movement for the remainder of the war.

The states that rejected price controls at the Yorktown conference—New Hampshire, Massachusetts, Connecticut, Rhode Island, and New York— met twice again over the next nine months wrestling with the problem, first in Springfield in July, and then in January 1778 in New Haven. These states had been the seat of the war for three years, and it had challenged them. The delegates had seen too many good patriots make compromises to believe wholeheartedly that price fluctuations derived from a lack of virtue. They had also seen too many attempts to stabilize the value of the dollar fail to think that public will was wanting. The error, the delegates finally concluded, was that bills of credit had failed to align households' self-interest with the public good.

"When we see self-love, that first principle planted in the humane breast by the all wise Creator for our benefit and preservation, through misapplication and corruption, perverted to our destruction, we feel the

necessity of correcting so pernicious an error and directing the operation of it in such manner that our self and social love might be the same,"
the New Haven delegates concluded on January 30, 1778. The New
Haven convention was unable to articulate any alternative to price controls and more vigorous taxation, but they had made a key distinction
between loyalty to the currency and loyalty to the state. They were suggesting that America might lose its economic sovereignty but preserve its
independence, winning one war and not the other. They also seemed to
suggest that bills of credit's reliance on the ability to tax might prove their
fatal flaw. Reformation of the currency itself became an option. The question, ultimately, was how to make a revolution within the Revolution, a
revolution in self-interest.[43]

VIII. American Farmers Turn against the Dollar

The New Haven convention further concluded it was the quantity, not
the quality, of bills that was causing the problems. This proved influential to congressional thinkers, perhaps, because it was psychologically
convenient. Quantity was impersonal. It allowed patriot leaders to argue
that the army's supply difficulties stemmed from a technical rather than
a moral failure. Thus, proposals abounded in 1778 for new ways to get rid
of the money, either by limiting the number of new bills or eliminating
them altogether. One of the best ways to increase the dollar's value, Gouverneur Morris wrote in the Congress's address "To the Inhabitants of the
United States of America" on May 8, 1778, was to "collect the moneys" to
invest them in large loan-office certificates, or have legislatures "sink their
respective emissions" by taxing them in to be burned.[44] "To support the
War, it is indispensably necessary to restore the Value of Money by reducing the Quantity," Congress's new Committee on Finance—Robert Morris,
Elbridge Gerry, Richard Henry Lee, John Witherspoon, and Gouverneur
Morris, appointed August 27, 1778—reported to Congress on October 28.
These were Congress's most astute financial minds, and they increasingly
believed that they were up against a mathematical law of nature. That was
easier to swallow than the alternative—that Americans had lost faith in
the cause.[45]

On the battlefields around New York that fall, though, it was clear
that the relationship between the currency and loyalty was taking on a
new, emotionally charged significance. In early October 1778 John Hurring took a horse from the Continental army encampment at Fishkill,

New York, and rode into the hills toward Connecticut on a mission. Fishkill was at the head of the Hudson Highlands, the crags hugging the river north of New York City that had served as a barrier to British aggression since the summer of 1776. The town was roughly halfway between Boston and Philadelphia and had become a center of supply as the war devolved into a series of feints and counterattacks, with the British all but bottled up in New York. At Valley Forge in March, after more than two years in the Continental army, Hurring's officers selected him for George Washington's "Life Guard," a unit Washington formed in March 1776 "as a guard for himself and his baggage." Guards were selected for their "sobriety, honesty and good behavior," above-average height, good looks, and cleanliness. Washington wanted men who were "clean and spruce," he wrote on March 11, 1776, "handsomely and well made."[46]

In October, the Hudson Valley becomes one of the most beautiful places in the world. Even before the trees erupt with color, the sky is a pennant-crisp blue, the light golden and rich. Riding west with a pass that allowed him to pass Continental patrols, Hurring likely had his mind on the task. The harvest was coming in, and he had been ordered to find fresh food for Washington and his aides. It might not have been easy. In 1778 loyalties this close to New York City were mixed. Many farmers had the option of selling their harvest to British agents farther south for coin and were increasingly unlikely to welcome a visit from a Continental purchasing agent—even one wearing the distinctive bearskin helmet and cockade of Washington's guards.

Near the Connecticut border, Hurring rode up to the farm of Israel Howland, a Quaker who had been born in Massachusetts but migrated to the New York Highlands in the 1750s, settling at Oblong Meeting near Pawling, less than a mile from the Connecticut border in an area still called "Quaker Hill." Howland lived with his son Prince, who at twenty-three had already served a year in the Continental army, and Prince's wife, Mary. Israel Howland's health was failing, and he couldn't walk far. He would die three years later, but he probably met Hurring at the gate.[47]

He was also, Hurring later told campmate Elijah Fisher, "an old Tory," a supporter of British rule. The confrontation between Hurring and Howland was brief. Hurring asked whether Howland would be willing to sell part of his harvest or any of his warm winter clothing to the army. He probably mentioned Washington's name. Israel refused. Perhaps further words were exchanged, even insults. The farm was evidently prosperous. Refusing to sell marked Howland as disloyal, and Hurring might have said so. To a soldier like Hurring, who had lived through the starving winter at Valley Forge the year before, there was no other excuse. In New Jersey, some patriots were already arguing they had a "perfect right to plunder" anyone who had put themselves beyond the protection of Revolutionary law.[48] Hurring talked to Israel long enough, he later recalled, to have seen "several things that he wanted" before returning to camp.

On the night of October 3, Hurring, Moses Walton, Elias Brown, and John Herrick returned to Howland's farm. They broke in, seizing silver spoons, some silver dollars, a bit of continental currency, a thick coat, and a variety of other clothing. By dawn, they were back in Fishkill, some twenty miles away. Two days later they raided another farm, owned by a man named John Hoag, stealing more clothing and silver in addition to £450 in continental bills.

The day after the second robbery, Fisher, who had been visiting family in Connecticut, returned to camp. He immediately recognized that his messmates, the men he had slept, ate, and served with since Valley Forge, were better dressed and better fed than he had left them. At first, he thought that they had somehow come into some money, perhaps from back pay or a settled debt. If so, that was good news. Herrick owed Fisher $16. But as others came in from the day's work, they told Fisher about their previous week's work. Fisher, who had noted every crime and every punishment he had witnessed during his service in his diary, was suddenly afraid. "I said that whether [Israel] be a tory or not if it should be found out . . . some or all [of] you will be hung." Two weeks later, Prince Howland rode into camp asking after the stolen items taken by a man wearing a distinctive military hat—a member of the Life Guard.[49]

Brown, Walton, and Hurring were sentenced to death at a court-martial on October 22. Herrick testified against them, receiving a reduced sentence of one hundred lashes "on his bare back well laid on." "Men who are called out by their Country to defend the Rights and Property of their fellow Citizens who are abandoned enough to violate those Rights and plunder that Property deserve and shall receive no Mercy," Washington wrote, approving the punishment. The condemned men were each to be hanged in front of separate divisions to spread the deterrence, but Brown and Walton escaped that night. Washington eventually pardoned Brown, at the request of his father. Walton fled west and was never heard from again. Hurring was hanged at Fishkill less than three weeks after he started toward Oblong in his bearskin cap.[50]

For soldiers like Hurring, the decline of the continental dollar was anything but a theoretical exercise. Along the front line, where American troops regularly repelled British raiders and captured spies, some carrying counterfeit currency from British presses in New York, the currency was a matter of life or death. The fate of the army itself, in a sense, hung on whether farmers, like the Howlands, were willing to sell to men like Hurring. Farmers, meanwhile, were fed up. "The majority of the people of this state wish to see [the money] perish," James Watson of Connecticut wrote in January 1779. Then, at least, they could return to the old regime, moneyless, helpless, but less chaotic. But where would the United States be when the money was gone? The money was its only way to supply the army. Even Watson acknowledged that "the prospect is certainly most gloomy, whether our currency lives, or dies."[51] The desire to preserve it was leading to violence, but doing away with it would leave Congress powerless.

IX. Pelatiah Webster and the Bill of Credit as American Autonomy

The northern states' conference led to further proposals to reform the currency. Some hoped to replace bills of credit with silver borrowed from abroad. On September 19, 1778, Congress's Finance Committee suggested authorizing a £5 million sterling loan in Europe to procure specie for use in America, ultimately as a substitute for the continental dollar. Congress agreed to the plan immediately.[52] Just as quickly, there was pushback.

One of the most significant voices against the loan was Philadelphia merchant Pelatiah Webster. Webster's own war had ended early. In the spring of 1777 he had loaded his ship with bar iron and flour, planning to run the British blockade and bring badly needed supplies into Massachusetts. On April 6 off Long Island, the *Orpheus*, a twenty-six-gun British frigate, sighted his vessel. There is no record that Webster put up a fight. The *Orpheus* took Webster's ship and cargo into occupied Rhode Island. Webster was confined for a month before being freed in a prisoner exchange. He returned home to Philadelphia to find one of his two daughters sick with smallpox and the British army advancing on the capital. Unwilling to leave a sick child, Webster stayed on when the British took the city, only to be jailed for bringing food and clothing to American prisoners of war "at a time when their distresses were beyond all description." Webster was imprisoned for 132 days, until June 17, 1778, the day before the British evacuated the city.[53]

His health was broken from "close confinement" and "grievous oppression," his business and affairs in ruins. Unable to continue his mercantile business, he turned to an earlier vocation. In 1746 Webster had graduated from Yale in the same class as Ezra Stiles and Lewis Morris, a future New York delegate to the Continental Congress. He was ordained in 1749 and served as the minister in Greenwich, a small town along the Swift River in western Massachusetts. The pay, however, proved insufficient. In 1755 he resigned his position, turning to "*mercantile* business" more out of "necessity than inclination. My old habits of reading and thinking could not easily be shaken off, and I was scarce ever without either a book or some subject of discussion ready prepared, to which I could resort, the moment I found myself at leisure with other business."[54]

The summer of 1778 was just such a moment. With little left to do but think, read, and write, he realized that the Revolution itself was an object worthy of study. "The powerful pressures of the *British* force during the war, and the obstinate and determined defence of the *Americans,* soon threw every thing into disorder, and produced every day *new occurrences* and *new problems,* which *America* had never seen before, and, of course knew not how either to obviate or solve them," Webster later wrote. "I conceived the most important and alarming of these events and questions were those which respected *our resources,* and especially the *state of the Continental money,* which was the *sole supply* of the public treasury at the time."[55] He would pursue this course of study for the next decade, advising the Continental Congress and future presidents like Washington and Madison. His home in South Philadelphia became a salon for like-minded Americans, besieged by both fans and critics. "Such as cheerfully join in company" were always welcome, he wrote in February 1780, "begging this favor at the same time of the rest, who do not like our employment, that they would not come into the room to interrupt us."[56]

Webster's early writing elaborated on a version of the quantity theory then coming into vogue. "The value of money is nothing in itself, it is a *mere relation,* it is the proportion between the medium of trade and the objects of trade: Therefore, if the medium of trade be increased, whilst the objects of trade continue the same, the money must depreciate; if the medium of trade increases and objects of trade decrease, the objects will alter fast, and the depreciation will increase, in double proportion, which I take the to be the case at present," he wrote.[57] For Webster, like the delegates at Springfield and New Haven, no object of trade had or should have a fixed value, neither the gold or silver used in anonymous long-distance trade nor the dollars the Continental Congress had used to purchase supplies and transport. Everything was relative. Fixing value in law, he argued, was doubly pernicious; it did not help and often did active harm. "*Let trade be as free as air,*" Webster wrote.[58] Restricting trade or fixing prices, he wrote, was an *"infernal means . . . opposed to heaven and its laws"* and "most repugnant to natural principles of *equity*, which are all derived from *Heaven,* and most destructive of the *rights* of human nature."[59]

Webster was opposed to almost every kind of economic interventionism except one: he believed in the necessity of American political control over money. This, indeed, was the only kind of coercion he viewed as legitimate and necessary for the operation of the state. "You may lead with a *thread* what you cannot drive with *whips* and *scorpions*," Webster wrote. "The *Britons* have found this to their cost, in the unnatural means they have pursued to preserve and recover their dominions in *America*. I wish we might be made wise by their errors."[60] He believed that American money was failing because it was not useful. To save it, Congress must create a money whose usefulness was "grounded in evidence and reason which the mind can see and believe," Webster wrote. This necessary "confidence" was "no more subject to the action of force, than any other passion, sentiment, or affection of the mind; any more than faith, love, or esteem."[61]

Webster recoiled at the idea that more metal, like the kind Congress might secure with a loan in Europe, was the answer. The value of money should be founded, Webster wrote, not on gold and silver but on the *"real wealth"* of the nation. What was necessary was creating institutions that aligned this "real wealth" with the needs of central authority. For Webster, the wealth of the nation, like the wealth of a colonial household, was founded on the productive capacity of its inhabitants and its property. This was what progressive British thinkers like Adam Smith had been saying for years. American bills of credit proved, Smith wrote, that a nation could send out all "the gold and silver which comes into it" for a half century or more, and yet see "its real wealth, the exchangeable value of the annual produce of its lands and labour," increase significantly. From a national standpoint, precious metals were not wealth, Smith was arguing, it was a means of putting that wealth in circulation, and one should not confuse the former for the latter. And indeed, in the seventy years when bills of credit had been in use, the American population had risen sixfold and productivity per person had roughly doubled.[62]

On these terms, Webster argued, America was wealthy regardless of its money problems. "This *real wealth,* considered as national, has very little connection with the public funds or stocks; for should they all fall . . . this would not destroy the *houses, fields, cattle, &c.* of the country."[63] In this regard, he noted, Americans had a significant advantage. They had little overseas debt, meaning they controlled their own standards of value, much as the colonies had before the war. "The American States owe nothing to any body but themselves, and employ no ships, soldiers, &c. but their own, so that they contract no foreign debt; and I take it to be a clear maxim that no state can be ruined, bankrupted, or indeed much endangered by any debt due to itself only; nor can it much be impoverished by any war, if the war and other casualties do not destroy mankind faster than women produce them."[64] Foreign loans, then, were an insane undertaking, particularly if, as proposed, Congress used them to promote the silver value of the continental dollar. "To solicit *France* for money to pay the *interest of loans* from our own people, certainly has a bad look," Webster wrote. "If a son should demand security of a stranger for monies lent to his father, people would certainly say something."[65]

The basis for Webster's analysis was his understanding of wealth as emanating from the propertied household. Father and son were in the same family, even if one was a dependent of the other. The son, by analogy, stood in the same relation as citizens to the new national government. To look for outside support in managing this relationship implied that the household and the relationships within it had dissolved. Even loans within the state made little sense, as they reversed the natural relationship within it. "Every idea of a *loan* either at home or abroad . . . directly tends to increase our distress," Webster argued.[66] A foreign loan, however, was more dangerous, as it would signal a failure of internal government. "I *abhor* and *execrate* every idea of a *foreign loan* to purchase necessaries produced among ourselves; it may be necessary to borrow in *Europe* money sufficient to purchase what we must export from thence" like guns, powder, ammunition, and clothing for the army, "but to borrow money in *Europe* to pay for supplies produced here among ourselves, appears to me to be the height of absurdity: this exposes our weakness to all the world; not only our *weakness* in the point of *supplies*; not the exhausted state of our country, for that is full of everything we want, clothing and military stores excepted; but the weakness of our *counsels* and *administration*, that our *domestic economy* should be so bad, that we should not be able to call into public use the very supplies in which the country abounds, is *shameful*," he wrote.

"*Domestic economy*," indeed, was the object.[67] The household that surrendered its financial independence because of demands from one of its members was fundamentally unsound, Webster argued, and could not be independent. The destruction of American credit abroad, he argued, would be better than soliciting foreign money for domestic use, which implied foreign domination. "It is manifest beyond any need of proof, that the nation who is in debt to a superior power, cannot be free and independent, but is ever liable to demands the most insulting and inconsistent with freedom and [safety]."[68] Taking on a silver currency implied a dependence on outside sources of value, of breaking the link between American money and American wealth that the bill of credit, a temporary form with no value of its own, had established. The management of money, of "the relationship between the medium of exchange and its object," was fundamental to the notion of a nation-state, a sovereign right and responsibility. Congress only contemplated surrendering that right, he wrote in later years, because of the pressure it was under to see the army clothed and fed. "This seems to have been a period of distress and madness," Webster concluded.[69]

For Webster, the continental dollar was fundamentally a credit instrument, a contract whose value was related to time. The only way to make it work as "money," as something that circulated at a stable value, drawing wealth into the public sphere, was to ensure that people needed it. His central recommendation was a new and heavy tax denominated in continental dollars. A tax, he argued, would create a demand for it as a currency above and beyond its commodity value as a questionable promise to pay. Then, and only then, would American farmers be willing to part with their "real wealth" in exchange for paper. "The only possible method then of giving value or credit to money is to give it such qualities, and clothe it with such circumstances, as shall make it a sure means of procuring every needful thing," Webster reasoned. "For money that will not answer all things, is defective, and has not the full nature and qualities of money."[70] Congress did not have to borrow silver to pay continental dollar holders in silver to prop up the dollar's value. It did not have to convince Americans that new national supplies of specie were imminent. Rather, it only had to tax in sufficient bulk to make American paper a necessity everywhere American law extended.

What Webster had hit upon, finding his way through logic rather than history, was the first principle of bills of credit themselves. The structure of the bills, the way they had been written into law almost a century earlier, required taxes to make them work. The bills had no meaning without the taxes passed first to establish the debt that citizens would use the bills to pay.

Webster, however, took the relationship between money and taxes to be a universal truth. This idea followed from his premises and had a good deal of truth in it more generally. What, after all, was the money of any particular country if not what its government would accept in payment? By that logic, Britain's imperial project, taxes charged in silver bullion, could be read as a plan to reshape American money—which, in fact, it was, if somewhat less directly. But his leap, while insightful on its own, mistook a structural quality of the bills themselves—their inherent legal relationship to taxation—for a universal policy prescription. Webster was not suggesting that Congress fulfill its specific obligations by taxing continental dollars out of existence, as had been planned, at least for the first run, since 1775. He was suggesting that any taxes, planned or unplanned, inherent to the bills' structure or not, would increase demand for bills such that it would increase their value.

If Congress could use taxes to make the continental dollar a needful thing, it might avoid "the danger of sinking under the weight of war."[71] A tax would both eliminate excess currency and make existing bills more valuable without any need for coin. "It would be more for the interest of the Thirteen United States to *call in and sink* their Continental bills as fast as they issue," Webster wrote, "than to receive a *sum of gold* every year equal to the money they issue, from some foreign power, as a perfect gift never to be repaid." Congress, he argued, should make the continental dollar valuable because it was money, not money because it could be exchanged for a silver coin. He envisioned an American state taxing and spending in its own currency, circulating its own wealth internally, beholden to no one but itself. All Congress would have to do was to tax and, if that failed, to tax some more.[72]

X. Congress Triples Taxes to Save the Dollar

In 1779 Congress followed Webster's advice. The first taxes scheduled in 1775 were coming due, and Congress resolved to make them a success. It pled, argued, and attempted to persuade the states to help it tax in and burn as much currency as it could. The congressional statements issued on January 13, May 26, and September 13, 1779, in letters to the states were almost manifestos, grand statements meant to elicit support and inspire resistance to other forces it saw in play.

The January 13 letter explained Congress's January 2, 1779, decision to begin taxing in significant quantities, $15 million in 1779 and at least $6 million every year thereafter, while calling in nearly half of all existing bills—some $41.5 million out of $101.4 million issued by Congress thus far—to combat counterfeiting. The goal, Congress wrote, was to reduce the bills' quantity using a variety of different measures and to honor commitments it had made when printing the first bills of credit, four long years earlier.[73]

The mention of counterfeiting signaled that Congress was becoming more alert to another, more deliberate side of Britain's war against American money. British troops and loyalists operating "from their Garrison at New York" had long been counterfeiting American bills of credit, offering them at cost to all comers. These counterfeiting operations, begun early in the war to outfit spies and disrupt finances around New York, had grown increasingly sophisticated, especially after the conquest of Philadelphia. There, the British army had apparently captured the printing presses, paper, inks, and etching plates used to produce real continental dollars, and had begun printing counterfeit bills that were all but indistinguishable from the originals. This led to creative tactics in what was unquestionably economic warfare. General William Howe, the British commander at Philadelphia, had even tried to smuggle a wagonload of counterfeit bills to the troops captured at Saratoga. American general Daniel Roberdeau likened it to a Trojan Horse, "not filled with men but most probably with the more dangerous Enemy, Counterfeited Continental money."[74]

"In despair of subduing the free spirits of America by force of arms or the intrigues of negotiation" (Congress had just rejected a peace proposal offering new guarantees for colonial rights), "as their last effort they have resorted to fraud," the address read. Congress declared that British forces had deployed "their emissaries . . . in a variety of artifices to debase our money, and to raise the price of commodities" while alarming the populace through "misrepresentation" about the money and, on orders from "our enemies of the highest rank," reproducing it besides.[75] Congress wanted to assure Americans, in Webster's terms, that paper money was not, in itself, a problem. The people had created it and would, eventually, destroy it. "Without public inconvenience or private distress, the whole of the debt incurred in paper emission to this day may be cancelled by taxes" like those Congress had long proposed. America could destroy its currency and fulfill the promise to tax that bills of credit represented.[76]

By May, congressional leaders came to believe that their five-month-old plan was insufficient. The reason, again, was military action. Between March and May, the value of the currency dropped precipitously as word spread that a 3,500-strong British expeditionary force from New York had captured Savannah, the Revolutionary capital of Georgia, with loyalist help on December 29, 1778.[77] Britain, with one blow, had taken an entire state off the board, making the idea of collecting $15 million in taxes increasingly fanciful. Disruption, it was clear to the American leadership, was becoming central to British war plans. "Nothing I am convinced but the depreciation of our currency . . . has fed the hopes of the enemy & kept the Arms of Briton in America untill [*sic*] now," Washington wrote James Warren on March 31, 1779. The British were waiting for the money to fail, at which point "we shall be our own conquerors," Washington wrote.[78]

Congress's response, in a May 26 letter drafted by John Dickinson, who had been reelected to Congress, was to triple down, demanding a further $45 million in continental taxes in 1779 alone, for a one-year total of $60 million. The new $45 million would not be burned, at least not yet. It would be a forced loan from the states to Congress, paying 6 percent per year, to be recirculated in lieu of new bills. The total, however, represented a sea change in congressional demand. Prewar taxes, between 1770 and 1774, averaged $0.41 per person per year, or roughly $2.05 per household. The January 1779 taxes were about $6.60 per capita. The May 1779 taxes, if collected, would amount to roughly $26.40 for every free inhabitant of the United States, or roughly $132 per household—sixty-four times higher than prewar levels.[79]

Or it would have been if the bills were trading at anything like face value. In fact, the bills were trading in Philadelphia at closer to twenty for one, meaning the taxes Congress demanded amounted, in silver terms, to just $6.60 per household or $1.32 per person—just over three times prewar levels. The charges would be painful, Dickinson acknowledged, but not as much as continued depreciation. "We will remember what you . . . said at the commencement of the war," Dickinson wrote. "Persevere, and you ensure peace, freedom, safety, glory, sovereignty, and felicity, to yourselves, your children, and your children's children."[80] Dickinson compared America and Britain to David and Goliath. The paper money had been the sling to bring the giant down. The only difficulty, Henry Laurens observed, was that some regions, like South Carolina, which was currently facing down a British army and fleet, might not be able to levy any taxes at all. He worried that the "burthen would be too much at this time." Perhaps more importantly, with the extra taxes, Congress had abandoned the internal logic of the continental dollar as a bill of credit. What made bills of credit work was not merely that taxes drove circulation but that each bill would be matched by a tax debt of equal value. The massive increase in taxes implied that Congress accepted the acknowledged fact that bills were worth less than it had intended, that Congress too had broken faith. The fact that the additional $45 million took the form of loans suggested Congress hoped to sort out the difference later, at a less perilous moment, once there were fewer dollars in the system. But the structural fact remained. Devaluing the taxes meant devaluing the bills still further.[81]

XI. The British Invasion of the South Sparks a Tragic Turn

The quadrupling of wartime taxes, taking them from $15 million to $60 million, including the money meant to be loaned by the states, proved a bridge to far. Rather than strengthening American sovereignty, Dickinson and Congress ended up exposing its limits. Laurens and the other delegates had not considered that Congress would soon face another, more pressing challenge. Over the course of four years of fighting, America's soldiers and thousands of tradespeople involved in the war effort had created what was, in effect, America's first broad-based, self-conscious, wage-earning class. Over the war years, wages in bills of credit or coin increasingly replaced payments traditionally received in credit or in kind— in food, lodging, clothing, or other goods, particularly in Philadelphia, the center of the broader effort. And that shifted the relationship ordinary people had to money as an institution. When money was obviously the shadow of a tax, like bills of credit, its value was less important than one's ability to get enough of it to avoid losing the farm in a sheriff's auction. Agitation over money before the Revolution had usually been about just that: pressuring colonial governments to make more of it, to ease the pain of a system where bills became scarcer with every year's scheduled burn. The Revolutionary government's failure to prop up the currency's value created a sea change in popular sentiment. Preserving the value of existing currency—the money that was being paid to soldiers, officers, carters, and farmers, and increasingly used to purchase daily necessities rather than saved for a tax payment—was becoming a popular obsession. For urban wage earners, the problem was existential. The dollar's failure meant their families had to live on charity, steal, or starve.[82]

By 1779, Philadelphia was the financial center of the continent. Philadelphia merchants were the first to hear of new policy developments and the first to make moves in the market in response. They were also the first to profit from the falling value of the continental dollar, buying them cheap, near the enemy, and selling them where the value still held. Congress printed most of its dollars there or nearby. Prices in Philadelphia markets, disseminated by blockade-running ships to New England or the Carolinas, "governed" the "Value of money" elsewhere.[83] Philadelphians were "the best judge being on the spot," one Boston merchant wrote to his counterpart in the city. Everywhere else in the colonies was at least one step, one letter, rumor, or announcement removed. Philadelphia merchants had long been in a position to affect policy—several, like Robert Morris, served in government—and now its wage-earning workers believed they might be as well.[84]

Congress's policy decisions in 1779 accelerated the rise of this new Revolutionary consciousness. With the continental dollar trading at a tiny fraction of its face value, Congress issued more than $90 million in a single year, bringing the total by the end to $199.98 million. Philadelphia was awash with bills of credit, and wage earners—soldiers included—faced abundant but extremely uncertain cash wages. The uncertainty produced a Revolutionary politics of its own. In 1779 ordinary people took to the streets of American cities as they hadn't since the protests over the Stamp Act and the Townshend Duties. This time, however, working men and soldiers made common cause against what they saw as elite mishandling and manipulation of *their* monetary institutions.[85]

On Tuesday, May 25, 1779, one day before Congress approved the wildly implausible tax figure of $60 million for 1779 alone, ordinary Philadelphians gathered in the wooded yard behind the state house where Congress was meeting, in what promoters billed as "a General Meeting of the Citizens of Philadelphia, and Parts adjacent."[86] General Daniel Roberdeau, the Pennsylvania member of the Continental Congress who had written an earlier account of British counterfeiting and the sacred significance of the continental dollar, took the chair. Roberdeau had popular credibility on the money issue. In 1776 he had exchanged 22,000 Spanish silver dollars, out of "five bags of silver coin and plate" captured by his privateers *Congress* and *Chance*, in return for continental currency. The dollars, meanwhile, had likely been sent to Canada and Schuyler's doomed campaign.[87] He addressed the assembled gathering. Taxes and sinking the currency were fine, but the real problem—as it had always been—Roberdeau stressed, was the lack of virtue in the mercantile community. "The dangers we are now exposed to arise, from evils created among ourselves," Roberdeau told the crowd. The only way to cure it, Roberdeau argued, was to limit prices, to restore the value of the dollar to its silver standard. The next day a committee drew up a list of prices and resolved that anyone who resisted it would not "be suffered to remain among us," comparing the merchants who raised prices week after week to witches.[88] On May 27, 1779, the same day Roberdeau's speech ran in the *Pennsylvania Packet*, Congress advertised that it had "already burned near half a million of Dollars" gathered in taxes. Roberdeau was implying that it was not just money that should be burning.[89]

The great irony of the movement that emerged was how much it shared, theoretically, with the congressional call for a new silver currency imported from France, opposed by Webster. Both wished to remove the relationship between the value of the new nation's currency and time, to make it, in effect, a permanent store of value. Instead of the temporary instrument imagined in Massachusetts, decades earlier, they wanted the bills to act just like the dollars their name invoked. The only difference was they wanted the bills to act like silver through an act of popular will. To recover that value, the Philadelphia committee suggested on June 29, 1779, Americans would have to remember the value a dollar was supposed to express. Laws could support money's meaning, the committee argued, but money was not maintained by laws alone. People had to support it in their private, political capacity as citizens. The people who raised prices were "governed by avarice," the committee argued. Laws could not move quickly enough to keep up with them. The committee could. The right to oppose price increases as "citizens organized" was the same right mobilized to oppose the British invasion.[90]

"The condition of an invaded country sufficiently proves the exercise of such a power necessary," the committee wrote. It added, moreover, that it saw its powers as temporary and distinct from "legal government." "We are likewise of the opinion that the laws already in being, would derive great support from the reinstitution of Committees," like the committees of safety at the start of the war, and that "such a reinforcement of power to the powers of government is necessary in an invaded country." The British invasion motivated them to continue their work and organizing. The committee repeated what had become conventional wisdom since France had joined the war: "The hope of the enemy appears to be principally fixed on what they would stile the bankruptcy of the Continent, occasioned by the failure of the currency," they wrote. The British would only succeed if Americans failed to take matters into their hands, enforce existing laws, collect taxes, and remember the true value of the dollar. "The money is our own. No power is bound to make it good, if we, whose property it is, make it otherwise," the committee concluded. "We ought to reflect, that the public faith, or the United States is but another word for ourselves."[91]

Other towns caught the "Philadelphia spirit," as the idea of popular rule by extralegislative "committees" dedicated to price regulation spread. The June 29, 1779, the *Packet* reported committees forming in New York, New Hampshire, Connecticut, Massachusetts, and Maryland to limit prices. The *Packet* further reported that in Boston, on June 17, handbills signed "VENGEANCE" had been put around town calling on Bostonians to gather at Old South Meeting House, where they had gathered fourteen years earlier to protest the Stamp Act, to form an association to lower prices. At the meeting, the inhabitants resolved "neither to buy nor sell silver and gold" and to report anyone that did.[92] A letter from Albany dated June 16, 1779, reported that citizens there had chosen a committee as well "to remedy the evil which threatened destruction to the land." The committee had decided that "Hard money is not to pass here any more," the letter read. "We have lately hung and burned in effigy a dealer in hard money."[93]

XII. The Money War Comes to Philadelphia

The Continental army, though, was the largest and most influential group of wage earners in the country, and inarguably those that had suffered the most from the dollar's rapid decline. The popular movement to restore the money soon reached soldiers eager to lend their support. On May 27 a battalion of Maryland militia stationed at the Head of Elk, where British troops had landed to march on Philadelphia two years earlier, swore "under the strictest ties of virtue and honor" to enforce the laws and "restore things again to rights, and to recover the credit of our currency." It was a premonition of bolder moves to come.[94]

On July 1 the officers of the first company of Philadelphia Militia Artillery, John McGinley, William Thorne, William Robinson, Samuel Powel, and John Dean, published a manifesto in the *Packet*. The company had received the resolves of the committee to reduce prices while they were stationed at the fort on Mud Island, just south of Philadelphia on the Delaware River, and they worried that the committee might not be able to bring off a reduction in prices without deploying the force of arms. "We are very sorry to observe, that designing and interested persons endeavor by every means to elude your judicious intentions, and that something more *poignant* and *striking* must at length bring them to reason." After their replacements arrived on Mud Island, the militia marched on the city on June 28. They declared themselves "ready and willing" to support the committee, "and if by reason of the obstinacy and perverseness of individuals, your Committee find themselves inadequate to the task, *our drum shall beat to arms*." Committee chairman William Henry assured the soldiers that the committee had the backing of the city for everything they did. The company gave "three cheers and fired three salutes, and were dismissed."[95]

Despite the efforts of the committees, paper money traded at ever-lower values, forcing Congress to print even more to support forces stretched thin across the continent. By the end of 1779, continental dollars were trading at fifty to one. The popular struggle to maintain its value through marches, demonstrations, and threats had done little to arrest its decline and contributed to elite skepticism that anything, at all, could save it. The decision to tax, the right one in the sense that it preserved the logic of bills of credit as a credit against a tax debt, had been hyperextended, exposing itself as a kind of ruse, a fraud because it demanded the impossible.[96]

Even the staunchest supporters of the dollar were wavering. "I have since considered this matter in every point of view my judgment enables me to place it, and am resolved to receive no more old debts; such I mean as were contracted and ought to have been paid before the War at the present nominal value of the money unless compelled to it, or it is the practice of others to do it," George Washington wrote to his cousin Lund Washington, who was overseeing his Virginia plantation in his absence, on August 17, 1779. Far from regulating committees, payment in bills worth one-fortieth their face value had become a travesty, contradicting the old notion of commercial justice as giving value for value. "The fear of injuring by any example of mine the credit of our paper currency if I attempted to discriminate between the real & nominal value of Paper money has already sunk me a large Sum." No man of "honor or common decency" would make such a demand, Washington wrote. He was obviously troubled by the decision, asking Lund to "consult Men of honor, honesty, & firm attachment to the cause—& govern yourself by their advice, or by their conduct" when it came to making a final decision to refuse payment. But even Washington, who had so much to lose personally in its failure, who repeatedly said Britain's only hope of victory was for the currency to fail, had privately given up on the Revolution's money.[97]

On September 1, 1779, Congress did the same, committing that it would limit net emissions to $200 million continental, declaring it was "inexpedient to derive the supplies for a continuance of the present war from emissions of bills of credit." All further finance would take the form of loans and the taxes that Congress had pledged at the beginning of the year. The final decision not to emit any more continental dollars was a bold one, as dangerous as it was untried. The war was still raging, in the South particularly, where a joint French and American force was gathering to retake Georgia.[98]

On September 13, 1779, John Jay, president of the Congress, decided to address the gathering crisis in American finance personally. Jay's declaration was a statement of defiance. Parliament's determination to quash the American "rebellion" rather than negotiate with its leaders in 1774 had created a choice of "either asserting your rights by arms, or ingloriously passing under the yoke. You nobly preferred war," he wrote. "Armies were then to be raised, paid, and supplied: money became necessary for these purposes. Of your own, there was but little; and of no nation in the world could you then borrow. The little that was spread among you could be collected only by taxes, and to this end regular governments were essential; of these you were also destitute. So circumstanced, you had no other resource but the natural value and wealth of your fertile country. Bills were issued on the credit of this bank, and our faith was pledged for their redemption." Thus far, Jay was only repeating a history everyone knew: that money as reinvented by the American colonies decades earlier had been central to the war effort, as essential in its way as arms and volunteers. However, Jay continued, the bills' ubiquity, for reasons he was still unclear about, had created a doubt that the bills which Congress had issued would ever be redeemed. This had created what he called an "artificial depreciation," meaning it had, in his view, no mathematical justification. This he attributed to the same masses who, all summer, had protested that very depreciation. "A distrust (however occasioned) entertained by the mass of people, either in the ability or inclination of the United States to redeem their bills, is the cause of it," Jay wrote. He set out to counter that distrust.[99]

No one doubted the United States' real physical wealth or its potential to rapidly increase in population once the war was over, Jay wrote. And it possessed a singular advantage in that its bills of credit would not have to be paid off in gold or silver. "Let it also be remembered that paper money is the only money which cannot 'make unto itself wings' and fly away. It remains with us, it will not forsake us, it is always ready and at hand for the purpose of commerce or taxes, and every industrious man can find it." It was entirely of America's creation and in its power to regulate internally. Great Britain, on the other hand, when the war ended, would "find herself in a very different situation," Jay wrote. "She must provide for the discharge of her immense debt by taxes to be paid in specie, in gold or silver perhaps now buried in the mines of Mexico or Peru, or still concealed in the brooks and rivulets of Africa or Indostan." Bills of credit conversely would be taxed in and respent, at first, and then destroyed. All it would take was a renewal of faith in the bills themselves. The massive nominal sums that Congress was levying were smaller than they appeared, when depreciation was considered. "[The bills] are to be found in every man's possession, and every man is interested in their being redeemed," he wrote. "We have resolved to stop the press, and to call upon you for supplies by loans and taxes. You are in capacity to afford them, and are bound by the strongest ties to do it. Leave us not therefore, without supplies nor let in that flood of evils which would follow such a neglect." Jay's final words, though, contained a hint of the desperation he and other leaders were beginning to feel, besieged by new forces unleashed by the money they had created. "Let it never be said," he concluded, "America had no sooner become independent than she became insolvent, or that her infant glories and growing fame were obscured and tarnished by broken contracts and violated faith, in the very hour when all the nations of the earth were admiring and almost adoring the splendor of her rising." Not even Jay's appeal, though, could conceal the fact that Congress had begun the process of retiring its power to create bills of credit.[100]

Jay's address only seemed to increase volatility in the streets. Little more than two weeks later, on October 4, armed militiamen paraded through the streets of Philadelphia, intent on arresting disaffected merchants accused of ignoring price controls and banishing them from the city. The militiamen had already made four arrests when they marched past James Wilson's house on the corner of Walnut and Third Streets. Wilson suspected the mob planned to arrest him as well and had holed up with a number of other well-armed merchants in what they called his "fort." What happened next may have been a mistake. As the column disappeared down Walnut Street, one of Wilson's guests fired into it from behind. The column halted and returned with a vengeance, and a firefight began between the "fort" and the dollar vigilantes. In the ensuing melee, more than twenty people were killed or injured. Eventually, the Pennsylvania Light Horse, an elite militia company, broke up the fight with sabers bared.[101]

The rioters and their leaders were chastened. Paine, who had supported the committee and served on it, wrote an anguished letter to the *Pennsylvania Packet* declaring that the men who died had "paid a martyrdom to mistake, and distinguished themselves as the lamented victims of wasted bravery." Meanwhile, for the leading merchants who had barricaded themselves against the militiamen, the existence of a politically engaged mass of wage-earning citizens who recognized that in principle the Revolution gave them the right to control their money had become intolerable. It was easy to see the combination of the army and the popular committees as the kernel of a new mass movement. If money was a sovereign domain and the people were sovereign, then popular sovereignty extended to money. The people who earned it could control it. They did not want the currency destroyed. They wanted to maintain it on their own terms, to regulate their new wage-earning republic. On a deeper level, they also seemed to recognize that the wave of money, while disruptive, had freed them from dependence on wealthy households that might otherwise have taken them into service for little or no pay. They wanted prices stabilized and profiteers punished. They wanted their wages to mean something, and they were determined to enforce that meaning themselves.

Wilson and his comrades, on the other hand, had taken advantage of the Revolution to become wealthy, buying estates, ships, and stock-in-trade, while stuffing away bills acquired at basement prices. From their perspective, eliminating the currency was perfectly acceptable. A variety of means might serve their ends. Higher taxes would force those who had less to sell more property in return for the paper Wilson and his allies had collected through their connection to the Revolution. Destroying the bills would leave them with bigger estates, more property, and a more prominent position when the money was gone. The popular Philadelphia committee saw increased taxes as yet another way to oppress those who already suffered most from the depreciation, stating that it could "never think it right that one part of the community should be taxed to make fortunes for the other." Meanwhile, the merchants argued, that "either the limitations [on prices] will become by unanimous consent destroyed, or that the paper currency will be destroyed by a consent as unanimous."[102]

What became known as the "Fort Wilson Riot" was a point, simultaneously, of divergence and radical convergence in the internal politics of the American Revolution. It was the point at which American elites largely abandoned any notion that money and loyalty had any strict, necessary relationship—a belief that the rioters and their supporters in the vast American countryside, with their deep sense of the relationship between money and the state, never relinquished. At the same time, it was the moment when those same elites came to believe that something like what the rioters demanded—a revolution in American money that would break the link between American currency and time, re-creating money as a store of value—was inevitable. It was the moment when they, like the rioters, began searching for a break from the old system and began to search for a new one—and with it a new money.

XIII. Britain Wins the Money War

That fall, the news of the combined French and American armies' loss to British defenders at Savannah "sent the value of money hurtling down" in New England, lower than many believed was possible. For many, this was the continental dollar's "final blow" and, in effect, Britain's final victory in its battle with American money. No amount of patriotism would allow taxes to be collected in states with no functioning Revolutionary government. The British had finally succeeded, not in winning the war or recovering its colonies, but in convincing many in Congress that their paper money was founded on principles that could not survive the war—just as the rise of a politically active, self-aware, wage-earning class threatened any return to the prewar social order.[103]

Meanwhile, tax receipts for the hoped-for $60 million were arriving. They were brutally disappointing. The tally made the cost of British disruptions in the South manifest. Some of the states had done heroic work. Massachusetts, by the original requirements laid out in January 1779, owed $2.4 million in taxes. In September the state loan officer, Nathaniel Appleton, delivered some $6.63 million worth of bills to Philadelphia to be burned. Some of those bills had been converted to a loan, paying interest. They were not taxes. But the amount was still heartening. Rhode Island provided $195,018 in tax receipts, against a bill of $195,000, and just over $746,372 in loan receipts. Connecticut's treasurer turned over bills worth $1.4 million against a bill of $1.66 million, and another $1.56 million in loan office receipts. Delaware sent $374,527 against a tax bill of $166,000. Other states were less successful; notably all but New Hampshire were war zones. New York and New Jersey sent no tax receipts, only bills returned to their loan office. Pennsylvania only sent taxes worth $166,000. Virginia sent no taxes but $4.85 million from its loan office. Maryland, Georgia, North Carolina, and South Carolina sent nothing at all. Britain's efforts, raiding from New York and campaigning across the South, had cut off roughly two-thirds of the colonial population—the entire South, New York, and New Jersey—from its already overambitious tax effort. And where the taxes were collected, the effects had been brutal. Elizabeth Drinker, in Philadelphia, recorded tax collectors seizing a tea table, six walnut chairs, brass andirons, and two kettles to settle a tax of £235 in July 1780. With the dollar trading at sixty for one, she suspected that they would sell the furniture for more than the debt and pocket the difference.[104]

The idea of bills of credit as a credit against a tax debt, it seemed, had failed on the national level. The only thing to do was to start over. "Whereas, the present fluctuating state of the Paper Currency, is productive of evils which cannot be effectually remedied, without calling in and sinking the whole," Congress's Committee on Finance wrote in a report dated February 26, 1780, Congress should call in all of the existing currency and burn it. The Committee on Finance also suggested that eliminating the paper was not enough. Money itself should be transformed in the United States. Congress's new financial instruments would not be bills of credit, implicitly subject to public power. They would be bonds promising payment in gold or silver, paying annual interest of 5 percent.[105]

On March 18, 1780, Congress adopted a version of the finance committee's plan. It gave the states one year to surrender all $180 million in continental dollars then outstanding. All were to be burned. Congress also reset the nominal value of the dollar, at one-fortieth of the bills' stated silver value, and decreed that any new bills it might issue would be paid off—not burned—in six years, in milled silver dollars, committing itself to a new, permanent standard. It recommended that states revise laws making continental dollars a legal tender "as they judge most conducive to justice."[106]

Thus, Congress designed the law to eliminate the popular committees along with the continental dollar. Without tender laws or its commitment to the value expressed in the dollar, the popular committee's price regulations would have no legal basis. Without a paper currency in circulation, wage-earning laborers, mechanics, and militia would have nothing to regulate, no obvious means to exert influence on the currency. Rather than a plentiful, ephemeral, temporary money backed by the people's pledge and power of the popular consent, Congress's specie basis meant that the new money would be scarce and permanent, with a source of value that was external to the United States. At the same time, in a manner of speaking, Congress had given into the popular committees' demands. The committees had wanted a currency that held its value, that would be a stable form of wealth for wage earners, something permanent. They had hoped to get there by other means, by popular control rather than a form of money itself, but the aim, the goal, was the same. Britain had won the money war. Instead of a monetary regime based on what both Webster and Jay had called the "true" basis of national wealth—its land, its people, and its products—Congress's money would now be based on precious metal. No one had any idea where it might come from or whether the war could still be fought now on Britain's terms.

CHAPTER NINE

Transformations

I. The Revolt of the Connecticut Line

On May 25, 1780, the Connecticut Line of the Continental army mustered in front of their log and mud huts and began packing to go home. The cold had lingered behind the Watchung Mountains in Morristown, New Jersey; the food had not. The Connecticut soldiers had spent the winter on the front lines, in towns along the North River, Arthur Kill, and Sandy Hook. There was nothing to eat but Indian meal—ground, dried corn or "hog's fodder," as their enemies called it. The enemies there were not British soldiers but American "Refugees": loyalists fled to New York, boat raiding from Staten Island. They picked off American soldiers by night, sneaking through the swamps after the setting of the moon and rushing out of the reeds with bayonets. The winter was particularly harsh, and the spring brought no relief. To the south, on May 12, Charleston fell. Across Quebec, great wildfires raged so widely their smoke obscured the sun. On May 19 the day was so dark from the northern fires, Connecticut private James Plumb Martin later wrote, that "cocks crew and the whip-poor-wills sung their usual serenade" at noon, people carried candles all day long, and "the night was uncommonly dark as the day was."[1]

That week, Martin and the line crossed the Great Swamp to Baskin Ridge to join the main army, outside Morristown in the high hills to the west. "Here, the monster Hunger, still attended us; he was not shaken off by any efforts we could use, for here was the old story of starving, as rife as ever."[2] So, at the end of a bright, hungry day, after being called to roll, the soldiers refused to leave the parade ground. Instead, they shouldered their arms and began a short-lived march north. Headed off by other companies, they turned back to their huts as night fell. "But the worm of hunger knawing [*sic*] so keen kept us from being entirely quiet," Martin recalled. "We therefore kept upon the parade in groups, venting our spleen at our country and government, then at our officers, and then at ourselves for our imbecility, in staying there and starving in detail for an ungrateful people."[3]

The collapse of the continental dollar created a wave of desperation. It left the United States with no way of matching its still-impressive agricultural abundance with the needs of maintaining an army in the field. Temporary money had been abandoned and replaced with nothing at all. The result was a stark, brutal reminder of what bills of credit had allowed Americans to create, a continental movement for independence, and what might have awaited them if they had not had an ingenious monetary tradition to draw on: no army, no resistance, helplessness. American leaders and future leaders, many of whom were in camps like those in Morristown, blamed this condition on bills of credit and resolved to create a new, permanent alternative that would have value wherever the army served, even if that meant transforming every American's relationship to money.

The revolt of the Connecticut Line was just one of several between 1777 and 1780. In November 1777 soldiers stationed near West Point refused to march because of "Distress for Money." Congress had not paid them in over half a year. In the midst of the mutiny, a captain ran a private "thro' the Body" with his sword. The man shot and killed the captain before dying.[4] In 1778 soldiers in Providence, Rhode Island, mutinied over a lack of pay and flour and Virginians in Charlottesville revolted over a lack of supplies.[5]

But the 1780 revolt was more extreme. No one had paid the Connecticut Line in five months, and the soldiers were close to starvation. There was no money to pay them in any case. Congress and the British army's actions over the previous year had seen to that. It seemed at first as if there was no alternative means to feed them either. Their goal, in revolt, had been to go home, where their families—farmers who provided for themselves and each other—would share what they had. The continent, seemingly, had nothing more to offer. In abandoning the dollar, Congress declared itself powerless. In a plea to the states for supplies and taxes on April 4, 1780, Congress warned that, without the states' support, "the army must disband . . . or provide for themselves," precisely the position that the

Connecticut Line had come to on their own. States would have to take on the responsibility of supporting their companies, and none had any obvious means of doing so.[6]

After the revolt, later that evening, Colonel Walter Stewart of the Pennsylvania Line and a few other officers came to speak to the Connecticut troops, gathered around their campfires. The soldiers explained their position: "We were unwilling to desert the cause of our own country, when in distress; we knew her cause involved our own," Martin recalled in his memoir. "But what signified our perishing in the act of saving her, when that very act would inevitably destroy us, and she must perish with us."[7] Stewart replied that he and the other officers had no money either. "We all suffer," he told them. The result was a sense of impotence and fear, spreading through the ranks. "This is a decisive moment," George Washington wrote to Pennsylvania Assembly president Joseph Reed from Morristown on May 28, 1780, "one of the most (I will further say *the most*) important America has seen."[8]

II. Thomas Paine Devises a Plan

Thomas Paine read Washington's letter aloud in the Pennsylvania Assembly a few days later. The room went silent. One member rose, Paine recollected years later. "'If,' said he, 'the account in that letter is a true state of things, and we are in the situation there represented, it appears to me vain to contest the matter any longer, we may as well give up at first as at last.'" Silence fell again. Another rose: "'Well, well,' said he, 'don't let the House despair. If things are not so well as we wish, we must endeavor to make them better.'"[9] The mood seemed to lift. Discussion turned to ways that Philadelphians could salvage the war effort on their own.

That weekend, the first of June 1780, Paine wrote one letter to prominent Philadelphia merchant Blair McClanaghan and another to Reed, president of the Pennsylvania Assembly. On Saturday, as he was writing, word arrived that Charleston had fallen. The lesson was clear. The current system of government was faltering. For Paine, there was a further lesson. However unpleasant it was, American patriots should give up their power to create and regulate money, and give it to wealthy men. As for the wealthy, "If they have any spirit, any foresight of their own interest and danger, they will promote a subscription of either money or articles," Paine wrote. For Paine, the Americans' chief difficulty had always been Congress's "empty treasury." The notion itself implied that gold and silver were the only true wealth for, in Paine's view, it had never been full. Paine had been willing to support bills of credit while they were effective, but now the matter was different. The line's revolt proved finally that people could not make paper money, in Paine's view, without courting disaster. Popular power did not extend that far. There was "something radically wrong" when governments put "paper in the room of money,"[10] Paine wrote. This lesson, he reflected in later years, had been repeated over and over down through history: "Gold and silver will, in the long run, revolt against depreciation and separate from the value of paper; for the progress of all such systems appears to be that the paper will take the command in the beginning, and gold and silver in the end."[11] In the long run, he believed, there was no alternative.

Paine acknowledged that money was theoretically subject to the will of the people. He was friendly with Webster. His whole career in America rested on such claims. The year before, he had served on the committee in Philadelphia seeking to regulate prices. But that did not mean, he argued, that money should or could be made on the people's own terms, conforming with their own concerns and preexisting ways of life. The committees of 1779 had tried just that, and in Paine's view they had failed. Money was a form of political organization, and "the people of America understand *rights* better than *politics*," Paine wrote. The thing to do, Paine wrote Reed, was to gather the "richer inhabitants of the city" and ask them "to deposit their plate to be coined for the pay of the Army, crediting the government for the value, by weight."[12] The merchants' "hard money," whether garnered through speculation in paper currency, trade abroad, or dealings with the British, would likely be forfeit anyway if the British won, Paine wrote. "Property is always the object of a conqueror, where he can find it," he observed. Merchants may as well put their precious metal and their credit to work before they lost it.[13] Getting silver or gold for public purposes was the key. Paine seems to have been disillusioned. In 1776 he had celebrated living in a country that could support itself with its own resources, making a money that, as paper, would never be worth a conqueror's time and effort. For him, the war had proven the inadequacy of that early hope. He recalled a German farmer, likely during Washington's starving winter at Valley Forge, remarking that "*money is money, and paper is paper.*" That was as much philosophizing, he later wrote, "as the whole subject requires."[14]

Redefining money, from the spring of 1780 on, became, for him, a matter of recognizing reality, that money was gold and silver and nothing else. Crucially, he did not believe that he was, in fact, redefining anything.

Rather, he was recovering an understanding of money that he had received in his youth, enforced as a tax collector, abandoned in brief Revolutionary excitement, and recovered in his late-war sobriety. Money, for him, was an ontological proposition, a fixture within his eighteenth-century cosmology. The irony was that this was one of the few things that had not changed. He was still the individual who would go on to write *The Rights of Man* and *The Age of Reason*. He still believed in the infinite improvability of human affairs, the malleability of governments, and the Revolutionary project he had done so much to advance in America. He had merely circumscribed his radicalism, placed a limit around its application. Money had become the boundary to radical action rather than, as in 1775 and 1776, its necessary adjunct.

The irony was that Paine's version of natural money—of money as gold and silver—was the revolutionary concept in an American context. Paine was writing and working in what was still Blackwell's America, where money was a creature of the state. The notion that America was subject to the monetary limits that had defined life in the Britain of his childhood was itself a radical notion. Paine was suggesting, implicitly, that context did not matter. Bills of credit, as Paine wrote in his letters that weekend, were still the American tradition, what the historian E. James Ferguson rightly called America's "ancient system," its foundational monetary form. They had failed under immense pressure, to be sure, but they had not been replaced. From that perspective, Paine's abrupt call for a monetary transformation—couched in the language of scientific necessity—was less out of character than it might first appear. He still believed in the necessity of revolutionary change, only this time it was a reformation of America's money, the necessary condition for its Revolution in the first place, that he was proposing. The degree of change was no less.[15]

III. The First Bank

Paine's letter to McClanaghan was a private appeal to the merchant elite, as deliberate as it was ironic. Paine had served on the committee to regulate prices the previous fall, supporting the new paper economy opposed by the bulk of the merchants. Now he exhorted the wealthiest Philadelphians to contribute metal to the cause. "The whole currency in circulation is scarcely equal to a year's expences of the war, and could all the Taxes be instantly collected, they would not at present prices purchase the supplies. How then is the army to be recruited, clothed, fed and paid?" he asked. The merchants would have to provide an answer, Paine wrote. He enclosed $500 of his own Pennsylvania currency in the envelope as his contribution to whatever McClanaghan organized. McClanaghan proved right for the job. On June 8, 1780, he took Paine's letter to the merchants' Coffee House and read it aloud, calling for a new establishment and contributions. By the end of the evening Philadelphia merchants had subscribed "two hundred pounds hard money," Paine recalled with pride in 1783. America's first bank was on its way.[16]

On June 17, when the first subscribers met in the Coffee House again, they had made little progress. The city's mercantile elite had pledged just 400 Pennsylvania pounds "hard money" and some 101,360 pounds in continental money—hardly a significant stock. The amount was nothing on the scale of the army's needs. Whatever Paine had thought wealthy Philadelphians were capable of, there did not appear to be enough silver and gold among them to be useful on its own. Moreover, subscribers complained that mixing paper and specie contributions was incoherent. Both the specie and the paper cash were measured, ostensibly, in Pennsylvania pounds, but their market values were of completely different orders. The former was solid or rising, the latter soft and sinking. So, the subscribers resolved to abandon their original scheme—and with it, Paine's contribution.[17]

By July there was a formal plan, published in the *Pennsylvania Gazette*. The bank opened its doors on Front Street in Philadelphia on July 17, 1780, with a capital of £300,000, "Pennsylvania Currency, in Specie," meaning at the face value of the Pennsylvania pound rather than the rate state paper traded for, "at the rate of seven shillings and six-pence for a Spanish dollar," or 90 pence in a dollar. On its face, £300,000 was a difficult sum to raise. At £44 a day, the rate McClanahan and Paine managed in their first week collecting subscriptions, it would have taken more than eighteen years. Crucially, however, the bank's promoters soon changed the terms of the deal. Now subscribers could pay just 10 percent up front in kind and "the residue from time to time as it should be needed." The idea was that if things went well, it never would be.

The new deal meant the bank would only have at most 81,000 in Spanish silver dollars on hand, a paltry sum in comparison with the army's requirements. But it also meant that investing in the bank might prove immensely profitable. Every subscriber would be able to leverage any specie they had or could get ten to one. A £100 investment became £1,000 worth of bank securities. Even the most jaded speculator could see the possibilities. If the partnership was successful, they could sell shares at an immense gain. The risk was substantial, of course. Subscribers were personally liable for the bank's credit and the other nine-tenths of the stock, but another aspect of the new plan mitigated this risk. Congress, the merchants hoped, would commit to repay any banknote loans in coin, turning the bankers' pledge into a vastly larger pile of paper currency. The idea went like this: Congress would borrow from the bank to purchase food and rum. The bank subscribers would use banknotes to make the purchase, float the supplies up the Delaware to Trenton, and transport them from there overland to the army. Meanwhile, Congress would pledge to refund the costs in silver when it could get some.[18] Everyone directly involved would win. Subscribers got a security with a face value of ten times what they had paid. Congress got supplies. The army would eat. Within a few days, ninety-two subscribers had pledged the full amount. McClanaghan and fellow merchant Robert Morris led the way, pledging £10,000 Pennsylvania apiece.[19] Before the plan was published, the bank had already begun buying flour on credit to send up the Delaware River to the troops, promising payment when the new harvest came in.[20]

The merchants pledged not to "derive the least pecuniary advantage" from the "bank." Of course, this promise should not be taken on faith. But the form of the bank itself suggests that the Philadelphians had no intention of "making money" in any usual sense if they did not plan to sell their shares. Most circulating money, for all intents and purposes, still consisted of the devalued continental dollar and new state issues. Subscribers pledged their private property and credit for a certain amount of the bank's "capital"—ranging from £1,000 to £10,000—if necessary. There were no deposits, no plan to charge interest or discount bills—in sum, no profit center in the bank's plans. Depositors did not receive interest. The bank builders thought depositors would give the bank paper currency in return for its banknotes, because the banknotes were denominated in "Pennsylvania Currency, in Specie," making the bank's paper, at least in theory, a more stable store of value than the notes they deposited. Depositors, in other words, traded a volatile, risky asset for a stable one supported by some of the largest private fortunes in Pennsylvania. That, not interest, was the attraction. The bank had no plans to lend the bills it collected and does not seem to have done so.[21]

Thus, the 1780 plan for the Bank of Pennsylvania described an institution that did not look like a bank, in the sense of the Bank of England, at all. In essence, it was a food bank. Contemporaries noticed the difference. The new Pennsylvania Bank was founded "on the joint credit of the public and individuals," twenty-three-year-old Alexander Hamilton wrote in a letter to James Duane dated September 3, 1780, but did "not seem to be at all conducted on the true principles of a bank," because it borrowed on the private credit of its subscribers rather than purchasing with banknotes.[22]

The bank's attempt fell short of its goal. The bank did get some flour to Washington's camp, but as soon as mid-August it was already falling short of subscribers' "early expectations." Their plans had run into numerous difficulties, including laws that prohibited transporting flour across state lines, designed to keep American farmers from supplying the British. These difficulties, in turn, seem to have convinced many of the subscribers that something further had to change. These changes would entail a new plan for a bank. The Bank of Pennsylvania would be transformed into the grander-sounding Bank of North America. More significantly, it involved reshaping money's role in the institution and, if possible, American society.[23]

IV. Robert Morris Joins the Fray

The key figure in that transformation was Robert Morris, whose early investment in the Bank of Pennsylvania had proved so crucial. Morris was born in Liverpool in 1734 to an unwed mother and a slave- and tobacco-trading father, who soon left to establish a trading post in Maryland, on the eastern shore of Chesapeake Bay. Morris joined his father when he was thirteen. When he was fifteen, his father sent him to Philadelphia. The elder Morris died the next year, leaving Morris a fortune worth £2,500 sterling, which—coupled with the new friends he had made working with the Willing family's shipping company—set the young man up in business. In 1757 Morris and the English-educated Thomas Willing founded Willing, Morris & Company, which quickly became one of the most successful trading ventures in the city. Their business was bound labor, enslaved Africans and hundreds of German, Welsh, Irish, and English "servants" who sold years of their lives to merchants like Morris, in return for passages to America that, too often, became death sentences on crowded, disease-ridden ships. Willings's own father died of an indentured servants' shipborne fever in 1754.[24]

They were both deeply interested in finance and its implications for the British Empire. In 1765 Morris and Willing had been prominent opponents of the Stamp Act. Willing signed an open letter from the "Merchants of Philadelphia," declaring that they were "cut off from all Means of supplying our selves with Specie enough even to pay the Duties imposed on us, much less to serve as a medium of Trade." The next year, they joined with seven other Philadelphia firms in an attempt to create a private currency, issuing £5 notes and promising to pay whoever held them within nine months, along with 5 percent interest, but the scheme failed to secure a charter.[25]

When the war began, Willing and Morris immediately set out to profit from it, advancing some £25,000 sterling on their own account to procure gunpowder. By the fall of 1775, they were the principal supplier of gunpowder to the American forces, having secured tons of it in Europe and distributed it throughout America. The risk was considerable, but so were the returns. The profits on a single congressional contract came to £12,000, or would have, the firm claimed, if Willing and Morris's ship hadn't been turned away in Europe. War also brought power. By March 1776, Morris was the head of the secret committee charged with importing arms from the continent.[26]

When the Philadelphia committee movement began in 1779, Morris was one of their first interviews. Thomas Paine was among the group that visited Morris at his home and, ultimately, accepted his explanation for rising prices. Morris was also in James Wilson's house on October 4, barricaded inside against the popular militia. Never a political thinker, the experience pushed Morris to refocus on his private affairs, which were, by then, considerable. A French visitor to Philadelphia estimated his personal net worth mid-war at several hundred thousand pounds sterling.[27]

One opportunity that presented itself was the Spanish trade, the trade of North American foodstuffs for silver in the Spanish Caribbean that George Grenville accidentally quashed in 1765. In June 1779 Spain entered the war on the side of France and the United States. That meant Caribbean ports were, again, open to American traders. Morris, as usual, was quick to see an angle. Working with Spanish consul Francisco Rendón, Morris secured a special license from Congress to export 3,000 barrels of flour to Havana in 1780. Rendón promised it would fetch Spanish silver at prices of at least $30 a barrel, six times what it cost to purchase in Philadelphia, delivering a tremendous profit almost miraculously in silver coin.[28]

The arrival of all that silver at the same time that the finances of the Revolution were crumbling created a kind of dissonance between the increasingly prosperous merchant community of Philadelphia and the finances of the state itself. The Bank of Pennsylvania proposed by Paine and carried through by merchants like Morris was intended as a stopgap, bridging the two. But its failure suggested to many, as Paine had indeed warned, that merchants like Morris should take a more direct hand in government. In his June 4 letter to Joseph Reed, who had proved a stalwart supporter of price controls and other measures to address the decline of the continental, Paine had made the foundation of his new system clear, in terms he must have found painful to write.

"While the war was carried on by emissions at the pleasure of Congress, any body of men might conduct public business, and the poor were of equal use in government with the rich," Paine wrote. "But when the means must be drawn from the country the case becomes altered, and unless the wealthier part throw in their aid, the public measures must go heavily on." The time of money subordinate to the popular will was over, Paine intuited. Men like Morris would be given the means to rule.[29]

V. Morris Moves to Reform and Replace American Money

Morris got his chance at the beginning of 1781. On February 7 Congress established a new position, the "Financier" or "Superintendent of Finance," to "examine into the state of the public debt, the public expenditures, and the public revenue, to digest and report plans for improving and regulating the finances, and for establishing the order and economy of the expenditure of public money." Morris seemed to dither in accepting the office. He demanded the right to keep all of his ongoing business associations and the ability to fire his subordinates, both of which Congress eventually accepted. In fact, he was laying plans that he felt matched the scale of the crisis. "All we have to fear is that the want of money may disband the army, or so perplex and enfeeble our operations as to create in the people a general disgust and alarm, which may make them clamour for peace on any terms," Alexander Hamilton wrote Morris on April 30, 1781.[30] Morris's plan was to create a new money to replace bills of credit. He accepted the post on May 14, 1781. On May 17 he submitted a blueprint for a national bank he called "the Bank of North America" for congressional approval.[31]

Morris's plan, at least in theory, was innocuous. It was an attempt to corral some of the new metallic wealth flowing into Philadelphia and turn it to a public purpose. The capital, Morris wrote George Washington on July 2, was awash in "many Spanish dollars" from the grain trade to Havana. The bank would put them to work, making loans to Congress anticipating tax revenues, much (though he didn't say so) as the Bank of England had since 1694. On the most basic level, the changes Morris proposed were twofold. First, the plan scrapped the bank's reliance on personal credit, operating on a strictly metallic basis. The Bank of North America would ask investors to pay for their shares up front in actual gold and silver on the initial capital of $400,000. Second, the BNA allowed shareholders to profit from bank operations. The bank planned to pay dividends out of its profits of 5 to 6 percent on each subscriber's investment. Subscribers would not be able to profit on their personal credit, however. Where subscribers to the Bank of Pennsylvania had been asked to pay 10 percent of their subscriptions up front in paper or coin and the rest only if necessary, investors who purchased $400 shares in the Bank of North America were forced to pay in full and in coin on subscriptions up to $2,000. Larger investors were allowed to pay one half up front "in gold or silver" and the rest within three months. The effect was to replace the Bank of Pennsylvania's long-term credits on reputation and property, the basis of most pre-Revolutionary economic life, with short-term credit for only the wealthiest subscribers—those with more than $2,000 in coin to invest. As for state paper, the new bank would not even receive it on deposit. In the Bank of North America's plan, references to Pennsylvania currency in the Bank of Pennsylvania's plan disappear, with "dollars" and "gold and silver" taking their place.[32]

The reason was ambition. Morris's longer-term plan for the Bank of North America was to transform the role of money in American life. Money in colonial anglophone America meant many things, but as a matter of political economy, it had come to mean the short-term bills of credit designed to be taxed in and eliminated once the crisis passed. The war had revealed the bills' temporary nature as a weakness. Each deadline, in effect, became a possible point of failure. The states' failure to collect their tax quotas in 1779 had proved to Morris and others that bills could be reformed on their own terms. A new money was necessary, one that would last.

Morris made no secret of his goal. On May 29 he wrote Philip Schuyler, whose expedition to Canada had foundered on the sovereign limitations of the continental dollars as bills of credit, that he would never have accepted the office of financier if he had not been "pressed by the *Necessity, the absolute Necessity* of a change in our Monied System." On June 11 he wrote Thomas Jefferson, asking for his personal aid in getting the bank off of the ground. "All the Publick Bodies in America, have more or less, lost the Confidence of the World as to Money Matters, by trying Projects and applying Expedients to stop a Course of depreciation which Original errors had fixed too deep to Admit of any radical Cure," he wrote. The solution was a bank that, using banknotes backed by actual silver coin, could make loans to government in a "Paper that Cannot depreciate." The ongoing difficulties that the states faced—gathering in the discredited bills—did not concern him, Morris wrote General Horatio Gates on June 12. "I shall leave the paper and the projectors of it to take care of each other," he wrote, "provided I can introduce such a Medium for War and Commerce as will stand the test of time."[33]

Banknotes were the medium he had in mind, each one redeemable at the bank in actual coin, gathered in Havana fresh from American mines and the mint in Mexico City. The notes, the twelfth clause of his May 17 plan declared, would be "payable on demand" for coin and, more aspirationally, "receivable in the duties and taxes of every state in the union, and from the respective states, by the treasury of united states, as specie." His whole plan, however, relied on his ability to collect coin—the whole $400,000 described in his plan—so that the bank could actually begin operation. He had no doubt, he wrote Gates, that his plan could produce this new monetary medium, "if People can be induced to make the first experiment which I have offered to their consideration by Subscribing to the bank."[34]

Morris hoped that the war would mark a sea change in American financial forms, institutions, and the relationships they established between the American state and its people. In his view, the bills of credit were ineffective because of American pre-war ignorance. The bills were not "capable of drawing [America's] resources to the true point of Exertion," he wrote in a letter to his French counterpart, Jacques Necker, on June 15, 1781. The new bank money was intended to fix precisely this point: to make a money that would always be able to mobilize North America's sprawling population in the event of a war with a European power. He reasoned, coolly, from experience. Gold and silver had not become less valuable in the face of invasion and occupation; they had become more so. If he could create a new money that was not the temporary expression of the value of a tax debt but rather a definite, imperishable promise to deliver a dollar on demand, it would have the same power to command "resources" as coin, while maintaining practicable flexibility. Morris never sent the letter, perhaps, because it was overly confessional. "You will observe, sir, we set out in this war without Arms, Ammunition, Cloathing or Stores of any kind, without Money or Credit (except with our own people), that despising the practices of the most experienced Nations, We determined to pursue the purest principles of Oeconomy in our own way, untill we have by dear bought experience learned that we knew nothing of the matter." He still needed to borrow from France, and ignorance was not becoming.[35]

Finding local subscribers proved more difficult than Morris hoped. The pace of his letters advertising the bank's plan suggests he had hoped to make up subscriptions from the Havana silver within weeks. Instead, subscriptions came in unsteadily over long, dragging months. The silver that merchants like Morris had gained in the Spanish trade was being turned around and put back into trade itself. Few were willing to put their faith in an untried scheme, even if its author, Morris, was one of their own. Morris seems to have underestimated the novelty of his plan, but his peers did not. No bank had previously existed in North America. Even Morris's closest advisers were not quite sure how it might work. Three years later, in 1784, Thomas Willing, Morris's business partner and close associate, admitted in a letter to founders of a new bank in Boston that he, Morris, and the other early schemers had been in "a pathless wilderness" with "little known" about what banks were or did, and no book explaining "the Interior Arrangements or Rules Obeyed in Europe." According to Willing, the Philadelphians had never even seen a banknote before. They only discovered their correct, meaning British, form later through "Accident." "All was to us a mystery," Willing wrote, "but something was necessary to be done to assist the Public Measures."[36]

Outside of Philadelphia, the war was not going well. Over the course of the year, it had expanded dramatically. The British force that took Charleston, South Carolina, had also captured the bulk of the United States' southern army under Major General Benjamin Lincoln. In August, Cornwallis routed another American army near Camden, South Carolina, killing, wounding, or capturing more than half the rebel forces. From there, British troops ranged north, raiding into North Carolina by the end of the year and, beginning in 1781, into Virginia. To be sure, the British had more success in taking territory than in keeping it. As soon as they left an area, patriot militias would begin probing into it, punishing those who tried to maintain British rule. Outside of fortified Savannah and Charleston, the only place British writ extended uncontested was where Cornwallis's army was actually present. "To possess territory demands garrisons," General Henry Clinton wrote George Germain, the Viscount Sackville, who was serving as secretary of state for the colonies in 1780, and the British did not have the manpower.[37]

If Philadelphia merchants would not have faith in one of their own, Morris would have to look elsewhere for his metal. Again, the war had changed things. One option was from the British themselves. The British army had hoped to conduct their invasion and occupation on credit, buying supplies from farmers with bills of exchange on London, just as they had during the colonial period, or in kind with British manufactures. But that proved impossible. Between 1778 and 1781 alone, the British army spent some £8 million sterling to supports its armies in North America, almost all of it in gold and silver.[38] The army in New York had tried to "hold back the money," one German officer wrote home on December 19, 1780, "one prefers now to let them have tea, linen, cloth, etc. in exchange." But to no avail. "Passionately anxious for gold and silver, they constantly brought us cattle and other provisions from the outset" and had succeeded in getting it, the officer wrote. "The War has made the inhabitants of this city and the neighbourhood rich, and New York is for its size one of the wealthiest cities in the world. The sums which the army consumes here are incredible."[39]

American farmers did not accept British credit because they did not, all things being equal, accept British rule. Loyalism was widespread in theory but often weak in practice. At best, the British general William Howe wrote shortly before he resigned his post in America, loyalists could be counted on for "an equivocal neutrality." In 1780 John Adams told an Amsterdam merchant with pride that unlike the Americans, the British had been forced to pay with gold and silver everywhere they went: Boston, Rhode Island, Long Island, Staten Island, "those parts of New York and New Jersey where they have been able to carry on clandestine Trafick," and Philadelphia. "They are doing the same now more or less in South Carolina and Georgia, and they can't go into any Part of America, without doing the Same," Adams added. The implication was that unlike the Continental Congress, which had been able to pay for the first four years of the war with paper, the British had been forced to pay in kind. All of it, Adams argued, would end up as a "Resource" for the Americans.[40]

The American refusal to accept anything but gold and silver in payment had created logistical difficulties for the British. In South Carolina, on December 22, 1780, Cornwallis, who assumed command in the American South after Charleston fell, wrote Clinton in New York that "The Want of Specie in this Province put us under the greatest Difficulties. Every method has been pursued to keep the Money in the Hands of the Contractors of Government, and to prevent the Imposition of the Merchants. But the Sum actually in the Province is so inadequate to the necessary Demands, that we have scarcely been able to pay the Subsistence of the Troops."[41] "Subsistence" was the coin paid out to troops that allowed them to purchase food from local merchants and farmers. Clinton, meanwhile, was facing money problems of his own. Still, he promised to send "£50,000 in Specie" by the next ship.[42] The only substitute for gold and silver that South Carolina merchants would accept were bills of exchange on London sold below the market rate then current in New York—allowing the South Carolinians to simply send the bills north to make a profit.[43]

VI. Morris Steps into a Void

On April 12, 1780, the *Pennsylvania Journal* published a confidential letter from Clinton to George Germain, the British secretary of state. It had been captured, the *Journal* reported, by an American privateer. The letter dated January 30, 1780, in Savannah, Georgia, suggests the impotence Clinton felt even on the verge of his most celebrated victory. Bills of credit had soldiered on despite British efforts.[44] "No experiments suggested by your Lordship; no assistance that could be drawn from the power of gold, or the arts of counterfeiting have been left unattempted," the letter read. Still, Americans had persisted. "Every day teaches me the futility of calculations founded on [the money's] failure."[45] Instead, Clinton and the British leadership hoped for victory with the support of loyalists in the South. Ultimately, the letter concluded, "if [the money] is to be destroyed at all, it can only be by Congress; and in this case it will undoubtedly be succeeded by some substitute, more valuable and permanent."[46]

That was, of course, what Morris was attempting, even as the war effort grew more precarious all around him. Without a functional alternative, the continental dollar had been replaced with nothing at all. Congress and its purchasing agents had resorted to asking states for specific supplies, like grain and cattle in lieu of taxes. Army purchasers had taken to paying in IOUs, without any practical limit or sense of what, in fact, Congress had promised. The states, meanwhile, had been left to come up with their own strategies to fill the vacuum in centralized financial strategy.[47]

Everywhere, the story was repeated. Paper faded and reordered relations in its wake. In August 1780 delegates from Massachusetts, Connecticut, and New Hampshire convened in Boston to discuss means of maintaining the new order and to "forward the most vigorous exertions of the present campaign."[48] Congress had asked the states to provide supplies—and beef in particular—for the support of the army, but without using currency and the market it supported, there was no obvious means to extract cattle from the citizenry without violence. The army, meanwhile, resorted

to force. When they could, they took supplies from loyalists without paying. In New York, the young private Elijah Fisher recorded Continental
infantry raiding across enemy lines and bringing back "considerable Cattle
and other articles" as plunder.[49] Still, the New England delegates concluded, there was no substitute for a system that had "a tendency to induce
people to bring plentifully to market and to sell at reasonable prices."[50]
The measure they settled on was a tax payable "in silver and gold, or the
produce of the country." They knew which was more likely to be paid.
Rather than purchasing supplies for the army and injecting more bills into
the countryside, the state delegates hoped the new tax would force people
to give what the army needed.[51]

States soon moved to put the plan into practice, demanding either gold
and silver or precisely what the army needed, according to Congress. In
August 1781, for example, the Rhode Island General Assembly passed a
tax that illustrated how the new regime would function. The stated goal
of the act was to provide the army with "Fresh Beef," based on Congress's
demand for a monthly supply. Rhode Island's requisition took the form
of taxes levied in gold and silver. The idea was that towns could pay tax in
either gold and silver or beef. Since there was still little gold and silver,
the state expected towns to deliver cattle. And if they did not, the state
empowered county sheriffs to "seize and restrain double the quantity of
Beeves, or Neat Cattle, as will make the weight required and assessed" and
deliver them to the army. The tax turned the logic of the Stamp Act on its
ear: Rhode Island asked its citizens for the impossible, for "bricks without
straw," but did so to force them into giving up cattle the assembly knew
they had. New Englanders had found a way to use specie scarcity to the
state's advantage, to force an exchange in kind.[52]

After Morris's initial attempts to secure investors in America came to
naught, securing foreign silver on loan became his top priority. The opportunity was presented by America's new and growing alliances in Europe.
Following the advice of Pelatiah Webster and others, Congress had
rejected the idea of borrowing money to spend in America, but borrowing
to fund a bank was another thing altogether. That would turn the coin into
a broader source of funding, deploying it as part of an institutional mecha-
nism rather than frittering it away. On July 3 Congress cleared Morris "to
pursue such measures he may think proper for exporting and importing
goods, money and other articles, at the risque and for the account of the
United States." The next day Morris wrote John Jay, then serving at the
court of Spain, to ask for "a considerable Sum of Money from Spain" to be
delivered from Havana directly to the bank. America had been successful,

Morris wrote, in the "patient Resistance whose Opposition must at length weary the Enemy into granting our Independence." But the "vigorous active Operations" needed to conquer occupied New York, Charleston, or Savannah were another matter. "Money is necessary for the latter, and I can say with Confidence that Money alone is necessary," Morris wrote.[53]

On July 17 Morris wrote the governor of Cuba, Juan Manuel de Cagigal, with more specific requests. He asked for $400,000 in Spanish silver in return for a load of flour and bills of exchange drawn directly on the Spanish crown. "I have commenced my Administration with a Proposal to establish a national Bank, the Plan of which I take the Liberty to enclose," Morris wrote. He wanted the silver, he wrote, in part to "induce further Subscriptions among our own Countrymen. For when they see and feel the use of an Institution, which they are yet unacquainted with, they will cheerfully and liberally support it." Congress gave Morris the *Trumbull*, the last of the navy's original thirteen frigates, to carry the five hundred barrels of flour, Morris's letter, and bills of exchange to Havana. Caught in a storm, the *Trumbull*, under Captain James Nicholson, lost a mast and, after a short, brutal fight, fell into the hands of a chasing British fleet. The Spanish loan never materialized.[54]

VII. Paine Seeks a Loan of Silver, While Morris Founds a Bank to House It

That left Thomas Paine. Paine had been thinking of leaving the United States since the demise of the Philadelphia Committee to regulate prices in 1779. All his plans reeked of desperation. On one hand, many leading Americans still respected him as the clearest voice for independence and the country's stalwart defender in the press in his ongoing series *The American Crisis*. On the other, he had made a number of influential enemies. The most important of these was Silas Deane, a merchant who had also served as the United States' first unofficial representative to France, whom Paine had accused, essentially, of embezzling. Deane had set out, at great risk, for France in 1776 with equally great ambitions. Britain, Deane wrote in August 1776, was only rich because of the trade with its colonies. "The colonies, therefore, offer their commerce to France," Dean wrote, "offering, in effect, the principal part of British wealth and power, with all the advantages of sovereignty, but none of the costs of sovereignty." The French were understandably intrigued and set up a covert channel sending weapons, powder, and other war matériel to the Americans through Deane. Paine had accused Deane of claiming commission on goods that were meant as a gift to the new republic. Deane counter-claimed, accurately, that the "gifts" could not be "gifts" because they were given before France had officially joined the war. They had, instead, taken the form of commercial transactions facilitated by Deane, which were thus subject to commission. The debate tarnished Paine's reputation as a sage in Philadelphia and soured him on service in a time when Deane's friends found themselves firmly in power.[55]

Paine's first plan was to return to England to serve as a kind of local propagandist for the American cause, but he abandoned it as too danger-ous. He also planned to begin writing a history of the American Revolu-tion but determined that it would be impossible to do so without records that were only available in England. In January 1781, however, he got another opportunity to leave and took it. Congress had enlisted Colonel John Laurens, a young, dashing South Carolinian, to go to France to bad-ger the French court into sending actual coin to the United States. Lau-rens was an idealist who dreamed of creating and leading an all-Black unit in the Continental army as the final proof that slavery, which had built his family fortune, was a crime against the human spirit. He knew Paine and admired him. Knowing Paine longed to leave and needed a job, he asked Paine to come on the trip as his secretary and sounding board. Thus, in February 1781 Paine set out to France with Laurens to ask King Louis XVI for silver. "A loan of money is the *sine qua non*," Alexander Hamilton wrote Laurens as he embarked on the mission. Without that, nothing.[56]

Paine and Laurens left Boston on Sunday, February 11. Four days later they awoke in a field of ice, "a tumultuous assemblage of floating rolling rocks, which we could not avoid and against which there was no defense," Paine recalled. The ship survived and, after rescuing a pirated Venetian trader from a Glaswegian cutter, made landfall at the port of L'Orient in northwest France on March 9. The French, warned of Laurens's arrival, offered a gift of 2 million livres, slightly more than half a million Span-ish dollars, credited against goods already being sent in other words, wiping out some American debt but not providing specie. Laurens, over two months of increasingly fraught negotiations, warned that would not be enough. The bank and the army would need more. Laurens told the French foreign minister that it would be impossible to maintain a "paper credit without a foundation of specie" that only the French could provide. The French were unimpressed. They had never been convinced by Amer-ican descriptions of the continental dollar as a bill of credit. Laurens's main interlocutor, Charles Gravier, compte de Vergennes, had written

John Adams the previous year in a huff about the forty-to-one revaluation of the continental dollar. He had understood the dollars as a debt, owed by Congress, that it would pay off in actual silver dollars. Adams tried in vain to reeducate him. Bills of credit were "a Subject peculiar to America, no Example entirely similar to it," Adams wrote. The Abbé Guillaume Thomas François Raynal repeated the claim that the continental dollar was a debt, rather than a credit *against* a tax debt, in his history of the Revolution that same year. This time it was Paine, with the benefit of having observed Laurens's efforts, who tried to correct him. Raynal, Paine wrote, "speaks as if the United States had contracted a debt upwards of forty million pounds sterling, besides the debts of the individual states." And indeed, Paine wrote, "it must be extremely difficult to make foreigners understand the nature and circumstances of our paper money, because there are natives who do not understand it themselves." But, Paine wrote, "to suppose as some did, that, at the end of the war, it was to grow into gold or silver, or become equal thereto, was to suppose that we were to get two hundred millions of dollars by going to war, instead of paying the cost of carrying it on," getting things precisely backward. Regardless, the exchange had soured Vergennes on American credit.[57]

Laurens's badgering style eventually won out, to his fellow ambassadors' chagrin, and the French government agreed to deliver specie via two frigates to America. Paine, meanwhile, was reluctant to leave France, where he found that his writings had been well received in translation. Laurens convinced him to join the voyage to what was now, even Paine admitted, his home. They set out on June 1 and arrived in Boston on August 25, 1781, with 2.5 million livres in Spanish silver. It took fourteen wagons and fifty-six oxen more than two months to haul the silver to Philadelphia.[58]

It arrived far too late to contribute to the decisive battle of the war. In October, Washington cornered Cornwallis at Yorktown while the French fleet cut him, his army, and the thousands of formerly enslaved people who had fled to British lines off from supply by sea. Josiah Atkins, a private from Waterbury, Connecticut, remembered being shocked to learn, when he marched south near Washington's home at Mount Vernon, that Washington had "two or 300 Negroes to work on it as slaves. Alas! That persons who pretend to stand for the *rights of mankind* for the *liberties of society,* can delight in oppression, & that even of the worse kind. . . . *While they promise liberty, they themselves are the servants of* [*corruption*]," he wrote in his diary. On June 10 Atkins received "one months [*sic*] pay in hard money," likely from French officers who had been escorting their own troops to battle. The siege lasted the better part of a month. On October 19, 1781, Cornwallis surrendered, ending the last major British offensive of the American Revolution. Morris, meanwhile, used almost half of the French silver, $254,000, to complete the capital for his new bank investing on the account of the United States which became an equity partner.[59]

Congress incorporated the Bank of North America on December 31, 1781. The charter gave Morris and the other directors of the bank the right to raise a capital of $10 million "of Spanish silver milled dollars." Congress also named Morris's partner, Thomas Willing, as president. The bank opened on January 7, 1782. On January 8 Morris wrote to John Dickinson, who had just been elected president of the state of Pennsylvania. The bank's notes, he wrote, "will afford the individuals of all the States a medium for their intercourse with each other, and for payment of Taxes, more convenient than precious metals, and equally safe." On January 12 Philadelphia merchant Joseph Pemberton reported to his correspondent John Wilson that vessels returning from Havana had paid in $80,000 in silver dollars on deposit in the first week alone, in addition to another $100,000 paid in December, before the bank had officially opened its doors. Within a month, Boston merchants were asking their correspondents in Philadelphia for bank bills in lieu of local bills of exchange. By the end of the year, the same merchants were pressing their correspondents for "what Money you have left lodge[d] in the Bank at Philadelphia."[60]

The initial public response was relief at the difference between this bank, with its notes and its silver, and everything that had come before. There seemed no doubt that the bank could do what it said it would: take silver on deposit in return for notes that were payable on demand. Bankers could not afford to have people treat their notes as anything less than a permanent form of wealth, and the bank's public and private backers immediately switched to the language of money as specie. The subscribers' plan described initial specie down payments as "a fund to begin with," using "fund" in the British sense of a money hoard. Clerks recorded the bank's notes and ledgers in terms of the Spanish silver dollar, broken down into 90ths, not Pennsylvania pounds or continentals. Slivers of silver took the place of long-standing American monies of account.[61] The bank, likewise, took pains to emphasize the physicality of its specie-denominated wealth. According to one account, customers were greeted with "a display of silver upon the counter, and men employed in raising boxes containing silver, or supposed to contain silver, from the cellar into the banking room, or lowering them from the banking room into the cellar." The bank presented money as a scarce commodity, which it alone commanded.[62]

Meanwhile, the subscribers directed their purchasing agent, or factor, appointed to purchase rations and liquor on the government's account, to "pass as many notes in payment as possible, until Congress can reimburse the Bank," to avoid facing specie demands.[63] This was alchemy. The notes might not be silver, but the bank did everything to ensure people would treat the notes as if they were until Congress could find the specie to make it real. But the real transmutation was the fact that, at the center of its new nation, Morris's bank, so difficult to create and impossible without government help, was shifting what money meant, one depositor at a time. Where money had meant a bill of credit, something temporary, representing a debt that citizens owed the public, it now was coming to mean silver, or a promise of silver. The specie was less important, though, than the shift it represented for the new nation's relationship to money. Public money, bills of credit, had been temporary. Bank money, a debt payable in silver on demand, would be a permanent form of wealth, as would every new financial instrument or share in an institution built with the new money as the seed pattern for the financial world Morris and his friends already envisioned.[64]

For Paine, the shift was a relief. The paper money, he wrote early in 1782, was more than a "stone in the bridge, that has carried us over" with thus "a claim upon our esteem." It "was a corner-stone, and its usefulness cannot be forgotten." Americans could be grateful for it and still not lament its passing. The cornerstone had been removed, with "silver and gold supplied in its place," Paine wrote. Money's fate, he concluded, "is now determined."[65]

VIII. Britain Secures a Victory in Paris

British negotiators in Paris, though, were not so sure. Even after it had been defeated at Yorktown, Great Britain was anything but a spent force. It still held New York, Savannah, and Charleston—all key cities if the United States was going to be governable. It still controlled the far West, where its alliances with Native American nations, who hoped to secure themselves against American expansion, had continually bloodied the states' western reaches. Arguably, with its naval victories over the French and Spanish at the close of the war, Britain was ascendant. But it, too, had financial concerns. The war had been expensive, and it had long been clear that the British strategy, which relied on a light military footprint backed by loyalist forces that never seemed to materialize, was not going to succeed. The question, after Yorktown, was not whether the war would end but on what terms, and for Britain that meant finally settling the question of American money.[66]

When talks began in earnest, in the fall of 1782, the first concern of the principal American negotiators—Benjamin Franklin and John Jay—was getting the British to recognize the independence of the United States. Jay, in particular, had been humiliated in Madrid, his diplomatic post, after the continental dollar debacle when the Spanish court refused to recognize him as the representative of an independent power or offer anything substantial in the way of specie loans. He was eager to secure British recognition as recompense. Neither negotiator wanted to enter into a settlement that implied that Britain retained any sovereignty over its former subjects. All summer Franklin and Jay demanded official recognition up front and refused to treat on the subject of debts or other "confiscations," saying those were state matters, even as British negotiators sweetened their terms in the hopes of luring the Americans away from their allies the French.[67]

Then, in early September, Franklin and Jay's British counterparts seemed to give way all at once. On September 3, 1782, Thomas Townshend wrote Richard Oswald, the Scottish merchant, military contractor, and large-scale slave trader, who had testified against the Americans during the Stamp Act hearings sixteen years earlier but now was serving as Britain's primary negotiator. Parliament, Townshend wrote, had agreed to drop demands that the debts owed British merchants and the claims of loyalist refugees be settled before the question of independence. Townshend wrote that the king was hopeful for an "equitable Determination" but would waive settling them as a condition for peace. The letter was everything Franklin and Jay could have wished for except diplomatic recognition.[68] They did not have to wait long for that either. On September 19, 1782, George III authorized Oswald to treat with "Persons vested with equal Powers, by and on the part of the Thirteen United States of America," making Jay and Franklin's new nation, the United States of America, an official part of the diplomatic record. Recognition had been achieved. After more than eight years of war, the king of England had countersigned the Declaration of Independence.[69]

With that, the commissioners got to work. Within two weeks, they had hammered out a treaty that might as well have been an American wish list. It contained no clauses addressing prewar debts or the estates of fugitive loyalists. Rather, its substance was a treaty of free trade, offering most of the North American continent east of the Mississippi and south of the St. Lawrence River valley, and pledging that neither Britain nor the American states would charge duties on the other's ships that they did not charge their own. It was essentially a treaty of commercial union, concluded on the best possible terms. It would restore trade with Britain, the lifeblood of the colonies before the war, while giving the new nation extensive latitude to maneuver.[70]

Jay could hardly have been more excited. He expressed it in almost feverish conversations that Oswald recorded and, without Jay's knowledge, sent to his superiors in London. Jay's enthusiasm was understandable to Oswald. Recognition was a real coup, the realization of years of painstaking labor and hard fighting, and for Jay the achievement of a grand ambition at substantial risk and personal sacrifice. The combination left him gushing. In early October, before the treaty draft was finished, Jay even pushed Oswald to encourage Parliament to invade America's ally, Spain, and seize the mouth of the Mississippi. British ports then, Jay enthused, would become "the Mart or Center of a great part of the Trade of America to the Southward," just as Quebec would be to the northward, Oswald reported. "By which means, upon the whole, England, having those two keys in its hand, may still enjoy an exclusive Monopoly of a large share of north american Commerce." If it could conclude the peace on good terms, and seize the key port of the American West, Jay had observed, Britain "may not happen to be, in point of Trade, so great a Loser by the change, as is generally imagined." In a letter sent along with the draft treaty on October 5, Oswald reported that in the final negotiations, Jay had gone still further. Jay suggested that under the terms they were negotiating, Britain would be the real winner of the war. It would, in effect, retain its commercial empire in North America. "We should lose no thing, & should be saved the Expense & trouble of gouverning them," Oswald wrote. He seemed a little taken aback at Jay's enthusiasm. "These are his words," Oswald wrote. He wanted to be sure the ministers would believe him. He was not making up the American's thirst to restore part of the British trade monopoly.[71]

Jay's enthusiasm seems to have prompted reflection in Whitehall and the Privy Council. When the draft treaty arrived, the council had prepared a positive response. But after reading Oswald's conversations with Jay, they reconsidered. They thought his invitation to invade Florida was a trap and doubted Oswald's generosity. If Britain was to reestablish its trading relationship with America, on what terms should it do so? These discussions brought the money problem back to the fore. Britain had begun the war almost ten years earlier because it believed that Americans would never submit to taxes and a regulatory regime that the empire deemed necessary to make them good customers. Sensing a giddiness in the

American negotiators, Townshend moved to trade the diplomatic recognition of the United States for American recognition of the pound sterling. He and his advisers also seem to have concluded that Oswald had become too chummy with his counterparts, too eager to make concessions. With their new instructions, the council sent a new negotiator.[72]

The negotiator was Henry Strachey. His mission was to secure Britain's victory in the money war, to win from the states with independence what they had never ceded as colonies: the right to determine what money was within their borders. In 1765 he had followed Robert Clive to India to secure the Diwani, beginning the train of devastating accidents that had begun with famine in India, continued with the East India Company's bankruptcy, and ended with tea in Boston Harbor. Strachey was a hardened imperial operative and an intensely single-minded negotiator. His mission was clear. Reactionary elements in Parliament were already suggesting that Britain was giving everything away in its negotiations and gaining nothing. "The Clamour likewise will scarcely be withstood, if some Recognition is not obtained in favor of the Debts Contracted before 1775," Prime Minister William Petty, the Second Earl of Shelburne, wrote. Of all the points of negotiation, he continued, "the debts require the most serious attention,—that honest debts may be honestly paid in honest money—no Congress money." Shelburne had given Oswald the same instructions, suggesting that he frame the debts as a moral issue "which can never be sufficiently dwelt and insisted upon."[73]

John Adams accidentally helped matters along. He arrived in Paris late in October 1782 and proceeded to upend the American negotiating position. Regarding the debts, he told Franklin in an early meeting, he "had no Notion of cheating any Body." In the back of Adams's mind, he later noted in his diary, was a conversation that morning with Oswald and Strachey, where he had mentioned his idea about honoring British debts on the terms of British merchants. Oswald, for his part, seemed pleased, but Adams's words struck Strachey "with peculiar Pleasure, I saw it instantly smiling in every Line of his Face," Adams wrote on Sunday, November 3, 1782.[74] Adams had naïvely all but conceded what the British commissioners now wanted most: to bring the newly independent nation back into the British fold on British terms. If the moral question was conceded, all that was left were the details.[75]

After Adams had given British negotiators the moral edge, Jay and Franklin believed that fighting it might put the treaty at risk. The next day Adams, Jay, Strachey, and Oswald hammered out an agreement stipulating that even British debts confiscated by rebel colonies could be recovered by British creditors, at the "full value, or Sterling Amount of such bona fide Debts as were contracted before the year 1775." The language in the final treaty was somewhat more stringent, prescribing "Sterling Money" rather than "Sterling Amount." From Adams's notes, there is little doubt it was Strachey who pushed for the language. Evidently, the British negotiators, if not all the Americans, were aware that something more than simple fairness was at stake. They knew they were giving up something, because the British had demanded it, but it seems that they were unclear precisely what. None, except Franklin, who was seventy-six years old, had any real financial expertise. Jay, who had overseen the final failure of the continental dollar while president of the Continental Congress, had something like the opposite. He was a hardheaded and tireless negotiator but may indeed have had something more than sympathy for the British position, as his willingness to abandon America's erstwhile allies suggests.

That position, in retrospect, seems clear. Strachey and the other British commissioners hoped to use the treaty to bring America back into Britain's financial sphere. Taxes were out of the question, but the millions of pounds of sterling debts contracted before the war might do much the same work. If Americans treated sterling money as an apparently abstract and unbiased standard it might become the benchmark for American value. It does not appear that the British wanted coin exactly; they wanted the relationships with American merchants and planters that had sustained the British Empire before the war. They wanted to be free from American juries and American legislatures that had proved troublesome when they were still colonies. And, just as before, they wanted to control the monetary terms of those relationships. The British only succeeded, in large measure, because some Revolutionary leaders, like Jay, had already come to the same conclusion.[76]

IX. The Aftermath Provokes Opposition and Despair

The change, though, was still to come. Morris may have hoped that the Bank of North America would put banknotes in the place of the continental dollar, but if that was the goal, the bank failed. Morris had hoped the bank would expand by lending to Congress against anticipated tax revenues, and those revenues failed to materialize. Congress had no power to tax on its own under the Articles of Confederation, and thus the bank had much less ability to lend than its British counterpart and few means to force its notes into circulation. In any event, under Willing, the bank was defined by its conservatism. In theory, the bank could have used its specie like the Bank of England, to multiply the means of payment by issuing more notes than the gold and silver it had in its vault, but it did not. The bank's hard-money policy paired with its supporters' official hostility to paper currency had the effect of constricting the Pennsylvania money supply, resulting in what one historian has called "a painful deflationary spiral." But the goal was to create pain. The difficulty involved in getting hold of the new bank currency that Morris had imagined—the labor, effort, shifted lifestyles, and occupations—would make the money real. The goal was not to provide money but to transform it into the permanent instrument Morris and his friends imagined.[77]

Morris, Paine, Washington, and many other influential Americans had all been convinced that bills of credit must be abandoned as a means of war funding. The Bank of North America had not succeeded in replacing bills of credit with a plentiful means of exchange, but it had shown America's new class of continental or "Federalist" statesmen a way forward, laying a pattern for bank-led financial expansion. It created a template: first, for other merchant banks, starting with Boston in 1784, and second, the outline of a national fiscal system a decade later that would place banks at its heart. Money would no longer be a service provided by the government in service of its people. Money would be produced at a profit in response to market pressures for the benefit of individuals whose business would profit the banks, rather than the other way round.[78]

With peace, too, a new kind of crisis had emerged along with the newly expanded class of landless laborers willing to work for wages. In the settled world of prewar farming households, one's social standing, ability to work, and property were usually sufficient to meet one's needs. If they were not, coin would be of little help far from merchants and markets. There had always been a significant group of migrants, sailors, and menial laborers in the largest American towns. After the Revolution, it had greatly increased in size, and with it demands for money wages.[79] In the North, the urban household, as such, was on the brink of dissolving. Families were unable to find servants willing to work as members of their family in return for food, lodging, and clothing, without offering cash wages. In cities where access to cash was becoming the most meaningful form of social standing, and strangers were doing business on a regular basis, it became more common to encounter people suffering from the lack of it—and fleeing to the countryside where they could reproduce something of the older, remembered way of life.[80]

In July 1780 Elijah Fisher, who had served in Washington's Life Guard, was working as a farm laborer when he heard that he was entitled to depreciation wages compensating him for the decline of the continental dollar over his three years in the army. On July 4 he walked nearly forty miles to Boston to see about it and, after some confusion, received £54 in new securities, on top of the £49 he already had. He was so inspired, he reenlisted.[81] After another year in the militia, he went back to working on farms, only to find farmers increasingly reluctant to pay the wages they had promised. Monetary scarcity, the effect of the new way of producing money, was making its way deep into the American hinterlands. Fisher found it increasingly difficult to support himself. Seeing few options, on Christmas Day 1782, Fisher signed on to a privateer, only to be captured by a British warship and imprisoned on the *Jersey* in New York harbor. On April 6, 1783, his jailers read the official proclamation of peace, negotiated in Paris. Fisher was sent ashore in New York, where he spent all night at a tavern. The next day, he began searching for a ship back to New England and home.

On May 14, 1783, he made it back to Boston, crossing to the peninsula where American money had been reinvented almost a century earlier, on the ferry from Charlestown. There, the full weight of the transformation became apparent to him for the first time. The city was overwhelmed with newly impoverished men like him, men who had earned the continental dollar and were now struggling to survive, scraping for food and shelter. "So many had come there from the army & from the sea, that had no homes that would work for little or nothing but to have vittles," he wrote. Payment was once again in kind. Fisher feared that when his own savings, collected from a deadbeat employer, were gone, he would become one of them.

On May 16, 1782, Fisher wrote, "I come down to the market and sits down all alone almost Discouraged, and begun to think over how that since I had been in the army what Ill Success I had met with." He continued, "But then came into my mind that there were thousands in far worse circumstances than I was." The city was full of them. He, on the other hand, still had the securities he had been paid out two years earlier. He went back to his boarding house and later sold them to a broker for approximately one-third of their face value. He put the money into supplies and a piece of land near what is now North Yarmouth, Maine, and began farming on his own account.[82]

X. Rebels and the Road to the Constitution

Disappointed men like Fisher did not merely return to the land. They banded together, voted, protested, and entered government in the hopes of securing a new monetary settlement within the states. There was no legal or constitutional impediment to them doing so. The Bank of North America was distant, the negotiations in Paris rumored and indistinct. The trauma felt by American leaders had not translated to an American public still steeped in the legacy of temporary money. The Articles of Confederation had left the states free to pursue their own monetary course, including the ability to create new bills of credit to replace those that had failed in the war. After the British army withdrew from Charleston, New York, and Savannah, there was no reason that bills of credit could not rise again.

The states had picked up the banner of temporary money as soon as Congress had dropped it. By 1786, Pennsylvania, Rhode Island, New Hampshire, New York, Delaware, North Carolina, South Carolina, Georgia, and New Jersey had all gone back to issuing bills of credit, leading to conflict between states and leaders who had been burned by the wartime experience. Rhode Island was the most notorious revivalist allowing debtors to pay their debts with bills at face value—even if the creditors were unwilling to show up in court. But it was far from alone. Beginning in 1782, New Hampshire began issuing "notes" and "certificates" to its soldiers, as a credit against a new £110,000 tax. The notes paid interest in certificates that were exchangeable for gold or silver unless the New Hampshire Treasury did not have any. Of course, it did not. In that case, more certificates would be given, "receivable in public taxes." Other states followed a similar course. Temporary currency, all but dead in 1780, was reemerging.[83]

Americans who knew about the monetary terms of the peace with Britain knew that there would be pushback from abroad, as states asserted their newly won economic sovereignty, making new bills, retiring wartime debts, and slowing debt collections. But the situation was inherently contradictory. The Treaty of Paris had secured a paper victory in the money war for Britain, but it had also secured independence and with it the right to self-determination. Many Americans apparently suspected that while they had gone to war, in the first place, to defend themselves, the assault had come because they had asserted the right, within the empire, to arrange money and taxation as they saw fit. Independence had secured the agency to do so. And yet the Treaty of Paris, so long as it remained extant, stood as a limit to that power.

Some, likely from states like Virginia where the colony had confiscated British debts as a wartime measure, hoped that further negotiations might secure monetary leeway. "I perceive that according to the Ideas of some, I am sent here to make a new Treaty of Peace, the old one not being agreeable to some Gentlemen who were in debt before the War," John Adams wrote Rufus King from London on June 14, 1786. "This I shall never be able to do." In fact, the British were clinging to their posts in the American

West and refusing promised compensation for the thousands of African Americans who had joined their side during the war in a heroic bid for freedom, in order to ensure that their prewar debts would be settled on the British Empire's monetary terms—in gold and silver or the sterling equivalent. "There will never be an end of Questions and Chicane, until the States repeal all the Laws which impede the Recovery of old Debts in America," Adams wrote.[84]

Yet despite the wartime experience and all of Morris's efforts, the notion of money as precious metal was still far from universal. Many Americans believed that their victory had created a republic that was distinct *because* of the way it had broken with the tyranny of gold and silver.[85] America was great because America was different, set up on a different financial basis. "No blood we shed / For metals buried in a rocky waste," the New Jersey poet Philip Freneau wrote in June 1786 in a poem entitled "The Rising Glory of America." America, he wrote, was "designed by nature for rural reign, / for agriculture's toil."

> *More Blessed are we, with whose unenvied soil*
> *Nature decreed no mingling gold to shine,*
> *No blushing sapphire, ruby, chrysolite,*
> *Or jasper red—more noble riches flow*
> *From agriculture, and the industrious swain,*
> *Who tills the fertile vale, or mountain's brow,*
> *Content to lead a safe, a humble life.*

Americans, Freneau believed, had despised an imperial world where the "thirst of gold," as he put it, had become an "All conquering motive of the human breast." The Revolution had secured the United States as an alternative to societies swamped, as Freneau saw it, by unproductive and violent greed. He was not alone. Freneau, who had become friends with James Madison at Princeton, would go on to edit the *National Gazette*, the leading newspaper of Thomas Jefferson's Democratic Republican Party. They, like Webster, had realized that giving up bills of credit meant giving over American economic sovereignty, surrendering, in effect, to the international system that the British were building. And though Morris and the negotiators in Paris had already laid the groundwork for the new system, they made sure that these men, none of them elected, would not have the final word on the matter.[86]

The reembrace of temporary money led to popular hostility against the institutions that were trying to keep it dead once and for all. Morris's Bank of North America came under attack in 1785. In Pennsylvania, new taxes payable either in banknotes or gold and silver had drained whatever surplus the war had left over, particularly in the western counties, and the bank was doing nothing to make up the difference. The bank's notes were not expanding in circulation, replacing the old bills of credit. They were pooling purchasing power in Philadelphia at the expense of anyone living further afield. To make matters worse, when the state restarted its loan offices, offering new bills of credit to farmers on mortgage in March 1785, the bank's directors refused to take the new bills of credit in deposit. The bank's conclusion was that bills of credit and notes backed by specie could not be set equal to each other.[87]

This had been precisely the position of the British government twenty years earlier. The result was a political firestorm. Most Pennsylvanians had not been privy to Morris and his allies' plans to remake money, and they objected to what they were learning. State lawmakers almost immediately began a review of the bank's charter. And on September 13, 1785, they voted to revoke it as "injurious to the welfare of the state."[88] When the bank and its directors appealed to the assembly, the stakes became clear: whether money in the new republic would be a permanent thing, outside of the state's control, or something responsive to democratic governance. For the bank's backers, the question was academic. The Revolution had made their case. Bills of credit were "the child of confidence—and of confidence alone," Robert Morris argued before the state assembly on the morning of Thursday, March 30, 1786. "That confidence has been destroyed." Others, however, were not so sure.[89]

As speakers rose against the bank, it became clear that the bank and its new money threatened something more fundamental, seemingly, than a paper currency. Permanent money, they charged, was remaking Pennsylvanians' very being, the way they moved in the world, and interacted with one another—just as it had in Britain almost a century earlier. "The human soul is affected by wealth, in almost all its faculties," Assemblyman William Findley from the far western Westmoreland County testified, in what has proved a lasting statement of popular protest against American banking. "It is affected by its present interest, by its expectations, and by its fears." Findley saw the bank as seeking to remake, not just money, but Pennsylvanian society. "The institution is inconsistent with our laws—our habits—our manners," he said. In a corporation like the bank, "principles of honour and generosity, &c., can have no place." It had "no principle but that of avarice," no aim but "to engross all the wealth, power, and influence of the state." Its logical end was conquest. "Democracy must fall before it," Findley concluded, if democracy allowed it to exist.[90]

Findley's analysis, like Dickinson's *Letters from a Farmer,* took for granted that property relied on government, on economic sovereignty generated by popular consensus to exist. The bank, however, had re-created wealth as a thing "not dependent on government," separate from the will of the people. This was no accident. In prospect, Findley believed, the bank and its supporters aimed at overturning the system of democratic government in preparation for an eventual assault on landed wealth like his. "So, by taking advantage of a scarcity of money, which they have so much in their power to occasion, they may become sole lords of the soil," and with it, lords of the state.[91]

The attack on the bank called Revolutionary penmen burned by the demise of the continental dollar back to the fray. Paine had retired to Bordentown, New Jersey, living on a $3,000 gratuity from Congress and the proceeds from a confiscated loyalist's farm gifted by the state of New York. In 1785 he was staying with friends on the second floor of a home overlooking the Delaware River, riding regularly, and working with local craftsmen to design a new kind of cast-iron bridge. But with the bank in peril, he again took up his pen. The result was a long essay entitled *Dissertations on Government: The Affairs of the Bank; and Paper Money* published in Philadelphia as a pamphlet on February 18, 1786. Money, Paine had come to believe, was the limit of democracy. It presented both an intractable physical reality and a trap for those who thought otherwise.[92]

Money, Paine acknowledged, was about class and power, a question not just of home rule, as one historian famously observed, but of who would rule at home. The crisis had taught Paine that "poor" men would have to be replaced by "the rich" in government because the rich understood how money really worked. "It was easy times to the governments while Continental money lasted," he wrote. "The dream of wealth supplied the reality of it; but when the dream vanished, the government did not wake." The bank was still shaking the dreamer. The war, Paine wrote, had proved that money *was* gold and silver. Anything else was a delusion or a fraud. "When an assembly undertakes to issue paper *as* money," he wrote, "the whole system of safety and certainty is overturned, and property set afloat." "It is," he wrote, "like putting an apparition in the place of a man; it vanishes with looking at it, and nothing remains but air." Again, Paine proved influential. His essay sparked a national debate as newspapers in virtually every state reprinted his argument, and helped elect a narrow majority of probank legislators in Pennsylvania who restored the bank's charter while preserving bills of credit alongside it.[93]

Now, American elites like Paine were saying, the nation was free except on the one central point that the states, as colonies, had fought for control: the arrangement of monetary affairs. A conflict was building. Assertions of monetary power had been central to the American Revolution itself, the cause of the protests against "taxation without representation" in the Stamp Act crisis, and the impetus for constitutional agitation within the empire in the unsettling decade that followed it. As Finley said in his protest against the Bank of North America, the idea of a permanent money, of money as naturally gold and silver, proposed that the opposite was true: that property in its most political, monetary form was something beyond democratic control. One side or the other would have to give.

The political crises that plagued the United States in the 1780s, from Shays's Rebellion in Massachusetts in the summer of 1786 to Mathew's Rebellion in Virginia a year later, revealed how radical Morris's wartime proposal to transform money into a permanent instrument for war and commerce was.[94] The conflict was not uniform or one-sided. It was merely ubiquitous. In some states, like Massachusetts, a hard-money legislature was opposed by a popular movement in favor of paper money that largely failed to achieve significant political power. In others, like Pennsylvania and New Jersey, popular majorities in the legislature adopted paper money over the objection of vocal elite minorities, many of whom cited the horrors of the Revolutionary experience. There was, as the historian Woody Holton has rightly observed, as much cause to lament a dearth of democracy—in terms of legislative support for temporary money—as there was an "excess of democracy," the phrase both Alexander Hamilton and Elbridge Gerry used to describe the failures of the Confederation years.[95]

A central point of rough elite agreement, by 1787, was that money lay at the root of many popular disorders, and those disorders might lead to conflict between the states. The aforementioned Rhode Island revival, where out-of-state creditors were forced to accept bills with only relatively small, local circulation helped to solidify the consensus. There are considerable debates about the Rhode Islanders' intent and the viability of their experiment, but the idea that one state might use its ability to create currency at the expense of other states proved far more compelling than any of the arguments for or against temporary money or gold and silver in one state or another. One widely republished southern writer called the Rhode Island legislature "dangerous to community at large." A Massachusetts author called the state's citizens "armed plunderers of their neighbours."[96]

The next spring and summer, delegates from all the Revolutionary states gathered in Philadelphia for a Constitutional Convention. On May 29, 1787, Edmund Randolph of Virginia gave the first speech of the convention on the necessity of national defense "supported by money." Article 1, Section 10 of the Constitution was the convention's answer to Randolph's challenge. It declared that "No State shall . . . coin Money; emit Bills of Credit; make any Thing but gold and silver Coin a Tender in Payment of Debts." South Carolina framer Charles Pinkney later called this "the soul of the Constitution." And many historians have read it as a repudiation of the monetary experiments of the previous half decade. However, it did not so much eliminate the possibility of bills of credit as move the power that many state legislatures had reclaimed from the local, state level to the federal government. This explains why section 10, despite its seemingly radical repudiation of states' monetary powers, was a relatively unimportant factor in the state ratification conventions over the next two years. Though the Constitution does not expressly authorize national bills of credit (a deliberate omission), it does give the new legislature the power to "lay and collect taxes," the only power necessary to emit them. If asked, supporters of the Constitution always suggested that while bills of credit had been denied the states, the new federal government would still have that power. Pinkney, perhaps the most articulate opponent of state-issued currencies, was clear on this point. "Besides, if paper should become necessary," he added at the end of a long speech against "paper money" in general at the South Carolina ratification convention, "the general government still possess the power of emitting it, and Continental paper, well-funded, must ever answer the purpose better than state paper."[97]

But, as we have seen, the debate had another dimension. Two broad constituencies were fundamentally opposed to all money conceived as a democratically responsive, temporary medium. The first were men like Morris, who served as a Pennsylvania delegate at the federal convention. These men were powerful, but not powerful enough to make gold and silver the money of the land on their own in the convention itself. They do not even seem to have tried. The other constituency, as we have seen, was the British Empire itself, which was still fighting in the wake of losing direct control in North America to have its prewar debts honored on sterling terms.

Thus, perhaps the key clause of the U.S. Constitution in creating the financial basis for what became, truly, a monied republic, was not Article 1, Section 10 but Article 6, Section 2. This clause provides that "all Treaties made, or which shall be made, under the Authority of the United States, shall be the supreme Law of the Land; and the Judges of every State shall be bound thereby, any Thing in the Constitution or Laws of any States to the Contrary notwithstanding." It was this clause, not Article 1, Section 10, that would prove controversial over the next decade and prove the judicial handmaiden to Hamilton's plans, as treasury secretary, to finish the job that Morris had begun. The early United States adopted a permanent money, becoming a monied republic, because of both internal pressures—the rule of the rich that Paine had both foretold and assisted, a group that founder James Wilson, as early as 1787, was calling "capitalists"—and external demands to join, and become powerful within, the emerging, imperial, European world system of capitalism. America had lost the second half of its double revolution, its money war, first in the rebellions of the Continental Line and again in Paris. Article 6, Section 2 wrote the terms of its surrender into the U.S. Constitution.[98]

To be sure, by the 1790s, many Americans who agreed on little else seemed eager to participate in the British-led international monetary system they had rejected as colonies less than thirty years earlier. Perhaps temporary money was a practice that could only subsist under the imperial aegis, as much a by-product of empire, or soft subsidy as it was any kind of counterhegemonic force. Without imperial protection, exposed to the hazards of invasion and, when the war had ended, to the possibility of a Babel-like confusion of monies, Americans leaders may have *needed* to abandon bills that relied on public faith, were temporary, and responsive to public demands, if only because the war had taught them that any such bills were vulnerable at precisely the moments when they were needed most. In abandoning temporary money, though, they had also abandoned the basis of their Revolution, the reason independence had been so pressing in the first place. America had revolted against Britain's plans to tax because Britain became hostile to the way that Americans had spent much of the century making money on their own terms. Americans had developed a Revolutionary theory that placed the right to self-determination within the empire ahead of property rights, creating a theoretical foundation for a unified Revolutionary movement. They had gone to war depending on their own institutional and physical resources with their money as their only financial support. When they abandoned that money, they also abandoned much of what had made America in the eighteenth century such a vital and prosperous place. It would take another revolution to replace what they had lost.

The Monied Republic

CAPITALISM AND THE AMERICAN REVOLUTION

FIG. 11. Liberty Dollar, United States, 1794, Obverse.

In the early spring of 1796, looking out over gardens just off Rue de Clichy in the northern reaches of Paris, Thomas Paine began to write what was, in his view, an act of revenge. Paine, at fifty-nine, had become famous as the "Apostle of Liberty," a veteran of two revolutions, author of *Common Sense* and *The Rights of Man*. Brilliant and irascible, he had been imprisoned by Robespierre on December 28, 1793, at the height of the Terror, and only freed on November 4, 1794, on the word of James Monroe, the new ambassador of the United States.[1]

By the time Monroe secured his release Paine was desperately ill, with a large pus-filled abscess on his side, angry and weak from nearly a year of hunger, cold, and constant fear, as fellow prisoners were carted away to quick trials and the guillotine. When Monroe offered his family's apartment as a place to recover, Paine gratefully accepted. Later, they all moved into Monroe's new lodging, the Folie de la Bouëxière, a white, light-filled pavilion set in ornamental gardens just inside the city wall filled with bronze statuary and gilt, painted ceilings, oversized mirrors, and topped with a sail-like rooftop tent for dinner parties and afternoon teas. There, Paine entertained all comers and began, again, to write. Like many old revolutionaries, Paine drank "like a fish," the thirty-three-year-old Irish rebel Wolfe Tone observed after meeting Paine in Paris. Still, he was a welcome guest. Paine was even wittier in person than he was on paper, Tone recalled, and far more fun. "He is vain beyond all belief, but he has reason to be vain, and for my part I forgive him. He has done wonders for the cause of liberty, both in Europe and America, and I believe him to be conscientiously an honest man."[2]

Paine's target that spring was the British financial system. He wanted to expose the web of banknotes, public debt, and private finance for what he believed it to be: a "monster of national fraud," "a farce," "a monument of wonder, not so much on account of the extent to which it has been carried, as of the folly of believing in it." Each new imperial war cost half again as much as the last, with no end in sight. The Bank of England's notes were worth less by the day, its capital a "slender twig" bending under the weight of its obligations. The British nation was "insolvent," Paine wrote, its treasury "empty." But Paine's aim was not exposé or reformation. Like Tone's in Ireland, where he would die in British custody in 1798, Paine's aim was revolution.[3]

Over Paine's two-decade career as a radical penman, he had noticed a pattern: "Every case of failure in finances" had "produced a revolution in governments, either total or partial," he wrote. "A failure in the finances of France produced the French Revolution. A failure in the finance of the assignats"—France's revolutionary currency—"broke up the revolutionary government, [and] produced the French Constitution. A failure in the finances of the Old Congress of America and the embarrassments it brought to commerce, broke up the system of the old confederation and produced the Federal Constitution." One by one, governments radical and conservative had fallen. "If, then, we admit of reasoning by comparison of causes and events, the failure of English finances will produce some change in the government of that country." Revolution, he hoped, yet again.[4]

In order to understand the American Revolution, we have to understand American money. That has been one of the premises of this book: that money—complex, abstract, and occasionally tedious—is a critical causal factor in American history. America's colonial money was distinct, as we have seen, in its relationship to time. It was temporary, a fact that emphasized its link to government, and made both its political character and unique vulnerabilities painfully clear. It was money to burn. During the Revolution, many Americans rejected that temporary character, longing for something stable and invulnerable, money as a permanent form of wealth. This was precisely what Britain had hoped to bring to America before the war, and the conceptual shift marked a British victory. In the Revolution's last years, American elites began writing that transformation into law, setting the specie basis for a new, permanent kind of money— the outlines of which persist today. Americans had stopped burning their money and began rebuilding their society around the necessities and institutions this new form presented.

Paine's point, worth remembering today, was that monetary revolutions are also social revolutions, but there is a sad irony at the heart of his analysis. In America, a shift in monetary thinking had been the necessary condition for independence. Yet it was precisely this kind of shift that Paine ended his career railing against. Paine was the revolutionary's revolutionary, someone who had broken with the cant of crown and cross, and, in doing so, had helped invigorate the cause of democracy immeasurably. And yet, despite this, he was unwilling or unable to see alternative possibilities for money. Money, for him, was nonnegotiable, the unmoved mover, an institution whose logic would reshape governments but could not, itself, be reshaped. The apostle of liberty could not see that accepting money as a given was a surrender, ceding economic sovereignty to the very forces he was fighting against. In that sense, Paine, like colonial America's burning money, was a casualty of the American Revolution.

It may seem inevitable that America would emerge independent just as it did, as an empire in waiting with a strong, British-influenced financial system, focused, as one historian has put it, on "war and violence" because these laid "the foundation for American greatness." While not disputing the relationship between American money and violence, what I want to argue in closing is that what we think of as American strength in the early republic, its nascent imperialism, was, in fact, a sign of profound weakness, the recognition of the ways that it, like Paine, had lost its battle with Britain in terms of money and finance. Strength is the ability to follow one's own path.[5]

Paine's analysis is useful, in part, because of the way it turned out to be wrong. Britain was able to survive the financial changes of the 1790s by following America's colonial example, at least on a superficial level, and, for a time, breaking the link between the pound sterling and precious metal. The pound arguably became even more prominent when stripped of its pretensions to solidity, a naked creature of the imperial state. It is remarkable, indeed, that the market for international debt centered in London, a material precondition for the classic gold standard, only developed after its victory over Napoleon and France. The nation's ability to reshape money, as it turned out, depended on its mastery of the broader, global system of exchange around it. Britain, with its position in India and China at the turn of the nineteenth century, had that power. America and revolutionary France did not. George Washington, in March 1780, had anticipated Britain might shrug off the limits it imposed on others. Even a "bankruptcy will probably be made a ladder to climb to absolute authority," he wrote. And that turned out to be the case.[6]

It is this broader, systemic power that historians of the early American republic and American capitalism have tended to underestimate. America, with its specie standard, emerged in the nineteenth century as a dependent country in the sense defined by the Brazilian economist and politician Enrique Cardoso, as one where "the accumulation and expansion of capital cannot find its essential dynamic component within the system." The essential component in this case was precious metal, which the proliferation of banknotes and counterfeiting in the early nineteenth century would only imperfectly supply. In establishing money as both permanent and metallic, America had instituted a need that only expansion to the Pacific, gold rushes in Georgia and California, and Nevada's Comstock Lode, would satisfy.[7]

America was born with a missing piece, a fact that helps us understand the inside-out nature of early American capitalism. America in the nineteenth century exported more than five times as much of its products as its peers, twice as much per capita as industrializing Europe. Slavery's capitalism was driven by the need to accumulate foreign exchange, credit and coin, open and positively eager to participate in imperial adventures like the genocidal push west, and the explosion of enslavement and violence in the Deep South. What these things had in common, other than that imperial impulse, was the fact they generated either coin or credit on terms Britain had established as necessary for participation in the trading world it increasingly dominated. Britain was early America's largest trade partner by far, and America was responsive to its demands, needing British credit and the pound sterling as much as the Lancashire mill owners needed the cotton grown by enslaved Black Americans. Indeed, the United States might be usefully defined as capitalist precisely because of the way its monetary needs laid it open to external influence.[8]

Temporary money, perhaps like the British Empire itself, had served as a cushioning barrier between the European commercial system and the states'—previously the colonies'—internal economies. Stripped of that protection, as Paine suggested, America's monetary revolution became a collective compulsion. Monied wealth in the United States was distinctive from colonial wealth in that it was not a product of the household. As the historian Ann Daly has put it, America's new "paper sat on a bedrock of coin. But, before gold could become that bedrock, it had to be dug out of rock." For those Americans who did not turn miner, that meant engaging in markets beyond their control. The household in the early republic stood in relation to America's new money much as the United States as a whole did to foreign coin. It would have to go out to bring money back in. This led to epochal shifts in market relations and household organization, as farmers increasingly raised crops for sale rather than use, traveled farther to sell them, and moved west to grow more. It gave rise to a large and permanent class of wage laborers, men and women who would spend their lives working outside the home in order to earn money. It began a transformation in gender roles as privileged families sought to establish the home as a place apart from the demands of money and gendered women as somehow in need of protection from it. The new money provided a naturalizing rhetoric for race and underpinned the financialized postwar slavery. None of these transformations can be considered as distinct from the monetary form that pervaded them. Monied wealth, once woven into the social fabric, would permanently warp it.[9]

From the perspective of the Revolutionary era, though, the most regrettable transformation was the way that America had lost command of its own ideas. The American Revolution was a tragedy for economic thought, a moment of prematurely foreclosed possibilities that it would take the better part of two centuries to reopen. By the end of the war, very few American politicians seem to have even understood their own monetary system, much less Britain's. But Britain had, over the previous century, created a vast intellectual apparatus that served as a resource to

FIG. 12. Liberty Dollar, United States, 1794, Reverse.

American thinkers, giving them the tools, however imperfect, to follow in their erstwhile enemy's footsteps when their own, imperfectly documented folkways failed them.

The significance of ideas in this moment of change suggests the possibility of a path not taken. What would the government of the United States be like—and with it the world—if American finances had not failed? If Congress, in the midst of war, had stayed the course on the continental dollar and a different, perhaps more hopeful, Constitutional Convention had written its alternative understanding of money into America's fundamental law rather than that of its opponent? The result might have been disaster, an invitation to further invasions and the dissolution of the union. That is certainly what the Federalists feared. America needs banks because "the millennium is not yet come," James Wilson wrote in 1786, but other futures were possible as well.[10]

Without the desperate need for international exchange, we might imagine the United States emerging as a counterweight to the European capitalist system, centered in London, rather than its willing accomplice. We might imagine an American economy where slavery had been abandoned because northern financiers and southern slavers never made the linkages with British capital that fueled the cotton boom. We might imagine, as well, a world where the Monroe Doctrine of European noninterference preserved the Americas as a region of experimental political economy and alternative global connectivity, rather than as a reserve for Anglo-American mercantile and financial interests. It is possible, in sum, that the United States would have emerged over the course of the nineteenth century as a powerful alternative form of empire, one implicitly dedicated to the negation of capitalism's stark utopia, putting markets and money in service of humanity, rather than the other way around.[11]

Little in America's colonial history gives one hope that this would have succeeded, or even been tried, but our own ideas about money, shaped by the Revolutionary settlement, perhaps makes that utopian vision of America less imaginable than it was. Money is a human institution. Its history reveals it as a far more malleable social tool than is typically thought. The shape it took in antebellum America, the monied republic, was not necessary for American growth. America had been prosperous with temporary money, with money to burn. It was force, not foresight, that created America's monetary regime. American money, as this history shows, has its roots in imperial ambition, violence, and fear. It was an adaptive response to a capitalist system at war. American money has carried something of that history of violence with it ever since.

ACKNOWLEDGMENTS

This book has survived two deaths, two births, two countries, three nations, a couple of mental breakdowns, a global pandemic, and the academic job market. It bears a few scars. I have been helped along the way by more people than I could possibly acknowledge, none of whom are responsible for the deliberate idiosyncrasies or inadvertent mistakes it may retain. I have tried to pay that generosity forward, both here in this book and in my daily life as a teacher and father.

The person to whom I am most grateful is my wife, Mariel Kessel, a brilliant historian, potter, and editor in her own right. She kept me and our family afloat during the long years of graduate and postgraduate insecurity with charm, intelligence, and the same ferocity I saw in her when we met more than a decade ago in Josh Wolff's Histories of American Capitalism seminar at Columbia University.

At Columbia and Barnard, Dorothy Ko, Elizabeth Blackmar, Mae Ngai, and Eric Wakin instilled in me a passion for history as a nontraditional student arriving from a career in journalism. This book would not exist without Betsy's encouragement and mentorship, and Mae remains a model of every aspect of academic life. They are what I aspire to be as a teacher and scholar. Carl Wennerlind has become a wonderful mentor in the years since. At Princeton, Sean Wilentz taught me that the arc of historiography is long, and a historian's job is to bend it. His generosity toward what were then wild ideas about the Stamp Act set me on my course, and he remains an inspiration in the dogged defense of his ideals. We fought and still fight over everything; I hope I've proved a worthy opponent. Jeremy Adelman, through his leadership of the Global History Lab, introduced me to a world of scholarship and inquiry. His support has been critical to making a career in the UK. I am forever grateful. David Bell was a wonderful mentor and generous co-teacher. Jonathan Levy, too, has been a brilliant colleague, advocate, and interlocutor over the past decade. I am immensely grateful for his generosity, more times than I can count, and his intellectual example. Alan Stahl was a lovely part-time boss and the source for many of the images in this book. Dirk Hartog not only introduced me to Christine Desan but also to the legal history that forms the backbone of this work.

Chris McKenna, Rowena Olegario, and Charles Wilson made it possible for me to be the first Career Development Fellow in the Global

History of Capitalism at Brasenose College, Oxford. That fellowship, in turn, allowed me to work with incredible colleagues, collaborators, and friends, including Peter Hill, Juan Neves-Sarriegui, Sonia Tycko, Joanna Innes, Joseph la Hausse de Lalouvière, Arnaud Petit, Gillian Hamnett, Simon Shogry, Dan Luban, Bill Wood, the late Aaron Graham, Eduardo Posada-Carbó, Damian Clavel, Robert Iliffe, Silvia Elsner, the unstoppable Horns of Plenty, the Henry Road mafia, Joe Davies, and many, many others. I am forever in their debt.

Academia would never be worth it without the comrades we make along the way. Emily Kern, Merle Eisenberg, Joel Suarez, Sean Vanatta, and Heath Pearson remain my dearest friends and, along with Mariel, proved to be the most insightful readers of this manuscript. Christian Flow, Matthew Chan, Robyn Radway, Margarita Fajardo, Paula Vedoveli, Morgan Robinson, Wangui Muigai, Aaron Stamper, and so many others made our time in New Jersey wonderfully memorable.

The world of early American monetary history has also left me with more debts than I can adequately repay here. Ann Daly, Katie Moore, Jeffrey Sklansky, Simon Middleton, Mara Caden, Farley Grubb, and Chris Desan especially have all had a huge impact on my academic life and thought. Farley was generous from the start and remains a beacon of intellectual integrity. Chris's generosity in debate and critical camaraderie has been one of the great treasures of my intellectual life. Of the many things they taught me, the most rewarding was to learn that I was not alone.

Most of this book was written with support from the New School for Social Research's Currency and Empire - Monetary Policy, Race, and Power Seminar and the University of St Andrews. I would like to thank all my colleagues for St Andrews' generous teaching leave for new staff, and especially Bridget Heal for bringing me north. The philosopher Quentin Pharr was my first reader. All of my students at Oxford, Princeton, and St Andrews have made crucial contributions to my thinking on the American past. I would like to especially thank Kevin Lee for helping to prepare the manuscript and the members of my seminar on the Global History of Money, 2024–25, for their insights. Anna Vrountas and William Finlator proved, in effect, indispensable. They are the reasons I love to do this work. I would also like to thank all the librarians and archivists at Firestone, the NYPL, Butler, Kew, the Bodleian, St Andrews, the Library Company, NYHS, Mystic Seaport, the Library of Congress, Archives du Ministère des affaires étrangères, and state archives and historical societies of assistance. Georgia, North Carolina, Virginia, Maine, Massachusetts, New Jersey, New York, and Pennsylvania for keeping knowledge of the past alive in an increasingly hostile world. No new understanding of the past would be possible without their dedication.

At PUP, I would like to thank Rob Tempio for his couches (still kicking), his Oxford flat, and for introducing me to the press. Eric Crahan was wonderful enough to buy this book. Priya Nelson did brilliant and empathetic work driving it through the review process. Also, she is a bit of seer. Daniel Simon did a heroic and beautiful job copyediting the manuscript, and the entire team has been a pleasure to work with throughout a long, hard bit of work. Thank you all.

Finally, I must thank Daniel and Augusta for allowing me to type these words on a Saturday morning, despite the loss of a wee dagger pin we bought in the shops, my brothers Charles and Sam, for their constant encouragement, and my mother, Julie, and her wonderful husband, Don, for their patience and support. Charles read an early draft and provided crucial comments, as did Erica Nelson, my oldest friend in the world. Bill and Betsy Kessel were the best in-laws ever, throughout, and Nick Paskert provided critical pine-related support. Sam listened to an early version of this argument in the canyons of Marin County and helped me to imagine what it might become. I am eternally grateful.

Introduction

1. Robert Darnton, *The Great Cat Massacre and Other Episodes in French Cultural History* (New York: Vintage Books, 1985), 5.

2. John Russell Bartlett, ed., *Records of the Colony of Rhode Island and Providence Plantations in New England* (New York: AMS Press, 1968), 8:458–477. The best books on taxation in early America are: Robin Einhorn, *American Taxation, American Slavery* (Chicago: University of Chicago Press, 2006); Alvin Rabushka, *Taxation in Colonial America* (Princeton: Princeton University Press, 2008); Katie A. Moore, *Promise to Pay: The Politics and Power of Money in Early America* (Chicago: University of Chicago Press, 2024).

3. Susan Carter et al., eds., *Historical Statistics of the United States Millennium Edition Online* (New York: Cambridge University Press, 2006), tables 302–314; Farley Grubb, "The Circulating Medium of Exchange in Colonial Pennsylvania, 1729–1775: New Estimates of Monetary Composition, Performance, and Economic Growth," *Explorations in Economic History* 41, no. 4 (2004): 329–360.

4. Writs 1764, Box III, Folder 2, Pownalborough Court House Collection (Maine Historical Society, Portland ME). The bills are "IOUs," of course, if the "I" in question is the citizenry and not the government. But without that recognition the error quickly compounds. The confusion can lead to misreading the colonial monetary record as one of repeated bad faith, where colonies seem to promise to exchange bills for "specie" only to repeatedly renege. It also leads to the mistaken view that colonists used paper money "in lieu of taxes," when bills of credit's legal existence was predicated on the power to tax. Mihm's entry on colonial finance in the *Oxford Handbook of the American Revolution* is a particularly regrettable example. Mihm repeatedly asserts that colonial taxes and other payments were meant to be "in specie," when those payments were designed to be paid in paper currency—hence all the burning. Congress's promise to redeem all the bills in silver dollars came after the continental dollar had been all but abandoned and was never implemented. Stephen Mihm, "Funding the Revolution: Military and Fiscal Policy in Eighteenth-Century America," in *The Oxford Handbook of the American Revolution*, ed. Jane Kamensky and Edward Gray, 327–351, esp. 329, 332–333 (New York: Oxford University Press, 2013); Farley Grubb, *The Continental Dollar: How the American Revolution Was Financed with Paper Money* (Chicago: University of Chicago Press, 2023), 208–224.

5. For example, see New York's fortification issue in 1743 and Pennsylvania's lighthouse, loan-office, and jail building issues from 1773 to 1775 in Eric Newman, *The Early Paper Money of America*, 5th ed. (Iola, WI: Krause, 2008), 279, 348–350. On taxes as the driving force in colonial money and, arguably, all money, see Christine Desan, *Making Money: Coins, Currency and the Coming of Capitalism* (Oxford: Oxford University Press, 2014); Christine Desan, "From Blood to Profit: Making Money in the Practice and Imagery of Early America," *Journal of Policy History* 20,

no. 1 (2008): 26–46. The work of economic historian Farley Grubb is indispensable for understanding bills of credit as an economic institution. See especially Grubb, *The Continental Dollar*; Farley Grubb, "Colonial Virginia's Paper Money, 1755–1774: Value Decomposition and Performance," *Financial History Review* 25, no. 2 (2018): 113–140. Moore's Promise to Pay is indispensable. The classic works of E. James Ferguson, Leslie Brock, and John McCusker are also valuable sources: E. James Ferguson, "Currency Finance: An Interpretation of Colonial Monetary Practices," *William and Mary Quarterly* 10, no. 2 (1953): 154–180; Leslie Brock, *The Currency of the American Colonies, 1700–1764: A Study in Colonial Finance and Imperial Relations* (New York: Arno Press, 1975); John McCusker, *Money and Exchange in Europe and America, 1600–1775* (Chapel Hill: University of North Carolina Press, 1992).

6. Christine Desan, "The Constitutional Approach to Money: Monetary Design and the Production of the Modern World," in *Money Talks: Essays in Honor of Viviana Zelizer*, ed. Nina Bandelj and Fred Wherry (Princeton: Princeton University Press, 2017); Rebecca Spang, "The Currency of History: Money and the Idea of Progress," *World Policy Journal* 33, no. 3 (2016): 39–44, esp. 41. The works touching on the cultural, political, and economic importance of early American money are too numerous to list in full, but indispensable contributions over the last six decades include: Katherine Smoak, "The Weight of Necessity: Counterfeit Coins in the British Atlantic World, circa 1760–1800," *William and Mary Quarterly* 74, no. 3 (2017); Claire Priest, *Credit Nation: Property Laws and Institutions in Early America* (Princeton: Princeton University Press, 2022); Jeffrey Sklansky, *Sovereign of the Market: The Money Question in Early America* (Chicago: University of Chicago Press, 2017); K-Sue Park, "Money, Mortgages, and the Conquest of America," *Law & Social Inquiry* 41 (2016): 1006–1035; Ellen Hartigan-O'Connor, *The Ties That Buy: Women and Commerce in Revolutionary America* (Philadelphia: University of Pennsylvania Press, 2009); Terry Bouton, *Taming Democracy: "The People," the Founders, and the Troubling End of the American Revolution* (New York: Oxford University Press, 2007); Margaret Newell, *From Dependency to Independence: Economic Revolution in Colonial New England* (Ithaca: Cornell University Press, 1998); Joseph Ernst, *Money and Politics in America, 1755–1775: A Study in the Currency Act of 1764 and the Political Economy of Revolution* (Chapel Hill: University of North Carolina Press, 1973).

7. Mary Douglass, *Purity and Danger: An Analysis of Concepts of Pollution and Taboo* (London: Routledge, 2001), 70. London anticapitalist activists make this point explicitly at their semiannual "Church of Burn." The group, which gathers in a pub, charging a sliding admission fee that ends up on the pyre, seeks to recast participants' relationship to civilization itself by burning money in order "to transgress its logic" through a "powerful sacrament" that is "both symbolic and real." "Church of Burn," *Finance and Society Network*, http://financeandsocietynetwork.org/church-of-burn-2020 [accessed April 25, 2024].

8. Farley Grubb, "Chronic Specie Scarcity and Efficient Barter: The Problem of Maintaining an Outside Money Supply in British Colonial America," *National Bureau of Economic Research Working Paper Series* (2012), www.nber.org/papers/w18099; Michael Merrill, "Cash Is Good to Eat: Self-Sufficiency and Exchange in the Rural Economy of the United States," *Radical History Review* 13 (1977): 42–71.

9. The literature on the American "transition to capitalism" is vast. Start with: Melvyn Stokes and Stephen Conway, eds., *The Market Revolution in America:*

Social, Political and Religious Expressions, 1800–1880 (Charlottesville: University of Virginia Press, 1996); Charles Sellers, *The Market Revolution: Jacksonian America, 1815–1846* (New York: Oxford University Press, 1994); Gordon Wood, *The Radicalism of the American Revolution* (New York: Vintage, 1993); Winifred Rothenberg, *From Market-Places to a Market Economy: The Transformation of Rural Massachusetts, 1750–1850* (Chicago: University of Chicago Press, 1992); James Henretta, *The Origins of American Capitalism: Collected Essays* (Boston: Northeastern University Press, 1991); Christopher Clark, *The Roots of Rural Capitalism: Western Massachusetts, 1780–1860* (Cambridge: Harvard University Press, 2001); Joyce Appleby, *Capitalism and a New Social Order: The Republican Vision of the 1790's* (New York: NYU Press, 1984).

10. On the significance of *The Stamp Act Crisis* and Bailyn's *Ideological Origins* (see below) to twentieth-century American historiography, see Jack Rakove, "Rebel Without a Cause—A Narrow Approach to the American Revolution," *New Republic* (Nov. 30, 2012). Edmund Morgan and Helen Morgan, *The Stamp Act Crisis: Prologue to Revolution* (Chapel Hill: University of North Carolina Press, 1953), esp. 73.

11. Bernard Bailyn, *The Ideological Origins of the American Revolution* (Cambridge, MA: Belknap Press, 1992 [1967]), esp. 94–95.

12. Daniel Rodgers, "Republicanism: The Career of a Concept," *Journal of American History* 79, no. 1 (1992): 11–38, esp. 21–22; Jack Rakove, "Got Nexus?" *William and Mary Quarterly* 68, no. 4 (2011): 635–638; Woody Holton, *Forced Founders: Indians, Debtors, Slaves, and the Making of the American Revolution in Virginia* (Chapel Hill: UNC Press Books, 1999); Gary Nash, *The Unknown American Revolution: The Unruly Birth of Democracy and the Struggle to Create America* (New York: Viking, 2005); Marjoleine Kars, *Breaking Loose Together: The Regulator Rebellion in Pre-Revolutionary North Carolina* (Chapel Hill: University of North Carolina Press, 2002); T. H. Breen, *The Marketplace of Revolution: How Consumer Politics Shaped American Independence* (Oxford: Oxford University Press, 2004); Michael McDonnell, *The Politics of War: Race, Class, and Conflict in Revolutionary Virginia* (Chapel Hill: University of North Carolina Press, 2010).

13. Rodgers, "Republicanism," 22, 34; Jack P. Greene, *The Constitutional Origins of the American Revolution* (Cambridge: Cambridge University Press, 2010), xvi; Patrick Spero, "A Negotiated Revolution," *Reviews in American History* 41, no. 1 (2013): 31–38; Spero and Michael Zuckerman, eds., *The American Revolution Reborn* (Philadelphia: University of Pennsylvania Press, 2016).

14. John Hancock to Barnard and Harrison, August 8, 1765, Hancock Family Papers, Volume JH-6 (Baker Library Historical Collections, Harvard Business School); John Adams, "Original Draft: Instructions to the Representative of Braintree against the Stamp Act 1765," Sept. 24, 1765, in *The Adams Papers Digital Edition* (Charlottesville, VA: Rotunda, 2021), http://rotunda.upress.virginia.edu/founders /ADMS-06-01-02-0054-0002 [accessed Oct. 26, 2012]; *Journal of the First Congress of the American Colonies in Opposition to the Tyrannical Acts of the British Parliament Held at New York, Oct. 7, 1765* (New York: E. Winchester, 1845), 29. This is a tiny sampling of what, as we shall see, was a ubiquitous theme. For a fuller accounting, read on to chapter 4 or see Andrew David Edwards, "Grenville's Silver Hammer: The Problem of Money in the Stamp Act Crisis," *Journal of American History* 104, no. 2 (2017): 337–362.

15. Robert Thomas, "A Quantitative Approach to the Study of the Effects of British Imperial Policy upon Colonial Welfare: Some Preliminary Findings," *Journal of Economic History* 25, no. 4 (1965): 615–638; Edwin Perkins, *The Economy of Colonial America* (New York: Columbia University Press, 1988), 199–200; Robert Middlekauff, *The Glorious Cause: The American Revolution, 1763–1789* (New York: Oxford University Press, 1982); T. H. Breen, "Ideology and Nationalism on the Eve of the American Revolution: Revisions Once More in Need of Revising," *Journal of American History* 84, no. 1 (1997): 13–39, esp. 31; Bernard Bailyn, "The Central Themes of the American Revolution: An Interpretation," in *Essays on the American Revolution*, ed. Stephen G. Kurtz and James H. Hutson, 3–31, (Chapel Hill: University of North Carolina Press, 1973), esp. 12–13.

16. Thomas Paine, *The American Crisis* (London: R. Carlisle, 1819), 137; *Journal of the First Congress*, 29; Charles Chauncy, *A Discourse on "The Good News from a Far Country"* (Boston: Kneeland and Adams, 1766), 13; Newton Dennison Mereness, ed., *Travels in the American Colonies* (New York: MacMillan, 1916), 405.

17. The language in question is usually borrowed from economics: Farley Grubb, *The Continental Dollar: How the American Revolution Was Financed with Paper Money* (Chicago: University of Chicago Press, 2023); Dror Goldberg, *Easy Money: American Puritans and the Invention of Modern Currency* (Chicago: University of Chicago Press, 2023).

18. Lawrence Stone, "The Revival of Narrative: Reflections on a New Old History," *Past & Present*, no. 85 (1979): 3–24, esp. 3. On a previous attempt to revive narrative history, see James West Davidson, "The New Narrative History: How New? How Narrative?" *Reviews in American History* 12, no. 3 (1984): 322–334.

19. Foundational works in this emergent field include: Desan, *Making Money*; Rebecca Spang, *Stuff and Money in the Time of the French Revolution* (Cambridge: Harvard University Press, 2015); Stefan Eich, *The Currency of Politics: The Political Theory of Money from Aristotle to Keynes* (Princeton: Princeton University Press, 2022); Sklansky, *Sovereign of the Market*; Stephen Mihm, *A Nation of Counterfeiters: Capitalists, Con Men, and the Making of the United States* (Cambridge: Harvard University Press, 2007).

20. "Whence arose the illusions of the monetary system? To it gold and silver, when serving as money, did not represent a social relation between producers, but were natural objects with strange social properties." Karl Marx, *Capital: A Critique of Political Economy*, trans. Samuel Moore and Edward Aveling (New York: Modern Library, 1906), 94–95.

21. Lindsay Schakenbach-Regele, "A Brief History of the History of Capitalism, and a New American Variety," *Enterprise & Society* 25, no. 1 (2024): 2–26.

22. Sebastian Conrad, *What Is Global History?* (Princeton: Princeton University Press, 2016).

23. What I mean here is analogous to what Adelman refers to as a "global regime" and Arrighi calls the "Modern Interstate System," both in reference to Wallerstein's notion of a modern "world-system." Jeremy Adelman, "Mimesis and Rivalry: European Empires and Global Regimes," *Journal of Global History* 10, no. 1 (2015): 77–98; Giovanni Arrighi, *The Long Twentieth Century: Money, Power, and the*

Origins of Our Times (London: Verso, 1994), 37; Immanuel Wallerstein, *The Modern World System* (New York: Academic Press, 1974).

24. Nancy Fraser, "Behind Marx's Hidden Abode," *New Left Review* 86 (2014): 55–72; Douglass North, *Institutions, Institutional Change and Economic Performance* (Cambridge: Cambridge University Press, 1999), 3.

25. It would be disingenuous to say that this book is a "global history" of the American Revolution. It is, however, a history of the American Revolution written from a global perspective, in Conrad's sense that it "takes the interconnected world as its point of departure, and the circulation of things, people, ideas, and institutions" as its key subjects. Conrad, *What Is Global History*, 5; Arrighi, *Long Twentieth Century*, 52.

26. Abraham Lincoln to Henry L. Pierce and others, April 6, 1859, in *The Collected Works of Abraham Lincoln*, ed. Roy P. Basler, 3:375 (New Brunswick, NJ: Rutgers University Press, 1953).

27. Thomas Piketty, *Capital in the Twenty-First Century* (Cambridge: Harvard University Press, 2014); Ellen Meiksins Wood, *Democracy against Capitalism: Renewing Historical Materialism* (Cambridge: Cambridge University Press, 1995).

Chapter One

1. Samuel Green, ed., *Two Narratives of the Expedition Against Quebec A.D. 1690, under Sir William Phips* (Cambridge: J. Wilson, 1902), 10–16, esp. 16; Emerson W. Baker and John G. Reid, *The New England Knight: Sir William Phips, 1651–1695* (Toronto: University of Toronto Press, 1998), 99.

2. Some accounts give the number of ships as thirty-four, but Phips's log lists only thirty-two. Green, *Two Narratives*, 29–31.

3. Cotton Mather, *Magnalia Christi Americana* (London: Thomas Parkhurst, 1702), 2:51–53.

4. *Calendar of State Papers, Colonial Series, America and West Indies, 1689–1692, Volume XIII* (London: Longmans, 1860-), 369, 376–377; K. A. J. McLay, "Wellsprings of a 'World War': An Early English Attempt to Conquer Canada during King William's War, 1688–97," *Journal of Imperial and Commonwealth History* 34, no. 2 (June 2006): 155–175; Robert Earle Moody and R. C. Simmons, *The Glorious Revolution in Massachusetts: Selected Documents, 1689–1692* (Boston: Colonial Society of Massachusetts, 1988), 300. Before 1751, the English new year officially began on March 25, placing January in 1690 under the Old Style. For clarity, I have opted to use the reformed calendar throughout and translate seventeenth-century dates accordingly.

5. "Journal of Dr. Benjamin Bullivant," *Proceedings of the Massachusetts Historical Society* 16 (1878): 104–105. Wohawa is also referred to as Hope-Hood, Hoope Whood, and Wayhamoo, among other variations, by seventeenth-century colonial writers. Franklin B. Dexter, "Influence of the English Universities in the Development of New England," *Proceedings of the Massachusetts Historical Society* 17 (1879–1880), 352, 355; Harald E. L. Prins, "Chief Rawandagon, Alias Robin Hood: Native 'Lord of Misrule' in the Maine Wilderness," in *Northeastern Indian Lives, 1632–1816*, ed. Robert Steven Grumet, 113 (Amherst: University of Massachusetts Press, 1996).

6. *State Papers, Colonial Series, 1689–92*, 377, 263–264; "Journal of Dr. Benjamin Bullivant," 104.

7. Craig Muldrew, *The Economy of Obligation: The Culture of Credit and Social Relations in Early Modern England* (New York: Macmillan, 1998); Peter Laslett, *The World We Have Lost: Further Explored* (London: Routledge, 2000); Wendy Warren, *New England Bound: Slavery and Colonization in Early America* (New York: Norton, 2016); Aaron Fogelman, "From Slaves, Convicts, and Servants to Free Passengers: The Transformation of Immigration in the Era of the American Revolution," *Journal of American History* 85, no. 1 (June 1998): 43–76.

8. Akinobu Kuroda, "Anonymous Currencies or Named Debts? Comparison of Currencies, Local Credit, and Units of Account between China, Japan and England in the Pre-Industrial Era," *Socio-Economic Review* 11, no. 1 (2013): 57–80; Michael Merrill, "Cash Is Good to Eat: Self-Sufficiency and Exchange in the Rural Economy of the United States," *Radical History Review* 13 (1977): 42–71; Jane Guyer, *Marginal Gains: Monetary Transactions in Atlantic Africa* (Chicago: University of Chicago Press, 2004); Daniel Richter, *Ordeal of the Longhouse: The Peoples of the Iroquois League in the Era of European Colonization* (Chapel Hill: University of North Carolina Press, 1992), 84–87; George S. Snyderman, "The Functions of Wampum," *Proceedings of the American Philosophical Society* 98, no. 6 (1954): 464–494. On the variety of non-European exchange generally, see David Graeber, *Debt: The First 5,000 Years* (New York: Melville House, 2012).

9. Craig Muldrew, *The Economy of Obligation: The Culture of Credit and Social Relations in Early Modern England* (New York: St. Martin's Press, 1998). Specific examples drawn from Joseph Olden, Accompt Book, MSS Co199 no. 773 (Rare Books and Special Collections, Princeton University, Princeton, N.J.), 49; Jeremiah Tinney, "Jeremiah and Ebenezer Tinney Account Book" (Mystic Seaport Collections Resource Center, Mystic CT).

10. John Winthrop, *The History of New England from 1630 to 1649*, ed. James Savage, 2:7 (Boston: Phelps and Farnham, 1825). Park shows how colonists mobilized this innovation: the ability to seize land for debt as a pretextual legal means to dispossess Native Americans from their land. Park, "Money, Mortgages, and the Conquest of America," 1006–1035.

11. Winthrop, *History*, 2:7; Nathaniel B. Shurtleff, ed., *Records of the Governor and Company of the Massachusetts Bay in New England* (Boston: W. White, 1853), 1:302. Massachusetts first set a value on wampum in November 1637. In the 1637 act, the white shell beads were valued at 6 per penny for debts less than 12 pence, or 1 shilling. The 1640 act revalued white wampum to 4 a penny and set the value for blue at 2 a penny, but still only for debts of less than 1 shilling. In June 1641 the colony reset the value for all beads at 6 a penny and stopped accepting them in tax payments in 1649. In 1661 the colony repealed wampum's official valuation for small debts altogether, ending the experiment. Ibid., 1:208, 302, 329, 2:279, 4:4. Several colonies found it difficult to keep good shells in circulation, as they were typically most valuable in the trade with Native Americans. In 1652, for example, residents of New Haven complained that "little but refuse wampum" were traded in the town. Curtis P. Nettels, *Money Supply of the American Colonies* (New York: A. M. Kelley, 1964), 212.

12. Winthrop, *History*, 2:219. On the seventeenth-century English household economy, see Laslett, *The World We Have Lost*; Craig Muldrew, "'Hard Food for Midas': Cash and Its Social Value in Early Modern England," *Past & Present* 170 (Feb. 2001): 78–120; Estelle Stewart, *History of Wages in the United States from Colonial Times to 1928* (Washington, D.C.: U.S. Government Printing Office, 1934), 13. For examples of colonial thought on the importance of maintaining class hierarchy, see Joseph Dorfman, *The Economic Mind in American Civilization* (New York: A. M. Kelley, 1966), 1:25–45.

13. Stewart, *History*, 15–16.

14. John Cotton, "Gods Praise to His Plantations" (1630), in *University of Nebraska–Lincoln, Electronic Texts in American Studies*, ed. Reiner Smolinski, http://digitalcommons.unl.edu/cgi/viewcontent.cgi?article=1022&context=etas [accessed January 9, 2018].

15. William Wood, *New England's Prospect* (London: John Dawson, 1639); Alison Games, *Migration and the Origins of the English Atlantic* (Cambridge: Harvard University Press, 1999), 103.

16. Wood, *New England's Prospect*, 41–42, 46. I have modernized Wood's idiosyncratic spelling for the reader's ease.

17. Thomas Hinkley to William Blathwatt, June 28, 1687, in *Collections of the Massachusetts Historical Society*, ser. 4, vol. 5 (Boston: The Society, 1861), 155; T. H. Breen, *Puritans and Adventurers: Change and Persistence in Early America* (New York: Oxford University Press, 1980), 88–89; Einhorn, *American Taxation, American Slavery*, 66–70.

18. To be clear, the poll tax portion of each rate was 20 pence, so six rates would equal 120 pence. Each shilling contained 12 pence, so at 5 shillings, 6 pence per bushel, each bushel of wheat was good for 66 pence in taxes. Two bushels, then, would fetch 132 pence, covering the poll tax portion of six rates with 12 pence left over. Moody & Simmons, *Glorious Revolution*, 172–173.

19. "Journal of Dr. Benjamin Bullivant," 106; Breen, *Puritans*, 89. On the mint, see Louis Jordan, *John Hull: The Mint and Economics of Massachusetts Coinage* (London: University Press of New England, 2002), esp. 45; Mara Caden, *Mint Conditions: The Politics and Geography of Money in Britain and Its Empire, 1650–1730* (PhD diss., Yale University, 2017).

20. J. P. Baxter, ed., *Documentary History of the State of Maine* (Portland, ME: Baily and Noyes, 1897), 5:9, 50, 27, spelling modernized; Richard R. Johnson, *John Nelson, Merchant Adventurer: A Life between Empires* (London: Oxford University Press, 1991), 59; McLay, "Wellsprings," 161.

21. Baxter, *Documentary History*, 5:132; Baker and Reid, *New England Knight*, 104–105.

22. *State Papers, Colonial Series, 1689–92*, 377.

23. Mather, *Magnalia*, 2:51. On the significance of American paper money, see Christine Desan, "Monetary Design and the Creation of the Modern World," in *Money Talks*, ed. Bandelj and Wherry, 110–126; Dror Goldberg, "The Massachusetts Paper Money of 1690," *Journal of Economic History* 69, no. 4 (Dec. 2009): 1092–1106; E. James Ferguson, "Currency Finance: An Interpretation of Colonial Monetary Practices," *William & Mary Quarterly* 10, no. 2 (April 1953): 154–180.

24. John Gillies, trans., *Aristotle's Ethics and Politics* (London: A. Strahan and T. Caddell, 1797), 270; John Law, *Money and Trade Considered* (Glasgow: R. & A. Foulis, 1750), 6. Samuel von Pufendorf, writing in the mid-seventeenth century, seems to credit the idea of money as "the Common Measure of the Value of other things" to Michael of Ephesus, a prominent medieval commentator on Aristotle. Samuel von Pufendorf, *Of the Law of Nature and Nations*, trans. Basel Kennett (London: J. Walthoe et al., 1729), 469. On the many precedents for bills of credit, see Goldberg, *Easy Money*, 38–131.

25. Gillies, trans., *Aristotle's Ethics and Politics*, 270; Andrew Fitzmaurice, *Humanism and America: An Intellectual History of English Colonisation, 1500–1625* (Cambridge: Cambridge University Press, 2009); Quentin Skinner, *Reason and Rhetoric in the Philosophy of Hobbes* (Cambridge: Cambridge University Press, 1996), 22; Thomas More, *Utopia*, trans. Clarence H. Miller (New Haven: Yale University Press, 2014), 132, 134.

26. See, e.g., Carl Wennerlind, *Casualties of Credit* (Cambridge: Harvard University Press, 2011), 10–17; Mary Poovey, *A History of the Modern Fact: Problems of Knowledge in the Sciences of Wealth and Society* (Chicago: University of Chicago Press, 1998); William Derringer, *Calculated Values* (Cambridge: Harvard University Press, 2018); Desan, *Making Money.*

27. Moore, "The Blood That Nourishes the Body Politic," esp. 6–15; G. H. Turnbull, "Some Correspondence of John Winthrop, Jr., and Samuel Hartlib," *Proceedings of the Massachusetts Historical Society*, 3rd ser., vol. 72 (Oct. 1957–Dec. 1960), 36–67; John Winthrop Jr. to Samuel Hartlib (May 10, 1661), *The Hartlib Papers*, 32/1/10A–11B, www.dhi.ac.uk/hartlib/view?docset=main&docname=32A_01_10&term0=title_winthrop [accessed May 7, 2019]. On the significance of alchemy to seventeenth-century economic thought, see Wennerlind, *Casualties of Credit*. On American experiments with alchemy, see Walter Woodward, *Prospero's America: John Winthrop, Jr., Alchemy, and the Creation of New England Culture, 1606–1676* (Chapel Hill: UNC Press Books, 2011).

28. J. Hammond Trumbull, in *Proceedings of the American Antiquarian Society, New Series, Vol. III, October, 1883–April, 1885* (Worcester, MA: American Antiquarian Society, 1885), 270–275; Robert Charles Winthrop, ed., *Correspondence of Hartlib, Haak, Oldenburg & Others of the Founders of the Royal Society with Gov. Winthrop of Connecticut, 1661–1672* (Boston: John Wilson, 1878), 4, 17–18; Dorfman, *Economic Mind*, 1:93.

29. Dorfman, *Economic Mind*, 1:105; W. F. L. Nuttall, "Governor John Blackwell: His Life in England and Ireland," *Pennsylvania Magazine of History and Biography* 88, no. 2 (1964): 121–141.

30. On the date of Blackwell's return, see "Journal of Dr. Benjamin Bullivant," 107.

31. Nuttall, "Governor John Blackwell," 124–129.

32. John Towill Rutt, ed., *Diary of Thomas Burton, Esq.* (London: Henry Colburn, 1828),1:244, 2:102; Nuttall, "Governor John Blackwell," 129–135; J. Keith Horsefield, "The Origins of Blackwell's Model of a Bank," *William & Mary Quarterly* 23, no. 1 (1966): 135; David Farr, "Notes and Documents: John Blackwell and Daniel Cox: Further Notes on Their Activities in Restoration England and British North America," *Pennsylvania Magazine of History and Biography* 123, no. 3 (July 1999): 227–233.

33. Nicholas B. Wainwright, "Governor John Blackwell," *Pennsylvania Magazine of History and Biography* 74 (Oct. 1950): 457–472; James Hammond Trumbull, ed., *The Public Records of the Colony of Connecticut, May, 1678–June, 1689* (Hartford: Case, 1859), 246–247; John Frederick Martin, *Profits in the Wilderness: Entrepreneurship and the Founding of New England* (Chapel Hill: University of North Carolina Press, 2014), 93–94. According to Martin, Blackwell was involved in as many as four land ventures in his first three years in the colony. On Blackwell's financial career in London, see Horsefield, "Origins," 121–135; Viola Florence Barnes, *The Dominion of New England: A Study in British Colonial Policy* (New Haven: Yale University Press, 1923), 23.

34. "Dudley Records," *Proceedings of the Massachusetts Historical Society* (Nov. 1899), 248.

35. Trumbull, *Proceedings*, 277.

36. Moore, "Blood," McLay, "Wellsprings," 160–161; Wainwright, "Governor John Blackwell," 457–472. On Blackwell's 1686 bank, see John T. Hassam, "Bahama Islands: Notes on an Early Attempt at Colonization," *Proceedings of the Massachusetts Historical Society* 13 (March 1899): 24–25.

37. Andrew McFarland Davis, ed., *Colonial Currency Reprints, 1682–1751* (Boston: John Wilson & Son, 1910), 1:109, 118.

38. John Winthrop Jr. to Samuel Hartlib (May 10, 1661), *The Hartlib Papers*, 32/1/10A–11B, www.dhi.ac.uk/hartlib/view?docset=main&docname=32A_01 _10&term0=title_winthrop [accessed May 7, 2019]. On women's centrality in colonial households, see Laura Thatcher Ulrich, *Good Wives: Image and Reality in the Lives of Women in Northern New England, 1650–1750* (New York: Oxford University Presse, 1982); Jeanne Boydston, "Gender as a Question of Historical Analysis," *Gender & History* 20, no. 3 (2008): 558–583.

39. Park, "Money, Mortgages, and the Conquest of America,"; Jill Lepore, *The Name of War: King Phillip's War and the Origins of American Identity* (New York: Alfred A. Knopf, 1998), xi–xiii. On the idea that Native American warfare made it difficult to establish banks based on the value of land, see Dror Goldberg, "Why Was America's First Bank Aborted?" *Journal of Economic History* 71, no. 1 (March 2011): 211–222; Moore, "Blood,"; esp. 18; Goldberg, "Massachusetts Paper Money," 1096.

40. On the problem of colonial land tenure after the Restoration, see Viola Florence Barnes, *The Dominion of New England: A Study in British Colonial Policy* (New Haven: Yale University Press, 1923), 176–193; "Diary of Samuel Sewall," in *Collections of the Massachusetts Historical Society*, ser. 5, vol. 5 (Boston: Massachusetts Historical Society, 1878), 251–252; Moody and Simmons, *Glorious Revolution*, 287–288.

41. On household credit in colonial America, see Andrew David Edwards, *Money and the American Revolution* (PhD diss., Princeton University, 2018), esp. chapter 1; Farley Grubb, "Chronic Specie Scarcity and Efficient Barter," *National Bureau of Economic Research*, Working Paper 18099 (2012), www.nber.org/papers/w18099; Merrill, "Cash Is Good to Eat."

42. William Petty, *A Treatise of Taxes and Contributions* (London: Nathaniel Brooke, 1662), 17.

43. Petty, *Treatise*, 25; Poovey, *A History of the Modern Fact*, 4, 25–26, 129; Eli Cook, *The Pricing of Progress: Economic Indicators and the Capitalization of*

American Life (Cambridge: Harvard University Press, 2017), 29; Thomas Askew Larcom, *The History of the Survey of Ireland: Commonly Called the Down Survey, A.D., 1655-6* (Dublin: Irish Archeological Society, 1851), 158, 160. On Petty's influence in Britain's North American colonies, see Mark Valeri, *Heavenly Merchandize: How Religion Shaped Commerce in Puritan America* (Princeton: Princeton University Press, 2010), 134.

44. Poovey, *A History of the Modern Fact*, 73; Desan, *Making Money*, 20, 170; Luigi Einaudi, "The Theory of Imaginary Money," in *Luigi Einaudi: Selected Economic Writings*, ed. Riccardo Faucci and Roberto Marchionatti, 153–181 (New York: Palgrave Macmillan, 2006); Marie-Thérèse Boyer-Xambeu, Ghislain Deleplace, Lucian Gillard, *Private Money and Public Currencies: The Sixteenth Century Challenge*, trans. Azizeh Azodi (Armonk, NY: M. E. Sharpe, 1994); Aaron Graham, *Corruption, Party, and Government in Britain, 1702-1713* (Oxford: Oxford University Press, 2015), 53–56.

45. The best account of these competing bank plans, including Blackwell's, is still John Keith Horsefield, *British Monetary Experiments, 1650-1710* (London: London School of Economics, 1960). On the origins of Blackwell's plan in London financial projects, see John Keith Horsefield, "The Origins of Blackwell's Mode of a Bank," *William & Mary Quarterly* 23, no. 1 (1966): 121–135. On the intellectual origins of the bank, see Desan, *Making Money*; Wennerlind, *Casualties of Credit*; and especially Peter Dickson, *The Financial Revolution in England: A Study in the Development of Public Credit, 1688-1756* (New York: Macmillan, 1967).

46. *Calendar of State Papers, Colonial Series*, 13:287.

47. Moody and Simmons, *Glorious Revolution*, 182–183.

48. Moody and Simmons, *Glorious Revolution*, 290–291; Lawrence W. Kennedy, *Planning the City on a Hill: Boston Since 1630* (Amherst: UMass Press, 1992), 255.

49. On the importance of present-value calculations (the value now of an amount of money paid at some time in the future at a given rate of interest), see William Deringer, *Calculated Values* (Cambridge: Harvard University Press, 2018); Farley Grubb, "A New Approach to Explaining the Value of Colonial Paper Money: Evidence from New Jersey, 1709–1775," *NBER Working Papers no. 19903* (2014). Grubb's work suggests that colonial merchants came to value bills of exchange using time-discounting techniques in the eighteenth century.

50. "Diary of Dr. Benjamin Bullivant," 106.

51. *Calendar of State Papers, Colonial Series*, 13:377.

52. *Calendar of State Papers, Colonial Series*, 13:377, 384; Mather, *Magnalia*, 2:52.

53. Moody and Simmons, *Glorious Revolution*, 296–297, 311–312.

54. Moody and Simmons, *Glorious Revolution*, 296–297, 311–312.

55. *Calendar of State Papers, Colonial Series*, 13:385.

56. The first letter has traditionally been attributed to Cotton Mather, largely because *Some Considerations* is dedicated to John Phillips, the colony's treasurer from 1689 to 1692 and Mather's father-in-law. Additionally, Mather had already shown some interest in economic affairs with his 1690 sermon "The Serviceable Man." The attribution pivots on the false assumption that no one save Mather was likely to

have had the same combination of interest and access to Phillips. And yet Phillips had served on the committee to rethink the colony's economic institutions in 1686 that Blackwell chaired. Blackwell certainly knew him and in the letter refers to him as a peer. Moreover, Blackwell's ideas about money had crystalized in those discussions, where the colony's statesmen had "assembled to observe, inquire, examine, debate, consult, and consider all and every matter" related to trade with the man who had been Cromwell's treasurer at war. It was precisely the ideas about money first expressed in Blackwell's model for a bank in 1687 that the author of *Some Considerations* elaborated on in 1691 to explain the bills of credit.

Textual clues, moreover, point to Blackwell rather than Mather as the author. About halfway through the letter, the author recalls the aftermath of the English Revolution and Cromwell's invasion of Ireland. "I remember many years since, there was such a prank [played] in England and Ireland after the War," the author wrote, referring to the financial aftermath of the English Civil War. Blackwell was in a position to have experienced it directly. In 1647, when the worst of the fighting in England was over, he had joined the rest of Cromwell's regiment in petitioning for long-overdue back pay and, later, had been involved in designing a more tightly managed system of payments for soldiers serving in the disastrous (for the Irish) Cromwellian invasion. "Some," the author continued, "bought up the Soldiers Debenters at very low Rates, and then with half Debenters and half Money purchased great Estates in Kings and Bishops Lands, (a fine Trade they made if it had held), but God shook his Lap at this dishonest and interloping gain; and a great unexpected Revolution, made them lose both their Lands and Money. Thus, the woman shook her Dog by the Collar, till she made him Disgorge again all her Puddings." This vivid passage is best understood as the recollection of a participant in the events described, with a practiced eye for the financial doings of the Commonwealth era. Blackwell, tellingly, was the dog in the story. His father had purchased large estates while Blackwell served as treasurer at war, issuing the very debentures described. A royalist Parliament had stripped the family's English estates in the Restoration of 1660, forcing them to "disgorge" their "interloping gain" and flee to Ireland. Mather was born in 1663, years after the events described. The first historian to attribute *Some Considerations* to Cotton Mather was J. Hammond Trumbull in the 1884 proceedings of the American Antiquarian Society. In addition to the Phillips connection, Trumbull cited Cotton Mather's praise for bills of credit in his 1702 history of New England, *Magnalia Christi Americana*. Charles Evans, in his landmark bibliography of American imprints, notes that the attribution to Mather was "solely on the authority of Trumbull," implying, correctly, that there was no reason beyond Trumbull's authority pointing to Mather's authorship. In his *Colonial Currency Reprints*, Andrew McFarland Davis also explicitly followed Trumbull, adding, without clear attribution, that Trumbull felt that the style of emphasis in the first half of the pamphlet closely matched Mather's in *Magnalia*. Perry Miller seems to have followed Evans while noting that it seemed strange that Mather could get through an entire pamphlet without mentioning "the sins of New England." Modern library catalogs followed Evans as well, to the point of excluding Blackwell's co-authorship. Virtually all subsequent authors follow either Evans or Davis. None, other than Davis, note Trumbull's internal inconsistency. Trumbull noted that *Some Additional Considerations* contains direct echoes from Blackwell's plan for a bank of credit, but only in the second half. However, Trumbull discounts, or failed to consider, at least two additional points. First, the definition of money in *Some Considerations*, "a *Counter* or *Measure* of Men's Properties," is a paraphrase of the definition in Blackwell's 1687 pamphlet. It is possible, of course, that Mather was influenced by Blackwell, or vice versa. As we will see, Mather's argument in *Magnalia* draws directly from Blackwell's 1691 analysis. But the analytical similarities between the first half and Blackwell's 1687 plan, and the distinctiveness of Blackwell's position, leave room, at least, to question the Mather attribution. Moreover, as we have already seen, we have direct evidence that Blackwell's ideas about money were developed while he was in an official working group charged with discussing economic ideas, discussions the author seems to reference directly on page 3. It is, of course, possible that Mather and Phillips also had discussions about the nature of money, but there is no direct evidence of it that I am aware of, and none cited by Trumbull. This leaves the second half, which, in the pamphlet itself, is attributed to "a Gentleman that had not seen the foregoing letter," ruling out Blackwell if we attribute the first half to him and take the pamphlet's publisher at their word. Likewise, the identification at the end of the pamphlet excludes authors born in New England, ruling out a Mather/Blackwell collaboration. However, it would not exclude one likely author, the only colonial writer to publish on monetary theory in the 1680s other than Blackwell: namely, John Woodbridge, who was alive and serving in government just north of Boston. In addition, unlike Blackwell, Woodbridge matches the self-description the author of the second letter gives in the text: "*one who counts and loves* New-England *as his country, tho he was not Born and Bred in it.*" Woodbridge was born in England but died in Massachusetts. Blackwell left that spring. Additionally, unlike the first half of the pamphlet, the second half does not mention Blackwell's theory of money but instead, like Woodbridge, argues for extending the currency (not money) supply by means of credit without intervening in the orthodox sense of what money was: gold and silver coin. Furthermore, Blackwell and Woodbridge were both Puritan veterans of the English Civil Wars, with similar interests in new ideas about money and its institutions in America. A Blackwell/Woodbridge collaboration, then, is more plausible than the current attribution to Mather and Blackwell. *Proceedings of the American Antiquarian Society, New Series, Vol. III, October, 1883–April, 1885* (Worcester, MA: American Antiquarian Society, 1885), 270; Charles Evans, *American Bibliography* (Chicago: Blakely Press, 1903), 1:91; Davis, *Colonial Currency Reprints*, 1:196, 206; Perry Miller, *The New England Mind* (Cambridge: Belknap Press, 1982), 162; Moody and Simmons, *Glorious Revolution*, 479–480; *Calendar of State Papers, Colonial Series*, 13:412–418; [John Blackwell and John Woodbridge, usually attributed to Cotton Mather and John Blackwell], *Some Additional Considerations on the Bills of Credit* (Boston: Benjamin Harris, John Allen, 1691); Nuttall, "Governor John Blackwell," 125–135.

57. Blackwell, *Some Considerations*, 3; Moody and Simmons, *Glorious Revolution*, 479–480; *Calendar of State Papers, Colonial Series*, 13:412–419.

58. Blackwell, *Some Considerations*, 1.

59. The description of the bills of credit as "IOUs" is ubiquitous in the literature on the 1690 moment. This overlooks the distinction contemporaries made between

the bills and actual IOUs, like the debentures they replaced. See, e.g., Desan, "Monetary Design and the Production of the Modern World," in *Money Talks*, 118; Goldberg, "The Massachusetts Paper: 1098; Moore, "Blood," 3, 26.

60. Blackwell, *Some Considerations*, 2.

61. Ibid., 3.

62. Ibid., 3.

63. Ibid., 5; Petty, *Treatise*, 17.

64. Blackwell, *Some Considerations*, 6, 11. Blackwell was right about the Canadians. In 1684 the French failed to send supplies of coin to Canada. In June 1685 the French intendant Demuelles, at wit's end, issued money made of playing cards cut in four and signed and sealed them himself. The cards, though, had a very different financial structure than bills of credit. They were promises for gold and silver that were paid off as soon as a new shipment of specie came from France. Herbert Heaton, "The Playing Card Currency of French Canada,"*American Economic Review* 18, no. 4 (1928): 649–662.

65. Mather, *Magnalia*, 2:51–52; Moore, "Blood," 35–37.

Chapter Two

1. Wennerlind, *Casualties of Credit*; Goldberg, *Easy Money*, 26–131.

2. There is some disagreement in the sources as to the actual date of Fauquier's birth. He was baptized on July 11, 1703, at St. Andrew's Undershaft and likely born in June. America's temporary money would not have been out of place in seventeenth-century Britain, a place awash in all sorts of monetary experiments and bold new plans for financial institutions rooted in alchemical, mystical, mercantilist, even religious ideas. Within half a century, the life of a single man or woman, that would change. One way to trace it, then, is to turn explicitly to the biography of the man whose life and interests would intersect with virtually every development of Britain's eighteenth-century financial revolution and its attempted extension to the colonies. G. Woods Wollaston, "The Family of Fauquier," in *Proceedings of the Huguenot Society of London, Volume 13* (London: Spottiswoode, Ballantyne, 1886), 340–356; Pickering, *Statutes at Large*, 9:380–381.

3. William Scott, *The Constitution and Finance of English, Scottish and Irish Joint-Stock Companies to 1720* (Cambridge: Cambridge University Press, 1910), 1:313, 326–327; Larry Neal, *The Rise of Financial Capitalism: International Capital Markets in the Age of Reason* (Cambridge: Cambridge University Press, 1990), 11–14, 45. For the story of Phips's treasure hunt, see Scott, *Constitution and Finance*, 2:484–486.

4. Steven Pincus, *1688: The First Modern Revolution* (New Haven: Yale University Press, 2009), 369–372; G. M. Trevelyan, *England under the Stuarts* (London: Methuen, 1925 [1904]), 430.

5. Desan, *Making Money*, 304–308.

6. John Blackwell, *An Essay Towards Carrying on the Present War against France* (London: Blackwell, 1695), 1.

7. For a useful analysis of Parliament's quest for financial stability after the Revolution, see Deringer, *Calculated Values*, 43–78.

8. After Newton's final attempt at reforming the value of the coinage in December 1717, Parliament, beset with complaints from merchant groups, declared "that this House will not alter the standard of the Gold and Silver coins of this Kingdom in Fineness, Weight, or Denomination." Though other forms of financial maneuvering proliferated, Parliament kept its word on the coin for nearly a century. Craig, *Mint*, 219; Hopton Haynes, "State of the Mint When the Grand Coynage Began in 1696," ca. 1700, Lansdowne MS 801 ff. 69r–78v (British Library, London), via *The Newton Project*, ed. Rob Iliffe, www.newtonproject.ox.ac.uk/view/texts/normalized /MINT01099; Isaac Newton, "Fragment on Church History (section 7.3f)," 1707, Yahuda Ms. 7.3f (National Library of Israel, Jerusalem), via *The Newton Project*, ed. Rob Iliffe, www.newtonproject.ox.ac.uk/view/texts/normalized/THEM00421.

9. Luigi Enaudi, "The Theory of Imaginary Money;" *Cobbett's Complete Collection of State Trials and Proceedings for High Treason, and Other Crimes and Misdemeanors from the Earliest Period to the Present Time*, ed. Thomas Howell, (London: R. Bagshaw, 1809) 2:114–130, esp. 218.

10. Historians have long debated the significance of the Glorious Revolution to the rise of capitalism. North and Weingast famously argued that the key transformation was one of property rights. Thus, the story goes, that what William III gave up was his "confiscatory power"—the crown's ability to, under previous regimes, to "expropriate" subjects' wealth. Thus, William and his allies made a "credible commitment" to protect established property rights. The problem, as many have since argued, is that property rights per se were well established in Britain decades, even centuries, before 1689. The monarch had no legal "confiscatory power" before the Glorious Revolution, thus nothing to lose. What the monarch did lose, though, was control over money. Desan rightly argues that Parliament's subsequent attempt to create a money designed for and created by profit-driven enterprises is far more significant than any shift in property rights per se. For good overviews of the debate, see Geoffrey M. Hodgson, "1688 and All That: Property Rights, the Glorious Revolution and the Rise of British Capitalism," *Journal of Institutional Economics* 13, no. 1 (2017): 79–107; Anne L. Murphy, "Demanding 'Credible Commitment': Public Reactions to the Failures of the Early Financial Revolution," *Economic History Review* 66, no. 1 (2013): 178–197. On the broader transformation, see Desan, *Making Money*, 266–359; Douglass North and Barry Weingast, "Constitutions and Commitment: The Evolution of Institutions Governing Public Choice in Seventeenth-Century England," *Journal of Economic History* 49, no. 4 (1989): 803–832; D'Maris Coffman, Adrian Leonard, and Larry Neal, eds., *Questioning Credible Commitment: Perspectives on the Rise of Financial Capitalism* (Cambridge: Cambridge University Press, 2013).

11. William Lowndes, *A Report Containing an Essay for the Amendment of the Silver Coins* (London: Charles Bill, 1695), 119, 140; Joyce Appleby, "Locke, Liberalism, and the Natural Law of Money," *Past & Present* 71 (1976): 47. Appleby is mistaken in writing that the new coins would weigh 25 percent less than the old.

12. A. A. Hanham, "Lowndes, William (1652–1724)," *Oxford Dictionary of National Biography* (Oxford: Oxford University Press, 2008), https://doi.org/10.1093 /ref:odnb/17099.

13. Peter Laslett, "John Locke, the Great Recoinage, and the Origins of the Board of Trade: 1695–1698," *William & Mary Quarterly* 14, no. 3 (1957): 395; John Locke,

Several Papers Relating to Money, Interest and Trade (London: A. and J. Churchill, 1695), 4–5.

14. Locke, *Several Papers Relating to Money, Interest and Trade*, 2–21.

15. C. R. Fay, "Locke versus Lowndes," *Cambridge Historical Journal* 4, no. 2 (1933): 143–155.

16. Thomas Wagstaffe, *An account of the proceedings in the House of Commons in relation to the recoining the clipp'd money, and falling the price of guineas together with a particular list of the names of the members consenting and dissenting: in answer to a letter out of the country* (London: n.p., 1696), 2, in the digital collection *Early English Books Online* 2, https://name.umdl.umich.edu/A65922.0001.001 (University of Michigan Library Digital Collections) [accessed June 3, 2024].

17. Desan, *Making Money*, 170, 319–329, 337–359; Craig, *Mint*, 184–197, 218; Scott, *Constitution and Finance*, 2:208; Brodie Waddell, "The Economic Crisis of the 1690s in England," *Historical Journal* 66, no. 2 (2023): 281–302. On the broader transformation of the 1690s, see Desan, *Making Money*, 266–359; Douglass North and Barry Weingast, "Constitutions and Commitment: The Evolution of Institutions Governing Public Choice in Seventeenth-Century England," *Journal of Economic History* 49, no. 4 (1989): 803–832; D'Maris Coffman, Adrian Leonard, and Larry Neal, eds., *Questioning Credible Commitment: Perspectives on the Rise of Financial Capitalism* (Cambridge: Cambridge University Press, 2013); Mark Knights, "Charles Montague, of Jermyn Street, Westminster, and Bushey Park, Hampton Court," in *History of Parliament: The House of Commons, 1690–1715*, ed. D. Hayton and E. Cruickshanks (London: Boydell and Brewer, 2002), www.historyofparliamentonline.org/volume/1690-1715/member/montagu-charles-1661-1715#footnote26_i0qoam7.

18. Brodie Waddell, "The Economic Crisis of the 1690s in England," *Historical Journal* 66, no. 2 (2023): 281–302.

19. The East India Company alone shipped out 22.5 million ounces of silver, "enough for a coinage of £5,730,000 in the years 1700–1717." John Craig, *The Mint: A History of the London Mint from A.D. 287 to 1948* (Cambridge: Cambridge University Press, 1953), 215.

20. "Inflation Calculator," Bank of England, last modified April 16, 2025, www.bankofengland.co.uk/monetary-policy/inflation/inflation-calculator [accessed April 28, 2025].

21. J. G. A. Pocock, "The Mobility of Property and the Rise of Eighteenth-Century Sociology," in *Virtue, Commerce, History* (New York: Cambridge University Press, 1979), 103–123; B. R. Mitchell, *Abstract of British Historical Statistics* (New York: Cambridge University Press, 1988), 401; Scott, *Constitution and Finance*, 1:428; Helen Paul, *The South Sea Bubble: A Revision of the Gambling Mania Theory* (New York: Taylor & Francis, 2009).

22. Dickson, *Financial Revolution*, 282, 336.

23. Dickson, *Financial Revolution*, esp. 282–292; Ann Carols and Larry Neal, "The Micro-Foundations of the Early London Capital Market: Bank of England Shareholders During and After the South Sea Bubble," *Economic History Review* 59, no. 3 (2006): 498–538; Scott, *Constitution and Finance*, 1:439–440; Craig, *The Mint*, 215; Neil McKendrick, John Brewer, and John Harold Plumb, eds., *The Birth of a*

Consumer Society: The Commercialization of Eighteenth-Century England (Bloomington: Indiana University Press, 1982), 206.

24. Postlethwayt spent much of the 1740s lobbying Parliament for the Royal Africa Company, begging Whig MPs to pour public money into heavily fortified slave "castles" to protect British traffickers from their competitors. But wealth gathered from enslaving others, for Postlethwayt, was at least wealth gained from work. The power and influence money could command at the expense of more material interests, on the other hand, was as unearned as it was new and terrifying. On the political clout of "monied men," see, e.g., Paul Langford, *A Polite and Commercial People: England 1727–1783* (Oxford: Oxford University Press, 1994), 46; Malachy Postlethwayt, *Universal Dictionary of Trade and Finance* (London: W. Strahan, 1774), 2:295–296. On Postlethwayt's deployment of "political arithmetic" in service of the slave trade, see Marcus Rediker, *The Slave Ship: A Human History* (New York: Viking, 2007), 45–46.

25. [Daniel Defoe], *The Anatomy of Exchange-Alley* (London: E. Smith, 1719), 2. On the significance of Exchange Alley for British public finance, see Ann M. Carlos, Erin K. Fletcher, Larry Neal, and Kirsten Wandschneider, "Financing and Refinancing the War of Spanish Succession, and Then Refinancing the South Sea Company," in *Questioning Credible Commitment*, ed. D'Maris Coffman, Adrian Leonard, and Larry Neal (Cambridge: Cambridge University Press, 2013); Dickson, *Financial Revolution*, 245.

26. William Hogarth, *William Wollaston and His Family in a Grand Interior*, 1730, oil on canvas, 102.5×126.4 cm, Leicester Museum & Art Gallery, Leicester, https://artuk.org/discover/artworks/william-wollaston-and-his-family-in-a-grand -interior-81286.

27. William Wollaston, *The Religion of Nature* (London: Knapton, 1738), 52; John Burk, *The History of Virginia from Its First Settlement to the Present Day* (Petersburg, VA: Dickson & Pescud, 1804), 3:333–334; George Henkle Reese, ed., *The Official Papers of Francis Fauquier, Lieutenant Governor of Virginia, 1758–1768* (Charlottesville: University Press of Virginia, 1980), 1:418; Bernard Burke, *A Genealogical and Heraldic History of the Landed Gentry of Great Britain* (London: Harrison, 1900), 2:1542; Benjamin Wilson, *Francis Fauquier*, 1757, oil on canvas, 91.4×71.1 cm, Foundling Museum, London, https://artuk.org/discover/artworks/francis-fauquier -17041768-191970. In Burke's telling, Fauquier lost his inheritance to Lord Anson in a card game, so impressing the lord that he offered Fauquier his patronage and, eventually, Virginia. The timeline does not match, but it is instructive as folklore.

28. Jacob H. Hollander, ed., *Francis Fauquier on An Essay on Ways and Means (1756)* (Baltimore: Johns Hopkins Press, 1915), 3; Helen Julia Paul, "The South Sea Company's Slaving Activities," *Discussion Papers in Economics and Econometrics*, no. 0924 (University of Southampton, 2009); N. A. M. Rodger, "Anson, George, Baron," *Oxford Dictionary of National Biography* (Oxford: Oxford University Press, 2008), https:// doi.org/10.1093/ref:odnb/574; Francis Fauquier, *An Essay on Ways and Means for Raising Money for the Support of the Present War without Increasing the Public Debts* (London: M. Cooper, 1756), 17.

29. Brock, *Currency of the American Colonies*, 116; Thomas Cooper, ed., *The Statutes at Large of South Carolina* (Columbia: A. S. Johnston, 1836–1898), 2:210. For a good overview of the problems with *American Historical Statistics'* quantification of American colonial currency, see Grubb, "The Circulating Medium of Exchange in

Colonial Pennsylvania, 329–360. On South Carolina, see Dorfman, *Economic Mind*, 165; Cooper, *Statutes at Large*, 3:81, 190.

30. Brock, *Currency*, 272.

31. "A State of the Debts Incurred by the British Colonies in North America for the Extraordinary Expenses of the Last War," Jan. 28, 1766, T1/446/404 (National Archives, Kew); Sklansky, *Sovereign of the Market*, 43–45; Mary Schweitzer, *From Custom to Contract*; Henry Flanders and James T. Michell, eds., *Statutes at Large of Pennsylvania from 1682–1801* (Harrisburg: State Printer of Pennsylvania, 1896), 3:332.

32. George Berkeley, *Queries Relating to a National Bank, Extracted from the Querist: Also the Letter Containing a Plan or Sketch of Such Bank* (Dublin: George Faulkner, 1737), 3–4; James Livesey, "Berkeley, Ireland and Eighteenth-Century Intellectual History," *Modern Intellectual History* 12, no. 2 (2015): 454; C. George Caffentzis, "Why Did Berkeley's Bank Fail? Money and Libertinism in Eighteenth-Century Ireland," *Eighteenth-Century Ireland / Iris an dá chultúr* 12 (1997): 100–115; Jack Greene, *Pursuits of Happiness: The Social Development of Early Modern British Colonies and the Formation of American Culture* (Chapel Hill: University of North Carolina Press, 1988), 182–184; John McCusker and Russell Menard, *Economy of British America, 1607–1789* (Chapel Hill: University of North Carolina Press, 1985), 55; Alice Hanson Jones, "Wealth Estimates for the American Middle Colonies, 1774," *Economic Development and Cultural Change* 18, no. 4 (1970): 130.

33. Stacy L. Lorenz, "'To Do Justice to His Majesty, the Merchant and the Planter': Governor William Gooch and the Virginia Tobacco Inspection Act of 1730," *Virginia Magazine of History and Biography* 108, no. 4 (2000): 345–392; McCusker, *Money and Exchange*, 206; Hening, *Statutes*, 5:540.

34. Massachusetts's monetary history and pushback from Parliament is further explored in chapter 5. Robert Dinwiddie, "A Proclamation for Encouraging Men to Enlist in His Majesty's Service for the Defence & Security of This Colony," Feb. 19, 1754, in *Electronic Enlightenment: Scholarly Edition of Correspondence*, ed. R. V. McNamee (Oxford: Bodleian Libraries, 2008–2019), https://doi.org/10.13051/ee:doc /nelswiVH0010053a1d [accessed May 22, 2020].

35. George Washington's personal note on "A Proclamation for Encouraging Men to Enlist in His Majesty's Service for the Defence & Security of This Colony by Robert Dinwiddie," February 19, 1754, *Electronic Enlightenment*, https://doi.org/10.13051 /ee:doc/nelswiVH0010053a1d; Fred Anderson, *Crucible of War* (New York: Vintage, 2001), 42–50; Einhorn, *American Taxation, American Slavery*, 29–52; Breen, *Tobacco Culture*, 95–96; Jones, *The Wealth of a Nation to Be*, 132–134.

36. Ronald Lewis, "The Use and Extent of Slave Labor in the Chesapeake Iron Industry: The Colonial Era," *Labor History* 17, no. 3 (1976): 388–405.

37. Breen, *Tobacco Culture*, 93–100, esp. 102; Newton Dennison Mereness, ed., *Travels in the American Colonies* (New York: MacMillan, 1916), 404–405; Muldrew, *Economy of Obligation*, 98–100.

38. On the evolution of the Virginia pound, see McCusker, *Money and Exchange*, 206.

39. Joseph Ernst, "Genesis of the Currency Act of 1764: Virginia Paper Money and the Protection of British Investments," *William & Mary Quarterly* 22, no. 1 (Jan. 1965), 34.

40. Anderson, *Crucible*, 42–65.

41. Marc Egnal, *A Mighty Empire: The Origins of the American Revolution* (Ithaca: Cornell University Press, 1988), 97; A. Brock, ed., *The Official Records of Robert Dinwiddie, Lieutenant-Governor of the Colony of Virginia, 1751–1758* (Richmond: Virginia Historical Society, 1883), 21.

42. Hening, *Statutes at Large*, 6:467; McIlwaine, *Burgesses*, 8:231–232; Brock, *Dinwiddie*, 2:81–82, 86. The only exception to the notes' "legal tender" was the royal quit-rent—a 2 shilling tax each Virginian owed the king (or, in some cases, an English proprietor) on every 100 acres of land they owned. Anderson, *Crucible*, 95.

43. Aaron Graham, "Corruption and Contractors in the Atlantic World, 1754–63," *English Historical Review* 133, no. 564 (October 2018): 1093–1119, https://doi.org/10.1093/ehr/cey274; Ernst, "Genesis," 36.

44. Anderson, *Crucible*, 96–99.

45. Anderson, *Crucible*, 103; Farley Grubb, "Virginia's Paper Money Regime, 1755–1774: A Forensic Accounting Reconstruction of the Data," *Historical Methods* 50, no. 2 (2017): 99, 106.

46. Hening, *Statutes*, 7:81–84.

47. William and Francis Fauquier, "An Account of an Extraordinary Storm of Hail in Virginia," *Proceedings of the Royal Society London* (1757): 746–747.

48. For a representative example of the burgesses callously debating the worth of an enslaved person's life, see McIlwaine, *Burgesses*, 8:259.

49. "Francis Fauquier's Will," *William & Mary Quarterly*, ser. 1, vol. 8 (1899/1900): 175. To paraphrase my student Zach Barnes, there was no time when people did not know that slavery was wrong.

50. Francis Fauquier to Lords Commissioners of Trade and Foreign Plantations, January 5, 1759, in George Reese, ed. *Electronic Enlightenment*, https://doi.org/10.13051/ee:doc/fauqfrVH0010143a1c.

51. Ibid.

52. Ibid.

53. George Henkle Reese, ed., *The Official Papers of Francis Fauquier* (Charlottesville: University Press of Virginia, 1980), 1:145; Ernst, "Genesis," 53; Hening, *Statutes at Large*, 7:352.

54. On the general lack of hostility to bills of credit for much of the early eighteenth century, see Brock, *Currency*, 176–180.

55. Elizabeth Donnan, ed., *Documents Illustrative of the History of the Slave Trade to America* (Washington, D.C.: Carnegie Institute, 1931), 4:143; Fauquier to the Board of Trade, June 2, 1760, CO/5 1330 f. 17 (National Archives, Kew).

56. Hening, *Statutes*, 6:218, 6:466, 7:81, 7:281. Joseph Ernst and Farley Grubb's figures miss the first 5 percent tax, continued in February 1759. Grubb, "Colonial Virginia's Paper Money Regime," 105; Ernst, "Genesis," 52–53.

57. Fauquier to the Board of Trade, June 2, 1760, CO/5 1330 f. 17. Slave imports to Virginia and the Chesapeake (Virginia and Maryland) reconstructed with data from TransAtlantic Slave Trade Database, slavevoyages.org. On the sterling dock price of trafficked Africans, see Peter Mancall, Joshua Rosenbloom, and Thomas Weiss, "Slave Prices and the South Carolina Economy, 1722–1809," *Journal of Economic History* 38, no. 3 (2001): 616–639. Grubb estimates from later sources that taxes on slave imports amounted to £2,000 Virginia a year, based on a 5 percent tax.

58. *Black Prince,* Voyage IDs 17258, 17280, 17306, 17386, 17432, 17476, 17522, 17573, slavevoyages.org [accessed July 2020]; Patrick McGrath, ed., *Bristol in the Eighteenth Century* (Bristol: Bristol Historical Association, 1972), 174–175; Joseph Calder Miller, *Way of Death: Merchant Capitalism and the Angolan Slave Trade, 1730–1830* (Madison: University of Wisconsin Press, 1997), 1–8, 380–391, 419–420; Marcus Rediker, *The Slave Ship: A Human History* (New York: Viking, 2007), 37–40. While few dispute the violence of the Middle Passage, there are numerous different estimates of death rates. On 848 British flag slaving voyages between 1751–1800, the mean recorded death rate was 9.8 percent. Hebert Klein, Stanley Engerman, Robin Haines, and Ralph Shlomowitz, "Transoceanic Mortality: The Slave Trade in Comparative Perspective," *William & Mary Quarterly* 58, no. 1 (2001): 93–118, esp. table v. Average crew mortality rate for Liverpool slave ships trading to West-Central Africa between 1770 and 1775 was 16.3 percent. Overall, between 1770 and 1775, 4,660 crewmen enlisted on Liverpool slaving voyages, and 1,493 died, or 32 percent. Stephen Behrendt, "Crew Mortality in the Transatlantic Slave Trade in the Eighteenth Century," *Slavery & Abolition* 18, no. 1 (1997): 58, 61.

59. Voyage IDs 17386 and 17432, slavevoyages.org [accessed August 2020]; Mary Drummond, "Laroche, James [1734–1804], of Over, nr. Bristol, Glos," in L. Namier and J. Brooke, eds., *History of Parliament Online,* www.historyofparliamentonline .org/volume/1754-1790/member/laroche-james-1734-1804 [accessed August 2020]; Kenneth Morgan, *Bristol and the Atlantic Trade in the Eighteenth Century* (Cambridge: Cambridge University Press, 2004), 194; S. D. Smith, *Slavery, Family, and Gentry Capitalism in the British Atlantic: The World of the Lascelles, 1648–1834* (Cambridge: Cambridge University Press, 2006), 199; "Memorial of the Merchants of Liverpool Trading to Africa," Nov. 3, 1762, in Donnan, *Documents,* 2:517. Profits from the slave trade were highly variable, averaging from 7.8 percent and 19.8 percent for surviving Bristol accounts, and 8 to 10 percent in the final years of the British slave trade in Liverpool. Kenneth Morgan, "James Roger and the Bristol Slave Trade," *Historical Research* 76, no. 192 (2003): 215.

60. Toby Green, *A Fistful of Shells: West Africa from the Rise of the Slave Trade to the Age of Revolution* (London: Allen Lane, 2019), 186–239; "Thomas Clarkson's Efficiency of Regulation of the Slave Trade" (1789), in Donnan, *Documents,* 2:572.

61. "Thomas Clarkson's" and "New Items Relating to the Slave Trade, 1759," *Charleston Gazette,* in Donnan, *Documents,* 2:573, 4:374, 375; Voyage ID 17432, slavevoyages.org [August 2020]. On the price of trafficked Africans in sterling in British North America, see John Donald Duncan, *Servitude and Slavery in Colonial South Carolina 1670–1776* (PhD diss., Emory University, 1972), 155, table xiv. Statistics on human trafficking to Virginia compiled from slavevoyages.org; Ernst, "Genesis," 52–53.

62. Fauquier to the Board of Trade, April 8, 1762, CO/5 1330 f. 132; Hening, *Statutes,* 7:363, 383.

63. Grubb, "Colonial," 105.

64. Ernst, "Genesis," 52–56; CO/5 1330 ff. 131, 155.

65. CO/5 1330 f. 155.

66. Fauquier to Amherst, Sept. 25, 1762, *Electronic Enlightenment,* https://doi .org/10.13051/ee:doc/fauqfrVH0020802a1c [accessed June 3, 2020]; CO/5 1330 ff. 287–288.

Chapter Three

1. Peter Marshall, "Hill, Wills, First Marquess of Downshire," in *Oxford Dictionary of National Biography*, www.oxforddnb.com/view/10.1093/ref:odnb/9780198614128 .001.0001/odnb-9780198614128-e-13317; Walpole, *Memoirs of the Reign of George III*, 4:199.

2. Marshall, "Hill"; P. Roebuck, "The Making of an Ulster Great Estate," *Proceedings of the Royal Irish Academy* 79 (1979): 1–25; Arthur Collins, *Peerage of England* (London: Rivington, 1812), 5:97; "A new and correct Peerage of Ireland," *Gentleman's and London Magazine* (July 1785): 339.

3. Marshall, "Hill"; "A new and correct Peerage of Ireland," *Gentleman's and London Magazine* (July 1785): 339.

4. *Acts of the Privy Council*, 4:569.

5. Oliver Morton Dickerson, *American Colonial Government, 1696–1765: A Study of the British Board of Trade in Relation to the American Colonies, Political, Industrial, Administrative* (Cleveland: Clark, 1912), esp. 22–27; Laslett, "John Locke, the Great Recoinage, and the Origins of the Board of Trade," 370–402; Locke, *Several Papers*, 5.

6. Either Joshua Sharpe, a lawyer who often represented parties before the board, or John Sharpe, the colonial agent for Barbados.

7. Commissioners of Trade and Plantations, "Copy of All the Proceedings Had and State of the Viva Voce Evidence Taken before the Commissioners of Trade and Plantations Relating to the Trade Carried on by the British Northern Colonies with the Foreign Sugar Colonies," 1750, R Stanton Avery Special Collections (New England Historic Genealogical Society, Boston).

8. Charles McLean Andrews, *The Colonial Period* (New York: H. Holt, 1912), 136.

9. Presumably modern Sint Eustatius.

10. Dickerson, *Colonial Government*, 47–50.

11. John Brewer, *The Sinews of Power: War, Money, and the English State, 1688–1783* (Cambridge: Harvard University Press, 1990), xi.

12. Anonymous, *A Letter to a Member of Parliament, Wherein the Power of the British Legislature, and the Case of the Colonists, Are Briefly and Impartially Considered*, W. Flexney (London: n.p., 1765), 29.

13. McIlwaine, *Legislative Journals of the Council of Colonial Virginia*, 3:1281; CO/5 1330 ff. 129–130.

14. CO5/1330 234, 288. The account Fauquier included in the packet sent to the board did not include anticipated taxes for 1769. For those, see McIlwaine, *Burgesses*, 10:177–778.

15. Ibid. "Proceedings of the Virginia Committee of Correspondence, 1759–'67 (Continued)," *Virginia Magazine of History and Biography* 12, no. 1 (1904): 1–14; *Historical Statistics of the United States Millennial Edition*, table e.g. 429–442.

16. Akinobu Kuroda, "Concurrent but Non-Integrable Currency Circuits: Complementary Relationships among Monies in Modern China and Other Regions," *Financial History Review* 15, no. 1 (2008): 17–36.

17. "Currency Act of 1751," in *Statutes at Large*, ed. Danby Pickering, 20:306–309 (Cambridge: Joseph Bentham, 1765); Fauquier to Charles Wyndham, May 19,

1763, in Reese, *Electronic Enlightenment* (2013), https://doi.org/10.13051/ee:doc /fauqfrVH0020950a1c. The best account of the colonies' eighteenth-century debates with the Board of Trade over currency is Brock, *Currency of the American Colonies*.

18. Ernst, "Genesis," 52.

19. "Memorial of the Merchants of London Trading to Virginia," Undated, Read Dec. 22, 1762, CO 5/1330 ff. 129–130; "Address," CO 5/1330 ff. 230–232.

20. "Memorial," CO 5/1330 ff. 129–130. Ernst argues that the fluctuating rate of exchange amid a continuing postwar economic crisis explains the London merchants' position. Their own arguments, however, suggest a more fundamental discomfort with bills of credit in general. The merchants themselves admitted their real losses were negligible, a fact confirmed by colonial statistics. Ernst, "Genesis."

21. Desan, *Making Money*, 375–380; Richard A Kleer, "'A new species of money': British Exchequer Bills, 1701–1711," *Financial History Review* 22, no. 2 (2015): 179–203.

22. "Memorial," CO 5/1330 ff. 129–130.

23. "Address," CO 5/1330 ff. 230–232.

24. "Address," CO 5/1330 ff. 230–232.

25. Ibid.; *Journal of the Commissioners of the Board of Trade*, 11:331; McIlwaine, *Burgesses*, 10:190.

26. *Journal of the Commissioners of the Board of Trade*, 11:418.

27. Jack Sosin, *Agents and Merchants: British Colonial Policy and the Origins of the American Revolution, 1763–1775* (Lincoln: University of Nebraska Press, 1965), xiii.

28. Hill's thought processes—long considered a mystery—can be gleaned, as we shall see, from his subsequent report on American currencies to the Privy Council. It was completed, in Hill's own hand, on February 9, 1764, and contains evidence of a lengthy investigation, likely stretching back to the previous year. Sosin, *Agents*, 28; Ernst, "Genesis," 69. Complaints regarding North Carolina's paper money are the only ones, in addition to Virginia's, attached to Hill's report on the American currencies to the Privy Council. *Acts of the Privy Council*, 4:646.

29. "Extracts from the Carroll Papers," *Maryland Historical Magazine* 11, no. 4 (1916): 325; *Acts of the Privy Council*, 4:569.

30. *Journal of the Commissioners for Trade and Plantations*, 12:3–9.

31. *Journal of the Commissioners for Trade and Plantations*, 12:15.

32. *Journal of the Commissioners for Trade and Plantations*, 12:18

33. *Journal of the Commissioners for Trade and Plantations*, 12:21.

34. *Journal of the Commissioners for Trade and Plantations*, 12:24.

35. James Munro, ed., *Acts of the Privy Council of England: Colonial Series* (London: H. M. Stationery Office, 1911), 4:625.

36. Munro, *Acts*, 4:626–628, 630.

37. Martin Griffiths, "Joseph Harris of Trevecka," *Antiquarian Astronomer*, no. 6 (January 2012): 19–33.

38. Harris, *Essay*, 42–43n.43.

39. Ibid.

40. Joseph Harris, *An Essay upon Money and Coins* (London: G. Hawkins, 1757), 37–39, 43, 67, 91–93; Neil McKendrick, Brewer and Plumb, eds., *Birth of a Consumer Society*, 205–209.

41. Munro, *Acts*, 4:623–630.

42. Woodbridge and Blackwell, *Considerations*, 3.

43. Munro, *Acts*, 4:631.

44. *Journals of the House of Commons*, 29:1027–1056

45. Munro, *Acts*, 4:415; *Journals of the House of Commons*, 29:1027–1056.

46. McIlwaine and Kennedy, *Journals of the House of Burgesses of Virginia*, 10:249–252. The best account of the British merchants' position is Ernst, "Genesis," 33–74.

Chapter Four

1. Curtis Nettels, *Money Supply of the American Colonies* (Madison: University of Wisconsin Press, 1934), 274. This chapter incorporates elements from Andrew David Edwards, "Grenville's Silver Hammer: The Problem of Money in the Stamp Act Crisis," *Journal of American History* 104, no. 2 (2017): 337–362.

2. J. L. Bullion, *A Great and Necessary Measure: George Grenville and the Genesis of the Stamp Act, 1763–1765* (Columbia: University of Missouri Press, 1982), 52; Thomas Whately, *The Regulations Lately Made Concerning the Colonies, and the Taxes Imposed upon Them, Considered* (London: J. Wilkie, 1765), 42.

3. Pickering, *Statutes at Large*, 26:33–52.

4. Very few post-office payments were made. The first in fifty-four years came in 1764, and it amounted to £494. William Smith, "The Colonial Post-Office," *American Historical Review* 21, no. 2 (1916): 258–275.

5. Pickering, *Statutes at Large*, 26:49, 12:115–139; Thomas Whately, *Consideration on the Trade and Finances of the Kingdom; and on the Measures of Administration, with Respect to Those Great National Objects Since the Conclusion of the Peace* (London: J. Wilkie, 1766), 78.

6. Lawrence Henry Gipson, *Jared Ingersoll: A Study of American Loyalism in Relation to British Colonial Government* (New Haven: Yale University Press, 1920), 117; Henry McCulloh, *A Miscellaneous Essay Concerning the Courses Pursued by Great Britain in the Affairs of Her Colonies with Some Observations on the Great Importance of Our Settlements in America, and the Trade Thereof* (London: R. Baldwin, 1750).

7. William James Smith, ed., *The Grenville Papers: Being the Correspondence of Richard Grenville, Earl Temple, K.G., and the Right Hon. George Grenville, Their Friends and Contemporaries* (London: J. Murray, 1852), 2:374.

8. Henry McCulloh, "Draught for a Bill for Creating and Issuing Bills of Credit under the Denomination of Exchequer Bills of Union for the General Use of His Majesty's Colonies on the Continent of America Most Humbly Presented to His Grace the Duke of Newcastle," September 27, 1757, Add MS 32874 ff. 308–313 (British Library, London). On a series of similar proposals for a continental currency, see Aaron Graham, *Bills of Union: Money, Empire and Ambitions in the Mid-Eighteenth Century British Atlantic* (London: Palgrave, 2021).

9. Smith, *Grenville Papers*, 2:374; W. P. W. Phillimore and W. H. Whitear, eds., *Historical Collections Relating to Chiswick* (London: Phillimore, 1897), 153; Charles G. Sellers, "Private Profits and British Colonial Policy: The Speculations of Henry McCulloh," *William & Mary Quarterly* 8, no. 4 (1951): 535; Lawrence

Henry Gipson, *Jared Ingersoll: A Study of American Loyalism in Relation to British Colonial Government* (New Haven: Yale University Press, 1920), 117; London Customhouse Commentary on American Duties, July 21, 1763, T1/430/346 (National Archives, Kew).

10. John L. Bullion, *A Great and Necessary Measure: George Grenville and the Genesis of the Stamp Act, 1763–1765* (Columbia: University of Missouri Press, 1982), 21; Treasury Board, "An Acc:t Shewing the Cause of the Deficiency of the Grants for the Year 1764," 1764, T1/434/93 (National Archives, Kew); Mitchell, *Historical Statistics,* 390. On the contractors' desperation, see letters from George Colbrooke, S. Fludyer, and John Calerast, T1/434/133, 188, 190, T1/431/326-327 (National Archives, Kew). On the rumors of new taxes in Britain, see Anonymous [likely Thomas Whatley], *An Answer to the Budget Inscribed to the Coterie* (London: E. Sumpter, 1764), 15.

11. George Colbrooke, "Letter from George Colbrooke," Oct. 8, 1764, T1/434/188 (National Archives, Kew).

12. Mitchell, *Historical Statistics,* 401–402, 390; Eliga Gould, *The Persistence of Empire: British Political Culture in the Age of the American Revolution* (Chapel Hill: UNC Press Books, 2011), esp. 110, 109–118.

13. Gould, *Persistence of Empire,* 116–117; Board of Trade and Plantations, "State of the Debts Incurred by Such of the North American Provinces as Were Principally Engaged in the Service of the Late War," 1764, T1/433/402 (National Archives, Kew).

14. See, e.g., "List of Instruments Etca made use of in the Province of New Jersey," Oct. 27, 1764, T1/430/223-224 (National Archives, Kew); Henry McCulloh, "A State of the Several Articles Proposed by M. McCullo[h] to be Stamp'd," October 10, 1763, Add MS 35910 ff. 136–139 (British Library).

15. Massachusetts Historical Society, *Collections of the Massachusetts Historical Society: The Bowdoin and Temple Papers* (Boston: Wiggin and Lunt, 1897), 6:18–23. The information Whately did eventually receive on legal proceedings in the colonies was spotty and inconsistent. Reports from other colonies, including New Hampshire (at barely a half page), Maryland and New Jersey can be found in T1/430 (National Archives, Kew), ff. 170, 214, 222–224.

16. Charles R. Ritcheson, "The Preparation of the Stamp Act," *William & Mary Quarterly* 10, no. 4 (1953): 543–559; Pickering, *Statutes at Large,* 26:179–20; John Bullion, "British Ministers and the American Resistance to the Stamp Act, October–December 1765," *William & Mary Quarterly* 49, no. 1 (1992): 89–107.

17. Ritcheson, "Preparation," 552.

18. Robert Cholmondeley, "Report on Mr. Corbine's Memorial on the Rise of the Exchange in Virginia," July 11, 1764, T1/430/277 (National Archives, Kew). On the difficulties Americans associated with paying their own taxes in temporary money, see, e.g., Harold Selesky, *War and Society in Colonial Connecticut* (New Haven: Yale University Press, 1990), 141.

19. British customs officials estimated in 1763 that the Sugar Act of 1733 had brought in just £21,652, 10 shillings, and 11.25 pence in thirty years of operation, concluding "The Smallness of this Revenue Plainly proves that many Frauds have been & are Committed in that Country." T1/430 (National Archives, Kew), ff. 346.

20. Thomas Whately, *Considerations on the Trade and Finances of This Kingdom* (London: J. Wilkie, 1766), 77–79.

21. Whatley, *Considerations on the Trade and Finances,* 78–79.

22. Jack P. Greene, "'A Dress of Horror': Henry McCulloh's Objections to the Stamp Act," *Huntington Library Quarterly* 26, no. 3 (1963): 253–262.

23. Leonard Labaree, ed., *The Papers of Benjamin Franklin* (New Haven: Yale University Press, 1967), 11:234–240.

24. Jared Ingersoll, *Mr. Ingersoll's Letters Relating to the Stamp-Act* (New Haven: Samuel Green, 1766), 17–18.

25. "To Joseph Galloway," Oct. 11, 1766, in Labaree, *Franklin Papers,* 13:447–450.

26. Eliga Gould, "Thomas Pownall (1722–1805)," in *Oxford Dictionary of National Biography* (Oxford: Oxford University Press, 2004), www.oxforddnb.com [accessed August 24, 2021]; Labaree, *Franklin Papers,* 11:47–60; Michell and Flanders, *Statutes at Large of Pennsylvania,* 4:344–359; Simmons and Thomas, *Proceedings and Debates,* 2:24.

27. Labaree, *Franklin Papers,* 11:67, 14:76–87; Benjamin Franklin, "Remarks and Facts Relative to the American Paper Money," *Pennsylvania Chronicle,* May 27–June 1, 1767. There is a long tradition of scholarship arguing that Franklin was, in fact, in favor of the Stamp Act. Partially, this comes out of contemporary commentary from his opponents in Pennsylvania, along with rumor that someone with colonial experience had proposed the Stamp Act in the first place. The rumors, as it turns out, referred to McCulloh. It is true that Franklin, who was in London to free Pennsylvania from the Penns, had other priorities. The idea that Franklin was actually *for* the Stamp Act cannot withstand close scrutiny. In the final analysis, it depends on separating his efforts to oppose the act from his concurrent efforts to create a new pancolonial currency, when it is clear from context that the two efforts were directly linked. Theodore Thayer, *Pennsylvania Politics and the Growth of Democracy, 1740–1776* (Harrisburg: Pennsylvania Historical and Museum Commission, 1953), 111–115.

28. Ingersoll, *Mr. Ingersoll's Letters,* 31–32.

29. Peter D. G. Thomas, "Isaac Barré," in *Oxford Dictionary of National Biography* (Oxford: Oxford University Press, 2004), http://ezproxy-prd.bodleian.ox.ac.uk:2102/10.1093/ref:odnb/1509 [accessed August 10, 2021].

30. Ingersoll, *Mr. Ingersoll's Letters,* 32.

31. P. D. G Thomas and S. C. Simmons, eds., *Proceedings of the British Parliaments Respecting North America, 1754–1783* (Millwood, NY: Kraus International, 1982–1986), 2:8–17. The smuggled text of Barré's speech made it to America in a Feb. 11, 1765, letter from Connecticut agent Jared Ingersoll to Governor Thomas Fitch. Ingersoll, *Mr. Ingersoll's Letters,* 15.

32. Justin Du Rivage, *Revolution against Empire: Taxes, Politics, and the Origins of American Independence* (New Haven: Yale University Press, 2017); Ignacio Gallup-Diaz, Andrew Shankman, and David J. Silverman, eds., *Anglicizing America: Empire, Revolution, Republic* (Philadelphia: University of Pennsylvania Press, 2015); T. H. Breen, "An Empire of Goods: The Anglicization of Colonial America, 1690–1776," *Journal of British Studies* 25, no. 4 (1986): 467–499, esp. 497; James Deetz, *In Small Things Forgotten: The Archeology of Early American Life* (Garden City, NY: Doubleday, 1977), 38. John Murrin coined the term "Anglicization" in John M. Murrin, *Anglicizing an American Colony: The Transformation of Provincial Massachusetts* (PhD diss., Yale University, 1966).

33. John Wright, *The American Negotiator: or, The Various Currencies of the British Colonies in America; as Well the Islands, as the Continent* (London: J. Smith, 1765), i–lx.

34. Grenville has found many historical admirers. He was an efficient administrator and, though choleric in parliamentary combat, generally considered a thoughtful and decent man. The Stamp Act, then, might be understood as revealing his limitations. For a sympathetic portrait, see Philip Lawson, *George Grenville: A Political Life* (Oxford: Oxford University Press, 1984).

35. Anglo-Americanus [John Mercer], "To the Printer of the Virginia Gazette," *Maryland Gazette,* July 18, 1765; J. A. Leo Lemay, "John Mercer and the Stamp Act in Virginia," *Virginia Magazine of History and Biography* 91, no.1 (1982): 3–38.

36. Mercer, "To the Printer."

37. E.g. [Stephen Johnson], *Some Important Observations, Occasioned by, and Adapted to, the Publick Fast* (Newport, R.I.: Samuel Hall, 1766), 13; Charles Chauncy, *A Discourse on "The Good News from a Far Country"* (Boston: Kneeland and Adams, 1766), 13.

38. Edmund Morgan, "Colonial Ideas of Parliamentary Power, 1764–1766," *William & Mary Quarterly* 5, no. 3 (1948): 331–341.

39. Arthur P. Scott, "The Constitutional Aspects of the 'Parson's Cause,'" *Political Science Quarterly* 31, no. 4 (1916): 558–577.

40. James Fontaine, *Memoirs of a Huguenot Family* (New York: Putnam, 1853), 419–424.

41. William Wirt, *Life of Patrick Henry* (Philadelphia: James Webster, 1818), 65. Wirt confirmed this account with Jefferson. Jefferson shared his own description with Wirt in April 1812. Paul Leicester Ford, *The Writings of Thomas Jefferson, 1807–1815* (New York: Putnam, 1898), 339. The spy's diary was only discovered more than a century later in the French archives. "Journal of a French Traveller in the Colonies, 1765 I," *American Historical Review* 26, no. 4 (July 1921): 726–747; "Journal of a French Traveller in the Colonies, 1765, II," *American Historical Review* 27, no. 1 (October 1921): 70–89; Rhys Isaac, "Lighting the Fuse of Revolution in Virginia, May 1765: Rereading the 'Journal of a French Traveller in the Colonies,'" *William & Mary Quarterly* 68, no. 4 (2011): 657–670.

42. Francis Bernard, "Bernard's Speech to Both Houses," May 25, 1762, in "Massachusetts Bay: Journal of Assembly, 1761–1764," CO5/842/9 (National Archives, Kew).

43. The best overview of this process is still Arthur Meier Schlesinger, *The Colonial Merchants and the American Revolution, 1763–1776* (New York: Columbia University Press, 1918).

44. Barlow Trecothick to Samuel Abbot, December 23, 1763; September 5, 1764; June 12, 1765, Foreign Letters, Samuel Abbot Papers (Baker Library Historical Collections, Harvard Business School, Boston).

45. Samuel Abbot, *Samuel Abbot's New England Letter Book 1764*, Samuel Abbot Papers (Baker Library Historical Collections, Harvard Business School, Boston).

46. William B. Reed, ed., *The Life and Correspondence of Joseph Reed* (Philadelphia: n.p., 1847) 1:31.

47. Isabel Schnabel and Hyun Song Shin, "Liquidity and Contagion: The Crisis of 1763," *Journal of the European Economic Association* 2 (Dec. 2004): 929–68;

Jacob M. Price, *Overseas Trade and Traders: Essays on the Commercial, Financial and Political Challenges of British Atlantic Merchants, 1660–1775* (Brookfield, VT, 1996), esp. chap. 6. On the lack of liquidity in the colonies generally, see Wright, *Origins of Commercial Banking in America*, 19–36.

48. John Watts, *Letter Book of John Watts: Merchant and Councilor of New York, January 1, 1762–December 22, 1765*, ed. Dorothy C. Barck (New York: n.p., 1928), 186. For a good discussion of the colonial specie shortage, see Leslie V. Brock, "The Colonial Currency, Prices, and Exchange Rates," http://etext.virginia.edu/users/brock/brock34.htm.

49. Watts, *Letter Book of John Watts*, 204.

50. Ibid., 176.

51. Ibid., 345, 399, 403, 406.

52. Isaac, "Lighting the Fuse," 68; Colin Nicolson, ed., *The Papers of Francis Bernard* (Boston: Colonial Society of Massachusetts, 2015), 2:295–296; Edmund Morgan and Helen Morgan, *The Stamp Act Crisis: Prelude to Revolution* (Chapel Hill: University of North Carolina Press, 1953), 123–124.

53. Malcolm Freiberg, ed., *Journals of the House of Representatives of Massachusetts* (Boston: Massachusetts Historical Society, 1972), 42:108–109.

54. Milton Embrick Flower, *John Dickinson: Conservative Revolutionary* (Charlottesville: University of Virginia Press, 1983); Harold Trevor Moland, "The Historical Perspective of John Dickinson," *Early Dickinsoniana* (1961), 10.

55. John Dickinson, *The Political Writings of John Dickinson* (Wilmington, DE: Bonsal and Niles, 1801), 5, 21–31.

56. John Dickinson to Mary [Cadwallader] Dickinson, July 15, 1765, R. R. Logan Collection of John Dickinson Papers (Pennsylvania Historical Society, Philadelphia).

57. Bouton, *Taming Democracy*, 21–27.

58. David Barber to Thomas Hancock, April 24, 1762, series 1, box 1, Hancock Family Papers (Baker Library, Harvard Business School, Boston); Bouton, *Taming Democracy*, 21–27.

59. Abram English Brown, ed., *John Hancock: His Book* (Boston: n.p., 1898), 90; George Washington, "To Francis Dandridge," September 20, 1765, Papers of George Washington Digital Edition, http://rotunda.upress.virginia.edu/founders/GEWN-02-07-02-0250.

60. Merrill Jensen, *The Founding of a Nation: A History of the American Revolution, 1763–1776* (Cambridge: Hackett, 2004 [1968]), 108–110; Gary Nash, *The Urban Crucible: The Northern Seaports and the Origins of the American Revolution* (London: Harvard University Press, 1986), 185–187.

61. [Benjamin Church], *Liberty and Property Vindicated, and the St—pm-n Burnt* (Boston: n.p., 1765), 6–8; Ingersoll, *Ingersoll's Letters*, 28–31, 49.

62. Jensen, *Founding*, 113–117.

63. Francis Fauquier to the Lords Commissioners of Trade and Foreign Plantations [Board of Trade], November 3, 1765, *Electronic Enlightenment*, e-enlightenment.com [accessed Sept. 1, 2021].

64. Lawrence Lee, "Days of Defiance: Resistance to the Stamp Act in the Lower Cape Fear," *North Carolina Historical Review* 43, no. 2 (1966): 194.

65. Jensen, *Founding*, 120–121.

66. Clinton Alfred Weslager, *The Stamp Act Congress: With an Exact Copy of the Complete Journal* (Newark: University of Delaware Press, 1976), 181–197.

67. L. B. Namier, "Charles Garth, Agent for South Carolina: Part II (Continued)," *English Historical Review* 54, no. 216 (October 1, 1939): 647.

68. Thomas Fitch, *Reasons Why the British Colonies, in America, Should Not be Charged with Internal Taxes, by Authority of Parliament* (New Haven: B. Mecom, 1764), 4.

69. John Dickinson, "The Original Draft of the Resolves of the First Congress Held at New York in 1765" and "The First Draught of the Resolves of the Congress at New York in 1764," series 1, box 1, R. R. Logan Collection of John Dickinson Papers (Historical Society of Pennsylvania, Philadelphia).

70. *To the Merchants and Manufacturers of Great-Britain; The Memorial of the Merchants and Traders of the City of Philadelphia* (Philadelphia: n.p., 1765), 1.

71. The Printers, "Printing-Office, Quebec," May 29, 1766, *Quebec Gazette* (Archives de Montréal, Quebec).

72. The difficulty of explaining America's Revolutionary unity has motivated virtually all attempts to explain the causes of the American Revolution for the past two centuries. The most relevant literature has already been cited in the introduction to the present work, but it is perhaps useful to think through the difference between *Money and the Making of the American Revolution* interpretation and two recent distinguished attempts to do the same thing, T. H. Breen's *The Market Place of Revolution* and Jack Greene's *The Constitutional Origins of the American Revolution*. Breen's interpretation is particularly relevant, first because it is focused precisely on the problem of American unity, and second because it, too, argues that commercial concerns were at the center of the American crisis. For Breen, American resistance was both explained and facilitated by a shared consumer culture. Their participation in "a complex market economy" allowed them to appreciate "the capacity of consumer goods to mobilize strangers in political protest," which allowed them to build broad coalitions against "unconstitutional taxes and regulations" with boycotts and non-exportation agreements. Breen is undoubtedly right on the significance of consumer politics in the creation and maintenance of a shared Revolutionary project, but he has little to say about the reasons why that project came to seem necessary in the first place. In part, this is because Breen seems to accept the premise, derived in part from the Morgans' work on the Stamp Act crisis, that "pocketbook concerns," like money, "did not count for something in any systematic way." However, as I hope this chapter has sufficiently demonstrated, money was a central systematic issue in the Stamp Act crisis, and it continued to have systematic effects, albeit less obviously, throughout the Revolutionary period—particularly in the imperial center. This does not contradict Breen's work, however, so much as give it a deeper origin story, rooted not in consumption but in the terms of Atlantic exchange. Similarly, Greene is surely correct when he argues "that the American Revolution *principally* resulted from a dispute over the nature of the constitution of the British Empire, a dispute in which both sides had a legitimate case." My point is to show that the constitutional dispute, as we will see in the next chapter, had its origins in the problem of money in the Stamp Act crisis. In particular, it arose because of the way that the silver clause in the Stamp

Act forced Americans to consider the imperial constitution in a new and original way. Breen, *The Marketplace of Revolution* (Oxford: Oxford University Press, 2004), 10, 21; Greene, *The Constitutional Origins of the American Revolution* (Cambridge: Cambridge University Press, 2010), xiv.

Chapter Five

1. Paul Langford, *The First Rockingham Administration, 1765–1766* (Oxford: Oxford University Press, 1973), 7.

2. Langford, *First Rockingham Administration*, 5–8.

3. Langford, *First Rockingham Administration*, 15.

4. William Bollan, *The Mutual Interest of Great Britain and the American Colonies Considered* (London: W. Nicoll, 1765), 9.

5. Alice Hanson Jones's survey of probate inventories recorded just £1.8 in cash per head of household, compared with £5.9 for the colonies as a whole. There was too little silver or gold to break out as a separate category from "cash" as a whole, which Jones took, largely, to be paper currency. Jones, *Wealth of a Nation to Be*, 128.

6. John Hancock to Barnard & Harrison, Aug. 9, Sept. 11, Oct. 21, 1765, vol. JH-6 letter book (business) (Baker Library, Harvard Business School, Boston).

7. John Hancock to Barnard & Harrison, Aug. 9, Sept. 11, 1765, vol. JH-6 letter book (business) (Baker Library, Harvard Business School.

8. John Dickinson, *The Late Regulations, Respecting the British Colonies on the Continent of America Considered, in a Letter from a Gentleman in Philadelphia to His Friend in London* (London: J. Almon, 1765), 32.

9. Dickinson, *The Late Regulations*, 12.

10. Ibid., 13–14.

11. Ibid., 18.

12. Ibid., 41–42.

13. Ibid., 53–54.

14. John Wentworth to Marquis of Rockingham, R-65 ff. 11–13, Rockingham Papers, Sheffield Archive (East Ardsley: Microform Academic Publishers, 2014), microfilm 12565, Firestone Library, Princeton University.

15. Grenville's views on Rockingham are apparent from his speeches in Parliament at the time. See also Lawson, *George Grenville*.

16. Allan Christelow, "Contraband Trade between Jamaica and the Spanish Main, and the Three Port Act of 1766," *Hispanic American Historical Review* 22, no. 2 (1942): 309–343, esp. 320; Pickering, *Statutes at Large*, 25:345; George Grenville and the Treasury Board to George III, "May It Please Your Majesty," Nov. 1763, T1/430/332 (National Archives, Kew).

17. Nettels, *Money Supply*, 15–44; Simmons and Thomas, *Parliamentary Debates*, 2:84, 87–89, 135, 145.

18. Ibid., 318–321; Adrian Pearce, *British Trade with Spanish America, 1763–1808* (Liverpool: Liverpool University Press, 2007), esp. 44.

19. "Jamaica, May 5," *Gentleman's Magazine* 34 (July 1764), 337; Simmons and Thomas, *Parliamentary Debates*, 2:269; Pearce, *British Trade with Spanish America*, 41–79. On Grenville's antismuggling obsession, see J. L. Bullion, *A Great*

and Necessary Measure: George Grenville and the Genesis of the Stamp Act, 1763–1765
(Columbia: University of Missouri Press), chapters 3–4.

20. Simmons and Thomas, *Parliamentary Debates*, 2:205.

21. Ibid., 1:186.

22. Ibid., 2:194–196.

23. Ibid., 227; Benjamin Franklin, *The Examination of Doctor Benjamin Frank-lin, before an August Assembly, relating to the Repeal of the Stamp-Act* (Philadelphia: Hall and Sellers, 1766), question 14.

24. Simmons and Thomas, *Parliamentary Debates*, 2:185.

25. Simmons and Thomas, *Parliamentary Debates*, 2:185–190.

26. Simmons and Thomas, *Parliamentary Debates*, 2:122–123.

27. Martin Howard, *A Letter in Defense of the Said Letter from a Gentleman at Halifax to His Friend in Rhode-Island* (Newport: S. Hall, 1765), esp. 3. Justin du Rivage has argued that "many conservative colonists embraced Grenville's reforms," citing Howard's pamphlets and Yale president Ezra Stiles's observation that some 100,000 colonists "including northern Episcopalians, Quakers, and Crown officials" supported the Stamp Act. Stiles, though, had little direct knowledge of the support (or resistance to) the Stamp Act outside of Connecticut, and instead based his estimates on the numbers of his perceived religious enemies in other colonies. Du Rivage's analysis may be based on an archival error. He cites Stiles as recording there were "200,000 supporters of the act" when, in fact, Stiles believed there were 100,000 *potential* supporters in the colonies. These included, according to Stiles, 30,000 "[Northern] Episcopalians" (who were demonstrably not in favor of the Stamp Act, at least in large numbers) and 70,000 "Quakers and Crown [Officers]," all of whom might support "the Grenvillian system" of colonial government. We cannot take Stiles's back-of-the-envelope religious analysis of colonial politics at face value, however. Quaker opinions were not uniform, and many prominent Quakers (including the Philadelphia merchants who banded together to produce a nonimportation agreement) opposed the Stamp Act. Dickinson, perhaps the act's most prominent opponent in colonial legislative circles, came from a Quaker background. Crown officers, too, may have been professionally obliged to support an act of Parliament, but many, including Fauquier, sent letters of protest to Britain. Moreover, Stiles seems more concerned about the notion of American Episcopalian bishops than the Stamp Act per se. Justin du Rivage, *Revolution against Empire: Taxes, Politics, and the Origins of American Independence* (New Haven: Yale University Press, 2017), 124; Ezra Stiles, "Review of the Continental Provinces," *Ezra Stiles Papers at Yale University*, Princeton Theological Seminary microfilm 1988, Misc. Papers, reel 16, 372:67.

28. Simmons and Thomas, *Parliamentary Debates*, 2:121.

29. Burns had encountered Ramsay on her way across Scotland from Oswald's funeral in 1789. She stole his rooms at a country inn, forcing him to ride twelve more miles in the rain to shelter. Maurice Lindsay, "Oswald of Auchencruive, Mrs Mary (d. 1788)," in *The Burns Encyclopedia* (London: Robert Hale, 1959), 276–277; David Hancock, *Citizens of the World: London Merchants and the Integration of the British Atlantic Community, 1735–1785* (Cambridge: Cambridge University Press, 1995), 59–69, 172–221; Robert Scott Davis, "Richard Oswald as 'An American': How a Frontier South Carolina Plantation Identifies the Anonymous Author of

American Husbandry and a Forgotten Founding Father of the United States," *Journal of Backcountry Studies* 8, no. 1 (2014): 19–34.

30. Simmons and Thomas, *Parliamentary Debates*, 2:272–276.

31. Grenville's friends were right that reports were arriving that some of the wealthiest colonists, including, according to Fauquier, several Virginia merchants, were applying for trading documents and giving "Bond on Stampt paper." "This They do in great Secrecy out of fear of drawing the Colony on their Backs," Fauquier wrote. Fauquier to Henry Conway, March 12, 1766, *Electronic Enlightenment,* e-enlightenment.com [accessed October 5, 2022]; Simmons and Thomas, *Parliamentary Debates*, 2:287; Walpole, *Memoirs*, 295, 299.

32. Stiles, *Stiles Papers*, reel 16, 372:35.

33. Chauncy, *Discourse*, 6–7.

34. *Virginia Gazette*, June 20, 1766, p. 1; Stiles, *Stiles Papers*, reel 16, 372:35.

35. *Virginia Gazette*, June 20, 1766, p. 2

36. Chauncy, *Discourse*, 19, 11, 13.

37. Dickinson, *Political Writings*, 20; Pickering, *Statutes at Large*, 27:19–20.

38. Kennedy, *Burgesses*, 11:66. Grubb argues that Robinson's loans were at least partly in gold and silver, and nothing rules that out other than, circumstantially, the long-standing dearth of precious metal in the colony. However, the Virginia auditors themselves describe the money as having been "re-emitted," an explicit reference to notes. Grubb may also have overread the term "specie," which, in eighteenth-century America, often meant literally "in kind," meaning tobacco, coin, or any other good that the colony accepted in tax receipts as opposed to credit. See Farley Grubb, "Colonial Virginia's Paper Money Regime, 1755–74: A Forensic Accounting Reconstruction of the Data," *Historical Methods: A Journal of Quantitative and Interdisciplinary History* 50, no. 2 (2017): 96–117. For an explicit example of an in-kind "specie" tax, see Nathaniel Bouton, ed., *Provincial Papers: Documents and Records Relating to the Province of New-Hampshire* (Nashua: Orren C. Moore, 1873), 7:78–80; Fauquier to the Board of Trade, Dec. 18, 1766, *Electronic Enlightenment,* e-enlightenment.com [accessed May 12, 2022].

39. Edward Hoyt to John Dickinson, March 17, 1765, and June 1, 1767, R. R. Logan Collection of John Dickinson Papers (Pennsylvania Historical Society, Philadelphia).

40. Christopher Gadsden to John Dickinson, June 22, 1766, R. R. Logan Collection of John Dickinson Papers (Pennsylvania Historical Society. Philadelphia).

41. Jensen, *Founding*, 216–218.

42. Jensen, *Founding*, 219–221, 224–225.

43. Walpole, *Memoirs*, 3:39; Jensen, *Founding*, 219–220.

44. Horace Walpole, *Memoirs of George III* (New York: Putnam, 1894), 2:447, 3:30; Jensen, *Founding*, 226–227.

45. E. B. O'Callaghan, John Brodhead, and Berthold Fernow, eds., *Documents Relative to the Colonial History of the State of New York* (Albany: Weed, Parsons, 1853), 7:820, 831–832, 906–908.

46. Carl Becker, *The History of Political Parties in the Province of New York, 1760–1776* (Madison: University of Wisconsin Press, 1960 [1909]), 54–55; E. B. O'Callaghan, *Journal of the Legislative Council of the Colony of New-York* (Albany: Weed and Parsons, 1861), 2:1592.

47. William Cobbett, ed., *Cobbett's Parliamentary History* (London: Hansard, 1806–1820), 16:331–342; Simmons and Thomas, *Parliamentary Debates*, 2:423–426, 464.

48. Dickinson, *Political Writings*, 20.

49. Green, *Constitutional Origins*, ix.

50. John Dickinson, *Letters from a Farmer in Pennsylvania* (Philadelphia: J. Almon, 1768), 8, 17, 20,

51. Dickinson, *Late Regulations*, 32.

52. John Murrin, "A Roof without Walls: The Dilemma of American National Identity," in *Beyond Confederation: Origins of the Constitution and American National Identity*, ed. Richard Beeman, Stephen Botein, and Edward Carter, 333–348 (Chapel Hill: University of North Carolina Press, 1987).

53. Dickinson, *Letters*, 128–131.

54. For publication data, see Carl Kaestle, "The Public Reaction to John Dickinson's Farmer's Letters," *Proceedings of the American Antiquarian Society* 78 (1969): 323–359.

55. Dickinson, *Letters*, 129–130.

56. John Locke, *Two Treatises of Government* (London: C. and J. Rivington, 1824), 20, 75.

57. Worthington Chauncy Ford, ed., *Warren–Adams Letters* (Boston: Massachusetts Historical Society, 1917), 3; Bradford Alden, ed., *Speeches of the Governors of Massachusetts, from 1765 to 1775; and the Answers of the House of Representatives, to the Same* (Boston: Russell and Gardner, 1818), 134–135; Colin Nicolson, ed., *Papers of Francis Bernard* (Boston: Colonial Society of Massachusetts, 2015), 4:149–152, 5:63–64.

58. Kaestle, "Public Reactions," 354–355; McIlwaine and Kennedy, *Journals of the House of Burgesses*, 11:165–171; Nicolson, *Papers of Francis Bernard*, 4:149–152.

59. Richard Walsh, ed., *The Writings of Christopher Gadsden, 1746–1805* (Columbia: University of South Carolina Press, 1966), 65–68; Dickinson, *Political Writings*, 20.

Chapter Six

1. Sven Beckert, *Empire of Cotton: A Global History* (New York: Knopf, 2014), 18.

2. Narendra Sinha, ed., *Fort William–India House Correspondence, Vol. V: 1767–1769* (Delhi: National Archives of India, 1949), 605.

3. Irfan Habib, *Indian Economy under Early British Rule, 1757–1857* (New Delhi: Tulika Books, 2013), 31; Romesh Dutt, *The Economic History of India under Early British Rule* (London: Kegan, Paul, Trench, Trubner, 1906), 46; Sinha, ed., *Fort William*, 605–606.

4. P. J. Marshall, *Bengal: The British Bridgehead: East India, 1740–1828* (Cambridge: Cambridge University Press, 2006), 18.

5. Ghosh Kali Charan, *Famines in Bengal, 1770–1943* (Calcutta: Indian Associated, 1944), 1–2.

6. K. D. Bhargava, ed., *Indian Records Series Fort William–Indian House Correspondence, Vol. 6* (New Delhi: National Archives of India, 1960), 181, 192, 203, 228; *Parliamentary Register, Vol. 18* (London: J. Debrett, 1784), 277.

7. Clements Markham, *Narratives of the Mission of George Bogle to Tibet* (New Delhi: Asian Educational Services, 1999), cxxxv–cxxxvi; William Wilson Hunter, *The Annals of Rural Bengal* (London: Smith, Elder, 1872), 27–37.

8. The precise weight per rupee quoted was 120 to 140 and 15 Bengali seers, respectively. The seer is a weight slightly less than a modern kilogram.

9. [Anonymous], *The Gentleman's Magazine and Historical Chronicle, Vol. 41* (London: D. Henry, 1771), 402–404; Alexander Dow, *The History of Hindostan* (London: T. Becket and P. A. De Hondt, 1772), lxxi. On Dow's biography, see Upamanyu Pablo Mukherjee, *Crime and Empire: The Colony in Nineteenth-Century Fictions of Crime* (New York: Oxford University Press, 2003), 28. Historians have long discounted the British role in the Bengal famine of 1769–1770. Peter Marshall, perhaps the most influential historian of eighteenth-century India, emphasized the "continuity" of the British regime with the regional rulers that preceded it. In Marshall's view, the British were "actors in what was an essentially Indian play." However, recent years have seen a growing awareness of the fact that, while it may not have caused the famine, the East India Company surely exploited and exacerbated it. P. J. Marshall, "The British in Asia: Trade to Dominion, 1700–1765," in *The Oxford History of the British Empire: Volume II: The Eighteenth Century*, by Wm. Roger Louis, ed. P. J. Marshall and Alaine Low (Oxford: Oxford University Press, 1998), 497–98; Dutt, *The Economic History of India under Early British Rule*, 51; Sunderlal, *How India Lost Her Freedom* (Thousand Oaks, CA: Sage Select, 2018), 89; V. Damodaran, "Famine in Bengal: A Comparison of the 1770 Famine in Bengal and the 1897 Famine in Chotanagpur," *Medieval History Journal* 10, nos. 1–2 (2006): 149; Muḥammad Kāsim ibn Hindū Shāh Firishtah (Astarābādī.) and Alexander Dow, *The History of Hindostan* (London: T. Becket and P. A. De Hondt, 1772), lxxi; Niall Ferguson, *Empire: The Rise and Demise of the British World Order and the Lessons for Global Power* (New York: Basic Books, 2004), 39–40; Maya Jasanoff, *Edge of Empire: Lives, Culture, and Conquest in the East, 1750–1850* (New York: Vintage Books, 2006), 12, 28–32; Nicholas Dirks, *The Scandal of Empire* (Cambridge: Belknap Press of Harvard University Press, 2006), esp. 14, 180, 251; Linda Colley, *Britons: Forging the Nation, 1707–1837*, 2nd ed. (New Haven: Yale University Press, 2005). On the shift in consensus see, e.g., Benjamin Carp, *Defiance of the Patriots: The Boston Tea Party and the Making of America* (New Haven: Yale University Press, 2010), 11; Datta, "Rural Bengal," 107, 112–118; Nick Bunker, *Empire on the Edge: How Britain Came to Fight America* (New York: Vintage, 2015), 46–47; William Dalrymple, *The Anarchy: The Relentless Rise of the East India Company* (London: Bloomsbury, 2019).

10. Adam Smith, *The Wealth of Nations* (New York: Bantam, 2003 [1776]), 954–955 [book V, chap. 1, part 3]; Harry Verelst, *A View of the Rise, Progress and Present State of the English Government in Bengal* (London: J. Nourse, 1772), 81–82; Bhargava, *Indian Records*, 6:225, 227–228; Dutt, *Economic History*, 46–47; H. V. Bowen, *Revenue and Reform: The Indian Problem in British Politics, 1757–1773* (Cambridge: Cambridge University Press, 1991), 131.

11. Bowen, *Revenue and Reform*, 119; House of Commons, *Reports from Committees of the House of Commons* (London: n.p., 1803–1806), 4:359.

12. Simon Yang-Chien Tsai, *Trading for Tea: A Study of the English East India Company's Tea Trade with China and the Related Financial Issues, 1760–1833* (PhD

diss., University of Leicester, 2003), 82, 91–92, 111–112; Mitchell, *British Historical Statistics*, 388; Bhargava and Srinivasachari, *Indian Records Series*, 4:473.

13. Bowen, *Revenue and Reform*, 121–122.

14. Bowen, *Revenue and Reform*, 127–128; Commons, *Reports from Committees*, 4:400.

15. James Steuart, *The Principles of Money Applied to the Present State of the Coin of Bengal* (London: East India Company, 1772), 65; Mitchell, *British Historical Statistics*, 388.

16. Steuart, *Principles of Money*, 81.

17. Steuart, *Principles of Money*, 38.

18. Jesse Prinz, "The Return of Concept Empiricism," in *Handbook of Categorization in Cognitive Science*, ed. Henri Cohen and Claire Lefebvre, 680 (New York: Elsevier, 2005); Verelst, *A View*, 88.

19. Verelst, *A View*, 89.

20. Ibid., 90.

21. Ibid., 93.

22. Ibid., 95.

23. Ibid., 103.

24. Ibid., 103.

25. Steuart, *Principles of Money*, 67.

26. Bowen, *Revenue and Reform*, 151–153; P. D. G. Thomas, *The Townshend Duties Crisis: The Second Phase of the American Revolution, 1767–1773* (Oxford: Clarendon Press, 1987), 254–255.

27. Francis S. Drake, ed., *Tea Leaves: Being a Collection of Letters and Documents Relating to the Shipment of Tea to the American Colonies in the Year 1773, by the East India Tea Company* (Boston: A. O. Crane, 1884), 218, 220.

28. Josiah Quincy, *Memoir of the Life of Josiah Quincy, Jun., of Massachusetts* (Boston: Cummings, Hilliard, 1825), 73–76.

29. Quincy, *Memoir*, 75–81; Josiah Quincy, *Portrait of a Patriot: The Major Political and Legal Papers of Josiah Quincy Junior*, ed. Daniel R. Coquillette and Neil Longley York (Charlottesville: University of Virginia Press, 2005), 3:111–114.

30. Dickinson, *The Writings of John Dickinson*, 458.

31. Ibid., 459–60.

32. Ford, *Writings of John Dickinson*, 1:460; Emma Rothschild, "A (New) Economic History of the American Revolution," *New England Quarterly* 91, no. 1 (2018): 110–128; Arthur Meier Schlesinger, "The Uprising against the East India Company," *Political Science Quarterly* 32, no. 1 (1917): 60–79.

33. Benjamin Labaree, *The Boston Tea Party* (New York: Oxford University Press, 1964), 141, 154.

34. Thomas Pownall, *The Right, Interest, and Duty of the State, as Concerned in the Affairs of the East Indies* (London: S. Bladon, 1773), 10–11.

35. Thomas and Simmons, *Debates*, 4:37, 76.

36. Thomas and Simmons, *Debates*, 4:203–204.

37. Thomas and Simmons, *Debates*, 4:232–234

38. Bunker, *Empire on the Edge*, 338.

39. *Journals of the House of Commons*, 35:99; Bunker, *Empire on the Edge*, 360–361; Thomas and Simmons, *Proceedings and Debates*, 5:313, 359.

40. T. M. Devine, *The Scottish Nation, 1700-2000* (London: Penguin, 2000), 44–46; Bunker, *Empire on the Edge*, 347–348, 353, 364.

41. Bunker, *Empire on the Edge*, 281–288.

42. Bailyn, *Ideological Origins*, 219.

43. Breen, *Marketplace of Revolution*, 9.

44. Bunker, *Empire on the Edge*, 348.

45. Woody Holton, *Liberty Is Sweet: The Hidden History of the American Revolution* (New York: Simon & Schuster, 2021), 154.

46. Giovanni Arrighi, *The Long Twentieth Century*, 54–70; Verelst, *A View*, 103.

47. What Karl Polanyi calls the "utopian endeavour of economic liberalism to set up a self-regulating market system" seems to have its British roots in this imperial moment. As we will see, Britain became far better at constructing world systems after the American Revolution clarified the relevant levers of control. Polanyi, *The Great Transformation* (Boston: Beacon Press, 1957), 31.

Chapter Seven

1. Moncure Conway, *The Life of Thomas Paine* (New York: Putnam, 1892), 1:16–17.

2. Paine, *The Complete Writings of Thomas Paine*, ed. Philip Sheldon Foner (New York: Citadel Press, 1945), 1:143–144.

3. Ray Raphael and Marie Raphael, *The Spirit of 74: How the American Revolution Began* (New York: New Press, 2015); McCusker, *Money and Exchange*, 131.

4. A Citizen, *"To the Inhabitants of the State of Massachusetts-Bay. Friends and Fellow Countrymen! It Is with Concern and Attention That the House of Representatives Find That an Act, Intitled an Act for Drawing in the Bills of Credit"* (Boston: John Gill, 1777), 2. This pamphlet is the report of the Springfield Convention on New England currency held in 1777.

5. Bouton, *Provincial Papers.*, 7:75, 78.

6. Ibid., 7:78–79.

7. Ibid., 7:477.

8. Ibid., 7:481.

9. Ibid., 7:482.

10. Ibid., 7:477.

11. State of New Jersey, *Minutes of the Provincial Congress and the Council of Safety of the State of New Jersey [1775-1776]* (Trenton: Naar, Day & Naar, 1879), 234.

12. For a version of the carting and sledding economy, see Chapin family, "Chapin Family Business Records, 1782–1866" (Baker Library, Harvard Business School, Boston).

13. Caleb Stark and John Stark, *Memoir and Official Correspondence of Gen. John Stark: With Notices of Several Other Officers of the Revolution. Also, a Biography of Capt. Phinehas Stevens and of Col. Robert Rogers, with an Account of His Services in America During the "Seven Years' War"* (Concord, MA: Edson C. Eastman, 1877), 110.

14. Archelaus Lewis, "Archelaus Lewis's Diary and Orderly Books," July 20, 1775, Maine Historical Society, Portland.

15. Ibid., August 1, 1775.

16. Ibid., July 23, 1775.

17. Ibid., July 25, 1775.

18. Ibid., August 13, 1775.

19. Ibid.

20. Bouton, *Provincial Papers.*, 7:510.

21. Ibid.

22. Peter Force, ed., *American Archives* (Washington, D.C.: Congress, 1837), 4th ser., 2:1584; the best account of Connecticut's mobilization, including monetary issues, is Richard Buel, *Dear Liberty: Connecticut's Mobilization for the Revolutionary War* (Middletown, CT: Wesleyan University Press, 1980), https://bibdata .princeton.edu/bibliographic/50582.

23. Bartlett, *Records*, 7:320–321.

24. Ibid., 7:333.

25. Ibid., 7:470.

26. James P. Snell, *History of Hunterdon and Somerset Counties, New Jersey* (Philadelphia: Everts & Peck, 1881), 33.

27. *Minutes of the Provincial Congress*, 186.

28. Ibid., 223.

29. Ibid., 224–25.

30. Ibid., 226.

31. Ibid., 246.

32. Ibid., 249–50.

33. Thomas L. Purvis, "Hart, John," *American National Biography Online*, www .anb.org/articles/01/01-00378.html [accessed February 22, 2017].

34. *Minutes of the Provincial Congress*, 250.

35. Ibid., 252.

36. Ibid., 361.

37. Merrill, "Cash Is Good to Eat," 61, 63.

38. Purvis, "Hart, John".

39. James T. Mitchell and Henry Flanders, eds., *The Statutes at Large of Pennsylvania from 1682 to 1801* (Harrisburg: Clarence M. Busch, State Printer of Pennsylvania, 1896), 8:486, 489.

40. Ibid., 8:490.

41. Ibid., 8:494.

42. William Hand Browne, *Archives of Maryland* (Baltimore: Maryland Historical Society, 1892), 11:24, http://archive.org/details/archivesofmaryla11brow.

43. Ibid., 11:27.

44. Delaware, *Laws of the State of Delaware* (New-Castle, DE: Samuel and John Adams, 1797), 1:517, 617; Richard S. Rodney, *Colonial Finances in Delaware* (Wilmington: Wilmington Trust Company, 1928), 43.

45. Henry Read McIlwaine and John Pendleton Kennedy, eds., *Journals of the House of Burgesses of Virginia* (Richmond: Library Board, Virginia State Library, 1905), 13:274.

46. Elmer Beecher Russell, *The Review of American Colonial Legislation by the King in Council* (New York: Columbia University Press, 1915), 214.

47. McIlwaine and Kennedy, *Journals of the House of Burgesses of Virginia*, 13:278.

48. Ibid., 13:279.

49. Carl L. Becker, *The Declaration of Independence; a Study in the History of Political Ideas* (New York: Knopf, 1966), 181.

50. McIlwaine and Kennedy, *Journals of the House of Burgesses of Virginia*, 13:281–283.

51. Robert L. Scribner and William James Van Schreeven, eds., *Revolutionary Virginia, the Road to Independence* (Charlottesville: University Press of Virginia, 1973), 3:319, 330.

52. William Pitt Palmer et al., eds., *Calendar of Virginia State Papers and Other Manuscripts Preserved in the Capitol at Richmond* (Richmond: R. F. Walker, 1875), 1:267.

53. Hening, *The Statutes at Large*, 9:61–69.

54. Ibid., 9:67, 69.

55. Robert A. Rutland, ed., *The Papers of George Mason, 1725–1792* (Chapel Hill: University of North Carolina Press, 1970), 1:255–256.

56. William Laurence Saunders, ed., *The Colonial Records of North Carolina* (Raleigh, NC: Josephus Daniels, 1886), 10:194–195, http://archive.org/details/colonialrecordso10nort.

57. Allen Daniel Candler, ed., *The Revolutionary Records of the State of Georgia* (Atlanta: Franklin-Turner, 1908), 1:251–252, http://archive.org/details/revorecordsofgeor01candrich.

58. The nominal sum was large, in part, because South Carolina currency had long been valued at 7 to 1 in terms of pounds sterling, versus the 1⅓ to 1 of New England's "Lawful Money" standard. See McCusker, *Money and Exchange*.

59. William Edwin Hemphill, ed., *Extracts from the Journals of the Provincial Congresses of South Carolina, 1775–1776* (Columbia: South Carolina Archives Dept, 1960), 51.

60. Drayton's father, William Henry Drayton, had participated in the debates and left an account his son edited and published, after further research, as a memoir of the Revolutionary era. Drayton, *Memoirs of the American Revolution: From Its Commencement to the Year 1776, Inclusive, as Relating to the State of South-Carolina and Occasionally Referring to the States of North-Carolina and Georgia* (Charleston: A. E. Miller, 1821), 264.

61. Ibid.

62. David R. Chestnutt et al., eds., *The Papers of Henry Laurens* (Columbia: University of South Carolina Press, 1968), 10:185.

63. Joseph Ernst, *Money and Politics in America, 1755–1775: A Study in the Currency Act of 1764 and the Political Economy of Revolution* (Chapel Hill: University of North Carolina Press, 1973), 278; E. B. O'Callaghan, ed., *Documents Relative to the Colonial History of the State of New York* (Albany: Weed, Parsons, 1853), 8:72, 96–97, http://archive.org/details/documentsrelativ08brod; Commissioners of Statutory Revision, ed., *The Colonial Laws of New York from the Year 1664 to the Revolution* (n.p.: J. B. Lyon, 1894), 5:638–639.

64. *Journals of the Provincial Congress, Provincial Convention, Committee of Safety and Council of Safety of the State of New-York. 1775–1776–1777* (Albany: Thurlow Weed, 1842), 1:14.

65. Benjamin Franklin, "Remarks and Facts Relative to the American Paper Money," *Pennsylvania Chronicle*, June 25, 1767.

66. *Journals of the Provincial Congress*, 1:19.

67. Ibid., 1:18.

68. Force, *American Archives*, 4th ser., 2:1262–3; *Journals of the Provincial Congress*, 1:18.

69. Buel shows that Connecticut leaders saw the currency the same way. Taxing it in and destroying it—especially when it had already depreciated—was a cheap way to build up a strong creditor position vis-à-vis the Continental Congress. Buel, *Dear Liberty*.

70. Worthington C. Ford, ed., *Journals of the Continental Congress, 1774–1789* (Washington, D.C.: U.S. Government Printing Office, 1904), 2:88–91.

71. *Journals of the Provincial Congress*, 1:14.

72. On Wednesday, June 14, 1775, after one day of consideration on ways and means of raising money, Congress resolved the question of continental army pay in terms of dollars. Force, *American Archives*, 4th ser., 2:1847.

73. Ibid., 4th ser., 2:1254; Benjamin Franklin, "Of the Paper Money of America," ca. 1780, U.S. National Archives, http://founders.archives.gov/documents/Franklin/01-34-02-0156.

74. Ford, *Journals*, 2:103; Force, *American Archives*, 4th ser., 2:1854.

75. On the issue of translation between local currencies into dollars, see Ronald Michener and Robert E. Wright, "Development of the US Monetary Union," *Financial History Review* 13, no. 1 (2006): 24–25; *Journals of the Provincial Congress*, 1:48.

76. Ford, *Journals*, 2:103.

77. Force, *American Archives*, 2:1854.

78. Carl Wennerlind, "David Hume's Monetary Theory Revisited: Was He Really a Quantity Theorist and an Inflationist?" *Journal of Political Economy* 113, no. 1 (February 1, 2005): 223–37, https://doi:10.1086/426037.

79. Ford, *Journals*, 4:382–383.

80. Ibid., 2:221.

81. Ibid., 2:223.

82. Newman, *Early Paper Money of America*, 61–69.

83. Ford, *Journals*, 4:383.

84. *The Parliamentary Register* . . . (London: J. Almon, 1776), 3:501–488 [the final pages are misnumbered; after p. 502 it drops back to p. 479 and continues sequentially from there]; *Accounts of the Net Public Income and Expenditure of Great Britain and Ireland, 1688–1800; Receipts and Issues from Exchequer; Accounts of Gross Public Income and Expenditure, 1801–69,* 19th Century House of Commons Sessional Papers, vol. XXXV.1, 383 (House of Commons Parliamentary Papers Online, 2005), p. 174, https://parlipapers.proquest.com [accessed Oct. 28, 2018]. For good secondary analyses of contents of the *Accounts,* see Patrick O'Brien, "The Political Economy of British Taxation, 1660–1815," *Economic History Review* 41, no. 1 (1988): 1–32; Stephen Conway, *The British Isles and the War of Independence* (Oxford: Oxford University Press, 2002), 45–84.

85. *Parliamentary Register*, 3:487.

86. *Parliamentary Register*, 3:502.

87. *Parliamentary Register*, 3:501–488.

88. Pickering, *Statutes at Large*, 31:201–204; *Parliamentary Register,* 3:501–488; C. L'Estrange Ewen, *Lotteries and Sweepstakes* (London: Heath Cranton, 1932), 202–203. For an account of how demands for specie shaped the Bank of England's role in public borrowing, see Richard A. Kleer, "'A New Species of Mony': British Exchequer Bills, 1701–1711," *Financial History Review* 22, no. 2 (2015): 179–203.

89. *Parliamentary Register,* 3:501–488.

90. Pickering, *Statutes at Large*, 31:207–210.

91. Malachy Postlethwayt, *The Universal Dictionary of Trade and Commerce* (London: W. Strahan, J. and F. Rivington, 1774), 2:294.

92. Thomas Hansard, ed., *The Parliamentary History of England* (London: Hansard, 1813), 18:879.

93. Edward Larkin, ed., *Common Sense* (Peterborough, ON: Broadview Editions, 2004), 64.

94. Ibid., 65.

95. Thomas Jefferson, *A Summary View of the Rights of British America* (London: G. Kearsley, 1774), 42. The best single volume on the Declaration of Independence is Danielle Allen, *Our Declaration: A Reading of the Declaration of Independence in Defense of Equality* (London: Norton, 2014).

Chapter Eight

1. William B. Willcox, ed., *The American Rebellion: Sir Henry Clinton's Narrative of His Campaigns* (Hamden, CT: Archon Books, 1971), 109, 258; Great Britain, *The Parliamentary Register; or, History of the Proceedings and Debates of the House of Commons* (London: Wilson, 1802), 12:1–25, 424–434. There is a large recent literature on the loyalist experience emphasizing their numbers and significance. The British officers' complaint that only British-born men served is plausible. Some 19,000 men served in loyalist regiments. Roughly 90,000 British-born immigrants to America had arrived in the fifteen years prior to 1775. The more significant source of loyalist support, as mentioned by many recent authors, came from enslaved Americans who were promised freedom in return for their efforts. Maya Jasanoff, *Liberty's Exiles: American Loyalists in the Revolutionary World* (New York: Random House, 2012); Alan Gilbert, *Black Patriots and Loyalists: Fighting for Emancipation in the War for Independence* (Chicago: University of Chicago Press, 2013). The classic article is still Paul H. Smith, "The American Loyalists: Notes on Their Organization and Numerical Strength," *William & Mary Quarterly* 25, no. 2 (1968): 259–277; Aaron Fogelman, "Migrations to the Thirteen British North American Colonies, 1700–1775: New Estimates," *Journal of Interdisciplinary History* 22, no. 4 (1992): 691–709.

2. Grubb, *The Continental Dollar*, 11.

3. Winthrop Sargent, ed., *Loyalist Poetry of the Revolution* (Philadelphia: Collins, 1857), 71.

4. Ford, *Journals,* 2:237.

5. Force, *American Archives,* 4th ser., 3:242–243.

6. Ibid., 3:669–670.

7. Ibid., 3:738–740.

8. Ibid., 3:796–797.

9. Ibid., 3:1892–1894.

10. Ibid., 3:1093–1094, 1124.

11. Ibid., 3:1124. Schuyler wrote a short note sent by the Congress's dispatch riders—presumably the same ones that had been sent with Pennsylvania's small hoard. In it, Schuyler, tellingly, does not mention an acute need for specie.

12. For orders to collect gold and silver, see Ford, *Journals*, 3:179, 4:73; for a contemporary analysis of the Latin mottos and emblems, see Henry Phillips, *Historical Sketches of the Paper Currency of the American Colonies: Prior to the Adoption of the Federal Constitution* (Roxbury, MA: W. Elliot Woodward, 1865), 2:251–254; for the original source of the emblems, see Joachim Camerarius, *Symbola et Emblemata* (Mainz: n.p., 1668).

13. On New York currency in Quebec, see "An Ordinance for Regulating and Establishing the Currency of the Province," *Quebec Gazette*, Oct. 4, 1764; Herbert Heaton, "The Playing Card Currency to French Canada," *American Economic Review* 18, no. 4 (1928): 649–662.

14. The technical term for this is the "quantity theory of money," which states that MV=PT, or the money supply (M) times the velocity of circulation (V) equals the price level (P) times the number of transactions (T). All things being equal, it suggests, if the M rises, the price level will rise with it. The problem, which goes back to the infancy of quantitative research in colonial currency in the 1970s, is that the price of colonial bills of credit has practically no statistical relationship to their supply. Initially, this result was used against the quantity theory across the board. More recently, Farley Grubb and others have suggested that the difference can be attributed to the way that colonial bills of credit, in fact, differed from later forms of money. The best summary is Farley Grubb, "Colonial American Money and the Quantity Theory of Money: An Extension," *Social Science History* 43, no. 1 (2019): 185–207. Notable earlier entries in the debate include Roberg Craig West, "Money in the Colonial American Economy," *Economic Inquiry* 16, no. 1 (1978): 1–15; Ronald Michener and Robert Wright, "Development of the US Monetary Union," *Financial History Review* 13, no. 1 (2006): 19–41; Moore, Promise to Pay, 68–70.

15. Charles Calomiris, "Institutional Failure, Monetary Scarcity, and the Depreciation of the Continental," *Journal of Economic History* 48, no. 1 (1988): 47–68. More recently, historians have used a version of Calomiris's argument, as expanded by Desan and others, to explain the performance of the greenback dollar during the U.S. Civil War. Ariel Ron and Sofia Valeonti, "The Money War: Democracy, Taxes and Inflation in the U.S. Civil War," *Cambridge Journal of Economics* 47, no. 2 (2023): 263–288.

16. Douglas Southall Freeman, *George Washington, a Biography* (New York: Scribner, 1948), 4:278; Francis Wharton, ed., *The Revolutionary Diplomatic Correspondence of the United States* (Washington, D.C.: Government Printing Office, 1889), 2:233.

17. George Washington to John Hancock, December 16, 1776, *Papers of George Washington Digital Edition*, http://rotunda.upress.virginia.edu/founders/GEWN-03-07-02-0280 [accessed Feb. 21, 2017].

18. Richard K. Showman, ed., *The Papers of General Nathanael Greene* (Chapel Hill: University of North Carolina Press, 1976), 1:369.

19. Showman, *Papers of General Nathanael Greene*, 1:370–375.

20. Joanne B. Freeman, *Affairs of Honor: National Politics in the New Republic* (New Haven: Yale University Press, 2001); Joanne B. Freeman, "Dueling as Politics: Reinterpreting the Burr–Hamilton Duel," *William & Mary Quarterly* 53, no. 2 (1996): 289–318.

21. Wharton, *Revolutionary*, 2:234.

22. Ibid.

23. Ibid., 2:236.

24. Charles Janeway Stillé, *The Life and Times of John Dickinson, 1732–1808* (Philadelphia: Historical Society of Pennsylvania, 1891), 211.

25. Stillé, *Life and Times*, 401–403; Wharton, *Revolutionary*, 2:233; Council of Safety, *Minutes of the Council of Safety of the Province of Pennsylvania* (Harrisburg: Theodore Fenn, 1852), 92.

26. Paine, *Complete Writings*, 1:50; David Hackett Fischer, *Washington's Crossing* (Oxford: Oxford University Press, 2004), 142.

27. Grubb, *Continental Dollar*, 157.

28. Smith, *The Freedoms We Lost*, 209.

29. Ford, *Journals*, 4:49, 6:1045.

30. Ford, *Journals*, 7:33–37.

31. Ford, *Journals*, 7:123–125.

32. *Selections from the Correspondence*, 34–45.

33. *Selections from the Correspondence*, 39.

34. *Selections from the Correspondence*, 45.

35. Henry Biddle, ed., *Extracts from the Journal of Elizabeth Drinker* (Philadelphia: J. B. Lippincott, 1889), 71.

36. On the author's identity, see Samuel F. Batchelder, "Burgoyne and His Officers in Cambridge, 1777–1778," *Cambridge Historical Society Publications* 13 (January 22, 1918): 17–79. For the original German text, see August Ludwig Schlözer, ed., *August Ludwig Schlözer's Briefwechsel meist historischen und politischen Inhalts* (Göttingen: Bandenhoefschen, 1778–1782); Heinrich Urban Cleve, *Heinrich Urban Cleve Journal 1778*, Collection, series VIII D, entry 21, Peter Force Papers (Library of Congress).

37. Ford, *Journals*, 4:382.

38. Ray W. Pettengill, trans., *Letters from America, 1776–1779* (New York: Houghton Mifflin, 1924).

39. Pettingill, *Letters from America*, 127.

40. Pettingill, *Letters from America*, 127.

41. Joel Richard Paul, *Unlikely Allies: How a Merchant, a Playwright, and a Spy Saved the American Revolution* (New York: Penguin, 2010).

42. Chevalier d'Éon, "Mémoires sur les fluctuations de la Valeur de la Monnaye Continentalle leurs Causes leurs Effets," July 1778, Mf. 7281 V4 16–27 (Archives du Ministère des affaires étrangères, Paris).

43. Forrest Morgan and Charles J. Hoadly, eds., *The Public Records of the State of Connecticut* (Hartford: Case, Lockwood & Brainard, 1894), 1:613–618.

44. Ford, *Journals*, 11:480. For Gouverneur Morris's authorship, see ibid., 12:1284–1285.

45. Ford, *Journals*, for the report: 12:1073, for the appointment: 11:843.

46. Carlos Emmer Godfrey, *The Commander-in-Chief's Guard, Revolutionary War* (Washington, D.C.: Stevenson-Smith, 1904), 19.

47. "Prince Howland," *U.S., Sons of the American Revolution Membership Applications, 1889–1970*, Ancestry.com [accessed November 21, 2017]; "Israel Howland," *Lineage Book of the Charter Members of the Daughters of the American Revolution*, Ancestry.com [accessed November 21, 2017]; "Israel Howland," *Find a Grave Index*, Ancestry.com [accessed November 21, 2017]; "General Orders," October 23, 1778, *The Papers of George Washington Digital Edition* (Charlottesville: University of Virginia Press, Rotunda, 2008), http://rotunda.upress.virginia.edu/founders /GEWN-03-17-02-0549 [accessed November 21, 2017].

48. *Selections from the Correspondence of the Executive of New Jersey, from 1776 to 1786* (Newark: Daily Advertiser, 1848), 138.

49. Elijah Fisher, "Diary 1775–1785," Elijah Fisher Papers, Maine Historical Society, Portland.

50. George Washington, "General Orders, 23 October 1778," *The Papers of George Washington Digital Edition* (Charlottesville: University of Virginia Press, 2008–2017), http://rotunda.upress.virginia.edu/founders/default.xqy?keys=GEWN -print-03-17-02-0549 [accessed Nov. 21, 2017].

51. Buel, *Dear Liberty*, 166–167.

52. Ford, *Journals*, 12:929.

53. Pelatiah Webster, *Political Essays on the Nature and Operation of Money, Public Finances, and Other Subjects* (Philadelphia: Joseph Crukshank, 1791), 186.

54. Mary S. Lockwood, ed., *Daughters of the American Revolution Magazine* 16 (Washington, D.C.: National Society of the Daughters of the American Revolution, 1900), 70.

55. Webster, *Political Essays*, iii.

56. Ibid., 81.

57. Ibid., 14.

58. Ibid., 24.

59. Ibid., 131.

60. Ibid., 133.

61. Ibid., 132–133.

62. Adam Smith, *The Wealth of Nations* (New York: Bantam, 2003 [1776]), 627; John McCusker, "Estimating Early American Gross Domestic Product," *Historical Methods* 33, no. 3 (2000): 155–162. William Petty had made a related point in 1662 when he stated that though pounds, shillings, and pence were the usual English measures of wealth, the only "natural Denominations" were land and labor. William Petty, *A Treatise of Taxes and Contributions* (London: Nathaniel Brooke, 1662), 26.

63. Webster, *Political Essays*, 465–466.

64. Pelatiah Webster, *To the Stock-Holders of the Bank of North-America, on the Subject of the Old and New Banks* (Philadelphia: Joseph Crukshank, 1791), 1.

65. Webster, *Political Essays*, 41.

66. Ibid., 63.

67. Timothy Mitchell, "Fixing the Economy," *Cultural Studies* 12, no. 1 (1998): 82–101.

68. Webster, *Political Essays*, 62.

69. Ibid., 63.

70. Ibid., 133.

71. Ibid., 48.

72. Ibid., 111.

73. Ford, *Journals,* 12:1266–1267; Farley Grubb, "The Continental Dollar: How Much Was Really Issued?" *Journal of Economic History* 68, no. 1 (March 2008): 283–291.

74. Eric P. Newman, "The Successful British Counterfeiting of American Paper Money During the American Revolution," *British Numismatic Journal* 29 (1958–1959): 175–187, esp. 177. Ford, *Journals,* 13:60.

75. Ford, *Journals,* 13:59. Grubb calculates that the yearly tax needed, after factoring in the spending of 1779, would be $10.2 million for eighteen years. Grubb, *Continental Dollar,* 161–162. On counterfeiting, see also Albert Henry Smyth, ed., *The Writings of Benjamin Franklin* (New York: Macmillan, 1905–1907), 10:110.

76. Ford, *Journals,* 13:60.

77. Buel, *Dear Liberty,* 199–200.

78. George Washington to James Warren, March 31, 1779, *Papers of George Washington Digital Edition.*

79. Ford, *Journals,* 13:492–493, 14:626. For prewar per capita tax estimates, see Farley Grubb, "State Redemption of the Continental Dollar, 1779–90," *William & Mary Quarterly* 69, no. 1 (2012): 147–180, esp. 151. Household estimates derived from Jones's notion of "wealthholders" approximating free, taxable households: Jones, *Wealth of a Nation to Be,* 3–37. The idea of implausible overtaxing leading to devaluation originates with Farley Grubb, *Continental Dollar,* 102–171.

80. Ford, *Journals,* 14:656.

81. Buel, *Dear Liberty,* 199–200; Paul H. Smith, ed., *Letters of the Delegates to Congress, 1774–1789* (Washington, D.C.: U.S. Government Printing Office), 12:493–494.

82. Robert J. Steinfeld, *The Invention of Free Labor: The Employment Relation in English and American Law and Culture, 1350–1870* (Chapel Hill: University of North Carolina Press, 1991); Estelle Stewart and J. C. Brown eds., *History of Wages in the United States from Colonial Times to 1928* (Washington, D.C.: U.S. Government Printing Office, 1934), 13. For an analysis of how the British overcame similar payment difficulties in the late eighteenth century by aggregating and loaning out tax receipts to employers, see Craig Muldrew, "Wages and the Problem of Monetary Scarcity in England," in *Wages and Currency: Global Comparisons from Antiquity to the Twentieth Century,* ed. Jan Lucassen, 391–410 (New York: Peter Lang, 2007).

83. John Codman to William Turnbull, May 4, 1780, John Codman Letterbook, vol. 2, Records of Boston Merchants Engaged in Foreign Trade (Baker Library, Harvard Business School, Boston).

84. Ibid.

85. Smith, *The Freedoms We Lost,* 134–182; John K. Alexander, "The Fort Wilson Incident of 1779: A Case Study of the Revolutionary Crowd," *William & Mary Quarterly,* third series, 31, no. 4 (October 1, 1974): 589–612, https://doi.org/10.2307/1921605.

86. "Philadelphia, May 27," *Pennsylvania Packet,* May 27, 1779, 2.

87. Ford, *Journals*, 5:433; Robert Buchanan, *Genealogy of the Roberdeau Family* (Washington, D.C.: Joseph L. Pearson, 1876), 64.

88. "Philadelphia, May 27," *Pennsylvania Packet*, May 27, 1779, 2.

89. "General Loan-Office," *Pennsylvania Packet*, May 27, 1779, 3.

90. "Address of the Committee of the City and Liberties of Philadelphia; to Their Fellow Citizens throughout the United States," *Pennsylvania Packet*, June 29, 1779, 1, 4.

91. Ibid.

92. "Sons of Boston! Sleep no longer!" *Pennsylvania Packet*, June 29, 1779, 2.

93. "Extract of a letter from Albany, dated June 16, 1779, to a gentleman in this city," *Pennsylvania Packet*, June 29, 1779, 2–3.

94. "The following agreement . . ." *Pennsylvania Packet*, June 29, 1779, 2.

95. "To the Committee of the City . . ." *Pennsylvania Packet*, July 1, 1779, 3.

96. Grubb, *Continental Dollar*.

97. George Washington to Lund Washington, August 17, 1779, *George Washington Papers Digital Edition*, http://rotunda.upress.virginia.edu/founders/default.xqy?keys =GEWN-print-03-22-02-0142 [accessed July 23, 2017].

98. Ford, *Journals*, 14:1013.

99. Ford, *Journals*, 15:1052–1056, 1060–1061.

100. Ford, *Journals*, 15:1057–1062.

101. Alexander's article continues to be the standard source on this incident. For other recent accounts, see Bouton, *Taming Democracy*, 68–69; Smith, *The Freedoms We Lost*.

102. "The Committee to Whom Was Referred the Memorial of the Sundry Merchants," *Pennsylvania Packet*, September 10, 1779, 3; "To the Committee of the City of Philadelphia," *Pennsylvania Packet*, Sept. 10, 1779, 1.

103. Buel, *Dear Liberty*, 204–205.

104. Biddle, *Extracts*, 125; Grubb, *Continental Dollar*, table D.2; Ford, *Journals*, 30:22–24. The 1786 report that provides these number notes that bills destroyed in the individual states were not accounted for, meaning the sum may be substantially higher. However, the general trend is clear.

105. Ford, *Journals*, 16:205–207.

106. Ford, *Journals*, 16:268.

Chapter Nine

1. E. R. McMurry et al., "Fire Scars Reveal Source of New England's 1780 Dark Day," *International Journal of Wildland Fire* 16, no. 3 (2007): 266–70; James Sullivan Martin, *A Narrative of Some of the Adventures, Dangers and Sufferings of a Revolutionary Soldier* (Hallowell, ME: Glazier, Masters, 1830), 129–31.

2. Ibid.

3. Ibid., 134.

4. Israel Putnam to George Washington, November 7, 1777, *Papers of George Washington Digital Edition*, http://rotunda.upress.virginia.edu/founders/default.xqy ?keys=GEWN-print-03-12-02-0147 [accessed June 13, 2017].

5. James C. Neagles, *Summer Soldiers: A Survey and Index of Revolutionary War Courts-Martial* (Salt Lake City: Ancestry, 1986), 58–64.

6. Ford, *Journals,* 16:326.

7. Martin, *Narrative,* 134.

8. Reed, *Life and Correspondence,* 2:203.

9. Paine, *Complete Writings,* 2:383–384.

10. Paine, *Complete Writings,* 2:640.

11. Ibid., 2:660.

12. Ibid., 2:1186.

13. Reed, *Life and Correspondence,* 2:218.

14. Paine, *Complete Writings,* 2:404.

15. Ferguson, *Power of the Purse,* 24.

16. Paine, *Complete Writings,* 2:1183.

17. Samuel Hazard, ed., *Hazard's Register of Pennsylvania: Devoted to the Preservation of Facts and Documents, and Every Kind of Useful Information Respecting the State of Pennsylvania* (Philadelphia: W. F. Geddes, 1828), 2:259.

18. Lawrence Lewis Jr., *A History of the Bank of North America* (Philadelphia: J. B. Lippincott, 1882), 20.

19. Hazard, *Hazard's Register of Pennsylvania,* 2:260.

20. Ibid.; Bray Hammond, *Banks and Politics in America from the Revolution to the Civil War* (Princeton: Princeton University Press, 1957), 43; George Clymer to Samuel Meredith and Thomas Barclay, July 5, 1780, Bank of North America Records, letter book from 1780, vol. 643 (Historical Society of Pennsylvania, Philadelphia).

21. Hazard, *Hazard's Register of Pennsylvania,* 2:259–260.

22. McFarland, ed., *Colonial Currency Reprints,* 1:124; Hazard, *Hazard's Register of Pennsylvania,* 2:259. Hammond, like virtually every other writer on the Bank of Pennsylvania, argues that "Three hundred thousand pounds, Pennsylvania currency in specie" or "real money" likely meant "an amount of specie," suggesting a supply of physical gold and silver. Considering that the first advertisement of the bank admonished subscribers to bring their bills carefully bundled, however, it seems considerably more likely that the expression referred to the value of specie in terms of the Pennsylvania pound, a relationship long established by law. The idea seems to have been to detach the value signified by the term "Pennsylvania currency" from the fluctuating value of the bills. Hammond, *Banks and Politics,* 45.

23. George Clymer to George Washington, August 21, 1780, BNA Records, vol. 643.

24. Charles Rappleye, *Robert Morris: Financier of the American Revolution* (New York: Simon & Schuster, 2010), 1–15; Robert E. Wright, "Thomas Willing (1731–1821): Philadelphia Financier and Forgotten Founding Father," *Pennsylvania History: A Journal of Mid-Atlantic Studies* 63, no. 4 (1996): 525–560.

25. Wright, "Thomas Willing," 537, 542.

26. Rappleye, *Robert Morris,* 36–37, 52.

27. Rappleye, *Robert Morris,* 182, 184.

28. Rappleye, *Robert Morris,* 209; Peggy Liss, *Atlantic Empires: The Network of Trade and Revolution, 1713–1826* (Baltimore: Johns Hopkins University Press, 1983), 115–117.

29. Paine, *Complete Writings,* 2:1186.

30. E. James Ferguson, *The Papers of Robert Morris, 1781–1784* (Pittsburg: University of Pittsburg Press, 1973), 1:31.

31. Ford, *Journals*, 19:126; Ferguson, *Papers of Robert Morris*, 1:66–74.

32. Hazard, *Hazard's Register of Pennsylvania*, 259–160; "To the Public," May 28, 1781, James Wilson Papers, vol. 2, box 10, folder 10 (Historical Society of Pennsylvania, Philadelphia).

33. Ferguson, *Papers of Robert Morris*, 1:92, 142, 144.

34. [Robert Morris], "To the Public," James Wilson Papers, vol. 2, box 10, ff. 10, 87–97 (Historical Society of Pennsylvania, Philadelphia); Ferguson, *Papers of Robert Morris*, 1:144.

35. Ferguson, *Papers of Robert Morris*, 1:149–150.

36. Thomas Willing to William Phillips, Jonathan Mason, Isaac Smith, Thomas Russell, J. Lowell, and T. Higginson, January 6, 1784, BNA Records, vol. 2.

37. Jeffrey Crow and Larry Tise, eds., *The Southern Experience in the American Revolution* (Chapel Hill: University of North Carolina Press, 1978), 169.

38. Ferguson, *Papers of Robert Morris*, 1:59–60.

39. Pettengill, *Letters from America*, 232.

40. Crow and Tice, *Southern Experience*, 161; John Adams to Hendrik Calkoen, October 26, 1780, Founders Online, U.S. National Archives, last modified March 30, 2017, http://founders.archives.gov/documents/Adams/06-10-02-0117-0016. Original source: *The Adams Papers, Papers of John Adams, vol. 10, July 1780–December 1780*, ed. Gregg L. Lint and Richard Alan Ryerson, 238–239 (Cambridge: Harvard University Press, 1996).

41. Benjamin Franklin Stevens, ed., *The Campaign in Virginia, 1781* (London: n.p., 1888), 1:314.

42. Stevens, *Campaign*, 1:332.

43. Stevens, *Campaign*, 1:394.

44. The letter does not appear in the official record of Clinton and Germain's correspondence, in CO/5/97-99 in the National Archives, Kew. However, there are no letters in the official correspondence from December 15, 1779, to February 15, 1779, one of the longest breaks in the continuous record. Germain is known to have carried on secret, confidential correspondence on American affairs during his time as secretary of state for the American colonies that did not find its way into the official records. The bulk of the records housed in the Germain Papers at the Clements Library at the University of Michigan, which does not include this letter, come from this source, and therefore are missing from the official record in the National Archives. Relevant correspondence on reels 4–6 of module 5 of the Colonial Office paper microfilmed in the 1970s. "British Public Record Office Colonial Office, Class 5 Files," University Publications of America, 1972, microform 05485, Princeton University Library, http://cisupa.proquest.com/ksc_assets/catalog/10752_C.O.5FilesPt5.pdf.

45. The confidential letter matches Clinton's tone in his published correspondence. Newman, quoting J. Almon's *Remembrancer* from 1780, says that the letter appeared in the April 8, 1780, edition of the *Pennsylvania Journal and Weekly Advertiser*. In fact, it appeared on the first page of the April 12, 1780, edition. "Private No. 5," *Pennsylvania Journal and Weekly Advertiser*, April 12, 1780, no. 1335 (Philadelphia), 1–2; Newman, "Successful British Counterfeiting," 186; *The Remembrancer or Impartial Depository of Public Events* (London: J. Almon, 1780), 10:40.

46. "Private No. 5," *Pennsylvania Journal*, 2.

47. Ford, *Journals*, 16:326. On the use of IOUs, see Ferguson, *Power of the Purse*, 57–70.

48. Forrest, Hoadly, Labaree, *Public Records*, 3:560.

49. Fisher, "Diary," August 25, 1780.

50. Ibid., 561.

51. Ibid., 562.

52. Rhode Island General Assembly. "An Act for Proportioning the Supplies of Beef to the Several Towns in This State for the Support of the Army for the Months of October and November Next.," August 1781, An American Time Capsule, Library of Congress, http://memory.loc.gov/rbc/rbpe/rbpe16/rbpe165/16500800/001dr.jpg.

53. Ferguson, *Papers of Robert Morris*, 1:228–229.

54. Ferguson, *Papers of Robert Morris*, 1:311–315.

55. Author's translation. Silas Deane, "Mémoire," August 1776, F. 7280 V1 99–104 (Paris: Archives du Ministère des affaires étrangères); Paine, *Complete Writings*, 2:96–97.

56. Alexander Hamilton to John Laurens, February 4, 1781, *The Papers of Alexander Hamilton Digital Edition*, ed. Harold C. Syrett (Charlottesville: University of Virginia Press, 2011), http://rotunda.upress.virginia.edu/founders/default.xqy?keys=ARHN-chron-1780-1781-02-04-1 [accessed March 25, 2015].

57. Gregory Massey, *John Laurens and the American Revolution* (Columbia: University of South Carolina Press, 2000), 180; John Adams, "To the Comte de Vergennes," June 22, 1780, Adams Papers Digital Edition (Charlottesville: University of Virginia Press, 2020), https://rotunda.upress.virginia.edu/founders/default.xqy?keys=ADMS-print-06-09-02-0280-0004 [accessed Sept. 26, 2020]; Paine, *Complete Writings*, 2:228–229.

58. Paine, *Complete Writings*, 2:721.

59. Steven E. Kagle, ed. *The Diary of Josiah Atkins* (New York: Arno Press, 1975), 24–25, 28.

60. Ford, *Journals*, 21:1186–1190; Robert Morris to John Dickinson, January 8, 1782, box 20, f. 4, Dreer Collection, coll. 175 (Historical Society of Pennsylvania, Philadelphia); Codman and Smith, "Boston February 2, 1782, and Boston November 6, 1782," vol. 1, n.p., Records of Boston Merchants Engaged in Foreign Trade, 1739–1887 (Baker Library, Harvard Business School, Boston).

61. Lewis, *A History of the Bank of North America*, 39.

62. William M. Gouge, *The Journal of Banking from July 1841 to July 1842* (Philadelphia: J. Van Court, Printer, 1842), 237.

63. Hazard, *Hazard's Register of Pennsylvania*, 2:259.

64. Anne Bezanson, *Prices and Inflation During the American Revolution: Pennsylvania, 1770–1790* (Philadelphia: University of Pennsylvania Press, 1951).

65. Paine, *Complete Writings*, 2:228–229.

66. Gould, *Among the Powers of the Earth*.

67. Instructions to [Thomas] Grenville, April 30, 1782, FO 27/2/42–47 (National Archives, Kew).

68. Thomas Townsend to Richard Oswald, Sept. 3, 1781, FO 27/2/264–271.

69. Commission of Richard Oswald, Sept. 19, 1782, FO 27/2/290–293.

70. Draft Treaty, October 5, 1782, FO 95/511/93 (National Archives, Kew).

71. Richard Oswald to Thomas Townshend, October 2 and October 5, 1782, FO 27/2/300–305, 312–315; Richard Morris, *The Peacemakers: The Great Powers and American Independence* (New York: Harper & Row, 1965), 344–347.

72. Wilson, *Peacemakers*, 352.

73. Thomas Townshend and Lord Shelburne to Richard Oswald, October 11, 1782, and October 23, 1782, FO 27/2/338, 358–359, 352–359; Wilson, *Peacemakers*,

74. Adams, "Diary November 1782."

75. Oswald's Instructions, May 21, 1782, FO 27/2/87–90; Edmond Fitzmaurice, *Life of William, Earl of Shelburne, Afterwards First Marquess of Lansdowne, 1776-1805* (London: Macmillan, 1876), 3:283–83, 286; J. C. Fox to Mr. Grenville, June 10, 1783 FO 27/2/126–128; Benjamin Franklin to Richard Oswald, July 12, 1782, FO 27/2/189–190.

76. Morris, *Peacemakers*, 351–352; Christine Desan, *Making Money: Coin, Currency and the Coming of Capitalism* (Oxford: Oxford University Press, 2014), 293.

77. Terry Bouton, "Moneyless in Pennsylvania: Privatization and the Depression of the 1780s," in *The Economy of Early America: Historical Perspectives and New Directions*, ed. Cathy Matson, 221 (University Park: Penn State University Press, 2006).

78. Desan rightly identifies producing money for profit as a fundamental institutional foundation of European capitalism. Desan, *Making Money*, 296.

79. Allan Kullikoff, "The Progress of Inequality in Revolutionary Boston," *William & Mary Quarterly* 28, no. 3 (1971): 375–412, https://doi.org/10.2307/1918824.

80. Ellen Hartigan-O'Connor, "'She Said She Did Not Know Money': Urban Women and Atlantic Markets in the Revolutionary Era," *Early American Studies: An Interdisciplinary Journal* 4, no. 2 (October 12, 2006): 322–352; Michael Merrill, "The Anticapitalist Origins of the United States," *Review (Fernand Braudel Center)* 13, no. 4 (1990): 465–497.

81. Fisher, "Diary," July 4–July 26, 1780.

82. Fisher, "Diary," July 26, 1780–September 22, 1784.

83. Nathaniel Bouton, ed., *Provincial State Papers* (Concord, NH: Jenks, 1874), 8:925–927; William Hoskins to Payson, Johnson, and Haverly, n.d. [ca. 1786], Hancock Family Papers, series 2, vol. JH-7 (Baker Library, Harvard Business School, Boston); George William Van Cleve, "The Anti-Federalists' Toughest Challenge: Paper Money, Debt Relief, and the Ratification of the Constitution," *Journal of the Early Republic* 34, no. 4 (2014): 529–560; Mary M. Schweitzer, "State-Issued Currency and the Ratification of the U.S. Constitution," *Journal of Economic History* 49, no. 2 (1989): 311–322.

84. Charles King, ed., *The Life and Correspondence of Rufus King* (New York: Putnam, 1894), 1:184.

85. John Maynard Keynes, *Essays in Persuasion* (London: MacMillan, 1933), 319.

86. Philip Morin Freneau, "The Rising Glory of America," in *The Poems of Philip Freneau, Poet of the American Revolution*, ed. Fred Lewis, 1:49–84 (Princeton: Princeton University Library, 1902).

87. The best account of the revolt against bank money in Pennsylvania is Bouton, *Taming Democracy*.

88. Mitchell and Flanders, *Statutes at Large*, 12:57–58.

89. Mathew Carey, ed., *Debates and Proceedings of the General Assembly of Pennsylvania: On the Memorials Praying a Repeal or Suspension of the Law Annulling the Charter of the Bank* (Philadelphia: Mathew Carey, 1786), 37.

90. Carey, *Debates and Proceedings*, 65–66.

91. Ibid., 65–69.

92. Paine, *Complete Writings*, 2:393.

93. Paine, *Complete Writings*, 2:397, 404–405; Carl Becker, *The History of Political Parties in the Province of New York, 1760–1776* (Madison: University of Wisconsin, 1909), 22; Van Cleve, "The Anti-Federalists' Toughest Challenge," 540.

94. Woody Holton, *Unruly Americans and the Origins of the Constitution* (New York: Hill & Wang, 2007), 11–12; Ferguson, *Power of the Purse*, 245–250; Mary M. Schweitzer, "State-Issued Currency and the Ratification of the U.S. Constitution," *Journal of Economic History* 49, no. 2 (1989): 311–322.

95. Woody Holton, "An 'Excess of Democracy'—Or a Shortage? The Federalists' Earliest Adversaries," *Journal of the Early Republic* 25, no. 3 (2005): 339–382.

96. Van Cleve, "The Anti-Federalists' Toughest Challenge," 544–545.

97. James Madison, *The Debates in the Several State Conventions, on the Adoption of the Federal Constitution, as Recommended by the General Convention at Philadelphia, in 1787*, ed. Jonathan Elliot (Washington, D.C.: n.p., 1845), 4:335; Paul Kaminski and Gaspare Saladino, eds., *The Documentary History of the Ratification of the Constitution* (Madison: Wisconsin Historical Society Press, 1976–), 1:264, 275, 3:148.

98. James Wilson, "Prospectus for the Promotion of Immigration from Europe" [likely soon after 1787], box 1, vol. 2, ff. 46, James Wilson Papers 0721 (Historical Society of Pennsylvania, Philadelphia); On the ongoing significance of Article VI in the nineteenth century, see Woody Holton, "The Capitalist Constitution," in *American Capitalism: New Histories*, ed. Sven Beckert and Christine Desan (New York: Columbia University Press, 2019), chapter 1.

Conclusion

1. Paine, *Complete Writings*, 1:651–674; Audrey Williamson, *Thomas Paine: His Life, Work, and Times* (New York: St. Martin's Press, 1973), 213–250; Harry Ammon, *James Monroe: The Quest for National Identity* (New York: McGraw-Hill, 1971), 133–137; Moncure Daniel Conway, *The Life of Thomas Paine* (New York: G. P. Putnam, 1892), 2:232–235.

2. Theobald Wolfe Tone, *Memoirs of Theobald Wolfe Tone* (London: H. Colburn, 1827), 2:172–173; Guillaume-Martin Couture, "Garden Front of the Folie de la Bouëxière," in *The White House Historical Association Digital Library*, https://library.whitehousehistory.org/fotoweb/archives/5017-Digital-Library/Main%20Index/Presidents/James%20Monroe/1113318.tif.info [accessed April 4, 2021]; Aline Boutillon, "Folies, Tivoli . . . Et Rues Nouvelles," *9ème histoire*, www.neufhistoire.fr/articles.php?lng=fr&pg=2324 [accessed April 20, 2021].

3. Paine, *Complete Writings*, 1:651–674; Williamson, *Paine*, esp. 213; Patrick O'Brien and Nuno Palma, "Danger to the Old Lady of Threadneedle Street? The Bank Restriction Act and the Regime Shift to Paper Money, 1797–1821," *European Review of Economic History* 24, no. 2 (2020): 390–426.

4. Paine, *Complete Writings*, 1:664, 674.

5. Max Edling, *Hercules in the Cradle: Money, War, and the American States, 1783–1867* (Chicago: University of Chicago Press, 2014), 12; Andrew David Edwards, Fabian Steininger, and Andrea Tosato, "The Era of Chinese Global Hegemony: Denaturalizing Money in the Early Modern World," *L'Atelier du Centre de recherches historiques* 18 (2018), http://journals.openedition.org/acrh/8076.

6. Marc Flandreau and Juan H. Flores, "Bonds and Brands: Foundations of Sovereign Debt Markets, 1820–1830," *Journal of Economic History* 69, no. 3 (2009): 646–684; Mark Metzler, *Lever of Empire: The International Gold Standard and the Crisis of Liberalism in Prewar Japan* (Berkeley: University of California Press, 2006); Damian Clavel, "What's in a Fraud? The Many Worlds of Gregor MacGregor, 1817–1824," *Enterprise & Society* 22, no. 4 (2021): 997–1036; Worthing Chauncy Ford, ed., *The Writings of George Washington* (New York: G. P. Putnam's Sons, 1890), 8:293–299.

7. Ann Marsh Daly, "'Every Dollar Brought from the Earth': Money, Slavery, and Souther Gold Mining," *Journal of the Early Republic* 41, no. 4 (2021): 553–585; Enrique Cardoso and Enzo Faletto, *Dependency and Development in Latin America* (Berkeley: University of California Press, 1979), xx; Mae Ngai, *The Chinese Question: Gold Rushes, Chinese Migration, and Global Politics* (New York: Norton, 2021); Jeffrey Sklansky, *Sovereign of the Market: The Money Question in Early America* (Chicago: University of Chicago Press, 2017); Stephen Mihm, "Follow the Money: The Return of Finance in the Early Republic," *Journal of the Early Republic* 36, no. 4 (2016): 783–804; Stephen Mihm, *A Nation of Counterfeiters: Capitalists, Con Men, and the Making of the United States* (Cambridge: Harvard University Press, 2007).

8. Robert Lipsey, "U.S. Foreign Trade and the Balance of Payments," in *Cambridge Economic History of the United States*, ed. Robert Gallman and Stanley Engerman, 2:685–732 (Cambridge: Cambridge University Press, 2000); Douglass North, *The Economic Growth of the United States, 1790–1860* (Englewood Cliffs, NJ; Prentice-Hall, 1961).

9. Michael Zakim and Gary J. Kornblith, *Capitalism Takes Command: The Social Transformation of Nineteenth-Century America* (Chicago: University of Chicago Press, 2012); Melvyn Stokes and Stephen Conway, eds., *The Market Revolution in America: Social, Political, and Religious Expressions, 1800–1880* (Charlottesville: University of Virginia Press, 1996); Winifred Rothenberg, *From Market-Places to a Market Economy: The Transformation of Rural Massachusetts, 1750–1850* (Chicago: University of Chicago Press, 1992); Michael O'Malley, *The Entwined Histories of Money and Race in America* (Chicago: University of Chicago Press, 2012). Many historians celebrate this transformation as inherently beneficial and, ultimately, liberatory. My point is, without praise, to reemphasize its radicalism. Joyce Appleby, *Capitalism and the New Social Order: The Republican Vision of the 1790's* (New York: NYU Press, 1984); Gordon Wood, *The Radicalism of the American Revolution* (New York: Vintage Books, 1993).

10. Bird Wilson, ed., *The Works of the Honorable James Wilson* (Philadelphia: Lorenzo Press, 1804), 3:397.

11. Karl Polanyi, *The Great Transformation* (Boston: Beacon Press, 1957).

ILLUSTRATION CREDITS

FRONTISPIECE. Benjamin West, *The Expulsion of Adam and Eve from Paradise*, 1791, National Gallery of Art. www.nga.gov /collection/art-object-page.70986.html, public domain.

0.1. University of Notre Dame Continental Currency Collection, https: //coins.nd.edu/colcurrency/currencytext/CC-05-20-77.html, public domain

1. From Henry Phillips Jr., *Historical Sketches of the Paper Currency of the American Colonies* (1865), leaf 56AO, Firestone Library Special Collections, Princeton

2. From Henry Phillips Jr., *Historical Sketches of the Paper Currency of the American Colonies* (1865), leaf 56AO, Firestone Library Special Collections, Princeton

3. Photo by Emery May Holden Norweb, Smithsonian Institution, www .si.edu/object/1-new-england-shilling-massachusetts-1652:nmah _1076337, used under CC license

4. Photo by Emery May Holden Norweb, Smithsonian Institution, www .si.edu/object/1-new-england-shilling-massachusetts-1652:nmah _1076337, used under CC license

5. Photo by Ellen R. Feingold, Smithsonian Institution, www.si.edu /object/20-shillings-massachusetts-1690:nmah_472657, used under CC license

6. Leicester Museum & Art Gallery, https://artuk.org/discover/artworks /william-wollaston-and-his-family-in-a-grand-interior-81286, used under CC license

7. From Henry Phillips Jr., *Historical Sketches of the Paper Currency of the American Colonies* (1865), leaf 56AO, Firestone Library Special Collections, Princeton

8. From Henry Phillips Jr., *Historical Sketches of the Paper Currency of the American Colonies* (1865), leaf 56AO, Firestone Library Special Collections, Princeton

9. Smithsonian Institution, www.si.edu/object/1-continental -dollar-united-states-1776:nmah_1092980, used under CC license

10. Smithsonian Institution, www.si.edu/object/1-continental-dollar -united-states-1776:nmah_1092980, used under CC license

11. Photo by Chase Manhattan, Smithsonian Institution, www.si.edu /object/1-dollar-united-states-1794:nmah_835252, used under CC license

12. Photo by Chase Manhattan, Smithsonian Institution, www.si.edu /object/1-dollar-united-states-1794:nmah_835252, used under CC license

INDEX

Page numbers in *italics* indicate figures and tables.

GPSR Authorized Representative: Easy Access System Europe - Mustamäe tee
50, 10621 Tallinn, Estonia, gpsr.requests@easproject.com